An Introduction to R

An Introduction to R:
Data Analysis and Visualization

Mark Gardener

Pelagic Publishing

Published by Pelagic Publishing
20–22 Wenlock Road
London N1 7GU, UK

www.pelagicpublishing.com

An Introduction to R: Data Analysis and Visualization

A CIP record for this book is available from the British Library

ISBN 978-1-78427-337-8 Hbk
ISBN 978-1-78427-338-5 Pbk
ISBN 978-1-78427-339-2 ePub
ISBN 978-1-78427-340-8 PDF

https://doi.org/10.53061/THEE2596

Typeset by Deanta Global Publishing Services, Chennai, India

About this book

The modern world is awash with data. The R Project is a statistical environment and programming language that can help to make sense of these data. R is a huge Open Source project that has become enormously popular over the past few years. The rise of R is due to its power and flexibility. With R you can organize, analyze and visualize data. This book will help you learn how to use R from the ground up, giving you a start in the world of Data Science.

Acknowledgements

My thanks go to Richard Rowe, for introducing me to R all those years ago. Also, many thanks to Pelagic Publishing for being so fun and easy to work with, this book would not have been possible without their help. Thank you to all those students, who have kept me on my toes, much of this material has been "tried out" in a classroom somehow. Finally, a big thank you to the R Core Project team for their continuing great work in keeping R going.

Who this book is for

This book is an introduction to using R: The Statistical Programming Language. Regardless of your background or specialty – science, business, engineering, or social science – you'll find this book a starting point for learning about Data Science, that is, Data Analysis, Data Visualization, and Data Management. This book is not aimed at any particular educational level and should be accessible to anyone who wants to learn R, a powerful and flexible analytical toolbox.

What you will learn

In this book you will learn how to use the R program. You'll learn how to get started with R, in particular:

- making and importing data items
- exporting data
- managing and manipulating data objects
- summarizing and aggregating data
- visualizing data
- the basics of Data Analysis, including:
  - differences tests
  - correlation
  - association
  - regression
- R programming functions

This book is intended as a foundation course in using R for Data Science and a springboard for further exploration into Data Analysis and Data Visualization. Not every R command is shown (there are so many!), and the emphasis is on those that the author deemed most useful. I apologize in advance if you are an R user already, and your favorite function is missing.

Some R functions have lots of potential arguments, and not all of these have been illustrated, in order to make the learning journey simpler. Only the most "helpful" arguments are shown but you will see clearly if there are additional arguments you can use (you'll see as you read the book how easy it is to access the internal help system of R).

Author Biography

Mark is a scientist, lecturer and author. He likes to "tell stories with data", and he also likes to tell other people how to do that. It all started when Mark was at University studying Natural Sciences (as opposed to un-natural ones), and then later whilst doing a PhD in Ecology and Evolutionary Biology. Ecological data is really messy, which makes it fun but also frustrating. Mark discovered R at the end of his doctoral research, and the discovery sparked an interest in continuing to tell stories that continues to this day. Nowadays he writes textbooks and teaches people about Data Science (not just ecologists, but also people who earn their living indoors).

Mark enjoys fly-fishing and American Football, but not simultaneously. He currently lives in Sussex, with his wife, Christine, a biochemist.

Data Examples

All the examples in this book are from R itself. Many are from the basic datasets that come with R. Some are from the package: **MASS**, which comes with R but is not loaded by default. To load the package use:

```
library(MASS)
```

Support Material

Support material online can be found at the author's website. Visit: https://www.gardenersown.co.uk and follow links to *Publications* or *Resources*. In the text you'll also find some references to additional material, which will be indicated by the ↘ icon.

How this Book is Arranged

The chapters are laid out in what I thought was a sensible order, however it is nearly impossible to take a straight path and some ducking and diving was necessary at times. I hope you find the layout reasonably logical. Each chapter has a brief introduction giving an idea of what's to follow. Each chapter ends with a concise summary and some simple exercises (answers in the Appendix). I have tried to include plenty of examples and all the data is from within R itself, so there is no need to download anything else.

Notes and Tips:

At various points you'll see **Note** and **Tip** sections, giving some explicit information that I felt was important at the time.

Contents

1. A brief introduction to R

The R program is a free Open Source statistical environment. R is a programming language that carries out statistical computing and can produce high quality graphics. R can run on all major operating systems, e.g. Windows, Apple Macintosh and most Linux distributions. R started as an academic exercise at the University of Auckland in New Zealand. Now R has become a much larger international project with many people contributing to it.

R is highly customizable, and is now used by business, corporations, governments, academics and individuals around the world. R is used for many data science purposes; these might be as simple as adding together a few numbers, or more complicated multivariate statistical modelling.

What's in this chapter

» Obtaining and installing R
» Introduction to the R interface
» Getting help in and about R
» Extending R with additional command packages
» Alternative ways to run R

In short, this chapter is about getting and starting to use R.

Note: Support material

See the ⬊ for links to material on the support website.

1.1 Getting R

You can get R from the R Project website at https://www.r-project.org where you will find the download page (Figure 1.1).

Click on the appropriate link for your operating system and you'll be on your way. Once R is installed on your computer you will be able to run the program. If you use a Linux system, R runs via the terminal. On Windows or Macintosh you will find R like any other program.

1.2 The R interface

The main interface between R and you is the R console (Figure 1.2). When you run R this is what you'll see first. The console displays a "welcome" message and some additional "blurb", then waits for you.

The console is where you will type the commands required to "drive" R. You start typing at the > symbol. In the GUI (for Windows or Macintosh) there are some menus, which can help make using R a little easier (e.g. Figure 1.3).

The *Packages* menu for example (Figure 1.4) allows you to manage additional R command packages, which allow you to extend the (already extensive) capabilities of R.

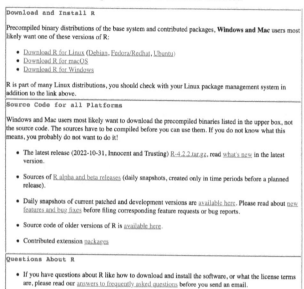

Figure 1.1 The installation page of the R website.

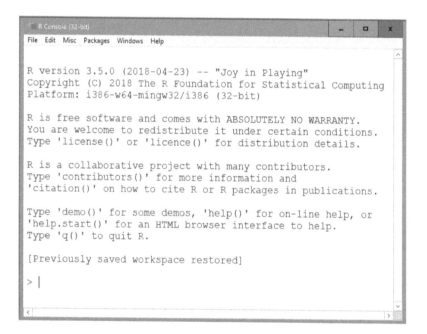

Figure 1.2 The R console in Windows.

If you produce any graphical output, this will appear in a separate window.

Tip: Command History

Use the ↑ to scroll back through previous R commands.

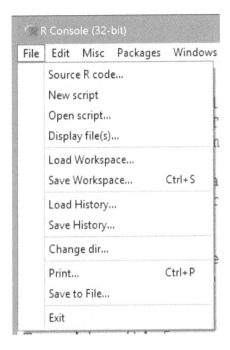

Figure 1.3 The File menu in the Windows GUI.

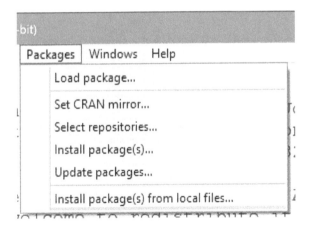

Figure 1.4 The Packages menu in the Windows GUI.

1.2.1 The help system

So, you are staring at the R welcome message and wondering what to type... there is plenty of help available in R but it can be hard to find what you want if you do not know the command name that you want help for!

In the Windows GUI version of R the main help system is displayed in your web browser (Figure 1.5). On a Macintosh the help system opens in a browser-like window, whereas in Linux the help entries are displayed directly in the console itself.

You can access the help entry for a command using the `help()` function. This works nicely if you know the name of the function for which you want help. You put the name of the function (in quotes) in the () brackets.

```
help("sum")
```

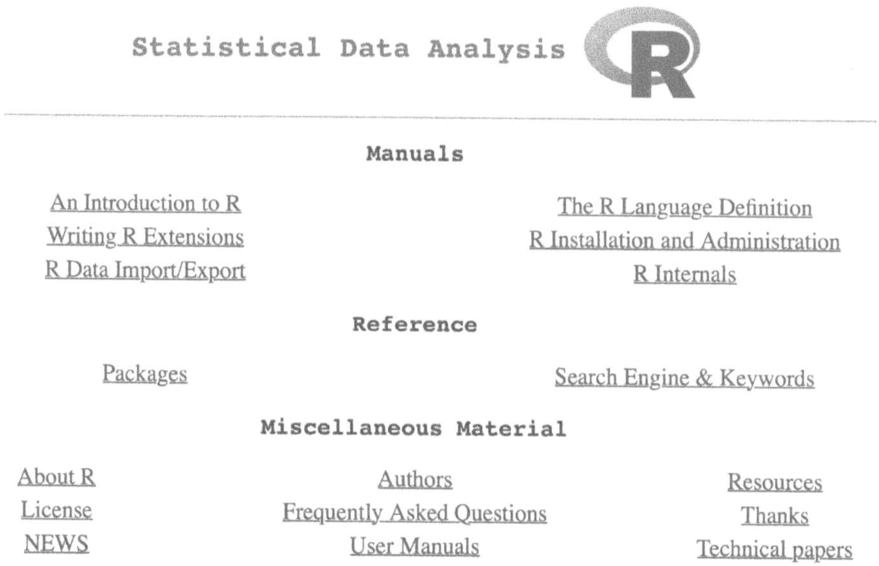

Statistical Data Analysis (R)

Manuals

An Introduction to R
Writing R Extensions
R Data Import/Export

The R Language Definition
R Installation and Administration
R Internals

Reference

Packages

Search Engine & Keywords

Miscellaneous Material

About R
License
NEWS

Authors
Frequently Asked Questions
User Manuals

Resources
Thanks
Technical papers

Figure 1.5 The R Help starting page in a web browser.

As a short-cut you can use ?name, where name is the name of the function (you do not need quotes).

```
?mean
```

If you do not recall the name of the function, but you think you know a bit of it, you can try apropos("partname"), where "partname" is the part you can recall, for example:

```
apropos("qq")
[1] "qqline" "qqnorm" "qqplot"
```

The result of apropos() is to show you all the functions that contain the "partword" you typed.

You can "force" R to open the help system in your default web browser using help.start(). This will open the starting page for the help system (Figure 1.5), regardless of the operating system you are using. Note that you do not need to type anything in the () brackets.

```
help.start()
```

Help entries from the terminal appear in the console by default. You can scroll up and down using the arrow keys, and quit by typing q from the keyboard.

Tip: Help from the Terminal

If you are using a terminal window (for example, if you are running Linux) and you want to open a help entry in a browser, add help_type = "html" to the help() command.

```
help(sum, help_type = "html")
```

You can set the default help-display type for your R session by using the options() function (note that R ignores lines starting with #, which are treated as comment lines):

```
# Default to HTML help
options(help_type = "html")
```

```
# reset to default
options(help_type = NULL)
```

R is loaded with analytical packages, not all of them are active (see section 1.3 *Extending R* for more details). You can search for help entries in any package, even if it is not "active", by using `help.search()`.

```
help.search(pattern = "mean")
```

If you know the name of the package you can access help on an individual command or view the index:

```
# Help on specific entry in package: MASS
help(lda, package = "MASS")

# Access index for package: MASS
help(package = "MASS")
```

Use ?? as a short-cut for `help.search()`, in which case quotes are not required.

```
??mean
```

R will search through all the R packages on your computer and show you matching entries.
     You can search the online R-help mailing list using the command `RSiteSearch()`. This opens your web browser.

```
RSiteSearch("mean")
```

Tip: Quotes or not?

If you use ? or ?? you generally do not need quotes. However, if your search term contains spaces you'll need to include them, e.g. ??"linear model".

Of course you can always use the Internet; adding "R" to your query will usually provide you with plenty of hits.

Anatomy of a help entry

Every help entry is supposed to conform to a standard. This means that when you look at typical help entries (e.g. Figure 1.6) they will always be set out in the same fashion.
     This set layout is summarized in Table 1.1, where you can see the various elements.
     The help system can be very helpful in reminding you of the exact parameters needed for each function. It can also help you explore other commands, as you can refer to the *See Also* and *Examples* sections.

1.2.2   Command history

R records the commands you type and stores them in memory. You can access the previous commands using the ↑ and ↓ keys. You can edit previous commands (use the mouse, arrow keys, delete and so on) and press ENTER to run them.
     You can also get a list of past commands using the `history()` function. This shows you the previously typed commands. If you are using the regular Windows GUI this opens in a new "R History" window, other GUI and systems vary in their output.

```
history(max.show = 25, reverse = FALSE, pattern, ...)
```

comment {base}   R Documentation

Query or Set a "comment" Attribute

Description

These functions set and query a *comment* attribute for any R objects. This is typically useful for `data.frame`s or model fits.

Contrary to other `attributes`, the `comment` is not printed (by `print` or `print.default`).

Assigning NULL or a zero-length character vector removes the comment.

Usage

```
comment(x)
comment(x) <- value
```

Arguments

x
    any R object

value
    a character vector, or NULL.

See Also

`attributes` and `attr` for other attributes.

Examples

```
x <- matrix(1:12, 3, 4)
comment(x) <- c("This is my very important data from experiment #0234",
                "Jun 5, 1998")
x
comment(x)
```

[Package *base* version 3.3.2 Index]

Figure 1.6 A typical entry from the R help system.

Table 1.1 Elements of a typical R help entry.

Section/title	Contents
Name {package}	The name of the help entry, this is usually the same as the command name but may be more generic. The package name appears in {}, giving the location of the entry.
Title	A general title.
Description	A brief description of the function(s).
Usage	This shows the general syntax (what you need to type into the console).
Arguments	A list of the various arguments that may be used.
Details	Additional information
Value	A brief note about what the result of the command is.
References	References to books or papers.
See Also	Links to related functions.
Examples	Examples that you can copy/paste into the console.

The `history()` function will show you the last 25 commands by default. However, you can alter the parameters (Table 1.2) to change the number of items and their order. You can also show entries that contain a pattern.

Table 1.2 Parameters of the history() command.

Parameter	Explanation
max.show	The maximum number of items to display (default = 25).
reverse	Set reverse = TRUE to display in reverse order. The default shows the last command at the bottom of the list.
pattern	A text pattern to match, this must be in "quotes".
...	Additional arguments can be passed to the pattern-matching.

> **Note: History display**
>
> The history() function includes the history() command you typed.

You can save the commands you type into a file using savehistory(), use a .txt file extension for the filename. You can also load a history file with loadhistory().

```
savehistory(file = ".Rhistory")
loadhistory(file = ".Rhistory")
```

You need to give the filename in "quotes" and include the pathway to the file. The default filename is a "hidden" file, in your working directory. You can see what this is currently set at using getwd(). See section 4.7.1 *Working directory* for more details on how to view and change the settings.

On the Windows GUI you can load or save the history from the *File* menu.

> **Note: Macintosh command history**
>
> The Macintosh R GUI has its own history system, which replaces the history() function and is not compatible with the "regular" system.

1.3   Extending R

R is powerful right "out of the box" but there are many additional "packages" you can add on to R to increase its capabilities. One of the great strengths of R is that you can customize it to suit your requirements. Many people have already done this and published their efforts as R packages on the *Comprehensive R Archive Network* (CRAN) at https://www.r-project.org.

The CRAN website gives a lot of information about the available packages, as well as access to the packages themselves. A particularly useful section is the *Task Views*, which is a link from the main CRAN page. This is a topic-led information section and gives comprehensive information about various topics and the R packages that are "useful" for those topics.

You can add and manage R packages quite easily using R, as you will see now.

1.3.1   Command packages

R is modular, although this is not generally apparent when you are using R. When you run R a default "set" of command packages are loaded into the memory of your computer. You can see what packages (or libraries) are currently loaded with the search() command.

```
search()
 [1]    ".GlobalEnv"        "package:stats"   "package:graphics"
 [4]    "package:grDevices"  "package:utils"   "package:datasets"
 [7]    "package:methods"    "Autoloads"       "org:r-lib"
[10]    "package:base"
```

The list you get will vary, depending what GUI you are running and if you've loaded any command packages. The example here is a "typical" minimum you get when running R from the terminal. You can get a "list" of packages that are on your computer system and "available" using installed.packages().

```
installed.packages()
```

The list can be very long indeed, and gives a range of information such as the version of the package and the location on your system. If you simply want a list of the names you can use:

```
rownames(installed.packages())
```

You can also use a menu if you are using the Windows or Macintosh GUI:

- Windows – *Packages > Load package…*
- Macintosh – *Packages & Data > Package Manager*

These will show you what R command packages (libraries) are available on your system.

1.3.2   Download packages

Most R command packages are on CRAN at https://www.r-project.org. If you go to the *Packages* section of the site, you can see the names and get other information about the packages that are available. You can get the packages onto your system in two main ways:

- Run the install.packages() command from R.
- Download a .zip archive from CRAN and then run an R command.

Once you know the name of a package you want you can use it in the install.packages() command like so:

```
install.packages("name")
```

In the command you give the "name" (in quotes) of the package you want to install. You will be asked to select a mirror site for the download; choose one local to you. The download will begin and the package will be added to your system.

Note: R Mirror Sites

The R website is mirrored at host institutions around the world. This lessens the "traffic" through each site, resulting in faster downloads for you.

If you are using a GUI you can use a menu for installation:

* Windows – *Packages*.
* Macintosh – *Packages & Data*.

Install from .zip

Using `install.packages()` allows you to access CRAN directly from R. However, it is possible to download a package using your web browser. You can download various items, including manuals (Figure 1.7).

Reference manual: abc.pdf
Vignettes: ABC
Package source: abc_2.1.tar.gz
Windows binaries: r-devel: abc_2.1.zip, r-release: abc_2.1.zip, r-oldrel: abc_2.1.zip
OS X binaries: r-release: abc_2.1.tgz, r-oldrel: abc_2.1.tgz
Old sources: abc archive

Figure 1.7 R Command Package download options.

You'll want to download the file that corresponds to your OS:

* Package source – for Linux machines (`.tar.gz` file).
* Windows binaries – ZIP files for Windows users.
* OS X binaries – TGZ archive files for Macintosh users.

Once you have the file on your system you will still need to install it using R. On Windows or Macintosh GUI you can try the following:

```
# Opens a file browser - you choose the file
install.packages(file.choose(), repos = NULL)

# For Windows GUI only
utils:::menuInstallLocal()
```

This will open a file browser and allow you to select the file you downloaded. The file will be opened and the R command package added to your system.

The `file.choose()` command only works if you are using a GUI. If you are using a terminal you need to use the full filename (in quotes) with its path.

Example:

Path names for different OS

```
# Windows
install.packages("C:/Users/Mark/Downloads/abc.zip")

# Macintosh
install.packages("Macintosh HD/Users/markgardenet/Downloads/
abc.tgz")
```

1.3.3 Prepare a package

Once an R command package has been "installed" it is on your system. However, it is not "active" until you tell R that you want to use it. To *activate* a command package use `library()` or `require()` commands, with the name of the package (quotes not required).

```
library(cluster)
require(cluster) # same thing
```

You can check on what packages are loaded with `search()`.

```
require(cluster)
search()
 [1]  ".GlobalEnv"         "package:cluster"    "package:stats"
 [4]  "package:graphics"   "package:grDevices"  "package:utils"
 [7]  "package:datasets"   "package:methods"    "Autoloads"
[10]  "org:r-lib"          "package:base"
```

Now the package is ready and the commands within it are available to use. If you are using a GUI you can use a menu command to "load" a package:

- Windows – *Packages > Load package…*
- Macintosh – *Packages & Data > Package Manager*

1.3.4 Remove a package

There are many command packages available and it might not be sensible to have them all "running" at the same time. Usually you would load only the package(s) that you need for a specific task. Once you are done you can "tidy up" and remove the package.

The `search()` command allows you to see what packages are loaded. When you type a command, R "looks" along the search path as defined in `search()` for the command that you've typed. The first entry on the search path is usually .GlobalEnv, which means your computer memory (think of it at your workspace). With so many command packages available it is inevitable that there will be duplication of command names. R will "select" the first entry it encounters on the search path. Each package you load gets to the front of the queue.

To "unload" a package use the `detach()` function.

```
detach(package:name)
```

You replace the name part with the name of the package to `detach`. Removing a package does not un-install it, it simply removes it from the current search path. The package is still on your system and can be loaded and unloaded as you need.

```
search()

 [1]  ".GlobalEnv"          "package:cluster"    "package:stats"
 [4]  "package:graphics"    "package:grDevices"  "package:utils"
 [7]  "package:datasets"    "package:methods"    "Autoloads"
[10]  "org:r-lib"           "package:base"

detach(package:cluster)

search()

 [1]  ".GlobalEnv"          "package:stats"      "package:graphics"
 [4]  "package:grDevices"   "package:utils"      "package:datasets"
 [7]  "package:methods"     "Autoloads"          "org:r-lib"
[10]  "package:base"
```

If you are using a Macintosh GUI you can use a menu to detach a package: *Packages & Data > Package Manager*. On Windows you must use the `detach()` command but see section 1.4 *Alternative ways to run R*.

1.3.5   Updating packages

From time to time the R command packages are updated. New features are added and bugs ironed out. You can check for newer versions of packages using `old.packages()`, which gives a (potentially long) list of packages that have suitable newer versions.

More usually you'll want to check and update; use the `update.packages()` command to do this.

```
update.packages(ask = TRUE, ...)
```

There are quite a lot of potential parameters but `ask` is the most useful. The default `ask = TRUE` will let you choose package-by-package which to update. If you set `ask = "graphics"` you'll get an interactive selector. Setting `ask = FALSE` will attempt to update all your packages without asking any further.

If you use a GUI you can also use a menu to help update your packages.

*   Windows – *Packages > Update packages…*
*   Macintosh – *Packages & Data > Package Installer*

Tip: Session Info

The `sessionInfo()` function can tell you about the "state" of your R system. It will show you the version of R, your operating system and what packages (and versions) are loaded.

1.4   Alternative ways to run R

When you download R for your computer from the R-Project website (https://www.r-project.org) you will get a version for your operating system.

*   *Windows*: The Windows R GUI.
*   *Macintosh*: The Mac Rapp GUI.
*   *Linux*: R runs from the terminal.

You can *always* run R directly, that is from a terminal or DOS window (Table 1.3), without using a GUI. However, this is not usually convenient!

Most of the time you'll want to use a GUI. The concept of an *Integrated Development Environment* is becoming increasingly popular. An IDE is a "wrapper" for R (or other program) that helps you manage your work-flow more easily. A good IDE will help you get the most out of R by making "housekeeping" tasks more straightforward (such as managing files and add-on packages). You can then focus on working with R.

Table 1.3 Running R from a terminal or DOS window.

OS	Terminal application
Linux	Open the regular terminal and type R
Macintosh	Open the Terminal.app or similar (e.g. iTerm) and type R
Windows	Look for the R.exe file in "C:\Program Files\R\R-xxx\bin", where R-xxx is a version of R. Then run the R.exe file.

There are several IDE around and a quick Internet search (e.g. "IDE for R") will reveal the options. The most widely used is called RStudio (https://www.RStudio.com).

1.4.1   RStudio: an Integrated Development Environment

RStudio (https://www.RStudio.com) is itself an Open Source project and is an attempt to make it easier for users to work with R.

RStudio forms an "Integrated Development Environment" (IDE), which is a big improvement over the basic Windows R GUI. RStudio allows you to focus on main "programming" tasks and undertakes "housekeeping" more easily than direct commands from the console.

RStudio is a wrapper for R and you must have R installed on your computer. When RStudio opens you see that the window is split into several areas (called panes, Figure 1.8).

Figure 1.8 The RStudio display is divided into 4 panes.

The panes display different kinds of information, some of the panes contain multiple items as tabs. The panes are:

Console

The main console is where "R lives" and where commands are entered and basic output generated. The left side of RStudio contains the console pane (but you can alter the configuration). In the default settings the pane above the Console holds the Script Editor window.

Script editor window

The top-left pane is the Script Editor window. This is the main area for text-based files that can be "run" as commands. This pane is also the area where data items can be "previewed". The script editor is a good place to keep your own learning notes.

Data/History/Files

The top-right pane is generally configured to show some "housekeeping" items:

- *Environment*: Shows you the "contents" of various environments. The default is the console itself, that is, the data currently in memory.
- *History*: Previous commands you've typed.
- *Files*: Access your computer file system.

Plots/Help/Packages/Help

The bottom-right pane contains some more "housekeeping" items, including:

- *Plots*: The output of graphical commands is shown here.
- *Packages*: This is where you can manage additional command packages to extend the capabilities of R.
- *Help*: The help system.

Customizing RStudio

You can control the layout of the panes and various other options from the Tools Menu. *Tools > Global Options....* You can alter the layout, colours and contents of the various panes to suit your needs.

EXERCISES:

Self-Assessment for Introduction to R

1. R is Open Source… TRUE or FALSE?
2. R is only available for Windows operating systems… TRUE or FALSE?
3. To open the help system in a web browser type ____ from the console.
4. To add a command package use the ____ function.
5. You can scroll back through previously typed commands by:
   a. Using `history()` command
   b. Using ↑ key
   c. Using `loadhistory()` command
   d. Using control & - keys

Answers to exercises are in the Appendix.

1.5 Chapter Summary: Introduction to R

Topic	Key Points
R is free	R is free and Open Source, with a large team supporting the project.
Downloading R	R is available from https://www.r-project.org for all major operating systems.
Commands	R is "driven" by typing commands into the console window.
Help system	R has extensive help, which usually opens in a web browser.
Extending R	Many additional R modules (command packages) can be downloaded and installed to extend the capabilities of R.
Running R	R can run via a terminal or its own GUI. The RStudio integrated development environment, is a popular way to run and manage R.

2. Basic math

R is a statistical programming environment, so you'd expect it to be able to perform in the math department. This chapter is an introduction to how to carry out some mathematical operations using R.

What's in this chapter

» Simple math
» Not so simple math:
  » logarithms
  » trigonometry
  » modulo math
» Making numbers look nicer:
  » rounding
  » exponent notation
  » significant figures
» Complex numbers

This chapter is about some of the more basic math, in later chapters you'll see more about statistics, summarizing data, hypothesis testing and modelling.

Note: Support material

See the ↘ for links to material on the support website.

The R program is really a giant calculator. You can type your math into the console and get the results. Start by typing some math at the > prompt in the R console.

```
2 + 7 - 4/3 * 8
[1] -1.666667
```

Notice several things:

- You get a result immediately.
- R generally ignores the spaces you typed (they are more for your benefit).
- The result starts with [1].

You need to type all your math on a single line; this means that the calculation order needs to be taken into account. Try the same values but with some parentheses:

```
(2 + 7 - 4/3) * 8
[1] 61.33333
```

Note: Math calculation order

Mathematical operations are carried out in a particular order: () then ^/* then +-.

Use `abs()` to get absolute value, that is ignoring any negative signs.

```
abs(14 - 37) # Absolute value
[1] 23
```

Use `factorial()` for factorials.

```
factorial(4) # e.g. 4 * 3 * 2 * 1
[1] 24
```

Use `sqrt()` for the square root.

```
sqrt(9) # Square root
[1] 3
```

Use ^ to raise something to a power e.g. x^y is x^y. The ^ operator is carried out alongside * and / operations, before + and – operations.

```
2^3 # 2 to the the power of 3
[1] 8
```

Tip: Check sign of result

You can check the sign of a number or result using `sign()`. The value returned depends on the value:

- −1 – value is negative.
- 0 – value is zero.
- 1 – value is positive.

```
sign(14 - 37)
[1] -1
```

2.1   Logarithms

Logarithms are used in many disciplines. You can compute logs with `log()`, which uses natural logs as the default base.

```
log(x, base = exp(1))
```

If you supply x only, then the natural log is the default.

```
log(100)
[1] 4.60517
```

Supply a base and that will be used.

```
log(100, base = 10) # Log base 10
[1] 2
```

There are several "helper" functions. Use `log10()` to use base = 10.

```
log10(1000)
[1] 3
```

The `log2()` function gives base = 2.

```
log2(16)
[1] 4
```

Use `log1p()` to add 1 to all values before taking (natural) log (i.e. `log(x + 1)`).

```
log1p(0.5)
[1] 0.4054651
```

To get the "reverse" of a logarithm you need either `exp()` (for natural logs) or `^`. Use `exp()` for the reverse of a natural log.

```
exp(4.60517)
[1] 99.99998
```

Use `expm1()` to reverse a natural log then subtract 1 (e.g. `exp(x)-1`).

```
expm1(0.4055)
[1] 0.5000523
```

Use `^` to "undo" a log to any base other than natural (`exp(1)`). You need `base^z` where base is the original base and z is the value you wish to "un-log".

```
10^3
[1] 1000
```

2.2 Trigonometry

Trigonometric functions work in radians. The main functions are:

- `sin()` `asin()` – Sine and arc-sine.
- `cos()` `acos()` – Cosine and arc-cosine.
- `tan()` `atan()` – Tangent and arc-tangent.

To get a result in degrees you need to multiply the angle by $\pi/180$ for the regular functions.

```
sin(45 * pi/180) # The sine of 45 degrees
[1] 0.7071068
```

For arc-functions you need to multiply the result by $180 / \pi$.

```
asin(0.7071068) * 180/pi # The arcsine of 0.7 in degrees
[1] 45
```

> **Note: The Value of π**
>
> R "knows" π, use pi in calculations.

2.3 Modulo math

Modulo math deals with fractions and remainders. For example, 100 / 11 = 9.091, which is 9 and one remainder in modulo terms.

Use %% to get remainders e.g. x %% y divides x by y and returns the remainder.

```
100 %% 11
[1] 1
```

Use %/% to get the divisor e.g. x %/% y divides x by y and returns the divisor.

```
100 %/% 11
[1] 9
```

Table 2.1 shows a summary of the basic math, trig and modulo functions.

Table 2.1 Summary of math, trig and modulo functions in R.

Function	Use
+ - / * ()	Add, subtract, divide, multiply and parentheses.
x %% y	Modulo math: the remainder of x÷y.
x %/% y	Modulo math: the quotient of x÷y.
pi	The value of π, which is approximately 3.142.
x^y	The value of x raised to the power of y.
sqrt(x)	The square root of x.
abs(x)	The absolute value of x.
factorial(x)	The factorial of x.
log(x, base = n)	The logarithm of x (default natural log).
log10(x)	Logarithm using base = 10.
log2(x)	Logarithm using base = 2.
log1p(x)	Add 1 to x before logarithm.
exp(x)	The exponent of x.
expm1(x)	Subtract 1 from exponent of x.
cos(x) acos(x)	The cosine (and arc-cos) of x.
sin(x) asin(x)	The sine (and arc-sine) of x.
tan(x) atan(x)	The tangent (and arc-tan) of x.

> ### Note: Matrix math
> R can do matrix math very easily. Much of this is done "under the hood". See $\searrow$ online support website for additional details about matrix math.

2.4   Making numbers look nicer

You commonly need to make numbers look "nicer", to make a display easier to read for example. There are several ways to "tidy" numbers:

- Exponents
- Rounding
- Scientific notation

2.4.1   Exponents

You can enter values using exponent notation, for example xEy or XeY. Use a positive value after the exponent for "big" numbers.

```
1e4
[1] 1000
```

Use a negative value after the exponent for "tiny" numbers.

```
1.5E-4
[1] 0.00015
```

> ### Note: Exponents and case
>
> You can enter an exponent as lower-case e or upper-case E, but R will always display exponents as lower case.

2.4.2 Rounding

There are various functions that allow you to manipulate decimal places:

```
round(x, digits = 0)
ceiling(x)
floor(x)
trunc(x)
```

Use the round() function to round values to a specified number of decimal places.

```
x <- 1.234567
round(x) # Default is zero decimals
[1] 1
round(x, digits = 4)
[1] 1.2346
```

Use ceiling() to round up to the nearest integer.

```
ceiling(1.234)
[1] 2
```

The floor() and trunc() functions lop off the decimal portion.

```
floor(1.789)
[1] 1
trunc(3.99)
[1] 3
```

> ### Note: Displayed digits
>
> By default R displays calculated values to seven digits. Use options(digits = x) to change the setting to x. This value is in force until you change it, or quit R.
>
> ```
> pi # Displays 7 digits (the default)
> [1] 3.141593
> options(digits = 4)
> pi
> [1] 3.142
> options(digits = 7) # Reset to default values
> ```

2.4.3 Significant figures

Significant figures are handled using the signif() function.

```
signif(pi, digits = 4)
[1] 3.142
```

When you have very large values R may switch into exponent display.

```
x <- 123456789
signif(x, digits = 4)
[1] 123500000
signif(x, digits = 3)
[1] 1.23e+08
```

You can control the likelihood of values being displayed in exponent style (scientific format) using options(scipen = x), where x is a control value (the default is 0).

- +^{ve} values tend to display as "regular" numbers.
- -^{ve} values tend to display as scientific format.

Example:

Increase likelihood of scientific number display

```
z <- 1234.56789
signif(z, digits = 3)   # Default display

[1]  1230

# Increase chance for exponent
options(scipen = -10)
signif(z, digits = 3)

[1]  1.23e+03

options(scipen = 0)   # Reset to default
```

Table 2.2 hows a summary of functions that help make numbers display "nicely".

Table 2.2 **Summary of functions to make numbers nicer.**

Function	Use
round(x, digits = 0)	Round numbers to digits decimal places.
ceiling()	Round up to next largest integer.
floor()	Round down to next smallest integer.
trunc()	Truncate decimal portion.
signif(x, digits = 6)	Show x to digits significant figures.
options(scipen = x)	Alter the likelihood of presenting numbers in scientific format, negative values for scipen are more likely to result in display of scientific format.

2.5 Complex numbers

Complex numbers can be used to solve various problems that regular math cannot. Complex numbers have a *real* part and an *imaginary* part. The *imaginary* part involves i, which is defined as: $i^2 = 1$ or alternatively: $i = \sqrt{-1}$.

You can make a complex number using the complex() function or simply type it "direct" using x+yi syntax.

```
complex(real, imaginary)
```

Example:

Make complex numbers

```
complex(real = 2, imaginary = 4)
[1] 2+4i

12-2i
[1] 12-2i

4+0.5i
[1] 4+0.5i
```

Table 2.3 Functions for complex numbers.

Function	Purpose
Re(z)	The *real* part of a complex number.
Im(z)	The *imaginary* part of a complex number.
Mod(z)	The modulus.
Arg(z)	The argument.
Conj(z)	The complex conjugate.

The functions in Table 2.3 extract a "component" form a complex number. You can use most of the "usual" mathematical operators on complex numbers, including trigonometry.

Example:

Complex numbers

```
z <- complex(real = 2, imaginary = 3)
z
[1] 2+3i
Re(z) # Real part
[1] 2
Im(z) # Imaginary part
[1] 3
Mod(z) # Modulus
[1] 3.605551
# Regular math on complex number
z * 10
[1] 20+30i
log(z)
```

```
[1] 1.282475+0.982794i
sin(z)
[1] 9.154499-4.168907i
```

Note: Non-numbers

R represents "missing" values as NA, which you can think of as "not available". The object NaN results from calculations that cannot resolve to a proper value, think of that as "not a number". Infinity ∞ is represented by Inf.

EXERCISES:

Self-Assessment for Basic Math

1. The calculation order is ____.
2. A convenience function for log to base 10 is ____.
3. You can only operate trigonometry in radians. TRUE or FALSE?
4. The result of floor(47.555) is:
   a.   48
   b.   47.6
   c.   47
   d.   47.5
5. The default number of decimal places for rounding via the round() function is

   ____.

Answers to exercises are in the Appendix.

2.6   Chapter Summary: Basic math

Topic	Key Points
Math order	Since calculations are "inline" you need to recall the precedence order of operators, () ^/* +-.
Math functions	There are many math functions including: abs(), sqrt() and factorial().
Logarithms	Use log(x, base = y) to get a logarithm. The default is natural log but you can use any base.
Trigonometry	R can handle all regular trig functions e.g.: sin(), cos() and tan(), as well as their inverse: asin() acos() atan(). Trig functions operate in radians.
Pi constant	R knows π via the pi constant.
Modulo math	Use %% and %/% for modulo math (remainders and divisors).
Rounding	Use round(), ceiling(), floor(), and trunc() functions for rounding operations.
Complex numbers	R can make with complex numbers via the complex() function. Other functions include: Re(), Im(), Mod(), Arg(), and Conj().

3. Introduction to R objects

R deals with *objects*, which usually means either *data* or *functions* (instructions to "do something"). These objects have to be stored, so you can use them when you need, and therefore things get names to help you deal with them. You've already seen various examples of names with some R functions.

An R object has some sort of name, it also has other attributes so that R "knows" how to deal with it. A data object for example could be stored as numbers or as text. Some R objects are stored as a single "row", others have multiple columns.

What's in this chapter

» Naming conventions for R objects
» Assigning results to named objects
» Constants, datasets and built-in R objects
» An introduction to the different kinds of R object

This chapter is a brief introduction to R objects. You'll see more about the properties (attributes) of objects in Chapter 6 R object types and their properties.

Note: Support material

See the ↘ for links to material on the support website.

3.1 Names for objects

Since R is an object-oriented language, everything gets a name. This allows things to be stored and managed. You need to know what is "allowed":

- You can use letters a–z or A–Z.
- R **is** case sensitive.
- You can use numbers 0–9.
- You can use . or _ (period, underscore).
- No other characters are allowed.
- A name **must** start with a letter.

It is possible to begin a name with . or _ but it is not generally advisable. On most operating systems things beginning with punctuation are hidden and/or system files.

Example:

R names that are "allowed". The following are all different as far as R is concerned.

```
data1
data.1
data _ 1
Data1
dAta1
```

Example:

R names that are "disallowed"

```
1Data
1.data
1_dAta
```

Tip: Check name availability

You can check if a name is already used by typing it into the R console. If you get some kind of "result", the name is taken. If you get an error, the name is "free".

```
xyz
Error in eval(expr, envir, enclos): object 'xyz' not found
```

Alternatively use `exists("name")` to return a `TRUE` or `FALSE` result:

```
exists("xyz")
[1] FALSE
```

Note that the name must be in quotes.

3.2   Saving results to objects

Earlier you saw how to do some basic math. The results were displayed but not stored in any way. You will usually want to assign results to named objects; this stores them and allows you to use them later.

To "store" something in R you need to assign the *something* to a name:

$$name = something$$

This *something* could be a calculation, some data or a function, for instance. Here is an example using some simple math:

```
ans1 = 23 + 8
ans2 =17-4
ans3 = ans2 / 4
```

Notice that the results are not displayed. You have told R to evaluate the math to the right of the = and assign the result to the object you give the name of. These result objects are available immediately, the final line shows a previous result used as part of the math.

In the example you can also see that R has ignored the spaces. Use spaces to help you see what was typed.

To see the result you type the name of the result object. The ; character mimics the enter key, so results are placed next to one another.

```
ans1
[1]  31
ans2 ; ans3
[1]  13
[1]  3.25
```

> ### Note: Overwriting
>
> If you assign a result to a name that already exists, the new object will overwrite the old one; there is **no warning**.

3.3 Object assignment

There are alternative ways to assign results to named objects. The = is not the only (or preferred) way. There are three methods:

- Use = for standard right to left assignment.
- Use <- for right to left assignment (the preferred method).
- Use -> for left to right assignment.

Example:

Object assignment variations

```
# How you'd use pencil & paper
ans3 = ans2 + 9 - 2

# The preferred method
ans4 <- 3 + 5
ans5 <- ans1 * ans2

# View results
ans3 ; ans4 ; ans5
[1]  20
[1]  8
[1]  403

# Reverse assignment
ans3 + 3 / ans4 -> ans6
ans6
[1]  20.375
```

The <- is the *preferred* method, and what you will usually see when looking at examples in help entries and on the Internet (your GUI or IDE may have a shortcut: alt + "-" is a common one). The = is usually kept for assigning parameter values inside the () of R functions.

> ### Tip: View result as you assign an object
>
> When you make an assignment, the result is stored but not presented. Enclose the entire command in () to have the result displayed (as well as stored).
>
> ```
> (ans3 + 3/ans4 -> ans6)
> [1]  20.375
> ```

3.4 Objects that are built-in

There are some items already built-in to R, these are:

- R command functions.
- Constants.
- Data examples.

You've seen some examples of R functions already. R command packages generally contain functions; some also contain constants and/or datasets. You'll see more examples of `function` objects throughout the text (see also Chapter 15).

3.4.1 Constants

The `base` package contains several built-in constants.

The only mathematical constant is; π (3.142). There are a few other constants (Table 3.1).

Table 3.1 Constants in the *base* package.

Constant	Result
pi	The value of π.
month.name	Names of the months of the year: `January - December.`
month.abb	Abbreviated month names: `Jan - Dec.`
letters	Lower-case letters a - z.
LETTERS	Upper-case LETTERS A - Z.

See Chapter 7 Working with data objects for details about how to "extract" one or more elements from the constants (and other data objects).

3.4.2 Datasets

R has lots of datasets built-in for practice and examples. Many of the additional packages also contain their own data examples. Use the `data()` command to view the available datasets (Table 3.2).

```
data(..., package = NULL)
```

Table 3.2 Some parameters of the *data ()* function.

Parameter	Explanation
...	Names of datasets to load (separated with commas). Most data does not need to be loaded but in some packages it does.
package	Where to look for datasets to list. The default will list data for packages currently loaded (that is visible with `search()`). Give the name of a package (in "quotes") to see data for a particular package.

Example:

Datasets

```
# View data in package: cluster
data(package = "cluster")

Data sets in package 'cluster':

agriculture  European Union Agricultural Workforces
animals      Attributes of Animals
chorSub      Subset of C-horizon of Kola Data
flower       Flower Characteristics
plantTraits  Plant Species Traits Data
pluton       Isotopic Composition Plutonium Batches
ruspini      Ruspini Data
votes.repub  Votes for Republican Candidate in Presidential Elections
xclara       Bivariate Data Set with 3 Clusters
```

In general you can "use" a dataset if the package containing it is loaded, i.e. if you see it with `search()`. However, with some packages you must use `data(name)` to load the dataset. You don't need quotes around `name` (but you can if you want).

If a package is not loaded onto the search path you may still be able to access the data by using `package::name`. If you get an error, try: `data(name, package = "pkgname")`. In other words, give the name of the dataset and use the `package` parameter to point to the relevant `package` name.

Example:

Load a dataset from a package not "loaded" on the search path

```
# Access the shrimp dataset from package:MASS
MASS::shrimp
 [1] 32.2 33.0 30.8 33.8 32.2 33.3 31.7 35.7 32.4 31.2 26.6 30.7 32.5 30.7 31.2
[16] 30.3 32.3 31.7
```

Tip: View all installed datasets

You can view all the datasets in all the packages installed on your R system:

```
data(package = .packages(all.available = TRUE))
```

3.5   Types of object: an introduction

R recognizes different sorts of object. These can have different properties and are potentially handled by R in different ways. There are two main ways that R objects can vary:

- The form (or class) of the object.
- The nature of the contents.

The form of an object is largely related to the "shape". R objects can generally be thought of in terms of their dimensions, so you get one dimensional, two dimensional and so on. There are other attributes too, and the overall form is called an object `class` in R. The `class` of an object affects how R deals with it.

The nature of the contents is (fairly obviously) related to what the objects is made up of. There are different kinds of data item, such as numbers or text.

3.5.1   Object form or class

The arrangement of the items in an object affects how R interacts with it and what you can do with it (Table 3.3) shows some of the classes of object that R handles.

See Chapter 6 R object types and their properties for more information about the properties of R objects.

3.5.2   Object contents: types of data

The contents of an R object can be one or more of several kinds or types (Table 3.4).

See the chapter Manipulating data objects for more details about making objects and type.

A `vector` object can be more or less of any type, but all the elements must be the same type.

Table 3.3 Some object classes recognized in R.

Class name	Details
vector	One-dimensional objects. A vector is displayed as a row but think of it as being like a single column in a spreadsheet.
data.frame	Two dimensional. A data.frame has rows (cases) and columns (variables). You can think of it like a spreadsheet.
matrix	Two dimensional. A matrix has rows and columns.
table	Two or more dimensions. A table is a summary of cross-classifying variables, and shows their frequencies.
array	One or more dimensions. An array can have any number of dimensions.
list	A list is a loose collection of other objects that are bundled together for convenience.
ts	A ts object is a time series, which is a series of data items with additional information about the time intervals. A ts object can be multidimensional, that is, you can have more than one dataset with the same time interval information.

Table 3.4 Some of the types of data used by R.

Data type	Description
numeric	Regular numbers (that is, double precision values).
integer	Numbers stored as integers.
double	Double precision numbers, which conform to IEC 60559 (you get a precision of around 53 bits).
character	Text values, displayed in "quotes".
logical	Logical values are represented as TRUE or FALSE.
factor	Grouping variables. A factor is a kind of "category" variable.

```
# A numeric vector
MASS::shrimp

 [1] 32.2 33.0 30.8 33.8 32.2 33.3 31.7 35.7 32.4 31.2 26.6 30.7 32.5 30.7 31.2
[16] 30.3 32.3 31.7

# A character vector
month.abb

 [1] "Jan" "Feb" "Mar" "Apr" "May" "Jun" "Jul" "Aug" "Sep" "Oct" "Nov" "Dec"
```

A factor is similar to a vector in that it is one dimensional. At first glance a factor may appear to be a numeric or a character but it has an additional attribute levels, and these are displayed when you "look" at a factor.

```
# A factor variable
PlantGrowth$group

 [1] ctrl ctrl ctrl ctrl ctrl ctrl ctrl ctrl ctrl ctrl trt1 trt1 trt1 trt1 trt1
[16] trt1 trt1 trt1 trt1 trt1 trt2 trt2 trt2 trt2 trt2 trt2 trt2 trt2 trt2 trt2
Levels: ctrl trt1 trt2
```

The `Levels:` part of the display shows you that the object is a `factor` and gives the labels for the different groupings. Notice too that there are no "quotes" around the data items. A `factor` may not have labels and appear to be numerical:

```
[1] 1 1 1 2 2 2 3 3 3
Levels: 1 2 3
```

However, the `Levels:` label shows you that this is a `factor`. See Chapter 8 Manipulating data objects for more details about `factor` variables.

A `data.frame` has rows and columns. Each column can contain a different type of data. A `data.frame` is strictly rectangular, so all columns are the same length.

```
# A data.frame with all numeric columns
BOD

  Time demand
1   1   8.3
2   2  10.3
3   3  19.0
4   4  16.0
5   5  15.6
6   7  19.8
```

A `matrix` has rows and columns but all the data **must** be the same type (e.g. all numeric or all character). A `matrix` is strictly rectangular.

```
# A numeric matrix
VADeaths
```

	Rural Male	Rural Female	Urban Male	Urban Female
50-54	11.7	8.7	15.4	8.4
55-59	18.1	11.7	24.3	13.6
60-64	26.9	20.3	37.0	19.3
65-69	41.0	30.9	54.6	35.1
70-74	66.0	54.3	71.1	50.0

A `table` can have >2 dimensions, in which case the `table` is displayed as several 2D elements.

```
# A table (three dimensions)
HairEyeColour

, , Sex = Male
```

	Eye			
Hair	Brown	Blue	Hazel	Green
Black	32	11	10	3
Brown	53	50	25	15
Red	10	10	7	7
Blond	3	30	5	8

```
, , Sex = Female
```

Hair	Eye Brown	Blue	Hazel	Green
Black	36	9	5	2
Brown	66	34	29	14
Red	16	7	7	7
Blond	4	64	5	8

A list is a loose collection of objects, bundled together for convenience. The elements of the list can themselves be different classes, shapes and so on.

```
# A list
MASS::shoes

$A
 [1] 13.2 8.2 10.9 14.3 10.7 6.6 9.5 10.8 8.8 13.3

$B
 [1] 14.0 8.8 11.2 14.2 11.8 6.4 9.8 11.3 9.3 13.6
```

A ts object is a time series. Usually the contents are numeric, but they don't have to be. A ts object contains additional information about the time, that is the start and end points and the frequency of observation.

```
# A ts (time series)
Nile

Time Series:
Start = 1871
End = 1970
Frequency = 1
 [1]  1120 1160  963 1210 1160 1160  813 1230 1370 1140  995  935 1110  994 1020
[16]   960 1180  799  958 1140 1100 1210 1150 1250 1260 1220 1030 1100  774  840
[31]   874  694  940  833  701  916  692 1020 1050  969  831  726  456  824  702
[46]  1120 1100  832  764  821  768  845  864  862  698  845  744  796 1040  759
[61]   781  865  845  944  984  897  822 1010  771  676  649  846  812  742  801
[76]  1040  860  874  848  890  744  749  838 1050  918  986  797  923  975  815
[91]  1020  906  901 1170  912  746  919  718  714  740
```

> **Note: The NA object**
>
> NA is an object in its own right in R. Think of it as a logical constant of length 1. It "signifies" missing values. See more about missing values in Chapter 7 section 7.2.5.

You'll see examples of different object classes and types throughout the text. Chapter 6 *R object types and their properties* and Chapter 8 *Manipulating data objects* also give additional information.

EXERCISES:

Self-Assessment for Introduction to R objects

1. R names must include at least one letter. TRUE or FALSE?
2. You can tell what kind an object is by using the ___ function.
3. A `matrix` object may have multiple columns but:
   a. they must be `numeric`
   b. they must be `character`
   c. they must all be the same kind
   d. they must be different kinds
4. A `factor` object is a kind of ___ or ___ variable.
5. The `logical` kind of object can only hold values 0 or 1. TRUE or FALSE?

Answers to exercises are in the Appendix.

3.6   Chapter Summary: Introduction to R objects

Topic	Key Points
Object names	All R objects have a name, which can use a-z, A-Z, 0-9, . and _ characters. Names are case sensitive and *must* start with a letter.
Object assignment	R prefers x <- y for assignment rather than x = y. In most cases = works (but there are some exceptions).
Built-in objects	There are different kinds of object built-in to R: command functions, constants, and data examples.
Object `class`	Different `class` objects have different properties.
Object form	Common `classes` of object are: `vector` (1 dimensional), `data.frame` (two dimensional), `matrix` and `list` (loose collection of stuff). There are several others.
Types of data	There are different types of data, including: `numeric`, `character`, `logical` and `factor` (there are others).

4. Making and importing data objects

So far you've done some simple math but not dealt with data objects in any meaningful way. In this chapter you'll learn how join things together to make larger data items and how to get data into R from external sources.

What's in this chapter

» Joining items
» Number sequences
» Repeated elements
» Enter data via the keyboard
» Import data:
  » Paste data from the clipboard.
  » Import data from a disk file (or Internet location).

See section 8.1 *Random numbers* in Chapter 8 *Manipulating data objects* for details about making random numbers and generally adding data to existing objects.

Note: Support material

See the ↘ for links to material on the support website.

4.1   Joining items

Most data items consist of more than one element. Joining things together to make larger items is a fundamental task that you'll need in many situations. The c() command is a very general one that can be used to join items together to make a longer item.

```
c(...)
```

In place of the ... you provide elements (e.g. numbers or text) separated with commas. In most cases you'll use c() to join elements to make a vector result. For example you can make a sample of numerical values:

```
data1 <- c(3, 5, 7, 5,3,2,6, 8, 5, 6, 9)
data1

[1] 3 5 7 5 3 2 6 8 5 6 9
```

Note that R ignores the spaces, they are for your benefit. You have now got a vector constructed by combining the numeric elements in the brackets (in the order they appear there). You can add to your sample:

```
data2 <- c(data1, 4,5, 7, 3, 4)
data2

[1] 3 5 7 5 3 2 6 8 5 6 9 4 5 7 3 4
```

In this case you added the new elements after the original, the order you type them is always the order they end up in. Note that in this example a new object data2 was specified. If you kept the original name the new assignment would overwrite the original data1 and there would be **no warning**.

Example:

Overwrite a data object

```
data1 <- c(data1, 4, 5, 7, 3, 4)
```

The evaluation happens within the execution of the c() function; the original data1 is taken and the additional values are appended, then the result is assigned to data1, which overwrites it. This means you need to **be careful!** The behavior might seem a bit strange if you are not used to programming, however, if you are running a program you do not want it to stop and ask you questions, you want it to run unsupervised.

Your data do not have to be numeric, a text input will work just fine. If you enter character values you have to enclose them in quotes, single ' or double " are fine as long as each element has "matching" quotes.

```
day1 <- c("Mon", "Tue", "Wed", "Thu", "Fri")
day1

[1] "Mon" "Tue" "Wed" "Thu" "Fri"
```

Note that whatever quote type you use, R will display the results enclosed in double " quotes unless you use noquote().

```
noquote(day1)

[1] Mon Tue Wed Thu Fri
```

Note: Enter text values without quotes

It is possible to enter text without quotes, using a custom function. There are some limitations though; you still need to separate with commas, and you cannot use characters other than those "allowed" in object names (which are regular letters, numbers, and . or _).

```
cc <- function(...) as.character(sys.call())[-1]
cc(This, is, text, 123, And. _ )

[1] "This" "is" "text" "123"  "And. _ "
```

The c() command is a very basic one and is used very widely in R. You won't generally use it to enter large quantities of data but you'll run across it in other contexts.

4.1.1   Add elements inside another

Using c() only allows you to append (or prepend) elements. Using the append() function however, allows you to insert elements starting from a position you specify.

```
append(x, values, after)
```

In the function you specify the position `after` which you want the new elements to be inserted. The default is to add elements at the end.

Example:

Insert elements

```
x <- c(1, 2, 3, 7, 8, 9)
x
[1] 1 2 3 7 8 9
append(x, c(4, 5, 6), after = 3)
[1] 1 2 3 4 5 6 7 8 9
```

4.2   Number sequences

The `c()` function is useful for joining things together but tedious if there are more than just a few elements. If you want sequences there are other ways to proceed.

Tip: Random numbers

Generate random numbers with `runif()`. You can also generate random variates from other distributions, see Chapter 8 *Manipulating data objects* for more details.

4.2.1   Integer sequences

You can make a simple `integer` sequence using `:`. You specify `p:q` where `p` is your starting value and `q` is your ending value.

Example:

Integer sequences

```
1:5
[1] 1 2 3 4 5
12:6 # Reverse direction
[1] 12 11 10 9 8 7 6
-1:-7 # Using negative values
[1] -1 -2 -3 -4 -5 -6 -7
```

Note: Integer sequences

The `p:q` does not *exactly* produce integer sequences, you can set `p` to a non-integer value but 1 will be added until `q` is reached (but not exceeded).

```
2.5:12.1
 [1]  2.5 3.5 4.5 5.5 6.5 7.5 8.5 9.5 10.5 11.5

2.7:-6
 [1]  2.7 1.7 0.7 -0.3 -1.3 -2.3 -3.3 -4.3 -5.3
```

4.2.2 Other numerical sequences

Using : works by adding 1 to your starting value in direct sequence. If you want other kinds of regular sequence you need `seq()`.

```
seq(from, to, by, length.out, along.with, ...)
```

There are options when using `seq()`, you should always give the starting and ending points but you can specify how the sequence is constructed (Table 4.1).

Table 4.1 Parameters of the *seq()* function.

Parameter	Explanation
from	The starting value (default = 1).
to	The ending value (default = 1).
by	The value to increment the sequence. If you give a value here the sequence will not extend beyond it, and may "fall short". The default is effectively 1.
length.out	The desired length of the result. If you give a value here the sequence will end exactly at the to point and the by interval will be calculated to make this happen.
along.with	Make the result the same length as this. Usually you point to another object that you want to match the length of.
...	Other parameters might be used.

The simplest kind of sequence uses a set interval, using the by parameter:

```
seq(from = 1, to = 100, by = 10)
 [1]  1 11 21 31 41 51 61 71 81 91
```

Note: The end of the sequence does not exceed the to parameter. In the preceding example the sequence stops at 91, rather than 101.

If you want to go "backwards" the by parameter needs to be negative.

```
seq(from = 90, to = 50, by = -3)
 [1] 90 87 84 81 78 75 72 69 66 63 60 57 54 51
```

You can fix the length of the result and let R work out the intervals using the `length.out` parameter:

```
seq(from = 1, to = 100, length.out = 10)
 [1]   1 12 23 34 45 56 67 78 89 100
```

You can also match the length of an existing data object by "pointing to it" with the `along.with` parameter:

```
data1 = c(3, 5, 7, 5, 3, 2, 6, 8, 5, 6, 9)
seq(from = 1, to = 100, along.with = data1)
 [1]   1.0 10.9 20.8 30.7 40.6 50.5 60.4 70.3 80.2 90.1 100.0
```

The parameter values do not have to be integers:

```
seq(from = 2.5, to = 20, by = 2.5)
[1]  2.5 5.0 7.5 10.0 12.5 15.0 17.5 20.0
```

Variations of seq() function

There are several "variants" of the seq() function.

```
seq.int(from, to, by, length.out, along.with, ...)
seq _ along(along.with)
seq _ len(length.out)
```

The seq.int() function is a "primitive" version of seq() and for most practical purposes you can consider it the same.

The seq _ along() function is designed to be a "counter" and produces an integer sequence, starting at 1, that matches the length of the argument.

```
data1
[1]  3 5 7 5 3 2 6 8 5 6 9
seq _ along(data1)
[1]  1 2 3 4 5 6 7 8 9 10 11
seq _ along(letters) # there are 26
[1]  1 2 3 4 5 6 7 8 9 10 11 12 13 14 15 16 17 18 19 20 21 22 23 24 25
[26]  26
```

The seq _ len() function is another "counter" that starts at 1 and ends at the value in the argument. It is generally faster to compute than seq(length.out =) but you are not likely to notice.

```
seq _ len(12)
[1]  1 2 3 4 5 6 7 8 9 10 11 12
```

4.3   Repeated items

You can use rep() to make repeats, which do not have to be numbers. The rep() function gives you three broad options:

```
rep(x, times = 1, each = 1, length.out = NA, ...)
```

If you specify times, the input x is repeated that many times.

```
rep(2, times = 10)
[1]  2 2 2 2 2 2 2 2 2 2
rep("Jan", times = 3)
[1]  "Jan" "Jan" "Jan"
```

If you specify each then each element of x is repeated that many times. This is assuming that x has more than one element of course.

```
# Simple repeat
rep(c("jan", "feb"), times = 3)

[1]  "jan" "feb" "jan" "feb" "jan" "feb"
# Repeat each element
rep(c("jan", "feb"), each = 3)

[1]  "jan" "jan" "jan" "feb" "feb" "feb"
```

If you specify `length.out` the output is modified to give a result of the length you specified.

```
rep(c("jan", "feb"), each = 3, length.out = 7)
[1] "jan" "jan" "jan" "feb" "feb" "feb" "jan"
```

There are two other versions of `rep()`:

```
rep.int(x, times)
rep _ len(x, length.out)
```

These are "convenience" functions and operate a little faster for the specific repeat "type", but you are unlikely to notice.

Note: repeats and object type

The `rep()` function will work "best" on `vector` objects but it can also make repeats of other things. However, the result may not be quite what you expect.

```
BOD # data.frame

  Time demand
1    1    8.3
2    2   10.3
3    3   19.0
4    4   16.0
5    5   15.6
6    7   19.8

rep(BOD, times = 2) # results in a list object

$Time
[1] 1 2 3 4 5 7

$demand
[1] 8.3 10.3 19.0 16.0 15.6 19.8

$Time
[1] 1 2 3 4 5 7

$demand
[1] 8.3 10.3 19.0 16.0 15.6 19.8
```

See also Chapter 7 *Working with data objects* section 7.2.6 *Duplicate cases*, were you can see how to create repeated elements using the `inverse.rle()` function.

4.4   Join by `paste()`

The `paste()` command allows you to "stick" items together, and then create a text output. You need to specify the items to join, and how, using the parameters (Table 4.2).

```
paste(..., sep = " ", collapse = NULL)
paste0(..., collapse = NULL)
```

The `paste0()` function (that is the number 0 not the letter O) is "convenience" function that can be useful under certain conditions; it uses `sep = ""`, and is reckoned to be marginally more "efficient".

Table 4.2 Parameters of the `paste()` command.

Parameter	Description
...	Items to be pasted, separated by commas. Usually these are `vector` objects.
sep	The separator character (in "quotes") to be used in the "join", the default is a space.
collapse	A character string (in "quotes") to use as a separator. If specified then, after elements are concatenated the result is "collapsed" down to form a single `character vector` with the elements separated using the specified character.

When the number of elements in each of the items you paste together match, you get a simple join:

```
# paste with : as separator
paste(letters, LETTERS, sep = ":")

 [1] "a:A" "b:B" "c:C" "d:D" "e:E" "f:F" "g:G" "h:H" "i:I" "j:J" "k:K" "l:L"
[13] "m:M" "n:N" "o:O" "p:P" "q:Q" "r:R" "s:S" "t:T" "u:U" "v:V" "w:W" "x:X"
[25] "y:Y" "z:Z"

# paste but collapse into a single vector
paste(letters, LETTERS, sep = ":", collapse = ", ")

[1] "a:A, b:B, c:C, d:D, e:E, f:F, g:G, h:H, i:I, j:J, k:K, l:L, m:M, n:N,
o:O, p:P, q:Q, r:R, s:S, t:T, u:U, v:V, w:W, x:X, y:Y, z:Z"
```

When the number of elements in one item is shorter, the elements are "recycled":

```
paste(1:10, "x", sep = "")
 [1] "1x" "2x" "3x" "4x" "5x" "6x" "7x" "8x" "9x" "10x"
```

Using `paste0()` is effectively the same as `paste(..., sep = "")`:

```
paste0(letters, 1:2)

 [1] "a1" "b2" "c1" "d2" "e1" "f2" "g1" "h2" "i1" "j2" "k1" "l2" "m1" "n2" "o1"
[16] "p2" "q1" "r2" "s1" "t2" "u1" "v2" "w1" "x2" "y1" "z2"
```

You can use `paste()` to "stick" things together in many creative ways; remember though, that the result is *always* text (that is, a `character vector`).

4.5   The `scan()` command

The `scan()` command is a flexible function that allows you to enter relatively small datasets from a variety of sources:

- Type from the keyboard.
- Read the clipboard.
- Data from disk.

```
scan(file = "", what = double(), sep = "", dec = ".", ...)
```

The various parameters control where, and how the data are imported (Table 4.3).

Table 4.3 Some parameters of the `scan()` function.

Parameter	Description
file	You can give a filename (in "quotes") to read a file from disk.
what	The kind of data expected. The default is numbers. Use what = "character" for text input.
sep	The separator character, the default is none (looks for whitespace). Specify "," for a comma, "\t" for a tab character.
dec	The decimal point character, the default is a period.
skip	How many lines to skip at the start of import.
na.strings	A character string giving values that are to be interpreted as "missing".
comment.char	A character string, lines beginning with this character(s) will be skipped.
...	Other parameters can be used.

The `scan()` command is designed for relatively small amounts of data, and the result is always a `vector`.

4.5.1 Enter data from keyboard with `scan()`

The `scan()` function allows you to enter data from the keyboard more rapidly than `c()`. The main advantage over `c()` is that you do not need to separate values with a comma , but can use spaces.

For numerical data the process is very simple:

1. Assign a data object with x <- scan().
2. Type your values, separated by spaces.
3. If you press ENTER, R will wait for further entry.
4. Finish the process by typing ENTER on a blank line.

Example:

Enter numeric data using `scan()`

```
data3 <- scan()
1:
```

R now waits for you to type something (if you change your mind press ENTER now), and the cursor changes from the default > to 1:. You can press ENTER and carry on, or press ENTER on a blank line to finish the process.

```
1: 6 7 8 7 6 3 8 9 10 7
11: 6 9
13:
Read 12 items
```

In this example 12 items were typed in. You can view the data by typing its name:
```
data3
[1] 6 7 8 7 6 3 8 9 10 7 6 9
```

If you want to enter text values you need to add `what` = `"character"` as a parameter. The process is the same as for numbers, you do not need commas or quotes. However, multi-words that contain spaces will be regarded as separate items.

```
day2 <- scan(what = "character")
1: Mon Tue Wed
4: Thu
5:
Read 4 items
day2
[1] "Mon" "Tue" "Wed" "Thu"
```

Tip: Enter text with multi-words using scan ()

You can enter text elements that contain spaces but you'll need to use a separator (e.g. sep = `","`). This can still save a lot of typing as you still do not need to use "quotes".

```
x = scan(what = "character", sep = ",")
1: hello you, what, are, you doing?
5:
Read 4 items
x
[1] "hello you" "what"    "are"    "you doing?"
```

4.5.2 Read the clipboard using scan()

You can access the clipboard using `scan()`, which makes it useful to transfer data from a spreadsheet, word processor, or text document (e.g. a web page).

The process is the same as if you were typing, the difference being that you paste from your clipboard instead of actually typing. You need to preview your data and check what separator character is used. If you are looking at a spreadsheet you can leave the `sep` parameter at its default. If you are copying from another document, you need to match the separator; use `sep` = `"\t"` for a Tab character.

Note: Rows from spreadsheet with scan ()

In general it is easier to copy columns than rows when using a spreadsheet. The regular Windows GUI does **not** like spreadsheet rows. However, an IDE like RStudio copes just fine. Similarly the basic Terminal does not handle spreadsheet rows "nicely"; a "substitute" terminal program (e.g. iTerm.app for Mac) can.

You should also check the contents of what you are pasting, so you know what you are dealing with. You will need to use `what` = `"character"` for copying text. It does not matter if the text is "quoted" or not, R will cope. However, R is not keen on curly quotes, and may either refuse to deal with them or not "recognize" them as quotes and you will end up with additional characters in your text.

4.5.3 Read data from a file using scan()

The `scan()` command can read data from a disk file (or URL), but only as a single variable. If you have data with multiple variables you need `read.table()`, see section 4.6 *Data files from disk*. In spite of this limitation `scan()` can be helpful in getting chunks of data into R.

You should preview the data to be imported, so you can determine the appropriate parameters to use (see Table 4.3). Table 4.4 lists some items you'll need to consider:

Table 4.4 Items to consider when using `scan()` for import from disk file.

Item	Parameter default	Parameter options
Data type	`what = double()`	Use `what = "character"` for text import.
Separator	`sep = ""`	Use *sep* = `"\t"` for Tab, `sep = ","` for comma.
Lines to skip	`skip = 0`	Use a number to state how many lines to skip.
Comment lines	`comment.char = ""`	Use `comment.char = "#"` to ignore lies beginning with "#".
Decimal point	`dec = "."`	Use `dec = ","` for European style decimal place.
Missing data	`na.strings = "NA"`	Give one or more "things" that are in the data that represent missing values, e.g. `na.strings = c(-1, "missing")`. These will be replaced by NA.

You can see an example of a datafile in Figure 4.1.

```
# These data are sizes in mm
# of beetles from a pond
# in Devon June 2013
34 35 33 26 35 35 35 32 38 29
32 34 33 29 37 37 31 37 31 28
30 38 34 33 33 32 29 35 29 30
36 32 31 33 35 35 31 34 29 29
36 34 37 28 27 32 28 32 36 32
36 31 33 38 33 32 36 33 34 31
41 34 30 27 34 34 29 27 37 31
35 34 27 35 28 31 31 36 32 32
30 33 36 34 29 33 28 34 37 34
34 33 31 30 36 26 29 35 34 35
```

Figure 4.1 A space separated data file with comment lines. Viewed in a web browser.

The final consideration is the file location. You need to specify the location of the file (in "quotes"), as a full path, relative to the current working directory (see section 4.7.1 *Working directory*). However, on most systems you can use `file.choose()` in place of a file name. This will invoke a file browser, allowing you to select the appropriate file. For example, the following would allow you to import the data shown in Figure 4.1.

```
beetles <- scan(file = file.choose(), sep = " ", comment.char = "#")
```

Once you press ENTER your system will open a file browser; you then select the file and `scan()` will continue. Type the name you assigned to view the result.

```
beetles
```

```
 [1] 34 35 33 26 35 35 35 32 38 29 32 34 33 29 37 37 31 37 31 28 30 38 34 33 33
[26] 32 29 35 29 30 36 32 31 33 35 35 31 34 29 29 36 34 37 28 27 32 28 32 36 32
[51] 36 31 33 38 33 32 36 33 34 31 41 34 30 27 34 34 29 27 37 31 35 34 27 35 28
[76] 31 31 36 32 32 30 33 36 34 29 33 28 34 37 34 34 33 31 30 36 26 29 35 34 35
```

You can use the other parameters (Table 4.4) to match the contents of the file. For example Figure 4.2 shows a simple comma-separated file, containing numeric data.

```
34,35,33,26,35,35,35,32,38,29
32,34,33,29,37,37,31,37,31,28
30,38,34,33,33,32,29,35,29,30
36,32,31,33,35,35,31,34,29,29
36,34,37,28,27,32,28,32,36,32
36,31,33,38,33,32,36,33,34,31
41,34,30,27,34,34,29,27,37,31
35,34,27,35,28,31,31,36,32,32
30,33,36,34,29,33,28,34,37,34
34,33,31,30,36,26,29,35,34,35
```

Figure 4.2 A simple comma-separated datafile. The contents are numeric and there are no comment lines or lines to skip.

You could import the data using something like the following:

```
mydata <- scan(file.choose(), sep = ",")
```

Note: Path separators

Windows users are used to back-slash \ as a separator between directories. However, in R you **must** always use forward-slash /, e.g. `"Users/Me/data/mydata.txt"`.

Note: Working directory

You can check what the current working directory is using `getwd()`. You can set the working directory using `setwd()` but Windows and Macintosh GUI have menus that make this task easy (also an IDE, such as RStudio).

4.6   Data files from disk

Most of the data you'll want to import from disk will be in spreadsheet-like layout, with rows and columns (e.g. CSV data). In this case the `scan()` function will not work for you and you'll need something that can manage multiple variables (columns).

The `read.table()` function is designed to help you import data from disk (or URL) that has a multi-column layout, where the columns represent different variables.

Files must be in plain text. You can specify separators, decimal point characters and other parameters in the command (Table 4.5).

```
read.table(file, header = FALSE, sep = "", dec = ".",
comment.char = "#", row.names, col.names, na.strings = "NA", ...)
```

Table 4.5 **Some parameters of** `read.table()`.

Parameter	Explanation
file	The filename (in quotes) with full path or relative to current working directory. You can specify a URL.
header	If TRUE the first row is considered to be column names. The default is FALSE.
sep	The separator character, the default is a space. Use sep = "\t" for Tab.
dec	The decimal point character. The default is dec = ".".
comment.char	Do not import lines beginning with the specified character (default is "#").
row.names	A vector of names to use for the rows. Use row.names = 1 to select the first column to act as row names. Alternatively you can specify names. The default uses a simple numeric index.
col.names	The default is to use the existing top row for names of columns (if header = TRUE). You can specify your own names.
na.strings	If a "cell" of the imported data is empty it will always be replaced with NA (not available). You can specify additional values/strings that will also be replaced by NA, the default being "NA".
…	Other parameters are available.

Note that in general the defaults of the `read.table()` command are very "conservative" and you will need to ensure that you specify all the appropriate parameters when you import data.

> ### Tip: Interactive file choice
>
> You can use file = file.choose() in place of a file name, in Windows or Macintosh, to interactively choose a file. This will *not* work if you run R from a terminal application.

4.6.1 Import CSV files

The `read.csv()` command is designed as a convenience function, with defaults that make it slightly easier to import CSV and other delimited files.

```
read.csv(file, header = TRUE, sep = ",", dec = ".", comment = "", ...)
```

In general you can use `read.csv()` on any occasion where you would have considered `read.table()`. The defaults for the parameters are such that you can generally avoid having to incorporate any except the `file` name.

There are several variants of `read.csv()`, these have subtly different parameter defaults, allowing you to import Tab separated for example. However, it is probably easier to stick to the `read.csv()` function and alter the appropriate parameter, than to remember the additional command names. The additional functions are:

```
read.csv2(sep = ";", dec = ",", ...)
read.delim(sep = "\t", dec = ".", ...)
read.delim2(sep = "\t", dec = ",", ...)
```

You can see that the main differences are in the `sep` and `dec` parameters.

Note: Importing `character` columns

In some versions of R `read.table()` would automatically convert `character` columns to `factor` variables. In later versions (4 and above), this changed and imported text remains as `character`. If you want to import text variables as `factor` you can do several things:

- Change the settings for the current session via: `options(stringsAsFactors = TRUE)`
- Use the parameter `stringsAsFactors = TRUE` in the `read.table()` command
- Change the columns you want into `factor` variables later:

  a. All text columns: `rapply(x, f = as.factor, classes = "character", how = "replace")` (see section 9.3)
  b. Single variable: `as.factor()` (see Chapter 8)

You can check the current option by typing: `default.stringsAsFactors()`

4.6.2 Script files

A script file is a plain text file where the contents are potential R commands. Script files can be very helpful in allowing you to "automate" certain tasks. A script file is usually saved with a `.R` file extension. The `source()` command is used to "read" a `.R` file:

```
source(file, ...)
```

4.6.3 RData files

A file with the `.RData` extension is readable only by R. It contains R objects, which could be data, results or custom functions. You can "import" an `.RData` file using the `load()` function:

```
load(file, ...)
```

You can also use the OS to `load` a `.RData` file "directly". You can double-click, (or right-click), or drag the file to the R icon. The result depends on the state of R at the time:

- If R **is** running: the objects contained in the `.RData` file are added to the workspace. Objects existing may be overwritten if their names match incoming objects. There are no warnings.
- If R is **not** running: R is opened and the objects contained in the `.RData` file are added to a "fresh" workspace (so it contains only the objects from the `.RData` file). In addition the working directory is set to point to the folder that contained the `.RData` file.

Note: Operating system and .RData files

Windows or Macintosh OS will generally associate `.RData` files with R. You can check which program is associated by right-clicking on the file icon.

4.7   Disk directories

You can access your computer's file system in various ways, for example:

- Examine the contents of disk directories.
- Create new disk directories.
- Delete files and/or directories.

In this chapter you'll see how to "look" at your file system, with a view to seeing what files you have that you may potentially import. See Chapter 5 *Managing and exporting data objects* for details about manipulating files and directories.

Note: R control over file system

It can be potentially "dangerous" to tinker with your file system from within R since you'll get few (if any) warnings.

4.7.1   Working directory

R uses a "default" directory (the working directory); this is where R "looks" for items to load and where it saves by default. You can check what the current working directory is with `getwd()`.

```
getwd()
[1] "/Users/markgardener"
```

The directory that you start with will depend of course on your operating system and your user set-up. However, note that R *always* uses forward slashes / as the separator between directory levels.

You can alter the working directory using `setwd()`. You need to type (in "quotes") the new path to point at the directory you wish to use. The new path needs to be relative to the current working directory, but there are a couple of "short-cuts" you can use to help.

- ".." – Steps up one level in the *path* hierarchy.
- "~" – Sets the *path* to the user default.
- "." – The current working directory.

If you are running R from a GUI (or IDE) there will also be an option to alter the working directory from a menu.

- Windows: *File > Change dir....*
- Macintosh: *Misc > Change Working Directory....*
- RStudio: *Session > Set Working Directory.*

Tip: Change working directory interactively in Windows GUI

In the Windows GUI you can use `choose.dir()` instead of a path to open a directory browser.

Example:

Working directory

```
setwd("~/Dropbox")
getwd()

[1] "/Users/markgardener/Dropbox"

setwd("..")
getwd()

[1] "/Users/markgardener"
```

4.7.2 View folder contents

You can access the file system to view the contents using `dir()` (or `list.files()`). You need to specify the path to the directory you want to view (in "quotes"), using / as path separators. You can use the same "short-cuts" (i.e. ".." and "~") as for altering the working directory.

Example:

Directory contents

```
dir("~/test")
[1] "Data-1.txt" "Data-2.csv" "Data-3.docx"
```

> ### Note: Empty directories
>
> If a directory is empty, `dir()` returns a result of `character(0)`.

See Chapter 5 *Managing and exporting data objects* for details about manipulating files and directories.

4.8 Excel and other format files

Aside from .RData (and .rds) files, which are coded representations of R objects, R will only import plain text files. However, there are add-on command packages (Table 4.6) that can read and import other file types, including Excel spreadsheets.

Table 4.6 Some R command packages that can import special format files.

Package	Function(s)	Imports
foreign	read.spss	SPSS .sav datafiles.
	read.dta	Stata datafiles.
	read.mtp	MiniTab portable worksheet.
xlsx	read.xlsx	Excel 2007 and Excel 97/2000/XP/2003 files.
openxlsx	read.xlsx	Excel 2007 files (not earlier .xls files).
readxl	read_excel	Excel .xls or .xlsx format files.

The package: **foreign** comes as part of the original distribution of R, so you do not need to install it. You will of course need to "launch" it using `library()`. The other packages will need to be installed (`install.packages()`) before you can use them, see section 1.3 *Extending R* for additional details.

Tip: View package functions

You can see the index page for a command package using `help()`. For example, the **foreign** package can also import other file types, look at the index for **foreign** for more details using:

```
help(package = "foreign")
```

4.9 Function objects

One of the strengths of R is that you can create your own custom functions. You can make a function using the `function()` command. There are three parts to a function:

- The name.
- The parameters (arguments).
- The body.

The name of the function should conform to the naming convention see section 3.1 *Names for objects* for a reminder.

The parameters are given in `()` and conform to a `name = value` convention. That is to say, you can give the name of a parameter and set a default `value`.

The body of the function refers to the input parameters and carries out the "business" of the function. If you need to use more than a single line (which is usual) you enclose the entire body of the function in curly brackets `{}`.

Example:

A simple R function

```
myfun <- function(x) x^3
myfun(x = 2)

[1] 8
```

The `myfun` function is now an object, currently stored in your workspace. You can "load" functions from disk in several main ways:

- Install and load a command package: `install.packages()` and `library()`.
- Run a script that contains the command lines to create the function: `source()`.
- Load a .RData file that contains a previously saved function object: `load()`.

You'll see examples of functions throughout the text and the topic of programming in general is covered in Chapter 15 *Programming tools*.

Note: Miscellaneous objects

It's possible to save R objects in text-form (ASCII), in a layout that allows the item to be human-read and also importable into R (see Chapter 5 *Managing and exporting data objects* for more details about the process).

You can read these miscellaneous ASCII text objects using dget().

```
dget(file)
```

EXERCISES:

Self-Assessment for Making and importing data objects

1. The ____ function is the simplest way to combine items.
2. You can use the ____ argument in seq() to make a sequence with a certain number of elements.
3. You can read disk files with which of the following functions:
   a. read.table()
   b. scan()
   c. load()
   d. source()
4. To import a tab separated file you specify the separator with ____.
5. You have to alter the working directory in order to read data or save items to disk.. TRUE or FALSE?

Answers to exercises are in the *Appendix*.

4.10 Chapter Summary: Making and importing data objects

There are various ways to make/import data items. Whichever method you use, make sure you've got what you expect! Type the name of the object you created to check that it looks "correct".

Topic	Key Points
Combine	Use c() to combine items.
Sequences	Make a sequence using seq(from, to, ...). Simple sequences only need a colon: p:q.
Repeated items	Use rep() to create repeated elements or items.
Paste	The paste() function sticks items together.
Clipboard	The scan() function can read the clipboard.
Import files	Use read.csv() for importing CSV files from disk.
Import R data	Files saved in R-format (.RData) can be loaded with load().
Directories	Use getwd() to see the name of the working directory. Set the working directory with setwd(). View directory contents using dir().

5. Managing and exporting data objects

This chapter is about managing your assets and exporting data and other items to disk. In the previous Chapter 4 *Making and importing data objects* you saw how to make and get data into R.

What's in this chapter

» View objects in your workspace
» Manage and remove objects from the workspace
» Manage files and folders on disk
» Export different kinds of object to disk files

In this chapter the focus is on managing data items, exporting to disk, and interacting with the file system.

Note: Support material

See the ⬊ for links to material on the support website.

5.1 Viewing items in the workspace

Managing your data and other R objects is important. You need to be able to see what data you have in your workspace, which you can do with `ls()`.

```
ls()
 [1] "ans1" "ans2" "ans3" "ans4" "ans5" "ans6" "cc"  "data1" "data2"
[10] "day1" "day2" "myfun" "x"
```

The result is a `vector` of all the R objects in your workspace. You can also use `objects()`, which is essentially the same thing. The R objects you see by default are those that correspond to data, results or custom functions in the `.GlobalEnv` part of the `search()` path. You can alter the "target" to point to other items on the `search()` path; so if you have additional command packages loaded you can look at the contents:

```
library(MASS)  # load library
ls(name = "package:MASS")  # view contents
```

5.1.1 List items that match a pattern

You can view only items in your workspace that match a `pattern`, so restricting the results you see. R uses *regular expressions* to carry out pattern matching.

```
ls(name, pattern)
```

In ls() the name is the part of the search() path you want to show, the default being .GlobalEnv, the workspace. The pattern parameter is a *regular expression* that is matched, with matches being displayed (Table 5.1).

Table 5.1 Some regular expressions used for pattern matching.

Pattern	Matches
"at"	Contains "at" in the order specified.
"a.a"	Period is a wildcard. This matches "a"(anything)"a".
"^a"	Caret ^ matches the start. This matches items beginning with "a".
"^da"	Beginning with "da".
"^[da]"	Elements in [] are treated independently (like OR). This matches beginning with "d" OR beginning with "a".
"^d|^a"	Use pipe character | as a logical OR. This is the same as above.
"^[^ab]"	Put caret ^ at start in [] to exclude. This matches items beginning with anything except "a" or "b".
"2$"	Use a following dollar symbol $ to match endings. This matches items ending with "2".
"[12]$"	Match items ending with "1" OR "2".
"[2-5]"	Use a dash – to give a range. This matches items containing numbers 2, 3, 4, or 5. This may not always work, so it is *safer* to use "[2345]".

Your pattern must always enclosed in quotes.

> ## Note: Regular expressions
>
> Regular expressions are used widely in computing (not just in R) and Table 5.1 only shows a few of the options available for regular expressions. There are many resources on the Internet that give more details about using regular expressions.

Example:

Use pattern in ls()

```
# Match only objects starting with 'a'
ls(pattern = "^a")

[1] "a"     "after"  "an.long"  "an.wide"  "ans1"  "ans2"  "ans3"
[8] "ans4"  "ans5"   "ans6"     "aq"
```

Find out more regarding *regular expressions* with:

```
help("regex", package = "base")
```

5.1.2   List objects and class

When you use ls() (or objects()), you get a character vector of names of the objects. This is useful but it does not tell you anything about the objects themselves. You can use sapply() to look at the class of every object, like so:

```
sapply(.GlobalEnv, FUN = class)
```

> ### Note: Object structure
>
> You can get more information about the objects in your workspace (or other packages) using `ls.str()` or `lsf.str()` functions. The former gives some details about individual objects, the latter only shows the function objects.

5.2 Removing items from the workspace

From time to time it is good to do some housekeeping. Generally this means getting rid of stuff you don't need. You can remove objects from your workspace using `rm()` (or `remove()`).

```
rm(..., list)
```

The simplest way is to give the names of the objects to be removed, separated by commas:

```
ls(pattern = "^ans")

[1] "ans1" "ans2" "ans3" "ans4" "ans5" "ans6"

rm(ans1, ans2)
ls(pattern = "^ans")

[1] "ans3" "ans4" "ans5" "ans6"
```

> ### Note: Removing "protected" objects
>
> You cannot use `rm()` to remove objects in R command packages.

5.2.1 Remove items that match a pattern

You can use a `list` to selectively remove objects with `rm()`. If you use `ls()` to make a selection you can bundle that inside a `list` like so:

```
# Remove all objects beginning with 'b'
rm(list = ls(pattern = "^b"))
```

Note that there are **no warnings** when you remove objects.

> ### Note: Clear everything
>
> You can clear **all** objects from your workspace with:
>
> ```
> rm(list = ls())
> ```
>
> There are **no warnings**. You can also clear the workspace using menus if you are using a GUI or IDE.

5.3 Managing the file system on your OS

You can save objects to disk in various formats, such as `.csv` or `.RData`. You'll see how to save/export to disk shortly – this section focuses on the file system of your OS.

You can manage files and directories from R. In the previous chapter you saw how to view the contents of disk folders. Here you'll learn how to make new folders, rename files and so on.

5.3.1 Create a new directory

You can make folders on your file system using dir.create(). You need to specify a path (in "quotes") to the folder you want to make. The same ".." and "~" short-cuts can be used as you've already seen. If the folder/directory already exists, you will get a warning, otherwise the folder is created without comment.

```
# Folder in home directory
dir.create("~/test-2")
```

> **Tip: Check a folder exists before making it**
>
> If a folder already exists, you'll get a warning. This can be "bothersome" if you are running a script, as you don't want any additional output. So, use if () to determine if the folder is already present. If it is not, then go ahead and make the folder.
>
> ```
> # Folder in working directory
> if (file.exists("./Temp") == FALSE) dir.create("./Temp")
> ```

5.3.2 Delete a directory

You can delete folders on your disk. This can obviously lead to potentially *awkward* situations! You need to use unlink(x, recursive = TRUE) to remove a directory called x.

Example:

Delete a disk directory/folder

```
unlink(x = "~/test-2", recursive = TRUE)
```

As with other "directory" commands you need the path in "quotes" (separators /) and can use the ".." and "~" short-cuts.

5.3.3 Manage disk files

There are various ways you can manage disk files (rather than folders). Table 5.2 shows some of the functions you can use to interact with the file systems.

When you use file.create() you create an empty file. If there was an existing file, it is overwritten with **no warning**. The only warning you get is if you try to create a file in an "unavailable" location.

You can copy a file from one location to another (potentially within the same folder) with file.copy(). Use overwrite = TRUE to force the replacement of a file with an existing name. Use recursive = TRUE to copy sub-folders.

> **Note: Symbolic links and path names**
>
> If you want to make a symbolic link, using file.symlink() the from path name needs to be "expanded" into its full form. Use normalizePath() to do this (or type it in full).
>
> ```
> file.symlink(from = normalizePath("oldpath"), to = "newpath")
> ```

Table 5.2 Some functions for managing disk files.

Command	Description/Result
file.create	Create an empty file. The function returns an on-screen message, indicating success or failure. If the file is *not* created there is also a warning, suppress this with showWarnings = FALSE.
file.exists	Check if a file exists. The result is either TRUE or FALSE.
file.append	Append one file to another: file.append(file1, file2).
file.remove	Remove a file.
file.rename	Rename a file: file.rename(from, to).
file.copy	Copy a file: file.copy(from, to, overwrite, recursive).
file.link	Make a "hard" link to a file: file.link(from, to).
file.symlink	Make a symbolic link to a file: file.symlink(from, to), to can be simply a directory.
file.info	File information. Returns a data.frame with various columns.
file.size	File size in bytes. A convenience function that returns one of the results from file.info.
file.mtime	Time and date a file was last modified. A convenience function that returns one of the results from file.info.

Example:

Make a "shortcut" on the user desktop of a file in the current working directory (for a regular Windows system).

```
file.symlink(from = normalizePath("Discover-R.pdf"), to = "~/
../Desktop")
```

There are other command functions that allow you to "tinker" with the file system. The commands you've seen here will give you a good starting point, but of course you should *proceed with caution* whenever you delve into your Operating System.

5.4 Saving and exporting data objects

So far you've had a look at how to deal with some files "incoming", and how to interact with the file system but you really need to know how to output items from R.

You can write data to disk in various ways (Table 5.3); exactly how will depend on the nature of the data or R object that you want to export.

- Binary files: readable by R but not by humans.
- ASCII files: readable by humans and computer programs (including R).

Broadly speaking save() and save.image() will write binary files, whilst the other functions will write ASCII (text) files.

5.4.1 Saving R data files

Binary files usually have an .RData file extension. They are readable by R and stored in a space-efficient manner.

Once you've imported data into R you'll most likely want to be able to save your data as .RData so that you can avoid having to import each time. There are two main functions:

Table 5.3 Some R functions that write/export to disk.

Function	Result
save	Exports R objects to .RData files. These are binary encoded and can be read into R using load().
save.image	Saves all R objects as .RData.
write	Saves vector objects or matrix to disk.
write.table	Saves data.frame objects, that is, two-dimensional data. Multidimensional objects are coerced to 2D before export.
write.csv	A convenience function for writing CSV files.
cat	Concatenates objects (usually vectors) and exports.
dput	Saves an ASCII text representation of an R object, which can be imported using dget().

```
save(..., list, file)
save.image(file = ".RData")
```

For save() you specify the R objects that you want to save, giving their names separated by commas. You can also give the names in a list (which would be a character vector of object names). You also need to specify a location (in "quotes"), remembering that the file path is relative to the current working directory.

Example:

Using save() to export R objects to disk

```
# Save to folder 'data' in current working dir
save(data1, data2, file = "data/working-files.RData")

# Save to folder in default working dir
save(list = c("ans3", "ans4"), file = "~/test/answer-files.RData")
```

To save everything you can use save.image(), this is equivalent to using save(list = ls()). If you don't specify a filename, a default file is saved.

You can "restore" R objects from disk using load(). Remember though, that any incoming objects could overwrite existing ones without warning. When you start R it will load the file called ".RData" if it finds it in your default working directory.

Note: Exiting and saving

When you exit R, using q() or via the GUI, R will ask if you want to save the workspace. Replying "yes" will cause the objects in your workspace to be saved to a file .RData in the *current* working directory (effectively save.image(file = ".RData"). When R opens, it looks for a .RData file in the *default* working directory and restores the data. It is therefore good practice to use save.image() and specify a named file (.RData file extension) to be sure.

5.4.2 Writing one-dimensional objects

There are times when you want/need to save objects to disk in ASCII (regular text) format. The function you require depends on the type of data object you are trying to export.

A vector object is one dimensional. You can use various functions to export vector objects, such as:

- write() – This is the "go-to" function for saving character separated files.
- cat() – Joins items together and then writes them.
- dput() – Saves character representations of R objects.

The write() function

Using write() is a good option if you have data as a single sample.

```
write(x, file, ncolumns, append, sep = " ")
```

The function takes your data x and writes it to the file you specify. You can specify how many columns (ncolumns) to create as part of the output and the separator, the default being a space. If you use append = TRUE, the data are added to the end of the file.

If you've written a datafile using write() it will generally be readable using scan().

The cat() function

The cat() function allows you to stitch objects together and then export them (Table 5.4).

```
cat(..., file = "", sep = " ", fill = FALSE, append = FALSE)
```

Table 5.4 Some parameters of the cat() function.

Parameter	Explanation
...	Objects to be joined, generally only vector objects can be handled.
file	The filename (in "quotes") for the destination of the output, the default goes to screen (the console).
sep	A separator character, the default is a space.
fill	The default (FALSE) does not add "newline" characters. Use fill = TRUE to split lines (according to screen width).
append	Use append = TRUE to add the result to an exiting file.

Note that the default does not send "newline" characters, you can specify one explicitly using "\n" as one of the objects. The cat() function is not really a serious contender for exporting data! It is more useful in programming, when you want to produce some output, such as an informative message.

The dput() function

The dput() function attempts to write a text representation of an R object. The result looks less like spreadsheet data and more like an R command.

```
dput(x, file = "")
```

You need to specify an R object x and a location (the default goes to screen). You can import the result of dput() from disk using the dget() command.

Example:

Write a vector using dput()

```
library(MASS)
DDT
```

```
[1] 2.79 2.93 3.22 3.78 3.22 3.38 3.18 3.33 3.34 3.06 3.07 3.56 3.08 4.64 3.34
```

```
dput(DDT, file = "")
```

```
c(2.79, 2.93, 3.22, 3.78, 3.22, 3.38, 3.18, 3.33, 3.34, 3.06,
3.07, 3.56, 3.08, 4.64, 3.34)
```

> ### Tip: Exporting multiple vectors as a single file
>
> The write() function can be used to send multiple vectors to disk as a single file. Instead of using append = TRUE you can make a new vector using c(), and export that.
>
> ```
> write(c(x, y, z), file = "")
> ```

5.4.3 Writing two-dimensional objects

The write() function is what you'll use to send single samples (vector objects) to disk. However, many of your data items will contain multiple variables. In other words they'll have columns where each column is a separate variable, and the rows will be cases, or observations (replicates).

In general your data will be in one of two main forms:

- data.frame – use write.table() to export.
- matrix – use write to export.

There are other forms of data, you'll see how to deal with those shortly.

Writing data.frame objects

The data.frame is a mainstay of data "form", this is the form of R object you get when you import data using read.csv(). It is a flexible form in that each column can be a different kind of data. You can think of a data.frame as being analogous to a spreadsheet worksheet, with rows and columns.

You can write data.frame objects to disk using write.table() and write.csv() functions (Table 5.5).

```
write.table(x, file = "", append = FALSE, sep = " ", na = "NA",
    dec = ".", row.names = TRUE, col.names = TRUE, ...)
write.csv(...)
```

The write.table() function is the main workhorse function but write.csv() can be used as a "quick" export convenience function. In reality this only saves you having to type the sep = "," parameter, so it is probably best to stick to write.table().

Table 5.5 Some parameters of `write.table()`.

Parameter	Explanation
x	The data to be exported. The function attempts to coerce x into a `data.frame`.
file	The filename (in "quotes") the default sends output to the console.
append	If TRUE output is appended to an existing file.
sep	The separator character. The default is a space, use "\t" for Tab or "," for comma.
na	The character to use for NA (missing) values, the default is the character string "NA".
dec	The decimal place character, the default is a period.
row.names	A vector of row names to use or a logical, the default is TRUE. Set to FALSE to have no row names.
col.names	The default uses the first row as column names. Set to FALSE to not export columns names or give a character `vector` of names to use instead.
...	Other parameters are possible.

Example:

Export a `data.frame`

```
BOD  # a data.frame

  Time demand
1   1    8.3
2   2   10.3
3   3   19.0
4   4   16.0
5   5   15.6
6   7   19.8


# default writes row names
write.table(BOD, file = "", sep = " ")

"Time" "demand"
"1"  1 8.3
"2"  2 10.3
"3"  3 19
"4"  4 16
"5"  5 15.6
"6"  7 19.8


# don't write row names
write.table(BOD, file = "", row.names = FALSE, sep = " ")

"Time" "demand"
1 8.3
2 10.3
3 19
4 16
5 15.6
7 19.8
```

> **Tip: End-of-line characters**
>
> The default end-of-line values are specific to your OS. You can specify `eol = "\r\n"` to mimic Windows style (CR+LF) when using `write.table()`.

Writing *matrix* objects

A `matrix` object is two dimensional but unlike a `data.frame` the columns cannot hold different kinds of data. So, a `matrix` must be all `numeric` or all `character` (or some other kind).

You can use `write.table()` to export a `matrix` object to disk. This is the simplest option and allows you to preserve the row and column names.

It is also possible to export a `matrix` using the `write()` function. Internally, R stores a `matrix` as a `vector` but with additional attributes, such as the number of rows and columns and their names.

When you use `write()` it takes the components of the `matrix` and exports it as if it were a `vector`. You can create the appearance of the original by setting the `ncolumns` parameter but all names (rows and columns) will be "lost". In addition to this, `write()` sends the values in the `matrix` out column by column. You can overcome this by transposing the `matrix` using `t()`.

Example:

Use `write()` to export a `matrix` without row/column names

```
# A matrix
VADeaths
```

	Rural Male	Rural Female	Urban Male	Urban Female
50–54	11.7	8.7	15.4	8.4
55–59	18.1	11.7	24.3	13.6
60–64	26.9	20.3	37.0	19.3
65–69	41.0	30.9	54.6	35.1
70–74	66.0	54.3	71.1	50.0

```
# transpose matrix to preserve col/row
write(t(VADeaths), file = "", sep = " ", ncolumns = 4)

11.7 8.7 15.4 8.4
18.1 11.7 24.3 13.6
26.9 20.3 37 19.3
41 30.9 54.6 35.1
66 54.3 71.1 50
```

> **Tip: Append extra `newline` to a file**
>
> Sometimes a datafile ends up without a final "return". This can cause an error when you attempt to import the data. If you do get an "incomplete final line" error you can append an extra "newline" character at the end of the file using `cat()`.
>
> ```
> cat("\n", file, append = TRUE)
> ```

5.4.4 Writing multidimensional objects

Some objects have more than two dimensions. An `array` or a `table` object, for example, can have more or less any number of dimensions. You cannot easily present a multidimensional object in two-dimensional space, such as in a spreadsheet or in the display of your console.

What R does when it displays a multidimensional object is to split it into several two-dimensional parts.

Other objects such as `lists` are a loose collection of "stuff", with elements that may be of widely differing form.

What you need to do is to rearrange your data so that it is in a two-dimensional form.

Writing `table` and `array` objects

You can try to export multidimensional data such as `table` or `array` objects using `write.table()`. What the function does is to try to rearrange the data into a two-dimensional layout first (see Chapter 10 *Tabulation* for more details). See also Chapter 8 *Manipulating data objects*.

In other words, `write.table()` first attempts to convert the object into a `data.frame()` and then exports the result. Now, the `as.data.frame()` function gets used to "reshape" your object into a `data.frame`; however, this may not always work, or at least not as you expect! You can always "preview" the result by either running `as.data.frame()` or by setting `file = ""` in the `write.table()` function.

If you have an `array`, R may need an additional step, conversion to a `table` using `as.table()`. If you have a `table` object R will rearrange the values into multiple columns, with variables corresponding to the various dimensions and with a variable `Freq`, which contains the "original" data.

The data that you manage to export can be re-imported using `read.table()` but will require "reshaping" back to the form you require. Generally the `xtabs()` function will be used for this, but see Chapter 10 *Tabulation* for more details.

Writing `list` objects

A `list` object is potentially useful, as it is a loose collection of items. Each element of a `list` can be different in shape, size, form and so on. In other words, a `list` is a handy way to bundle together miscellaneous items.

This flexibility can cause problems if you want to save a text representation of the data to disk. What you need to do is to reshape your data into some more "manageable" form, then export that. See Chapter 8 *Manipulating data objects*, and particularly section 8.13 *Altering data layout or form*, for more details.

If all else fails you can always fall back on `dput()`, which writes a structured text (ASCII) representation of an R object to disk.

5.4.5 Write a structured representation of an R object

Some objects are quite "difficult" to represent as text objects. Certain objects, such as R functions, are obviously not "data" as such, but are a series or R commands bundled together.

You can use `dput()` to write a human-readable (ASCII) version of an object to disk. Such exported text files are generally readable with `dget()`, which imports and "restores" the original object.

Saving R functions

In most cases you would write an R function in some kind of text editor. Both Windows and Macintosh GUI have script editors that can be used for this task. You would usually save your custom function as a plain text file with an `.R` file extension. The custom function can be "read" into R using the `source()` command.

If you have an R custom function in your workspace you can save it as a binary file with `save()`, and it can be reloaded with `load()`. If you want to make a text version then the `dput()` command will do the job.

When you import a custom function using `dget()` you need to ensure that you assign the incoming function to a named object.

See more in Chapter 15 *Programming tools*.

> ### Note: Function comments and `dput()`
>
> When you export a `function` using `dput()` any internal comments will be lost. If you need to retain comment lines (which can be a good idea), you should type the function name to view the command lines, then copy to the clipboard and paste to a plain text editor. See Chapter 15 for more details about writing and managing functions.

EXERCISES:

Self-Assessment for Managing and exporting data objects

1. You can view the contents of your workspace using ____ or ____ functions.
2. The `type()` function shows you the kind of object... TRUE or FALSE?
3. The `rm()` function will remove any item... TRUE or FALSE?
4. Which of these functions cannot save text representations of objects:
   a. dput()
   b. save()
   c. write()
   d. cat()
5. To export a `data.frame` object to disk you need the ____ or ____ functions.

Answers to exercises are in the *Appendix*.

5.5 Chapter Summary: Managing and exporting data objects

Topic	Key Points
View workspace	Use `ls()` or `objects()` to view the objects in your workspace. The `pattern` parameter can help you view item names matching the `pattern`.
Remove items	Use `rm()` to remove objects from the workspace, **note** this is irreversible and there is no warning! You can optionally use a `pattern` to match certain names.
Disk directories	Use `dir.create()` to make a disk folder. Use `unlink()` to delete a folder (be *careful*).
Disk files	You can carry out operations on files using various `file.___()` functions, e.g. `file.remove()`, `file.rename()` or `file.copy()`.
Export binary	Use `save()` or `save.image()` to export objects in the workspace to disk as R-encoded binary files. The usual file extension is `.RData`.
Export text	Use `write()` or `write.table()` to export objects as spreadsheet-like objects (i.e. human readable) to disk.

6. R object types and their properties

This chapter is about the properties of R objects and how you can view and alter them. So far you've seen that there are different kinds of R object, and had a brief introduction to them in Chapter 3 *Introduction to R objects*. In this chapter the focus is on the properties, such as names for rows and columns, and getting information about the size and shape of your data.

What's in this chapter

» Object class: how to see what it is and how to change it
» Size and shape: how to see the extent of your data object
» Names: how to view the names for rows, columns and so on, and how to alter them
» Preview: how to get an overviews of large datasets

See Chapter 8 *Manipulating data objects* for details about altering the contents of data objects.

Note: Support material

See the ⬧ for links to material on the support website.

6.1 Class

Every R object has a class attribute. This "tells" R what kind of object it is and this affects the sorts of things you can do with that object. In brief, the class of an object is a token that gives information about the form of the data (recall Table 3-3). The token (the class) doesn't hold any information itself, it is just a label, but this label is used by R functions so they can "deal" with the object correctly.

To view the class of an object you use the class() command with the name of the object. Note that with vector objects (one dimensional) the result shows you the type of contents, with everything else the class relates to the form of the data (i.e. its structure). The following examples are all from data built into R (use library(MASS) first):

Example:

Some object classes

```
library(MASS) # package of useful stuff
class(chem) # a vector

[1] "numeric"

class(letters) # a vector

[1] "character"

class(chickwts)

[1] "data.frame"
```

```
class(USPersonalExpenditure)

[1] "matrix" "array"

class(Titanic)

[1] "table"

class(AirPassengers) # time series

[1] "ts"
```

Tip: Get `class` of all elements of an object

To get the `class` of all the elements of an object, such as a `data.frame`, use the `sapply()` function like so:

```
sapply(Puromycin, FUN = class)

      conc           rate         state
  "numeric"      "numeric"     "factor"
```

This works for `data.frame` and `list` objects, but **not** `matrix` or `table` objects.

It is possible to write your own `class`, which can be useful in programming; see Chapter 15 *Programming Tools* for more details about that.

6.1.1 Testing object class

You can check out what `class` an object is using the `class()` function but sometimes you need to check if an object holds a particular `class`. You need to get a logical result, that is TRUE or FALSE. The easiest way is to use the `inherits()` function to carry out a "test" of `class` type.

```
inherits(x, what, ...)
```

You specify the object you want to test, x and `what` kind of `class` you wish to match. If the object has a `class` that does match, you get a TRUE result, otherwise you get FALSE.

Example:

Testing object `class`

```
inherits(cars, what = "data.frame")

[1] TRUE

inherits(cars, what = "matrix")

[1] FALSE
```

Testing object `class` can be important in cases where the following R commands need a particular `class` to function correctly. See Chapter 15 *Programming tools* for more details about scripts and custom functions.

> ### Note: Multiple `class` attributes
>
> Some objects can hold more than one `class`. The `inherits()` function gives you a positive match if *any* of the `classes` match, which is useful.
>
> ```
> class(mco) # object has 2 classes
>
> [1] "xtabs" "table"
>
> inherits(mco, what = "table")
>
> [1] TRUE
> ```

6.2   Changing object type

Once you know what kind of object you are dealing with, you may decide you need to alter it. In general the command `as.xxxx()` will do the job, where `xxxx` is the kind of object you want (Table 6.1). This does not always work, but R has a go at coercing the existing object into the kind you specified.

Table 6.1 Some of the functions used to coerce objects from one type to another.

Function	Result
as.numeric	Makes the object numeric, that is double precision numbers.
as.integer	Changes to integer number values.
as.character	Changes to text (character).
as.factor	Converts to a factor, that is a grouping variable.
as.data.frame	Attempts to coerce to a data.frame.
as.matrix	Converts to a matrix.
as.list	Converts to a list.
as.ts	Changes to a time series.

The simplest change is when you have a `vector` of some sort.

Example:

Alter the type of a `vector` object

```
library(MASS)
DDT

 [1] 2.79 2.93 3.22 3.78 3.22 3.38 3.18 3.33 3.34 3.06 3.07 3.56 3.08 4.64 3.34

as.character(DDT)

 [1] "2.79" "2.93" "3.22" "3.78" "3.22" "3.38" "3.18" "3.33" "3.34" "3.06"
[11] "3.07" "3.56" "3.08" "4.64" "3.34"

as.integer(DDT)

 [1] 2 2 3 3 3 3 3 3 3 3 3 3 3 4 3
```

When you have multidimensional objects, things may become more complicated. For instance, a matrix will easily be coerced to a data.frame (they are both two dimensional and "rectangular") but the conversion the other way may be problematic. A matrix can only contain data of the one type at a time, so your conversion may cause variables to be altered.

A table object has special attributes and also can have >2 dimensions. If you use as.data.frame() on a table you get a data.frame with variables corresponding to the dimensions of the table and a Freq column for the "contents", see Chapter 10 *Tabulation* for more details about dealing with table objects.

Example:

Coerce a table into a data.frame

```
as.data.frame(HairEyeColour)
```

```
    Hair    Eye   Sex  Freq
1  Black  Brown  Male    32
2  Brown  Brown  Male    53
3    Red  Brown  Male    10
4  Blond  Brown  Male     3
5  Black   Blue  Male    11
6  Brown   Blue  Male    50
```

Note: Multiple-step coercion

Some objects need to be converted to one type before they can be converted to something else! You can "nest" your as.xxxx() functions to achieve the desired result. Try the following example and then try each as.xxxx() function separately.

```
as.list(as.data.frame(VADeaths))

$`Rural Male`
[1] 11.7 18.1 26.9 41.0 66.0

$`Rural Female`
[1] 8.7 11.7 20.3 30.9 54.3

$`Urban Male`
[1] 15.4 24.3 37.0 54.6 71.1

$`Urban Female`
[1] 8.4 13.6 19.3 35.1 50.0
```

6.3   Changing object class

Sometimes the as.xxxx() function alters your object to a new form but fails to change the class attribute. You can alter the class of an object directly by assigning a new class with the class() function:

```
class(object) <- "newclass"
```

Altering the class does not alter an object's appearance but can alter how it is dealt with by R. A common use for altering class is in dealing with table objects, which retain their table attribute even if you use as.matrix() to "convert" them, as in the following example.

Example:

Changing class of a table object

```
# A simple table
ucb <- UCBAdmissions[, , 1]
ucb

          Gender
Admit      Male  Female
  Admitted  512     89
  Rejected  313     19

class(ucb)

[1] "table"

# Attempt to change to matrix
ucb <- as.matrix(ucb)

# Converts to a frequency layout
as.data.frame(ucb)

     Admit  Gender  Freq
1 Admitted    Male   512
2 Rejected    Male   313
3 Admitted  Female    89
4 Rejected  Female    19

# Because class is still table
class(ucb)

[1] "table"

# You need to change class explicitly
class(ucb) <- "matrix"

# Now you get a data.frame
as.data.frame(ucb)

          Male Female
Admitted   512     89
Rejected   313     19
```

In most cases the as.xxxx() "conversion" will work out, but for table objects you'll generally need this additional step.

The change of class will affect how R "deals" with an object, but sometimes the result retains additional attributes:

Example:

Change of class and retained attributes

```
# Copy the Nile time-series data
nile <- Nile
class(nile)

[1] "ts"
```

```
# Alter the class
class(nile) <- "numeric"

# The object acts like regular numbers but retains original
# time-series attributes
nile

 [1]  1120 1160  963 1210 1160 1160  813 1230 1370 1140  995  935 1110  994 1020
[16]   960 1180  799  958 1140 1100 1210 1150 1250 1260 1220 1030 1100  774  840
[31]   874  694  940  833  701  916  692 1020 1050  969  831  726  456  824  702
[46]  1120 1100  832  764  821  768  845  864  862  698  845  744  796 1040  759
[61]   781  865  845  944  984  897  822 1010  771  676  649  846  812  742  801
[76]  1040  860  874  848  890  744  749  838 1050  918  986  797  923  975  815
[91]  1020  906  901 1170  912  746  919  718  714  740
attr(,"tsp")
 [1] 1871 1970    1
```

So, changing `class` affects how R deals with an object, and it can sometimes be useful to alter the `class` directly to achieve a result, when a regular `as.xxxx()` would not work.

6.4   Size and structure

It is useful to be able to determine the nature of the R objects you are dealing with. The `class()` function tells you what kind of object you have but it does not tell much else. The size and structure of an object are useful attributes to know about.

6.4.1   Rows and columns

There are three main functions that can inform you about the "scale" of your R objects:

- `nrow()` – the number of rows.
- `ncol()` – the number of columns.
- `dim()` – the "dimensions".

Number of rows in an object

Use `nrow()` to get the number of rows in an object. This works best for `matrix` and `data.frame` objects, that are two dimensional. It will also work for `table` and `array` objects that may have >2 dimensions. It will *not* work for `vector` or `list` objects (you get a result of `NULL`).

Number of columns in an object

Use `ncol()` to get the number of columns in an object. This works best for `matrix` and `data.frame` objects, that are two dimensional. It will also work for `table` and `array` objects that may have >2 dimensions. It will *not* work for `vector` or `list` objects (you get a result of `NULL`).

The dimensions of an object

The `dim()` function returns a result giving the number of rows and columns of an object. The result itself is a `vector` and if you have a `table` or `array` with >2 dimensions you get >2 values. It will *not* work for `vector` or `list` objects (you get a result of `NULL`).

The result of `dim()` always gives rows first, then columns, followed by the other dimensions in an order that matches the structure of the `array` or `table`.

Example:

Numbers of rows and columns of various objects

```
# A data.frame
nrow(warpbreaks)
```

```
[1] 54
```

```
ncol(warpbreaks)
```

```
[1] 3
```

```
dim(warpbreaks)
```

```
[1] 54 3
```

```
# A table with 4 dimensions
dim(Titanic)
```

```
[1] 4 2 2 2
```

```
# A vector
nrow(DDT)
```

```
NULL
```

```
# A list
dim(shoes)
NULL
```

Tip: Number of "rows" and `vector` objects

The regular `nrow()` function returns `NULL` for `vector` objects. The `NROW()` function however (remember that R is case sensitive), treats a `vector` as a one-column `matrix`, so giving a "proper" result.

```
library(MASS)
nrow(shrimp)
```

```
NULL
```

```
NROW(shrimp)
```

```
[1] 18
```

6.4.2 Number of elements

The `length()` function tells you how many elements are in an object.

```
length(x)
```

```
length(x) <- value
```

What constitutes an element depends on the form (and therefore the `class`) of the object.

- vector – how many items.
- data.frame – how many columns.

- `list` – how many parts.
- `matrix` – how many items (rows x columns).
- `ts` – total number of observations.

You give x, the object you want to interrogate.

Example:

Use `length()` to get the number of elements of objects

```
# vector
length(galaxies)

[1] 82

# data.frame
length(airquality)

[1] 6

# matrix
length(VADeaths)

[1] 20

# table
length(Titanic)

[1] 32

# time series
length(Nile)
[1] 100

# list
length(shoes)

[1] 2
```

You can also set the length of an object by giving it a new value; this will either shorten the object, or lengthen it (using NA). See Chapter 8 *Manipulating data objects* for more information about this.

Missing values and `length()`

R objects can contain missing values. These are represented by NA, which is a special R object in its own right. Think of it as representing "Not Available".

Since NA is a "real" element it will be counted when you use `length()`. This may not be what you want.

```
nad <- c(NA, 2, 3, 6, 5, 4, 6, 8, 11, 9, NA, NA)
nad

 [1]  NA 2 3 6 5 4 6 8 11 9 NA NA

length(nad)

[1]  12
```

The `length()` function has returned a value of 12 in the preceding example, which is how many elements there are in total. To count *only* the non-missing values you need `na.omit()`:

```
length(na.omit(nad))

[1] 9
```

Now you get the number of non-missing elements. See Chapter 7 *Working with data objects* for additional notes about removing missing values. See Chapter 9 *Summarizing data* for more details about "taking care of" missing values when using summary statistics.

6.4.3   Object structure

You can use `str()` function to examine the internal *structure* of an R object. The function gives a kind of *preview* of any object, which can help you understand the nature of the object. The result of `str()` shows the first few items of each element of an R object, the following examples will suffice to show you how it works.

Example:

Using `str()` explore object structure

```
str(chem) # numeric vector

 num [1:24] 2.9 3.1 3.4 3.4 3.7 3.7 2.8 2.5 2.4 2.4 ...

str(month.name) # character vector

 chr [1:12] "January" "February" "March" "April" "May" "June"
"July" ...

str(chickwts$feed) # factor variable

 Factor w/ 6 levels "casein","horsebean",..: 2 2 2 2 2 2 2 2 2 2 ...

str(airquality) # data.frame

'data.frame':   153 obs. of 6 variables:
 $ Ozone   : int 41 36 12 18 NA 28 23 19 8 NA ...
 $ Solar.R : int 190 118 149 313 NA NA 299 99 19 194 ...
 $ Wind    : num 7.4 8 12.6 11.5 14.3 14.9 8.6 13.8 20.1 8.6 ...
 $ Temp    : int 67 72 74 62 56 66 65 59 61 69 ...
 $ Month   : int 5 5 5 5 5 5 5 5 5 5 ...
 $ Day     : int 1 2 3 4 5 6 7 8 9 10 ...

str(VADeaths) # matrix

 num [1:5, 1:4] 11.7 18.1 26.9 41 66 8.7 11.7 20.3 30.9 54.3 ...
 - attr(*, "dimnames")=List of 2
 ..$ : chr [1:5] "50-54" "55-59" "60-64" "65-69" ...
 ..$ : chr [1:4] "Rural Male" "Rural Female" "Urban Male" "Urban
Female"

str(LakeHuron) # time series

 Time Series [1:98] from 1875 to 1972: 580 582 581 581 580 ...

str(shoes) # list
List of 2
 $ A: num [1:10] 13.2 8.2 10.9 14.3 10.7 6.6 9.5 10.8 8.8 13.3
 $ B: num [1:10] 14 8.8 11.2 14.2 11.8 6.4 9.8 11.3 9.3 13.6
```

Note that the `str()` function does not produce a "real" result, the output is sent to the console and you cannot assign the result directly to a named object. It is possible to give additional parameters to `str()` that alter the appearance of the result; use `help(str)` if you want to explore those options.

> **Tip: Get `str()` for all objects in workspace**
>
> You can use `ls.str()` to "combine" the `ls()` and `str()` functions, to produce a listing of all objects in your workspace along with the *structure*. The output can be quite lengthy! You *can* assign the result to a named object:
>
> ```
> lst <- ls.str(pattern = "ucb")
> lst
>
> ucb : num [1:2, 1:2] 512 313 89 19
> ```

6.5   Name attributes

Most R objects can have named elements. The most obvious are the names for columns in a `data.frame` (the variables). There are several functions associated with names for elements of objects (Table 6.2). The various functions have subtly different (and overlapping) results.

Table 6.2 Functions for dealing with name attributes.

Function	Result
names	Names for elements of `vector` or `list` objects, as well as column names for `data.frame`.
colnames	Names for columns of `data.frame`, `matrix`, `table` and `array` objects.
rownames	Names for rows of `data.frame`, `matrix` and `table` objects.
row.names	Effectively the same as `rownames()`.
dimnames	Names for all the dimensions of an object. Note that `vector` objects do not have dimensions

The functions all operate in a similar fashion, allowing you to "see" the current name attribute or set a new one, as you'll see shortly.

6.5.1   General names

The `names()` command views or sets names for:

* columns of a `data.frame`
* elements of a `list`
* elements of a `vector`

The function is straightforward:

```
names(x)
names(x) <- value
```

If you give the name of an object you'll get the names. If there are no names the result is NULL. You can set new names by assigning them a new `value`, generally this will be a `character` `vector`. Note that you can "blank" (that is remove) names by assigning a value of NULL.

The most common use is probably in dealing with columns of a `data.frame`.

```
# Make a copy of BOD data.frame
(bod <- BOD)
```

```
  Time demand
1   1      8.3
2   2     10.3
3   3     19.0
4   4     16.0
5   5     15.6
6   7     19.8
names(bod)

[1] "Time"  "demand"

# Assign new names ('in quotes')
names(bod) <- c("time (days)", "Demand mg/l")
bod

  time (days) Demand mg/l
1           1         8.3
2           2        10.3
3           3        19.0
4           4        16.0
5           5        15.6
6           7        19.8

# Remove names
names(bod) <- NULL
bod

1 1  8.3
2 2 10.3
3 3 19.0
4 4 16.0
5 5 15.6
6 7 19.8
```

6.5.2 Column names

The `colnames()` command views and sets names for:

- Columns of a `data.frame`.
- Columns of a `matrix`, `table` or `array`.

The `colnames()` function works exactly the same as `names()` but on slightly different "targets". This pretty much means objects with rows and columns (but possible additional dimensions too).

Example:

View and alter column names of a `matrix` object

```
# Make a copy of the VADeaths matrix
(vad <- VADeaths)
```

	Rural Male	Rural Female	Urban Male	Urban Female
50–54	11.7	8.7	15.4	8.4
55–59	18.1	11.7	24.3	13.6
60–64	26.9	20.3	37.0	19.3
65–69	41.0	30.9	54.6	35.1
70–74	66.0	54.3	71.1	50.0

```
colnames(vad)

[1] "Rural Male"  "Rural Female" "Urban Male"  "Urban Female"

# Assign new names
colnames(vad) <- c("RM", "RF", "UM", "UF")
vad

        RM    RF    UM    UF
50-54 11.7   8.7  15.4   8.4
55-59 18.1  11.7  24.3  13.6
60-64 26.9  20.3  37.0  19.3
65-69 41.0  30.9  54.6  35.1
70-74 66.0  54.3  71.1  50.0

colnames(vad)

[1] "RM" "RF" "UM" "UF"
```

Note: Column names for `table` and `array` objects

You can use `colnames()` on an object with >2 dimensions. The "columns" are *always* the second dimension. You'll need `dimnames()` to view/set the "higher" dimensions.

6.5.3 Row names

Use the `rownames()` or `row.names()` commands for:

- Rows of a `data.frame`
- Rows of a `matrix`, `table` or `array`

These functions work exactly the same as `colnames()` but on the rows. The `rownames()` and `row.names()` are very similar, the latter is a little more "primitive" but in general use there is little material difference between them.

6.5.4 Dimension names

The `dimnames()` command is used to set names of multiple dimensions at one. This works for objects with multiple dimensions, including:

- `matrix`
- `table`
- `array`
- `data.frame`

You can view the current names or set new ones:

```
dimnames(x)
dimnames(x) <- value
```

If you set new names to an object with `dimnames()` the `value` has to be a `list` object. The elements of the `list` can be named, in which case they appear as a separate label in the final result.

Example:

Set multiple name attributes with `dimnames()`

```
# Make a copy of the VADeaths matrix
(vad <- VADeaths)
```

```
         Rural Male   Rural Female   Urban Male   Urban Female
50-54         11.7            8.7         15.4            8.4
55-59         18.1           11.7         24.3           13.6
60-64         26.9           20.3         37.0           19.3
65-69         41.0           30.9         54.6           35.1
70-74         66.0           54.3         71.1           50.0
```

```
# Current names
dimnames(vad)
```

```
[[1]]
[1] "50-54" "55-59" "60-64" "65-69" "70-74"

[[2]]
[1] "Rural Male"  "Rural Female" "Urban Male"  "Urban Female"
```

```
# Set names for rows and columns
dimnames(vad) <- list(age = c("<55", "<60", "<65", "<70", ">70"),
        category = c("RM", "RF", "UM", "UF"))
vad
```

```
      category
age      RM    RF    UM    UF
 <55   11.7   8.7  15.4   8.4
 <60   18.1  11.7  24.3  13.6
 <65   26.9  20.3  37.0  19.3
 <70   41.0  30.9  54.6  35.1
 >70   66.0  54.3  71.1  50.0
```

```
dimnames(vad)
```

```
$age
[1] "<55" "<60" "<65" "<70" ">70"

$category
[1] "RM" "RF" "UM" "UF"
```

Note: `dimnames()` result

The result of `dimnames()` is a `list`. If you use `name = value` pairs when assigning new values, the additional labels appear in the result, and as "extra" labels in the object.

6.5.5 Automatic names

You can assign semi-automatic names to columns or rows with `colnames()` or `rownames()` functions (but not with the `row.names()` function).

```
rownames(x, do.NULL = TRUE, prefix = "row")
colnames(x, do.NULL = TRUE, prefix = "col")
```

If the current names are NULL and you set do.NULL = FALSE, you can apply a prefix to the names (the suffix being a simple integer).

```
# Make a copy of the matrix
(uspe <- USPersonalExpenditure)

                      1940    1945    1950   1955   1960
Food and Tobacco     22.200  44.500  59.60  73.2   86.80
Household Operation   10.500  15.500  29.00  36.5   46.20
Medical and Health    3.530   5.760   9.71  14.0   21.10
Personal Care         1.040   1.980   2.45   3.4    5.40
Private Education      0.341   0.974   1.80   2.6    3.64

dimnames(uspe)

[[1]]
[1] "Food and Tobacco"  "Household Operation" "Medical and Health"
[4] "Personal Care"     "Private Education"

[[2]]
[1] "1940" "1945" "1950" "1955" "1960"

# Set names to NULL
dimnames(uspe) <- list(NULL, NULL)
# Semi-auto names
colnames(uspe, do.NULL = FALSE, prefix = "year")

[1] "year1" "year2" "year3" "year4" "year5"

rownames(uspe, do.NULL = FALSE)

[1] "row1" "row2" "row3" "row4" "row5"
```

6.5.6   Resetting name attributes

Assign a name attribute to NULL to remove/reset the attribute. This works for all the name functions you've seen so far.

```
# Copy the (named) vector
(Euro <- euro)

      ATS          BEF          DEM          ESP         FIM        FRF
13.760300    40.339900     1.955830   166.386000    5.945730   6.559570
      IEP          ITL          LUF          NLG         PTE
 0.787564  1936.270000    40.339900     2.203710  200.482000

# Remove names
names(Euro) <- NULL
Euro

[1]   13.760300    40.339900     1.955830  166.386000    5.945730  6.559570
[7]    0.787564  1936.270000    40.339900    2.203710  200.482000

# Copy matrix
vad <- VADeaths

# Remove names
dimnames(vad) <- list(NULL, NULL)
vad
```

```
      [,1]   [,2]   [,3]   [,4]
[1,]  11.7    8.7   15.4    8.4
[2,]  18.1   11.7   24.3   13.6
[3,]  26.9   20.3   37.0   19.3
[4,]  41.0   30.9   54.6   35.1
[5,]  66.0   54.3   71.1   50.0
```

6.5.7   Setting selective names

So far you've seen how to alter *all* the names at once. It is possible to use any of the naming functions to set just a single name, or whichever ones you want to view/alter. To do this you append [xyz] to the function and replace xyz with the number(s) of the name(s) you want to view/alter.

```
names(airquality)

[1] "Ozone"  "Solar.R" "Wind"  "Temp"  "Month"  "Day"

names(airquality)[2]

[1] "Solar.R"
```

The result of the naming functions is a vector, except for dimnames(), which is a list. The square brackets [] allow you to access a portion of the object you append it to. See Chapter 7 *Working with data objects* for more details.

6.6   General attributes

Objects can hold any "label" as an attribute, and in fact you can create your own labels. The class and various names are examples of basic attributes. One other potentially "useful" attribute is the comment. You can view and assign comment attributes using the comment() function.

```
comment(x)
comment(x) <- value
```

You can assign a comment, which should be a character vector, to more or less any R object.

```
y <- c(3, 4, 5, 4, 7, 6, 2)
comment(y) <- "My data sample."
comment(y)

[1] "My data sample."
```

6.6.1   Manipulating attributes

You can view and manipulate attributes using attributes() and attr() functions.

```
attributes(x)
attributes(x) <- value
```

When you assign attributes to an object the value should be a list. Note however that all existing attributes are removed. If you want to add a new attribute you can append $name to the function:

```
bod <- BOD
attributes(bod)

$names
[1] "Time"  "demand"

$class
[1] "data.frame"

$row.names
[1] 1 2 3 4 5 6

$reference
[1] "A1.4, p. 270"

attributes(bod) <- list(notes = "Some simple data")

# All previous attributes gone
bod

[[1]]
[1] 1 2 3 4 5 7

[[2]]
[1] 8.3 10.3 19.0 16.0 15.6 19.8

attr(,"notes")
[1] "Some simple data"

bod <- BOD

# Add an attribute
attributes(bod)$notes <- "Some simple data"
attributes(bod)
$names

[1] "Time"  "demand"

$class
[1] "data.frame"

$row.names
[1] 1 2 3 4 5 6

$reference
[1] "A1.4, p. 270"

$notes
[1] "Some simple data"
```

The attr() function allows you to view, alter or add any single attribute of an object.

```
attr(x, which, exact = FALSE)
attr(x, which) <- value
```

You can view a particular attribute of x using the which parameter (as a "quoted" string). The exact parameter allows partial matching (if set to FALSE) for queries. If you assign an attribute you'll overwrite anything with a matching name, otherwise a new attribute will be formed.

```
bod <- BOD

# partial match for 'reference'
attr(bod, which = "ref")

[1] "A1.4, p. 270"

# new attribute
attr(bod, which = "notelet") <- "A short note"
attributes(bod)

$names
[1] "Time"  "demand"

$class
[1] "data.frame"

$row.names
[1] 1 2 3 4 5 6

$reference
[1] "A1.4, p. 270"

$notelet
[1] "A short note"
```

There are other attributes that may be specific to particular objects, you'll see examples of these at appropriate places in the text.

6.7   Quick looks

It can be helpful to get an overview of an object, before you "do" anything meaningful. There are various ways you might undertake this, some of which you've already seen:

- Get an idea of the "size" of an object:
  - number of rows.
  - number of columns.
- View the structure of an object.
- View names for rows and columns.
- See the first few elements of an object.
- See the last few elements of an object.
- Summarize an object.

Of course you can simply type the name of the object to view it, but that will often lead to a lot of output that is hard to manage.

6.7.1   Top and bottom preview

You can get a "quick" view of top or bottom of objects using head() and tail() functions.

```
head(x, n = 6)
tail(x, n = 6)
```

The default is to set n = 6, which shows you the first (or last) six elements of x. The result you get depends on the nature of the object you are looking at (Table 6.3).

Table 6.3 Object types and the results displayed by head() and tail() functions.

Object class	What is displayed
vector	The first (or last) items.
data.frame	The first or last rows.
matrix	The first or last rows.
ts	Items in the time series.
table	If there are >2 dimensions, the table is converted to a vector and the elements displayed.
array	An array is converted to a vector if there are >2 dimensions.
list	The first or last elements.

The head() and tail() functions are particularly useful when dealing with large data.frame objects that have many rows.

```
dim(airquality)

[1] 153   6

head(airquality)
    Ozone   Solar.R   Wind   Temp   Month   Day
1      41       190    7.4     67       5     1
2      36       118    8.0     72       5     2
3      12       149   12.6     74       5     3
4      18       313   11.5     62       5     4
5      NA        NA   14.3     56       5     5
6      28        NA   14.9     66       5     6
```

You also see the first (or last) few rows when looking at a matrix but array and table objects are first converted to vector unless they only have two dimensions.

```
dim(HairEyeColour)

[1] 4 4 2

head(HairEyeColour)

, , Sex = Male

         Eye
Hair    Brown   Blue   Hazel   Green
  Black     32     11      10       3
  Brown     53     50      25      15
  Red       10     10       7       7
  Blond      3     30       5       8

, , Sex = Female

         Eye
Hair    Brown   Blue   Hazel   Green
  Black     36      9       5       2
  Brown     66     34      29      14
  Red       16      7       7       7
  Blond      4     64       5       8
```

6.7.2   Object summary

The summary() command gives you a summary of an object. The nature of the summary is dependent upon the class of the object. For example, if you have a numeric variable you get a numeric summary (including mean, quartiles), whereas non-numeric objects generally return information about levels of replication.

```
# A numeric vector
summary(abbey)

  Min. 1st Qu.  Median    Mean 3rd Qu.     Max.
  5.20    8.00   11.00   16.01   15.00   125.00

# A data.frame with numeric and factor columns
summary(InsectSprays)
     count          spray
 Min.:    0.00    A:12
 1st Qu.:  3.00    B:12
 Median:   7.00    C:12
   Mean:   9.50    D:12
 3rd Qu.: 14.25    E:12
   Max.:  26.00    F:12
```

Objects that are one dimensional, such as vector and factor will give a numeric summary or information about the replication. Two dimensional objects, such as data.frame and matrix are treated column-wise. You get a summary of each column, dependent upon the nature of the contents.

Other objects will return different kinds of summary. For example a table object will return a test for association.

```
summary(HairEyeColour)
Number of cases in table: 592
Number of factors: 3
Test for independence of all factors:
    Chisq = 164.92, df = 24, p-value = 5.321e-23
    Chi-squared approximation may be incorrect
```

The summary() function actually looks at the class of the object and runs a version of the function called summary.xxxx() where xxxx is the name of the class. If there is no matching function then summary.default() is used.

Note: Different summary() functions

The summary() command invokes a summary.xxxx() function to match the object class, you can try summary.default() to *force* a basic summary, or use a different kind of summary (i.e. with a different xxxx). This may not work as you expect. You can see the potential summary() variants available to you using:

```
methods(summary)
```

It is possible to write your own summary.xxxx() function, see Chapter 15 *Programming Tools* for more details about that. You'll see other examples of summary() used with statistical tests in Chapter 14 *Analyze data: Statistical analyses* and throughout the text.

EXERCISES:

Self-Assessment for Object types and their properties

1. To view the type of an object use ____, but to test for a particular type use the ____ function.
2. The `dim()` function show you the number of columns and rows.. TRUE or FALSE?
3. To view or alter the column names of a `matrix` object you use the ____ function.
4. Which of the following could you use to add a "citation" label to an object?
   a. `comment(my_data) <- "Gardener 2022"`
   b. `attributes(my_data) <- list(citation = "Gardener 2022")`
   c. `my_data$citation <- "Gardener 2022"`
   d. `attr(my_data, which = "citation") <- "Gardener 2022"`
5. You can set the number of rows of the preview in `head()` and `tail()` functions using the rows parameter... TRUE or FALSE?

Answers to exercises are in the *Appendix*.

6.8 Chapter Summary: Object types and their properties

Topic	Key Points
Object type	Use `class()` to determine the type an object is. You can use `inherits()` to test the `class` of an object. Note that objects can hold more than one `class`. You can also assign a new `class` to an object.
Changing type	You can coerce objects from one type to another with `as.____()` functions, e.g. `as.character()`, `as.factor()` or `as.matrix()`.
Object size	Get information about numbers of rows, columns, both using: `nrow()`, `ncol()` and `dim()` functions. The `length()` function shows the number of elements.
Object name elements	Use `names()`, `colnames()`, `rownames()`, `row.names()`, and `dimnames()` functions to view or alter element names.
Add comment	Use `comment()` to add notes to an object.
Attributes	The `attributes()` and `attr()` functions can help you add and manage object attributes.
Quick looks	Get quick overviews using: `head()`, `tail()`, and `summary()` functions. Note that the `summary()` function gives different results depending upon the `class` of the object.

7. Working with data objects

This chapter is about your data, specifically how to "slice and dice" objects. In other words, it's about how to extract bits of your data that you want/need to deal with and how to rearrange and sort your data into some kind of "sensible" order.

What's in this chapter

- » Elements within R objects
- » Subsets and selecting elements
- » Missing values and complete cases
- » Sampling
- » Rearranging data:
  - » sorting
  - » indexing
  - » ranking
- » Working with text (`character`) data
- » Working with `factor` objects

If you need to add data, remove elements, merge data, change data shape or layout, then the next Chapter 8 *Manipulating data objects* is what you'll need.

Note: Support material

See the ⬄ for links to material on the support website.

7.1 Elements within other objects

Many of the R objects you'll encounter will be composed of many smaller sub-units. For example, a `data.frame` will have various columns (the variables) and rows (corresponding to the replicates, or cases). You can see what the variable names are using the `names()` function.

```
names(BOD)

[1] "Time"  "demand"
```

However, if you try to access the separate elements you have a potential problem:

```
demand

Error in eval(expr, envir, enclos): object 'demand' not found
```

The "problem" is that the element you are trying to "get at" is inside another R object. Effectively its name is "hidden". You have several ways to "deal" with this:

- Use a suffix:
  - Append a $ to the object name, `object$element`.
  - Use square brackets `object[element]`.

- Add the object to the search() path:
  - attach() to search path.
  - Put the object in a local environment using wtih().

The solution you choose will depend upon the situation.

7.1.1   Get elements of objects using a suffix syntax

You can use a suffix syntax to "point" to an element of a larger R object. There are two methods:

- object$element
- object[element]

If you get a result when you use names() you can use the $. If the result of names() is NULL you cannot.

Get elements using $ suffix

The $ allows you to specify an explicit element within another, and to treat it as a "separate" object. You give the name of the "enclosing" object, with a suffix that includes a $ and the name of the element.

```
BOD$demand
[1] 8.3 10.3 19.0 16.0 15.6 19.8
```

The $ does not work for all object types. It *will* work for:

- Columns of a data.frame.
- Named elements of a list.

The $ syntax will *not* work with a matrix for example.

```
names(VADeaths)
NULL

colnames(VADeaths)
[1] "Rural Male"  "Rural Female" "Urban Male"  "Urban Female"
VADeaths$"Rural Male"

Error in VADeaths$"Rural Male": $ operator is invalid for atomic
vectors
```

If you don't get a result with names() then you can't use $ to access an element. If the result of names() is NULL then you need a different method.

Get elements of objects using [] suffix

The $ method of accessing elements only works for objects that have name() attributes. However, you can also use square brackets []. The syntax for using [] works for all R objects that have multiple elements (not function objects), including those with names().
    For a list you specify a single value in the [].

```
listobject[x]
```

There are two versions; using single [] returns the element and its name, using double [[]] returns the element *without* its name. Note that double [[]] only works for list objects.

```
shoes[1]
```

```
$A
 [1] 13.2 8.2 10.9 14.3 10.7 6.6 9.5 10.8 8.8 13.3
```

```
shoes[[1]]
 [1] 13.2 8.2 10.9 14.3 10.7 6.6 9.5 10.8 8.8 13.3
```

For multidimensional objects you need to give additional dimensions.

```
arrayobject[row, column, ...]
```

You can specify the row, column or other dimension(s) as a number or as a "name". Any element you omit will display "everything" in that dimension.

```
VADeaths[, "Rural Male"]
50-54   55-59   60-64   65-69   70-74
 11.7    18.1    26.9    41.0    66.0
```

```
VADeaths[, 2]
```

```
50-54   55-59   60-64   65-69   70-74
  8.7    11.7    20.3    30.9    54.3
```

```
dim(HairEyeColour)
```

```
[1] 4 4 2
```

```
HairEyeColour[, , "Female"]
         Eye
Hair    Brown   Blue   Hazel  Green
 Black     36      9       5      2
 Brown     66     34      29     14
   Red     16      7       7      7
 Blond      4     64       5      8
```

Note: Extract row elements with []

The square brackets allow you to extract any dimension of a multidimensional object, not just the columns. You specify the dimension you require explicitly and leave the other(s) empty.

```
VADeaths[1, ]
```

```
  Rural Male   Rural Female   Urban Male   Urban Female
        11.7            8.7         15.4            8.4
```

```
USPersonalExpenditure["Personal Care", ]
```

```
1940 1945 1950 1955 1960
1.04 1.98 2.45 3.40 5.40
```

See more about this in section 7.2.1 *Subsets and selecting elements.*

The [] will also work for data.frame objects.

```
BOD[, "demand"]

[1] 8.3 10.3 19.0 16.0 15.6 19.8

women[, 2]

 [1] 115 117 120 123 126 129 132 135 139 142 146 150 154 159 164
```

Remember that you can give either a column index number or the name, but the name *must* be in "quotes".

7.1.2   Attach an object to the search path

When you type the name of a function or object into the console, R "looks" for it in the search path, which you can see with search(). The search path starts with ".GlobalEnv", which is your current workspace (the computer RAM).

You can place some objects on the search path with the attach() function. This allows the contents of whatever you placed to be "findable". In general it is only data.frame and list objects that you can attach() (but see Chapter 15 *Programming tools* for information about environments). So, if you can get a result using names() you can use attach().

```
search()

 [1]             ".GlobalEnv"    "package:stats"    "package:graphics"
 [4]   "package:grDevices"    "package:utils"    "package:datasets"
 [7]     "package:methods"       "Autoloads"           "org:r-lib"
[10]           "package:base"

attach(BOD)

search()

 [1]             ".GlobalEnv"                  "BOD"    "package:stats"
 [4]   "package:graphics"  "package:grDevices"    "package:utils"
 [7]   "package:datasets"    "package:methods"       "Autoloads"
[10]              "org:r-lib"       "package:base"

demand

[1] 8.3 10.3 19.0 16.0 15.6 19.8

detach(BOD)
```

Once an item is on the search path, you can refer to any of the (named) elements within it.

Tip: Use detach()

It is a good idea to use detach() to remove an item from the search path once you've added it via attach() and then dealt with it. This avoids potential confusion with variables with identical names. Better still is to avoid attach() if possible, see with() in the following section.

Access an objects contents transiently

The with() function acts like a temporary attach(), and allows you to "access" the contents of a data.frame or list without the need to detach() afterwards.

```
with(data, expr, ...)
```

You specify the `data` you want to use as a temporary "environment", followed by the expression(s) you'd have used if you hadn't needed to use `attach()`.

```
names(BOD)

[1] "Time"  "demand"

demand

Error in eval(expr, envir, enclos): object 'demand' not found

with(BOD, demand)

[1] 8.3 10.3 19.0 16.0 15.6 19.8

names(airquality)

[1] "Ozone"  "Solar.R" "Wind"  "Temp"  "Month"  "Day"

summary(Ozone)

Error in summary(Ozone): object 'Ozone' not found

with(airquality, summary(Ozone))

  Min. 1st Qu. Median  Mean 3rd Qu.  Max.  NA's
  1.00  18.00  31.50  42.13  63.25 168.00   37
```

Using `with()` can be particularly useful if you have multiple `data.frame` objects with common variable names.

7.2 Subsets and selecting elements

You'll often want to extract a portion of your data from a larger dataset. This portion might be one (or more) column variables from a `data.frame` or it might be any rows for which a particular variable matches certain criteria. You may also want to get a random pick of data from a larger pool of options.

These things are all examples of sub-setting, which you can achieve in various ways, some of them you've already encountered:

- Use a `$` suffix.
- Use square brackets `[]` indexing.
- Use the `subset()` function.

A subset is just a smaller part of a larger object. The simplest subsets are entire columns or rows. More complicated subsets might involve multiple elements. More subtle subsets involve some kind of logical expression, which "chooses" which elements to include in the subset. Another kind of subset involves using random selections.

7.2.1 Selecting elements

The use of `$` is restricted to objects that have `names()` attributes, and returns the entire element. However, R uses an indexing system that involves square brackets `[]`, and this syntax works with *all* R objects that contain multiple elements.

Selecting parts of a *vector* object

A `vector` is one dimensional, to select one or more elements from a `vector` you need a single item "selector" in the square brackets:

```
x[i]
```

Where x is your vector and i is the element(s) you require. If i is a single value you'll get that element returned:

```
DDT

 [1] 2.79 2.93 3.22 3.78 3.22 3.38 3.18 3.33 3.34 3.06 3.07 3.56 3.08 4.64 3.34

DDT[1] # first element

[1] 2.79

DDT[4] # fourth element

[1] 3.78
```

If you want multiple elements you can give multiple values in the [].

```
# basic sequence from character vector
month.name[1:4]

[1] "January" "February" "March"  "April"

# numeric vector
abbey

 [1]    5.2    6.5    6.9    7.0    7.0    7.0    7.4    8.0    8.0    8.0   8.0  8.5
[13]    9.0    9.0   10.0   11.0   11.0   12.0   12.0   13.7   14.0   14.0  14.0 16.0
[25]   17.0   17.0   18.0   24.0   28.0   34.0  125.0

abbey[1:6]

[1] 5.2 6.5 6.9 7.0 7.0 7.0

# sequence 'backwards'
abbey[10:1]

 [1] 8.0 8.0 8.0 7.4 7.0 7.0 7.0 6.9 6.5 5.2

# non-sequential values
abbey[c(1, 4, 5, 9)]

[1] 5.2 7.0 7.0 8.0

# use a seq() to get alternate values
abbey[seq(from = 1, to = length(abbey), by = 2)]

 [1]    5.2   6.9  7.0    7.4  8.0   8.0   9.0 10.0 11.0 12.0 14.0 14.0
[13]   17.0  18.0 28.0 125.0

# negate values to 'exclude'
abbey[-1:-10]

 [1]   8.0   8.5   9.0   9.0 10.0 11.0 11.0 12.0 12.0 13.7 14.0 14.0
[13]  14.0  16.0  17.0  17.0 18.0 24.0 28.0 34.0 125.0
```

Recall the sections 4.3 on *repeated items*, and 4.2 *sequences*, in Chapter 4 *Making and importing data objects* for notes about making sequences of numbers.

More or less any item that has multiple elements can be dealt with in this fashion. For example, you may want to alter some of the names() of an object; you can do this using the [] notation.

```
(bod <- BOD)

    Time    demand
1     1        8.3
2     2       10.3
3     3       19.0
4     4       16.0
5     5       15.6
6     7       19.8

names(bod)[1] <- "Interval"
names(bod)

[1] "Interval" "demand"

names(airquality)

[1] "Ozone"   "Solar.R" "Wind"   "Temp"   "Month"   "Day"

names(airquality)[1:4]

[1] "Ozone"   "Solar.R" "Wind"   "Temp"
```

Selecting parts of a *list* object

A list object usually has multiple elements (although you can have a list with a single element). But because a list is a bundle of potentially disparate elements you cannot ascribe dimensions to a list. What you do know is that there is only one dimension of elements, although each element itself can be a different shape to any other element in the list. In short, list objects are useful but can be a pain to handle.

You can select an entire named element from a list using $. Potentially more usefully, you can use [] to pull out parts of the list. These [] can be daisy-chained to allow you access to "deeper" parts of a list.

Simple [] extract entire elements:

```
# make a list
L <- list(a = abbey, b = BOD, c = chem, d = DDT)
L[3:4]

$c
 [1] 2.90 3.10 3.40 3.40   3.70 3.70 2.80 2.50 2.40 2.40 2.70 2.20
[13] 5.28 3.37 3.03 3.03 28.95 3.77 3.40 2.20 3.50 3.60 3.70 3.70

$d
 [1] 2.79 2.93 3.22 3.78 3.22 3.38 3.18 3.33 3.34 3.06 3.07 3.56 3.08 4.64 3.34
```

To penetrate deeper you need to daisy-chain [], note however that you need [[]] for the first level.

```
L[1]  # named

$a
 [1]   5.2   6.5   6.9   7.0   7.0   7.0   7.4   8.0   8.0   8.0  8.0 8.5
[13]   9.0   9.0  10.0  11.0  11.0  12.0  12.0  13.7  14.0  14.0 14.0 16.0
[25]  17.0  17.0  18.0  24.0  28.0  34.0 125.0
L[[1]]  # un-named
 [1]   5.2   6.5   6.9   7.0   7.0   7.0   7.4   8.0   8.0   8.0  8.0 8.5
[13]   9.0   9.0  10.0  11.0  11.0  12.0  12.0  13.7  14.0  14.0 14.0 16.0
[25]  17.0  17.0  18.0  24.0  28.0  34.0 125.0
```

```
L[1][1:3] # not quite as expected
$a
 [1]    5.2   6.5   6.9   7.0   7.0   7.0   7.4   8.0   8.0   8.0  8.0 8.5
[13]    9.0   9.0  10.0  11.0  11.0  12.0  12.0  13.7  14.0  14.0 14.0 16.0
[25]   17.0  17.0  18.0  24.0  28.0  34.0 125.0

$<NA>
NULL

$<NA>
NULL

L[[1]][1:3] # works correctly
[1] 5.2 6.5 6.9
```

Note: Double square brackets [[]]

The double brackets [[]] return a result without any $name but they can only handle a single value/element at a time.

You can also use the name (in "quotes") rather than an index position, but this only selects a single (entire) element. The $ can also be used, and also daisy-chained.

```
L$a[1:3]
```

```
[1] 5.2 6.5 6.9
```

```
L$b$demand
```

```
[1] 8.3 10.3 19.0 16.0 15.6 19.8
```

```
L[[2]]["demand"]
```

```
   demand
1     8.3
2    10.3
3    19.0
4    16.0
5    15.6
6    19.8
```

```
L[[2]][, "demand"]
```

```
[1] 8.3 10.3 19.0 16.0 15.6 19.8
```

```
L["b"]["demand"]
```

```
$<NA>
NULL
```

Note that some methods don't work, and others produce a subtly different form of result. In the preceding example the 2nd element of the list is itself a two-dimensional object (a data.fra me). You'll see how to select from multidimensional objects in the following section.

Selecting parts of multidimensional objects

If you are dealing with multidimensional objects, such as matrix, data.frame or tables, you will need to use more than a single value in the [].

```
x[i, j, ...]
```

In short, you need to specify rows (i), columns (j) and any other dimensions as required (...). Other than the use of multiple dimensions, the methods of selecting are similar to those used for a vector. If you omit a dimension, the entire dimension is "selected". You can use a "name" to select a single (entire) dimension, or use index numbers (-^{ve} values are "deselected").

```
VADeaths
```

	Rural Male	Rural Female	Urban Male	Urban Female
50-54	11.7	8.7	15.4	8.4
55-59	18.1	11.7	24.3	13.6
60-64	26.9	20.3	37.0	19.3
65-69	41.0	30.9	54.6	35.1
70-74	66.0	54.3	71.1	50.0

```
# columns 3 & 4
VADeaths[, 3:4]
```

	Urban Male	Urban Female
50-54	15.4	8.4
55-59	24.3	13.6
60-64	37.0	19.3
65-69	54.6	35.1
70-74	71.1	50.0

```
# rows 1 & 2, but not column 1
VADeaths[1:2, -1]
```

	Rural Female	Urban Male	Urban Female
50-54	8.7	15.4	8.4
55-59	11.7	24.3	13.6

```
# name a row
VADeaths["55-59", ]
```

Rural Male	Rural Female	Urban Male	Urban Female
18.1	11.7	24.3	13.6

```
# table with three dimensions
dim(HairEyeColour)
```

```
[1] 4 4 2
```

```
# rows 1:2, all columns, 1st element of 3rd dim
HairEyeColour[1:2, , 1]
```

```
       Eye
Hair    Brown   Blue   Hazel   Green
  Black    32     11      10       3
  Brown    53     50      25      15
```

You can also daisy-chain the indices.

```
# same as VADeaths[1, 1:2]
VADeaths[1, ][1:2]
```

```
  Rural Male  Rural Female
        11.7           8.7
```

You can also mix and match "names" and indices.

```
USPersonalExpenditure[2:3, "1960"]
```

```
Household Operation   Medical and Health
               46.2                 21.1
```

```
USPersonalExpenditure[1:2, c("1940", "1950")]
```

```
                    1940 1950
Food and Tobacco    22.2 59.6
Household Operation 10.5 29.0
```

If the object has names() you can also mix $ and [].

```
airquality$Ozone[1:4]
[1] 41 36 12 18
```

Using [] allows you to access the various dimensions of R objects. So far you've only seen how to "get" explicit parts. The next step is to use a logical expression to select only certain elements; this is the topic of the following sections.

7.2.2 Matching elements

Matching returns a logical result, that is, TRUE or FALSE. There are several ways to set about matching:

- Use an expression and get TRUE or FALSE for each element.
- Get the index position of the first element that matches an expression.
- Find out if *any* element matches an expression.
- Find out if *all* elements match an expression.

Using conditional expressions is one way to extract a subset of your data.

Logical results and conditional expressions

R "recognizes" logical as a data class and therefore a type of data distinct from, say numeric or character. There are only two options:TRUE or FALSE, although you may abbreviate these to T or F (numeric values 1 and 0 may also be recognized).

Usually you will "generate" a logical result (often as a vector) by using a conditional expression, you'll then "know" which elements matched the expression. See also Chapter 8 *Manipulating data objects* for details about making logical vector objects "direct".

The simplest expressions use relational operators (Table 7.1).

```
chem
```

```
 [1]  2.90 3.10  3.40   3.40  3.70  3.70  2.80 2.50 2.40 2.40 2.70 2.20
[13]  5.28 3.37  3.03   3.03 28.95  3.77  3.40 2.20 3.50 3.60 3.70 3.70
```

```
chem > 3
```

```
 [1] FALSE  TRUE TRUE   TRUE  TRUE   TRUE FALSE  FALSE FALSE FALSE FALSE  FALSE
[13]   TRUE  TRUE TRUE   TRUE  TRUE   TRUE  TRUE  FALSE  TRUE  TRUE  TRUE   TRUE
```

The objects you "test" do not have to be numeric.

```
month.abb == "May"
```

```
 [1] FALSE FALSE FALSE FALSE  TRUE FALSE FALSE FALSE FALSE FALSE FALSE FALSE
```

Note that you need to double-up using ==, since the single = is for assignment.

Table 7.1 Some logical relational operators.

Operator	Description
>	Greater than.
<	Less than.
==	Equal to.
>=	Greater than or equal to.
<=	Less than or equal to.
!=	Not equal to.

You can use these operators (Table 7.1) with `character` variables, but the results will be somewhat dependent on your system language/locale.

```
month.abb > "Jun"
 [1] FALSE FALSE TRUE FALSE TRUE FALSE FALSE FALSE TRUE TRUE TRUE FALSE
```

Your conditional expressions can be daisy-chained to use multiple conditions, for which you need some additional logical operators (Table 7.2).

Table 7.2 Some logical operators.

Operator	Description
!	Logical NOT.
&	Logical AND. You can use && to step along the test object, only the first result is returned.
|	Logical OR. You can use || to step along the test object, only the first result is returned.

Note that there are two "versions" of | and &, you can double these to return a result for the "first" to match.

Example:

Logical results with linking (multiple) operators

```
chem # numeric vector
```

```
 [1]  2.90 3.10   3.40   3.40   3.70   3.70  2.80  2.50  2.40  2.40 2.70 2.20
[13]  5.28 3.37   3.03   3.03 28.95   3.77  3.40  2.20  3.50  3.60 3.70 3.70
```

```
# logical OR
chem > 3 | chem < 5
```

```
 [1] TRUE TRUE TRUE TRUE TRUE TRUE TRUE TRUE TRUE TRUE TRUE TRUE TRUE TRUE TRUE
[16] TRUE TRUE TRUE TRUE TRUE TRUE TRUE TRUE TRUE
```

```
# simple NOT
!chem > 3
```

```
 [1]  TRUE FALSE FALSE  FALSE FALSE  FALSE   TRUE   TRUE   TRUE   TRUE   TRUE   TRUE
[13] FALSE FALSE FALSE  FALSE FALSE  FALSE  FALSE   TRUE FALSE FALSE FALSE FALSE
```

```
# logical OR combined with a NOT
chem > 3 & !chem > 5
```

```
 [1] FALSE  TRUE  TRUE   TRUE  TRUE   TRUE FALSE FALSE FALSE FALSE FALSE FALSE
[13] FALSE  TRUE  TRUE   TRUE FALSE   TRUE  TRUE FALSE  TRUE  TRUE  TRUE  TRUE
```

```
# 'Step-along' OR, first result is returned
month.abb == "May" || month.abb == "Jun"
```

```
[1] FALSE
```

```
month.abb == "May" || month.abb == "Jan"
```

```
[1] TRUE
```

Exclusive OR

An exclusive OR is a test of "difference". The xor() function performs an exclusive OR test.

```
xor(x, y)
```

The function determines if x and y a different logical state; if they are different you get a TRUE result. The x and y must be logical variables, or something that produces one.

```
xor(TRUE, TRUE)
```

```
[1] FALSE
```

```
xor(TRUE, FALSE)
```

```
[1] TRUE
```

```
chem
```

```
 [1]  2.90 3.10  3.40   3.40  3.70  3.70  2.80  2.50  2.40  2.40 2.70 2.20
[13]  5.28 3.37  3.03   3.03 28.95  3.77  3.40  2.20  3.50  3.60 3.70 3.70
```

```
xor(chem > 3, chem < 5)
```

```
 [1]  TRUE FALSE FALSE  FALSE FALSE  FALSE   TRUE   TRUE   TRUE   TRUE   TRUE   TRUE
[13]  TRUE FALSE FALSE  FALSE  TRUE  FALSE  FALSE   TRUE FALSE FALSE FALSE FALSE
```

Is a result TRUE

The isTRUE() function allows you to carry out a simple test on an object.

```
isTRUE(x)
```

You supply x, which must be a single `logical` item.

```
chem > 3 || chem < 20

[1] TRUE

isTRUE(chem > 3 || chem < 20)

[1] TRUE

# result is a logical vector so returns FALSE
isTRUE(chem > 3)

[1] FALSE
```

Match elements to a conditional expression

The `match()` function returns the index of the first element that matches one or more conditions. The `%in%` operator is similar but returns a `logical vector`.

```
match(x, table, nomatch)
x %in% table
```

Here x is a `vector` that you want to "test" and `table` is a `vector` (which can be length 1) to match up to. The `nomatch` parameter gives the result (as an `integer`) that should be returned in the event of a non-match (the default is `NA`). The main difference between the function and the `%in%` operator is the kind of result, the former is an index of positions, the latter is a vector of `logicals`.

You have two items, a test subject x, and a `table` with the "conditions". The order you place them can have a profound effect on the result.

```
abbey

 [1]    5.2    6.5    6.9    7.0    7.0    7.0    7.4    8.0    8.0    8.0  8.0 8.5
[13]    9.0    9.0   10.0   11.0   11.0   12.0   12.0   13.7   14.0   14.0 14.0 16.0
[25]   17.0   17.0   18.0   24.0   28.0   34.0  125.0

match(7, abbey)

[1] 4

match(abbey, 7, nomatch = NA)

 [1] NA NA NA 1 1 1 NA NA NA NA NA NA    NA NA NA NA NA NA NA NA NA NA NA NA NA
[26] NA NA NA NA NA NA

7 %in% abbey

[1] TRUE

abbey %in% 7

 [1] FALSE FALSE FALSE    TRUE   TRUE    TRUE FALSE   FALSE FALSE FALSE FALSE  FALSE
[13] FALSE FALSE FALSE   FALSE  FALSE   FALSE FALSE   FALSE FALSE FALSE FALSE  FALSE
[25] FALSE FALSE FALSE   FALSE  FALSE   FALSE FALSE
```

Any element match for conditional expression

The `any()` function will give a `TRUE` result if any element in a `vector` is `TRUE`. In practice you'll use it with a conditional expression to get a `TRUE` result if there are *any* matches.

```
any(..., na.rm = FALSE)
```

You specify one or more vector objects or conditional expressions (...); these are concatenated and if na.rm = TRUE any NA elements are removed (the default is to keep them). If at least one element is TRUE, you get a TRUE result.

```
any(abbey < 7)
```

```
[1] TRUE
```

```
any(abbey > 1000)
```

```
[1] FALSE
```

Specifying multiple items is somewhat like using OR.

```
DDT
 [1] 2.79 2.93 3.22 3.78 3.22 3.38 3.18 3.33 3.34 3.06 3.07 3.56 3.08 4.64 3.34
```

```
chem
 [1]   2.90  3.10   3.40   3.40   3.70   3.70  2.80  2.50  2.40  2.40 2.70 2.20
[13]   5.28  3.37   3.03   3.03  28.95   3.77  3.40  2.20  3.50  3.60 3.70 3.70
```

```
any(DDT > 5, chem > 5)
```

```
[1] TRUE
```

```
any(DDT > 5, chem < 5)
```

```
[1] TRUE
```

All element matches for conditional expression

The all() function gives TRUE if *all* elements match an expression.

```
all(..., na.rm = FALSE)
```

It is similar to any() in that you specify multiple vector objects or conditions. You get a TRUE result only if *all* the elements are TRUE.

```
shrimp
 [1] 32.2 33.0 30.8 33.8 32.2 33.3 31.7 35.7 32.4 31.2 26.6 30.7 32.5 30.7 31.2
[16] 30.3 32.3 31.7
```

```
all(shrimp > 30)
```

```
[1] FALSE
```

```
all(shrimp < 40)
```

```
[1] TRUE
```

Specifying multiple items is somewhat like using AND.

```
DDT
 [1] 2.79 2.93 3.22 3.78 3.22 3.38 3.18 3.33 3.34 3.06 3.07 3.56 3.08 4.64 3.34
```

```
all(DDT > 2, DDT < 5)

[1] TRUE
```

Matching two complete objects

The identical() function compares two complete objects and returns TRUE if they are identical (otherwise FALSE).

```
identical(x, y, ...)
```

In the function you give two objects x and y to compare. There are other potential parameters. The most common use would be to compare two vector objects.

```
x <- 1:10
y <- 10:1

# Not matched as order different
identical(x, y)

[1] FALSE

y <- 1:10

# Now objects completely match
identical(x, y)

[1] TRUE
```

Note that the objects must match completely in every respect, see help(identical) for additional parameters that can "relax" the matching somewhat.

7.2.3   Index of elements

When you use a comparison operator you get a result that is a logical vector. You can inspect this vector and determine which elements matched the criteria. However, it can be useful to know which elements of an object meet your criteria directly. You can use which() to return an index for elements matching one or more conditions.

Essentially, the which() function "looks" at a logical vector and returns the index of those elements that are TRUE. So, you can use an expression that returns a logical vector as the argument of the which() function.

Example:

Index of matching elements

```
abbey

 [1]   5.2   6.5   6.9   7.0   7.0   7.0   7.4   8.0   8.0   8.0   8.0 8.5
[13]   9.0   9.0  10.0  11.0  11.0  12.0  12.0  13.7  14.0  14.0 14.0 16.0
[25]  17.0  17.0  18.0  24.0  28.0  34.0 125.0

which(abbey > 10)

 [1] 16 17 18 19 20 21 22 23 24 25 26 27 28 29 30 31

which(abbey == 8)

[1] 8 9 10 11
```

The expression you use can have multiple logical conditions:

```
# Index using <7 OR >100
which(abbey < 7 | abbey > 100)

[1] 1 2 3 31
```

If you combine `which()` with square brackets, you can "extract" the values:

```
abbey[which(abbey > 10)]

 [1]   11.0  11.0   12.0   12.0   13.7   14.0   14.0  14.0  16.0   17.0 17.0 18.0
[13]   24.0  28.0   34.0  125.0

abbey[which(abbey < 7 | abbey > 100)]

 [1]   5.2   6.5   6.9 125.0
```

If your data are something like a `data.frame` then you will need to use the square brackets to extract the rows you require.

Example:

Indexing rows to get a subset

```
# A data.frame
BOD

    Time    demand
1     1       8.3
2     2      10.3
3     3      19.0
4     4      16.0
5     5      15.6
6     7      19.8

# Regular logical vector result
BOD$demand > 15

[1]  FALSE FALSE TRUE TRUE TRUE TRUE

# Get index of matching rows
which(BOD$demand > 15)

[1] 3 4 5 6

# Use index to return subset
BOD[which(BOD$demand > 15), ]

    Time    demand
3     3      19.0
4     4      16.0
5     5      15.6
6     7      19.8
```

You don't have to use the "long command", it may be preferable to store intermediate components:

```
i <- BOD$demand > 15
j <- which(i)
BOD[j, ]
```

```
    Time    demand
3      3      19.0
4      4      16.0
5      5      15.6
6      7      19.8
```

Using a named index can be more useful, as you can potentially use the index for other operations.

Note: indexing and multidimensional objects

If your object is multidimensional you will need to use more specific about your index. A `matrix` or `array` object is treated like a `vector` and will be read column-wise. Similarly, a `data.frame` will be "read" column by column when using `which()`. So, use additional "identifiers" in the square brackets, `[row, column]`. For a `data.frame` or `list` you can also use `$` to select an element.

7.2.4 Subsets using the `subset()` function

The `subset()` function is a "convenient" way to get a subset from a `data.frame` (it can also work on other data types).

```
subset(data, subset, select, ...)
```

Table 7.3 Parameters of the `subset()` function.

Parameter	Description
data	The data from which you want a subset.
subset	A logical expression (multiple conditions can be used).
select	You can `select` the columns to be retained (or not). Use named columns or index positions, a – indicates a column to be not retained.
...	Other parameters are possible.

Example:

Using `subset()` on a `data.frame`

```
summary(warpbreaks)
```

```
         breaks      wool    tension
   Min.:   10.00     A:27    L:18
  1st Qu.:  18.25    B:27    M:18
  Median:  26.00     H:18
   Mean:   28.15
  3rd Qu.:  34.00
   Max.:   70.00
```

```
subset(warpbreaks, subset = breaks == 26)

   breaks  wool  tension
1     26     A       L
8     26     A       L
27    26     A       H
38    26     B       M
```

The select parameter can be used to retain (or drop) entire columns, but you can also use it to change the order.

```
subset(warpbreaks, subset = breaks > 50, select = c(1, 3, 2))

   breaks  tension  wool
3     54        L     A
5     70        L     A
6     52        L     A
7     51        L     A
9     67        L     A
```

You can specify multiple criteria using | and & for example, as you've already seen.

```
subset(warpbreaks, subset = wool == "A" & tension %in% "L")

   breaks  wool  tension
1     26     A       L
2     30     A       L
3     54     A       L
4     25     A       L
5     70     A       L
6     52     A       L
7     51     A       L
8     26     A       L
9     67     A       L
```

Use – to indicate variables you do **not** want to keep.

```
names(airquality)

[1] "Ozone"  "Solar.R" "Wind"  "Temp"  "Month"  "Day"

subset(airquality, subset = Month %in% "6" & Solar.R > 300,
                   select = c(-1, -Month))

   Solar.R  Wind  Temp  Day
41     323  11.5    87   10
45     332  13.8    80   14
46     322  11.5    79   15
```

Note that you can specify columns by their index position or by name, you can even mix methods (as in the preceding example).

You *can* use subset() with a matrix but you cannot "call" a column name directly as you would with a data.frame.

```
colnames(state.x77)

[1] "Population" "Income"   "Illiteracy" "Life Exp"  "Murder"
[6] "HS Grad"       "Frost"    "Area"
```

```
subset(state.x77, subset = state.x77[, "Murder"] > 12,
       select = Illiteracy:Murder)
```

```
             Illiteracy   Life Exp   Murder
Alabama         2.1         69.05     15.1
Georgia         2.0         68.54     13.9
Louisiana       2.8         68.76     13.2
Mississippi     2.4         68.09     12.5
Texas           2.2         70.90     12.2
```

> ### Tip: Subset based on columns instead of rows
>
> If you have a matrix you can transpose it using t () so that you can get a subset () of col-
> umns rather than rows. This *may* work with a data.frame but having columns of mixed
> types might give you problems!

7.2.5 Dealing with missing values

In R, NA is used to indicate "not available" and NA is an object in its own right (a logical constant). You'll have need to deal with NA items in a variety of circumstances.

- Identifying which elements are NA.
- Setting values to NA.
- Removing NA elements.
- Replacing NA with something else.
- Checking complete cases (that is rows that do not have NA).

You can identify NA elements with the is.na() function. This also allows you to specify elements to convert to NA. The anyNA() function returns TRUE if an object contains NA elements.

```
is.na(x)
is.na(x) <- value
anyNA(x, recursive = FALSE)
```

The is.na() function returns a logical vector as a result:

```
mv <- is.na(airquality$Ozone)
class(mv)
[1] "logical"
mv[1:12]

 [1] FALSE FALSE FALSE FALSE TRUE FALSE FALSE FALSE FALSE TRUE FALSE FALSE
```

You can get the index position of the NA elements by using which():

```
# How many are NA?
sum(is.na(airquality$Ozone))

[1] 37

# Which are NA?
which(is.na(airquality$Ozone))
```

```
 [1]  5 10 25  26  27 32  33 34 35  36 37  39   42  43  45  46  52  53 54
[20] 55 56 57  58  59 60  61 65 72  75 83  84  102 103 107 115 119 150
```

To replace NA elements with an alternative you first need to know which elements are NA, then assign them a new value.

```
aq <- airquality

# Look at 1st 20 of Ozone
aq$Ozone[1:20]

 [1] 41 36 12 18 NA 28 23 19 8 NA 7 16 11 14 18 14 34 6 30 11

# Alter NA to -1
aq[which(is.na(aq$Ozone)), ] <- -1

# View 1st 20 of result
aq$Ozone[1:20]

 [1] 41 36 12 18 -1 28 23 19 8 -1 7 16 11 14 18 14 34 6 30 11
```

You can set elements to NA by giving the index positions:

```
ddt <- DDT
is.na(ddt) <- c(1:3, 7)
ddt

 [1]   NA  NA  NA 3.78 3.22 3.38  NA 3.33 3.34 3.06 3.07 3.56 3.08 4.64 3.34
```

Use anyNA() to determine if an object contains NA. You get a TRUE result is any element contains NA. You can set recursive = TRUE to deal with objects, such as list, that contain multiple components.

```
anyNA(airquality)

[1] TRUE
```

Use na.omit() to return a copy of the original object without NA. The result "remembers" which elements were removed.

```
ddt <- DDT
is.na(ddt) <- c(2, 5:6)
ddt
 [1] 2.79  NA 3.22 3.78  NA  NA 3.18 3.33 3.34 3.06 3.07 3.56 3.08 4.64 3.34

na.omit(ddt)
 [1] 2.79 3.22 3.78 3.18 3.33 3.34 3.06 3.07 3.56 3.08 4.64 3.34
attr(,"na.action")
[1] 2 5 6
attr(,"class")
[1] "omit"
```

The na.omit() function will work on an entire data.frame too:

```
aq <- na.omit(airquality)
str(aq)
'data.frame':  111 obs. of 6 variables:
 $ Ozone   : int 41 36 12 18 23 19 8 16 11 14 ...
 $ Solar.R : int 190 118 149 313 299 99 19 256 290 274 ...
 $ Wind    : num 7.4 8 12.6 11.5 8.6 13.8 20.1 9.7 9.2 10.9 ...
 $ Temp    : int 67 72 74 62 65 59 61 69 66 68 ...
 $ Month   : int 5 5 5 5 5 5 5 5 5 5 ...
 $ Day     : int 1 2 3 4 7 8 9 12 13 14 ...
 - attr(*, "na.action")= 'omit' Named int [1:42] 5 6 10 11 25 26 27
32 33 34 ...
 ..- attr(*, "names")= chr [1:42] "5" "6" "10" "11" ...
```

You can check complete cases using the complete.cases() function. Most often you'll use it to check the rows of a data.frame or matrix but you can specify multiple objects in the function.

```
ccase <- complete.cases(airquality)
ccase[1:20]
```

```
 [1]  TRUE  TRUE  TRUE  TRUE FALSE FALSE  TRUE  TRUE  TRUE FALSE FALSE  TRUE
[13]  TRUE  TRUE  TRUE  TRUE  TRUE  TRUE  TRUE  TRUE
```

The result is a logical vector.

```
# Total rows in original data
nrow(airquality)
```

```
[1] 153
```

```
# How many complete rows
sum(complete.cases(airquality))
```

```
[1] 111
```

```
# Which rows are complete
which(complete.cases(airquality) == TRUE)
  [1]   1   2   3   4   7   8   9  12  13  14  15  16  17  18  19  20  21  22
 [19]  23  24  28  29  30  31  38  40  41  44  47  48  49  50  51  62  63  64
 [37]  66  67  68  69  70  71  73  74  76  77  78  79  80  81  82  85  86  87
 [55]  88  89  90  91  92  93  94  95  99 100 101 104 105 106 108 109 110 111
 [73] 112 113 114 116 117 118 120 121 122 123 124 125 126 127 128 129 130 131
 [91] 132 133 134 135 136 137 138 139 140 141 142 143 144 145 146 147 148 149
[109] 151 152 153
```

Use a simple ! as a NOT operation to determine incomplete cases:

```
sum(!complete.cases(airquality))
```

```
[1] 42
```

```
which(complete.cases(airquality) == FALSE)
 [1]   5   6  10  11  25  26  27  32  33  34  35  36  37  39  42  43  45  46  52
[20]  53  54  55  56  57  58  59  60  61  65  72  75  83  84  96  97  98 102 103
[39] 107 115 119 150
```

Of course, once you have an index of complete (or incomplete) rows, you can use that to make a subset using square brackets.

```
# Subset containing incomplete cases
aq <- airquality[!complete.cases(airquality), ]
```

> ### Note: Missing values in calculations
>
> Some functions allow NA items to be removed before computations via a na.rm parameter.

7.2.6   Duplicate cases

The duplicated() function shows you *which* elements are duplicated. The result is a logical vector.

```
DDT
```

```
[1] 2.79 2.93 3.22 3.78 3.22 3.38 3.18 3.33 3.34 3.06 3.07 3.56 3.08 4.64 3.34
```

```
duplicated(DDT)
```

```
 [1] FALSE FALSE FALSE  FALSE  TRUE FALSE FALSE FALSE FALSE FALSE FALSE FALSE
[13] FALSE FALSE  TRUE
```

```
which(duplicated(DDT))
```

```
[1] 5 15
```

If you run duplicated() on a data.frame or similar the result shows the rows that are duplicated.

```
head(iris, n = 3)
```

```
  Sepal.Length Sepal.Width Petal.Length Petal.Width Species
1          5.1         3.5          1.4         0.2  setosa
2          4.9         3.0          1.4         0.2  setosa
3          4.7         3.2          1.3         0.2  setosa
```

```
# How many duplicates?
sum(duplicated(iris))
```

```
[1] 1
```

```
# What are the row numbers
which(duplicated(iris))
```

```
[1] 143
```

```
# Show the duplicates
iris[which(duplicated(iris)), ]
    Sepal.Length Sepal.Width Petal.Length Petal.Width   Species
143          5.8         2.7          5.1         1.9 virginica
```

> ### Note: Duplicates and array objects
>
> For matrix and array objects you can specify an additional parameter MARGIN to execute the check for duplication over the specified MARGIN.

Finding runs

In some cases you may want to find out how many times items are repeated. The `rle()` function can provide the answer.

```
rle(x)
inverse.rle(x)
```

Essentially `rle()` returns the lengths of repeated elements and their values. The `inverse.rle()` function will "restore" the result of `rle()`.

Example:

Finding runs with `rle()` and making runs with `inverse.rle()`

```
x <- rep(10:6, 5:1)
x
```

```
[1]  10 10 10 10 10 9 9 9 9 8 8 8 7 7 6
```

```
rle(x)
```

```
Run Length Encoding
 lengths: int [1:5] 5 4 3 2 1
 values : int [1:5] 10 9 8 7 6
x <- list(lengths = c(4, 2, 3), values = c(TRUE, FALSE, TRUE))
class(x) <- "rle"
x
```

```
Run Length Encoding
   lengths: num [1:3] 4 2 3
   values : logi [1:3] TRUE FALSE TRUE
```

```
inverse.rle(x)
```

```
[1] TRUE TRUE TRUE TRUE FALSE FALSE TRUE TRUE TRUE
```

Unique cases

The `unique()` function returns a copy of an object with duplicates removed. If you are dealing with a `matrix` or `array` you can also specify the `MARGIN`.

```
DDT
```

```
[1] 2.79 2.93 3.22 3.78 3.22 3.38 3.18 3.33 3.34 3.06 3.07 3.56 3.08 4.64 3.34
```

```
unique(DDT)
```

```
[1] 2.79 2.93 3.22 3.78 3.38 3.18 3.33 3.34 3.06 3.07 3.56 3.08 4.64
```

7.2.7 Sampling

Sometimes you want a random sample from a larger dataset. There are many reasons for wanting/needing to do this, the simplest being you simply need to present a representative sample without showing all the data.

The `sample()` function carries out the "selection", there is also a variant `sample.int()` (Table 7.4).

```
sample(x, size, replace = FALSE, prob = NULL)
sample.int(n, size, replace = FALSE, prob = NULL)
```

Table 7.4 Parameters of the `sample()` function.

Parameter	description
x	The data from which to make the selection, usually a `vector`.
n	A positive number giving the number of items to choose from.
size	The size of the selection you require.
replace	Should elements be "replaced" and therefore be available for re-selection? The default is `FALSE`.
prob	A `vector` of probabilities giving a weighting. This should match the length of x (or n).

The `sample()` function is the more general of the two and allows selection from `numeric` and other types of data.

```
# A numeric vector
galaxies

 [1]  9172  9350  9483  9558  9775 10227 10406 16084 16170 18419 18552 18600
[13] 18927 19052 19070 19330 19343 19349 19440 19473 19529 19541 19547 19663
[25] 19846 19856 19863 19914 19918 19973 19989 20166 20175 20179 20196 20215
[37] 20221 20415 20629 20795 20821 20846 20875 20986 21137 21492 21701 21814
[49] 21921 21960 22185 22209 22242 22249 22314 22374 22495 22746 22747 22888
[61] 22914 23206 23241 23263 23484 23538 23542 23666 23706 23711 24129 24285
[73] 24289 24366 24717 24990 25633 26690 26995 32065 32789 34279

# Select 5 elements without replacement
sample(galaxies, size = 5, replace = FALSE)

[1] 26690 21701 19846 22747 23706

# Character vector
LETTERS[1:10]

 [1] "A" "B" "C" "D" "E" "F" "G" "H" "I" "J"

# Select 15 elements (need replacement)
sample(LETTERS[1:10], size = 15, replace = TRUE)

 [1] "C" "H" "J" "A" "J" "D" "H" "J" "I" "H" "A" "G" "E" "A" "I"
```

The `sample.int()` function only works on `numeric` data. You specify a value, n and the function chooses from `1:n`.

```
sample.int(100, size = 10)

 [1] 63 40 25 35 71 52 28 38 98 61
```

Weighted sampling

You can use the `prob` argument to set a weighting. Your weighting must be of the same length as your pool of data. This means you can alter the likelihood that elements will be chosen.

```
# A weighting vector
wt <- c(0.1, 0.1, 0.5, 0.5, 0.5, 2, 2, 2, 0.5, 0.5, 0.1, 0.1)

# Jun-Aug more likely, Jan-Feb Nov-Dec less likely
sample(month.abb[1:12], size = 8, prob = wt, replace = TRUE)

[1] "May" "Sep" "Aug" "Aug" "Jun" "Jun" "Jun" "Mar"
```

Note: Random start point

You can use the set.seed() function to control the random generating process. You give an integer value to the function, which allows you to "repeat" your randomness! This can be helpful for testing or teaching demonstration, for example.

```
set.seed(1)
sample.int(100, size = 4)

[1] 68 39 1 34

sample.int(100, size = 4)

[1] 87 43 14 82

set.seed(1)
sample.int(100, size = 4)

[1] 68 39 1 34
```

The value of the "seed" is set whenever you start R. Using set.seed() allows you an element of control.

Conditional sampling

In conditional sampling you set a logical condition and select from that pool, rather than the original dataset.

```
abbey

[1]    5.2   6.5   6.9    7.0    7.0    7.0    7.4   8.0   8.0   8.0  8.0   8.5
[13]   9.0   9.0  10.0   11.0   11.0  12.0   12.0  13.7  14.0  14.0 14.0  16.0
[25]  17.0  17.0  18.0   24.0   28.0  34.0 125.0

sample(abbey[abbey > 8], size = 10, replace = FALSE)

[1] 14.0 17.0 125.0 12.0 13.7 17.0 11.0 34.0 18.0 14.0

(dat <- 1:10)

[1] 1 2 3 4 5 6 7 8 9 10

sample(dat[dat > 5], size = 3)

[1] 10 6 7
```

If you omit the size parameter you get all elements that match the expression in a random order.

```
sample(dat[dat > 8])

[1] 10 9
```

However, there is a "problem" with the sample() function in cases where there is only one matching element:

```
sample(dat[dat > 9])

[1] 9 1 4 3 6 2 5 8 10 7
```

What you get is *all* the data, but in a random order. If that is what you wanted then that's okay but there is a workaround. You need to create a simple `function`:

```
resample <- function(x, ...) x[sample.int(length(x), ...)]
```

Now when you want conditional sampling you use the new `resample()` function instead.

```
resample(dat[dat > 8])

[1] 10 9
```

```
resample(dat[dat > 9])

[1] 10
```

Note: the `resample()` example is illustrated in the help entry for `sample()`.

7.3 Rearranging data

There are various ways to rearrange your data, here we'll focus on:

* Sorting – reassembling your data in a particular order.
* Ordering – getting an index so that you know the order of items.
* Ranking – the rank of elements in your data.

There are other ways to rearrange your data, such as altering the shape or form of your data, see Chapter 8 *Manipulating data objects* for more details about that.
   The simplest way to rearrange your data is to use the square brackets [] and give the index values you want explicitly (see section 7.2 *Subsets and selecting elements* for a reminder).

Example:

Rearrange data using square brackets

```
shrimp

[1] 32.2 33.0 30.8 33.8 32.2 33.3 31.7 35.7 32.4 31.2 26.6 30.7 32.5 30.7 31.2
[16] 30.3 32.3 31.7

length(shrimp)

[1] 18

# Reverse order
shrimp[length(shrimp):1]

[1] 31.7 32.3 30.3 31.2 30.7 32.5 30.7 26.6 31.2 32.4 35.7 31.7 33.3 32.2 33.8
[16] 30.8 33.0 32.2
```

What you put in the [] is an index, giving the explicit order you want. You match the number of "index" statements to the number of dimensions in the data you are rearranging.

The rev() function returns a copy of the original object in reverse order.

```
DDT
 [1] 2.79 2.93 3.22 3.78 3.22 3.38 3.18 3.33 3.34 3.06 3.07 3.56 3.08 4.64 3.34
rev(DDT)
 [1] 3.34 4.64 3.08 3.56 3.07 3.06 3.34 3.33 3.18 3.38 3.22 3.78 3.22 2.93 2.79
```

This generally only works for vector objects, although you can reverse the order of columns in a data.frame or elements in a list.

7.3.1 Sorting data

The sort() function allows you to shuffle your data into a 0–9 or A–Z order. The sort() function operates only on vector objects (Table 7.5).

```
sort(x, decreasing = FALSE, na.last = NA, ...)
```

Table 7.5 Parameters of the sort() function.

Parameter	Description
x	The data to sort, a vector.
decreasing	Which way to sort the data, the default FALSE sorts in ascending order.
na.last	How to deal with NA elements. The default omits them, alternatives are TRUE (places them last), or FALSE (places them first).
...	Additional parameters are possible.

Example:

Using sort()

```
(nad <- c(NA,20,30,60,50,40,60,80,110,90,NA,NA))
 [1] NA 20 30 60 50 40 60 80 110 90 NA NA
sort(nad) # NA omitted (default)
[1] 20 30 40 50 60 60 80 90 110
sort(nad, na.last = TRUE) # NA at end
 [1] 20 30 40 50 60 60 80 90 110 NA NA NA
sort(nad, na.last = FALSE) # NA at front
 [1] NA NA NA 20 30 40 50 60 60 80 90 110
sort(letters, decreasing = TRUE)
 [1] "z" "y" "x" "w" "v" "u" "t" "s" "r" "q" "p" "o" "n" "m" "l" "k" "j" "i" "h"
[20] "g" "f" "e" "d" "c" "b" "a"
```

You can only run `sort()` on a `vector`; if you want to sort a `data.frame` or similar object, you need an extra step that uses `order()`.

7.3.2 The order of data (indexing)

The `order()` function allows you to return the order of the data (Table 7.6); in other words, you get an index. You can use the index to re-sort your data, which is how you can sort a `data.frame` for example.

```
order(..., na.last = TRUE, decreasing = FALSE)
```

Table 7.6 Main parameters of the `order()` function.

Parameter	Description
...	One or more `vector` objects, separated with commas. The `order` of the first is used as the main `vector` and subsequent items are used as tie-breakers.
na.last	The treatment of `NA` elements. The default `TRUE`, places them at the end. Use `FALSE` to have them at the front and `NA` to omit them.
decreasing	The default `FALSE` returns the index in ascending order (use `TRUE` for the opposite).

Note that the default is to retain `NA` elements, placing them at the end. This ensures your index is the same length as the data.

```
(nad <- c(NA,20,30,60,50,40,60,80,110,90,NA,NA))

 [1] NA 20 30 60 50 40 60 80 110 90 NA NA

order(nad)          # NA items at the end

 [1] 2 3 6 5 4 7 8 10 9 1 11 12

order(nad, na.last = NA)  # NA items omitted

 [1] 2 3 6 5 4 7 8 10 9

order(nad, na.last = FALSE) # NA items first

 [1] 1 11 12 2 3 6 5 4 7 8 10 9
```

Once you have your index you can use square brackets [] to rearrange the data. This is how you'd sort a `data.frame` for example. You can use multiple variables, with subsequent variables being used as tie-breakers.

```
head(ToothGrowth)

   len  supp  dose
1  4.2   VC   0.5
2  11.5  VC   0.5
3  7.3   VC   0.5
4  5.8   VC   0.5
5  6.4   VC   0.5
6  10.0  VC   0.5
```

```
# Order by len with dose as a tie-breaker
i <- with(ToothGrowth, order(len, dose), decreasing = FALSE)
i
```

```
 [1] 1 9 4 5 10 3 37 38 34 40 6 36 7 8 2 17 35 18 49 31 13 20 39 11 12
[26] 14 16 33 22 19 41 45 48 32 28 53 15 60 42 29 43 21 54 55 46 24 51 47 44 25
[51] 52 57 27 50 58 59 30 56 26 23
```

```
head(ToothGrowth[i, ])
```

```
    len  supp  dose
1   4.2   VC   0.5
9   5.2   VC   0.5
4   5.8   VC   0.5
5   6.4   VC   0.5
10  7.0   VC   0.5
3   7.3   VC   0.5
```

You can use a - to reverse the order of variables. It is possible to order using numeric or character variables but factor variables *may* need additional treatment with xtfrm(), which "converts" a factor to an integer, allowing it to be sorted/ordered.

```
# attempt to order factor gives error
i <- with(ToothGrowth, order(len, -dose, -supp))
```

```
Warning in Ops.factor(supp): '-' not meaningful for factors
```

```
# Wrap factor in xtfrm()
i <- with(ToothGrowth, order(len, -dose, xtfrm(supp)))
j <- with(ToothGrowth, order(len, -dose, -xtfrm(supp)))
i
```

```
 [1] 1 9 4 5 10 3 37 38 34 40 36 6 7 8 2 17 49 18 35 13 31 20 11 12 39
[26] 14 16 33 22 19 41 45 48 28 32 53 15 60 29 42 21 43 54 55 46 51 24 47 52 57
[51] 25 44 27 58 50 59 30 56 26 23
```

```
j
```

```
 [1] 1 9 4 5 10 3 37 38 34 40 6 36 7 8 2 17 18 49 35 13 31 20 11 12 39
[26] 14 16 33 22 19 41 45 48 28 32 53 15 60 29 42 21 43 54 55 46 24 51 47 25 52
[51] 57 44 27 58 50 59 30 56 26 23
```

Note: Ordering factor variables

You *can* order a factor without using xtfrm() as long as all the variables are ordered in the same direction. So order(numeric, factor) works fine but order(numeric, -factor) does not. A "safe" option is to always use xtfrm() when ordering factor variables.

7.3.3 Data ranking

Ranking is similar to ordering, the rank() function carries out ranking (Table 7.7). The result gives the rank for each element in your vector.

```
rank(x, na.last = TRUE, ties.method = "average")
```

The ties.method parameters contains various options for how to deal with tied ranks (Table 7.7).

Table 7.7 Parameters for the rank() function.

Parameter	Description
x	The data to rank, a vector.
na.last	How to deal with NA elements, the default (TRUE) places them at the end. Use FALSE to have them at the beginning, or NA to omit them.
ties.method	How to deal with tied values, the default ("average") gives a mean rank. Other options are: "first", "last", "random", "max", "min".

The default ties.method = "average" is what is most generally used for "statistical" ranking. The "min" method is akin to sports ranking where tied values are given the minimum (joint) rank. There are different ways to deal with NA elements, with the default being to retain them but to place them last. The NA items always get unique ranks.

```
(nad <- c(NA,20,30,60,50,40,60,80,110,90,NA,NA))
[1] NA 20 30 60 50 40 60 80 110 90 NA NA

rank(nad, na.last = NA)   # omit NA
[1] 1.0 2.0 5.5 4.0 3.0 5.5 7.0 9.0 8.0

rank(nad, na.last = NA, ties.method = "min")
[1] 1 2 5 4 3 5 7 9 8

rank(nad, na.last = TRUE) # NA at end

[1] 10.0 1.0 2.0 5.5 4.0 3.0 5.5 7.0 9.0 8.0 11.0 12.0
```

The smallest values get the lowest ranks, whilst the largest values get the highest ranks. That is to say, small values get small ranks and big values get big ones. If you want to rank in the opposite direction use – in front of the vector name.

```
rank(-nad, na.last = NA)
[1] 9.0 8.0 4.5 6.0 7.0 4.5 3.0 1.0 2.0
```

Note: it is important to remember that the default is for lowest values to get lowest ranks.

7.4 Working with text and strings

There are many ways to deal with character variables, and R provides a range of functions to help carry out operations on text strings. In this section you'll get an introduction to some of the essentials.

R uses *regular expressions* to help manage text strings. A *regular expression* is a *pattern* that describes a set of character strings. R uses a POSIX 1003.2 standard and various extensions. Regular expressions are somewhat like math expressions and form a kind of mini-language. Regular expressions are used by many computer programs.

Most alphanumeric characters match themselves, so "ata" will find the pattern "ata" in a character string. Some characters are used to give special meanings, these are called meta-characters (Table 7.8).

Table 7.8 Some meta-characters used in regular expressions.

Meta-character	Description
.	A wildcard, the period . matches any character.
^	Matches the start of strings, so "^d" matches strings starting with "d". If used in [] it *negates* the list.
$	Matches the end of strings, so "a$" matches strings that end with "a".
?	The preceding item is optional and will be matched at most once.
*	The preceding item will be matched zero or more times.
+	The preceding item will be matched one or more times.
{n}	The preceding item is matched exactly n times.
{n,}	The preceding item is matched n or more times.
{n,m}	The preceding item is matched at least n times, but not more than m times.
\	An escape character, use "\." to find a period (which is usually a wildcard) for example. Other examples include tab: "\t", LF: "\n", CR: "\r".
|	Combines searches, somewhat like OR.
[]	Encloses lists of search terms, there are many options. Also, search *classes*, e.g. "[:digits:]" for digits (0–9). To use search classes you need double [[]], e.g. "[[:digit:]]" would match strings containing any number (digit).

You've already encountered several functions that use *regular expressions*, e.g.: dir(), ls() and apropos().

```
ls(pattern = "d.t") # wildcard

 [1] "dat"   "dat1" "dat2" "dat3" "data1" "data2" "data3" "ddt"   "dtt"
[10] "mydat"

ls(pattern = "^a") # beginning

[1] "a"     "after"  "an.long" "an.wide" "ans3" "ans4" "ans5"
[8] "ans6"  "aq"
ls(pattern = "2$") # ending

[1] "d2"    "dat2"   "data2" "day2"   "func12" "h2"    "m2"    "o2"
```

You can daisy-chain search parameters in two ways, use the | symbol or enclose in [].

```
ls(pattern = "^d|^a") # Start with d or a
```

```
 [1]  "a"        "after"    "an.long"  "an.wide"  "ans3"   "ans4"   "ans5"
 [8]  "ans6"     "aq"       "d1"       "d2"       "d3"     "dat"    "dat1"
[15]  "dat2"     "dat3"     "data1"    "data2"    "data3"  "day1"   "day2"
[22]  "ddt"      "deaths"   "dift"     "dtt"      "dv"
```

```
ls(pattern = "^[da]")  # Same as previous
```

```
 [1]  "a"        "after"    "an.long"  "an.wide"  "ans3"   "ans4"   "ans5"
 [8]  "ans6"     "aq"       "d1"       "d2"       "d3"     "dat"    "dat1"
[15]  "dat2"     "dat3"     "data1"    "data2"    "data3"  "day1"   "day2"
[22]  "ddt"      "deaths"   "dift"     "dtt"      "dv"
```

You can specify a range inside [] with the – character.

```
ls(pattern = "[0-9]")
```

```
 [1]  "ans3"    "ans4"    "ans5"    "ans6"    "d1"       "d2"       "d3"
 [8]  "dat1"    "dat2"    "dat3"    "data1"   "data2"    "data3"    "day1"
[15]  "day2"    "f19"     "f19a"    "f19b"    "f20"      "f3"       "f5"
[22]  "func10"  "func11"  "func12"  "func12a" "func12b"  "func13"   "func14"
[29]  "func16"  "func17"  "func18"  "func19"  "func19a"  "func19b"  "func20"
[36]  "func3"   "func3a"  "func4"   "func5"   "func6"    "func8"    "h2"
[43]  "h3"      "h4"      "m0"      "m1"      "m2"       "m3"       "m4"
[50]  "o2"
```

There are several search *classes* that can be specified:

- [:alnum:] – letters and numbers.
  - [:alpha:] – letters (both cases).
    - [:upper:] – upper case letters.
    - [:lower:] – lower case letters.
  - [:digit:] – numbers.
- [:punct:] – punctuation.
- [:space:] – space characters e.g. tab, newline, CR, LF.

There are others.

```
# Match any number
ls(pattern = "[[:digit:]]")
```

```
 [1]  "ans3"    "ans4"    "ans5"    "ans6"    "d1"       "d2"       "d3"
 [8]  "dat1"    "dat2"    "dat3"    "data1"   "data2"    "data3"    "day1"
[15]  "day2"    "f19"     "f19a"    "f19b"    "f20"      "f3"       "f5"
[22]  "func10"  "func11"  "func12"  "func12a" "func12b"  "func13"   "func14"
[29]  "func16"  "func17"  "func18"  "func19"  "func19a"  "func19b"  "func20"
[36]  "func3"   "func3a"  "func4"   "func5"   "func6"    "func8"    "h2"
[43]  "h3"      "h4"      "m0"      "m1"      "m2"       "m3"       "m4"
[50]  "o2"
```

```
# Start with upper case letter
ls(pattern = "^[[:upper:]]")
```

```
 [1]  "CW"   "Euro" "L"   "Mode" "NE"   "NH"   "Not" "PG"   "Td"   "WB"
[11]  "X"    "Yr"
```

The help entry for regular expressions `help("regexp")` gives a good deal more information. See also the website at *http://pubs.opengroup.org/onlinepubs/9699919799/basedefs/V1_chap09.html* for more notes about the POSIX 1003.2 standard.

Tip: Strings without quotes

The `noquote()` function displays `character` strings without quotes.

```
noquote(letters)
 [1] a b c d e f g h i j k l m n o p q r s t u v w x y z
```

7.4.1 Properties of character strings

There are several functions that deal with the properties of character strings:

- Count characters: `nchar()`
- Case:
  - Upper: `toupper()`
  - Lower: `tolower()`
- Starting: `startsWith()`
- Ending: `endsWith()`

Note: Unique strings

You can use `unique()` on a `character vector` to see the unique elements.

Counting characters

The `nchar()` function returns the number of characters in a string. The `nzchar()` function returns a `logical vector` with `TRUE` for elements that are non-zero (and `FALSE` for empty strings).

```
nchar(x, keepNA = NA, ...)
nzchar(x, keepNA = FALSE, ...)
```

The `keepNA` parameter controls what happens with `NA` elements. If you set this to `FALSE` then `nchar()` returns 2 for the length of `NA` elements. If you set `keepNA = TRUE` then `nzchar()` and `nchar()` return `NA` for `NA` elements.

```
nchar(month.name)
 [1] 7 8 5 5 3 4 4 6 9 7 8 8
(x <- c("some", "text", "", "as", "a", "test"))

[1] "some" "text" ""     "as"   "a"    "test"

nchar(x)

[1] 4 4 0 2 1 4

nzchar(x)

[1] TRUE TRUE FALSE TRUE TRUE TRUE
```

```
x[3] <- NA # make the 3rd element NA

nchar(x)

[1] 4 4 NA 2 1 4
nzchar(x, keepNA = TRUE)

[1] TRUE TRUE  NA TRUE TRUE TRUE
```

> **Tip: Trim string length**
>
> You can trim a string to a fixed length using the strtrim() function. See section 7.4.3.4 *Translate strings*.

Character case

You can alter the case of characters with toupper() and tolower() functions. The result is a new character vector with upper or lower case enforced respectively.

```
tolower(month.abb)

 [1] "jan" "feb" "mar" "apr" "may" "jun" "jul" "aug" "sep" "oct" "nov" "dec"

toupper(month.abb)

 [1] "JAN" "FEB" "MAR" "APR" "MAY" "JUN" "JUL" "AUG" "SEP" "OCT" "NOV" "DEC"
```

Starting and Ending characters

The startsWith() and endsWith() functions return a logical vector where the starting or ending matches the expression you employ.

```
month.name

 [1] "January"   "February"  "March"     "April"     "May"       "June"
 [7] "July"      "August"    "September" "October"   "November"  "December"

startsWith(month.name, prefix = "J")

 [1] TRUE FALSE FALSE FALSE FALSE TRUE TRUE FALSE FALSE FALSE FALSE FALSE
endsWith(month.name, suffix = "y")

 [1] TRUE TRUE FALSE FALSE TRUE FALSE TRUE FALSE FALSE FALSE FALSE FALSE
```

The prefix or suffix are often single characters but a more complicated regular expression can be used.

7.4.2 Split and Join character strings

You can split character strings into smaller sub-units. Conversely you can take separate elements and join them together to form a larger string.

Split character strings

You can split a `character` string into chunks (substrings) using the `strsplit()` function. The reverse, which is to join together substrings, is carried out using `paste()`. The `strsplit()` function can use *regular expressions* to carry out the splitting.

```
strsplit(x, split, fixed = FALSE)
```

In the function, x is a `character vector` to be `split`, being defined by one or more *regular expressions*. If you specify `fixed = TRUE` the split is carried out explicitly (i.e. not using a *regular expression*).

The result is a `list` with an element corresponding to the original x string. Each element of the `list` will be split as directed. You can use `unlist()` to view the results as a single vector.

```
x <- strsplit(month.name, split = "a", fixed = TRUE)
unlist(x)
```

```
[1]  "J"       "nu"        "ry"      "Febru"     "ry"        "M"
[7]  "rch"     "April"     "M"       "y"         "June"      "July"
[13] "August"  "September" "October" "November"  "December"
```

```
y <- c("a string that you want to split by spaces into separate
words.")
unlist(strsplit(y, "[[:space:][:punct:]]"))
```

```
[1]  "a"       "string"    "that"    "you"     "want"      "to"
[7]  "split"   "by"        "spaces"  "into"    "separate"  "words"
```

The `list` you get as a result can be dealt with in various ways:

* `unlist` – converts the `list` to a `vector`.
* `[]` – the square brackets allow you to extract the various elements.
* Other `list` manipulating functions – see section 8.7 *Manipulating* `list` *objects*.

Tip: White space

You can trim white space from strings with the `trimws()` function. See section 7.4.3 *Find and replace character strings* for more details.

Example:

Elements of a `strsplit()` result `list`

```
z <- strsplit(y, "[[:space:][:punct:]]")
str(z)
```

```
List of 1
 $ : chr [1:12] "a" "string" "that" "you" ...
```

```
z[[1]] # The entire element 1
```

```
[1]  "a"       "string"    "that"    "you"     "want"      "to"
[7]  "split"   "by"        "spaces"  "into"    "separate"  "words"
```

```
z[[1]][1:5] # Subset of element 1
```

```
[1] "a"    "string" "that"   "you"   "want"
```

See more about `list` objects in the following chapter in section 8.7 *Manipulating* `list` *objects*.

Note: Extracting bits of strings

You can use the `substr()` and `substring()` functions to extract portions of strings. See section 7.4.3 *Find and replace character strings* for more details.

Join character strings

The `paste()` function joins items together to produce a string. The function converts objects to `character` then concatenates them (Table 7.9).

```
paste(..., sep = " ", collapse = NULL)
paste0(..., collapse = NULL)
```

You can choose the separator character and optionally collapse the multiple elements to a single string (Table 7.9). The `paste0()` version of the function uses a default separator (`sep = ""`), which cannot be altered.

Table 7.9 Parameters of the `paste()` function.

Parameter	Description
...	R objects (separate names with commas), these will be coerced to `character vectors`.
sep	A character string used as a separator, the default is a space.
collapse	An optional character to use to split the result, which is collapsed to a single string.

If the items to be joined are the same length then they are simply stitched together.

```
paste(1:12, month.abb, sep = "-")
```

```
[1] "1-Jan" "2-Feb" "3-Mar" "4-Apr" "5-May" "6-Jun" "7-Jul" "8-Aug"
[9] "9-Sep" "10-Oct" "11-Nov" "12-Dec"
```

If one element is longer the shorter ones are "recycled" until the longer is "used up".

```
paste(letters, month.abb, sep = ":")
```

```
 [1] "a:Jan" "b:Feb" "c:Mar" "d:Apr" "e:May" "f:Jun" "g:Jul" "h:Aug" "i:Sep"
[10] "j:Oct" "k:Nov" "l:Dec" "m:Jan" "n:Feb" "o:Mar" "p:Apr" "q:May" "r:Jun"
[19] "s:Jul" "t:Aug" "u:Sep" "v:Oct" "w:Nov" "x:Dec" "y:Jan" "z:Feb"
```

The `collapse` parameter allows you to create a single element `vector`.

```
paste(1:12, month.abb, sep = ":", collapse = " - ")
```

```
[1] "1:Jan - 2:Feb - 3:Mar - 4:Apr - 5:May - 6:Jun - 7:Jul - 8:Aug
- 9:Sep - 10:Oct - 11:Nov - 12:Dec"
```

```
paste0(letters, LETTERS, collapse = " ")
```

```
[1] "aA bB cC dD eE fF gG hH iI jJ kK lL mM nN oO pP qQ rR sS tT uU vV wW xX yY zZ"
```

The paste0() function is slightly more efficient but you can only use the default sep = ""
(that is blank, *not* a space).

7.4.3 Find and replace character strings

There are various functions associated with finding and replacing operations:

- Find: grep() grepl()
  - Partial: pmatch() charmatch() match()
- Replace:
  - First: sub()
  - All: gsub()
  - White space: trimws()
- Extract: substr() substring()
- Translate: chartr() substr() substring() strtrim()

Some functions such as substr() and substring() fall into more than one category.

Find strings

The grep() and grepl() functions deal with the business of finding elements within strings
using *regular expressions* (Table 7.10).

```
grep(pattern, x, ignore.case = FALSE, fixed = FALSE, value = FALSE,
    invert = FALSE, ...)
grepl(pattern, x, ignore.case = FALSE, fixed = FALSE, ...)
```

Table 7.10 Some parameters of grep() and grepl() functions.

Parameter	Description
pattern	A regular expression or other character string.
x	A character vector to search for matches.
ignore.case	If TRUE the case is ignored (default = FALSE).
fixed	If TRUE the pattern is explicit (i.e. not a regular expression).
value	For grep, use value = TRUE to return the matching elements. The default (FALSE) returns a vector as an index for matching elements.
invert	For grep, use invert = TRUE to get non-matches (the default is FALSE).
...	Other parameters are available.

The two functions return slightly different results; grep() returns an index (or the original
values), whilst grepl() returns a logical vector.

```
grep(pattern = "y$", x = month.name)
```

```
[1] 1 2 5 7
```

```
grep(pattern = "y$", x = month.name, value = TRUE)

[1] "January" "February" "May"     "July"

grepl(pattern = "y$", x = month.name)

 [1] TRUE TRUE FALSE FALSE TRUE FALSE TRUE FALSE FALSE FALSE FALSE
```

Note: Other pattern-matching functions

There are other functions that pattern match, such as: regexpr(), gregexpr(), and regexec(). See help("grep") for the R help entry.

The match() function can also carry out matching (Table 7.11). You've seen the match() function earlier in section 7.2.2 *Matching elements*.

```
match(x, table, nomatch, incomparables)
x %in% table
```

The match() function returns the index of the first element in table that matches x. The %in% operator is similar but returns a logical vector (TRUE if there is any match and FALSE otherwise).

Table 7.11 Parameters of the match() function.

Parameter	Description
x	A vector of values to match.
table	A vector of values to be matched against.
nomatch	What value to be returned in the event of no match. The default is NA _ integer and if you give an alternative it must be an integer.
incomparables	A vector of values to "exclude" from matching. The default is NULL.

Note that match() does *not* use *regular expressions*.

```
match(c("Jun", "Feb", "Ju"), table = month.abb)

[1] 6 2 NA

match(c("Jun", "Feb"), table = month.abb,
      incomparables = c("Jan", "Feb"))

[1] 6 NA
c("Jun", "Feb", "Ju") %in% month.abb

[1] TRUE TRUE FALSE
```

Note that %in% *never* returns NA as a result, only TRUE or FALSE.

Partial matching

You can carry out partial matching using pmatch() and charmatch() functions.

The `pmatch()` and `charmatch()` functions seek for the first match of elements of x in a lookup "table" (Table 7.12).

```
pmatch(x, table, nomatch, duplicates.ok)
charmatch(x, table, nomatch)
```

Unlike `match()` these functions operate explicitly on `character vector` objects.

Table 7.12 Parameters of `pmatch()` and `charmatch()` functions.

Parameter	Description
x	The values to be matched, either a `character vector` or one that can be coerced to such.
table	The values to be matched against, either a `character vector` or one that can be coerced to such.
nomatch	What value to return in the event of no match or multiple partial matches. The default is NA _ integer. Any alternative must be an `integer`.
duplicates.ok	If TRUE elements in `table` can be used more than once, the default is FALSE.

The `duplicates.ok` parameter controls the behavior of the matching results. If FALSE (the default), once an element is matched from `table` it is removed from the "pool" for subsequent matches. If TRUE, exact matches are considered first, then unique partial matches. The positions of matches are returned as a `vector`. Empty strings cannot be matched.

The upshot is that you get a "positive" result only when you get a single match; no matches or multiple matches count as a "fail".

Example:

In the following example "Jun" gets matched (fully) on the first pass. It is then removed from `table` (the "pool") and the partial match "Ju" succeeds as only element 7 matches.

```
pmatch(c("", "Jun", "Ju"), table = month.abb, duplicates.ok = FALSE)

[1] NA 6 7
```

Example:

In the next example `duplicates.ok` is set to TRUE so "Jun" is matched fully but retained in `table` (the "pool"), meaning that the partial match "Ju" returns two results (6, 7) thus giving an NA result.

```
pmatch(c("", "Jun", "Ju"), table = month.abb, duplicates.ok = TRUE)

[1] NA 6 NA
```

The `charmatch()` function is similar to `pmatch()` with `duplicates.ok` = FALSE, however empty strings *are* matched and multiple matches return 0.

```
charmatch(c("Ja", "Ju", "Jun", "xxx"), month.abb)

[1] 1 0 6 NA
```

In the preceding example, "Ja" is matched partially at position 1, "Ju" matches twice (6, and 7) so returns 0, "Jun" is fully matched at position 6 and "xxx" is not matched at all, so returns NA.

Replace strings

The `sub()` and `gsub()` functions perform *pattern* recognition and replacement operations using *regular expressions*, whilst the `trimws()` function removes whitespace from the ends of strings (Table 7.13).

```
sub(pattern, replacement, x, ignore.case, fixed, ...)
gsub(pattern, replacement, x, ignore.case, fixed, ...)
trimws(x, which)
```

The `sub()` function replaces the first match only, whilst `gsub()` replaces all matches.

Table 7.13 **Parameters of** `sub()`, `gsub()` **and** `trimws()` **functions.**

Parameter	Description
pattern	A regular expression or other character string.
replacement	A replacement character string.
x	A character vector.
ignore.case	If TRUE the case is ignored (default = FALSE).
fixed	If TRUE the pattern is explicit (i.e. not a regular expression).
which	Which end of the string to strip white space, "both" (default), "left" or "right".
...	Additional parameters are possible.

Both `sub()` and `gsub()` return a character vector the same length as the original x.

Note: White space again

For `trimws()` a "space" can be a space, tab, line feed or carriage return.

Example:

First or all replacements using `sub()` and `gsub()`

```
# "me" is replaced in all elements
sub(pattern = "me", replacement = ".",
    x = c("mean", "median", "mode"))

[1] ".an"  ".dian" "mode"

# all m at start replaced
sub(pattern = "^m", replacement = ".",
    x = c("mean", "median", "mode"))

[1] ".ean"  ".edian" ".ode"
```

```
# m or e replaced but not both
sub(pattern = "[me]", replacement = ".",
    x = c("mean", "median", "mode"))

[1] ".ean"   ".edian" ".ode"

# m and e replaced
gsub(pattern = "[me]", replacement = ".",
     x = c("mean", "median", "mode"))

[1] "..an"   "..dian" ".od."
```

Note replacements are carried out from the start of each string.

Example:

Trim white space

```
txt <- " A text string. "
trimws(txt, which = "both")

[1] "A text string."

trimws(txt, which = "left")

[1] "A text string. "
```

Tip: Set string length

Use the `strtrim()` function to set the length of strings. See section 7.4.3.4 *Translate strings*.

Extract strings

The `substr()` and `substring()` functions allow you to extract substrings from `character` vectors (Table 7.14).

```
substr(x, start, stop)
substring(text, first, last = 1000000L)
```

These functions also allow you to translate the substrings into others (see the following section 7.4.3.4 *Translate strings*) for details of that.

Table 7.14 Parameters of the `substr()` and `substring()` functions.

Parameter	Description
x, text	A character vector.
start, first	An integer, the first element to be extracted.
stop, last	An integer, the last element to be extracted.

Giving a start/first position greater than the length of the string results in a "".

```
substr(c("a", "ab", "abc", "abcd", "abcde", "abcdef"),
       start = 3, stop = 6)
[1] ""    ""    "c"  "cd"  "cde"  "cdef"
```

If you provide a single value for the "section" of substring you want, the two functions return the same result.

```
substr(month.name, start = 1, stop = 3)
[1] "Jan" "Feb" "Mar" "Apr" "May" "Jun" "Jul" "Aug" "Sep" "Oct" "Nov" "Dec"
substring(month.name, first = 1, last = 3)
[1] "Jan" "Feb" "Mar" "Apr" "May" "Jun" "Jul" "Aug" "Sep" "Oct" "Nov" "Dec"
```

If you request "flexible" beginning/ending positions then the two functions give slightly different results.

Example:

Extract substrings using flexible endpoints

```
substr("abcdef", 1:6, 1:6)
[1] "a"
substring("abcdef", 1:6, 1:6)
[1] "a" "b" "c" "d" "e" "f"
substr("abcdef", 1:6, 6:1)
[1] "abcdef"
substring("abcdef", 1:6, 6:1)
[1] "abcdef" "bcde"  "cd"   ""     ""     ""
```

The substr() function uses only the *one* value for start and stop, whereas substring() expands first and last to give multiple values. However, when you have multiple strings multiple start and stop values will be used (and recycled):

```
substr(rep("abcdef", 4), 1:4, 4:5)
[1] "abcd" "bcde" "cd"  "de"
```

Remember that substr() always returns the same number of substrings as there were original strings but substring() *can* return more.

Translate strings

Character translation is similar to *find/replace*. However, you don't use *regular expressions* and specify exactly what you want to replace, and with what. There are several functions that deal with translation.

> ### Note: Case translation
>
> Changing case is a form of translation, see section 7.4.1.2 *Character case* for details of `tolower()` and `toupper()` functions.

```
substr(x, start, stop) <- value
substring(text, first, last) <- value
chartr(old, new, x)
strtrim(x, width)
```

You've seen `substr()` and `substring()` in the preceding section. The main difference in translation is that you can assign the substring(s) to a new `value`.

Example:

Translating substrings with `substr()`

```
mn <- month.name
substr(mn, 1, 1000) <- "X"
mn
```

```
[1] "Xanuary"   "Xebruary"   "Xarch"      "Xpril"    "Xay"       "Xune"
[7] "Xuly"      "Xugust"     "Xeptember"  "Xctober"  "Xovember"  "Xecember"
```

Note that you need to specify a `stop` value in `substr()`, use a larger value to overwrite/translate more characters. The `substring()` function has a default `last = 1000000L`.

The `chartr()` function allows you to switch old strings in x with new ones. Each corresponding character in `old` is replaced by its equivalent in `new`.

Example:

Character translation with `chartr()`

```
chartr(old = "ace", new = "XYZ", x = "abcdef")
```

```
[1] "XbYdZf"
```

You can specify ranges in `old` and `new` using –.

Example:

Ranges in character translation

```
txt <- rep("abcdef", times = 4)
chartr(old = "a-d", new = "P-S", x = txt)
```

```
[1] "PQRSef" "PQRSef" "PQRSef" "PQRSef"
```

Note that old and new *must* be the same length.

Use the `strtrim()` function to set the length of strings x to the desired `width`.

```
txt <- month.name
strtrim(txt, width = 3)
```

```
[1] "Jan" "Feb" "Mar" "Apr" "May" "Jun" "Jul" "Aug" "Sep" "Oct" "Nov" "Dec"
```

```
txt <- month.abb
strtrim(txt, width = 5)

 [1] "Jan" "Feb" "Mar" "Apr" "May" "Jun" "Jul" "Aug" "Sep" "Oct" "Nov" "Dec"
```

Note if you attempt to set a width longer than the original x, the result is simply truncated.

Note: Character abbreviation

The abbreviate() function will abbreviate character strings.

```
abbreviate(names.arg, minlength = 4, ...)
```

There are several potential parameters but the key one is minlength, which sets the desired length of the abbreviations.

```
state.abb <- abbreviate(state.name, minlength = 2, method = "both
.sides")
head(state.abb)
```

```
  Alabama      Alaska    Arizona   Arkansas  California  Colourado
     "Al"        "Aa"       "Ar"       "As"        "Cl"       "Co"
```

The function tries to abbreviate using the minlength you specify, but items that cannot be separated will have additional characters to make each item unique.

7.5   Working with factor objects

A factor variable is a special kind of vector that holds information about grouping. You can think of a factor as being a numeric vector with additional labels; these labels are called "levels".

There are a couple of useful functions to help deal with factor variables:

* nlevels – the number of different groups (levels).
* levels – the names of the levels.

Other functions are more appropriately dealt with in section 8.3 *Manipulating* factor *objects* of the following chapter.

```
summary(PlantGrowth) # group is a factor
```

```
       weight         group
    Min.:   3.590   ctrl:10
1st Qu.:   4.550   trt1:10
 Median:   5.155   trt2:10
   Mean:   5.073
3rd Qu.:   5.530
   Max.:   6.310
```

```
class(PlantGrowth$group)
```

```
[1] "factor"
```

```
str(PlantGrowth$group)

 Factor w/ 3 levels "ctrl","trt1",..: 1 1 1 1 1 1 1 1 1 1 ...

nlevels(PlantGrowth$group)

[1] 3

levels(PlantGrowth$group)

[1] "ctrl" "trt1" "trt2"
```

The levels() function allows you to view or alter the group labels (the levels). This also means you can merge levels by re-naming them.

```
pgg <- PlantGrowth$group
levels(pgg) <- c("C0", "T1", "T2")
pgg

 [1] C0 C0 C0 C0 C0 C0 C0 C0 C0 C0 T1 T1 T1 T1 T1 T1 T1 T1 T1 T1 T2 T2 T2 T2 T2
[26] T2 T2 T2 T2 T2
Levels: C0 T1 T2
```

Note: levels() and unique()

The levels() function is somewhat analogous to unique() but has additional features that are helpful in dealing with factor variables.

See the section 8.3 *Manipulating* factor *objects* in the following chapter for additional functions for dealing with factor objects.

EXERCISES:

Self-Assessment for Working with data objects

1. To access a variable in a data.frame you have to attach() to the search path.. TRUE or FALSE?
2. You can get the proportion of missing items using ____.
3. You can use the replace parameter in sample() to carry out sampling with replacement.. TRUE or FALSE?
4. To sort a data.frame you need to:
   a. Use sort()
   b. Get an index using order(), then use the index to re-order the data
   c. Get the rank() for the key column and use this to re-order using order()
   d. Use order() to give the key column(s) you want to sort by
5. You can convert to upper case with ____, or to lower case with ____.

Answers to exercises are in the *Appendix*.

7.6 Chapter Summary: Working with data objects

Topic	Key Points
Object elements	Variables/elements inside objects are "hidden": access using `x$element` or square brackets `x["name"]`.
Search path	Use `attach()` to place an object in the search path. Use `detach()` to remove an item. Use `with(x, ...)` to temporarily place an item in the search path (whilst ... is executed).
Subsets	Use `subset()` to get a subset. Alternatively use `x[]` square brackets.
Logical operators	Use operators to get logical results e.g.: `>` greater, `<` less, `==` equals, `!` not, `&` and, `|` or.
Matching	Use `match()` to return matches from a pool. Functions `any()` and `all()` return a logical value for any/all results of an expression. Use `identical()` to compare two items.
Indices	Use `which()` to get an index of items that match a logical expression.
Missing values	Missing values are shown as `NA`. Use `is.na()` to check for missing values, and `anyNA()` to return `TRUE`/`FALSE`.
Duplicates	Use `duplicated()` to look for duplicates. Use `unique()` to see unique elements.
Sampling	Use `sample()` and `sample.int()` to get random pick from a pool.
Sorting and ordering	Use `sort()` to rearrange data. Use `order()` to return an index showing the element positions in order. Use `rank()` to get the rank of elements.
Regular expressions	You can use regular expressions in searches.
Text properties	Count characters with `nchar()`. Change case with `toupper()` and `tolower()`. Identify start/end with `startsWith()` and `endsWith()` functions.
Text manipulation	Split text using `strsplit()`. Join text with `paste()`. Remove white space with `trimws()`.
Find/replace	Find with `grep()` and `grepl()`. Replace with `sub()` or `gsub()`.
Factor variables	A `factor` is a grouping variable. Use `nlevels()` to see how many categories (levels), and `levels()` to see category labels.

8. Manipulating data objects

This chapter is concerned with the manipulating of data objects and changing them in some manner. This might involve adding new variables or cases, or perhaps deleting them. Topics include how to merge datasets and how to alter the layout or "shape" of data objects. It is important to manipulate and organize your data before conducting any analysis!

What's in this chapter

- » Random variates
- » Making "empty" objects
- » Adding new elements:
  - » adding variables
  - » adding rows/cases
- » Removing elements
- » Merging datasets
- » Transforming elements:
  - » transforming contents
  - » altering data layout or shape

In earlier chapters you learnt something about the properties of some R objects and how to get subsets of data. In this chapter you'll learn more about how to make and tinker with a range of commonly used R objects.

Note: Support material

See the ⬂ for links to material on the support website.

8.1 Random numbers

In the previous Chapter 7 *Working with data objects* you saw how to "extract" a random sample from a data object. However, it can be useful to create a random set of values *de novo*. There are various types of distribution built-in to R and this means you can create a set of random values using an underlying distribution type. The distribution (shape) of your data will affect the kinds of analysis that can be carried out (see more about this in Chapter 14).

The basic function is rxxxx(), where the xxxx is the name of the distribution, e.g. rnorm() for the normal (Gaussian) distribution.

Each kind of distribution is defined by certain parameters, and you must give these parameters when you "request" a sample – for example:

```
rnorm(n, mean = 0, sd = 1)
```

For rnorm() you must specify the mean and the sd (standard deviation) of the underlying distribution you want to get n random variates from. Other distribution functions have different parameters.

Example:

Random variates from different distributions

```
set.seed(1)
rnorm(n = 10, mean = 5, sd = 1) # Normal
```

```
[1] 4.373546 5.183643  4.164371  6.595281   5.329508  4.179532 5.487429 5.738325
[9] 5.575781 4.694612
```

```
runif(n = 10, min = 1, max = 50) # Uniform
```

```
[1] 46.800556 11.394984 32.932015  7.152200  14.093813 19.919591  1.656126
[8] 19.737010 43.614851 17.677101
```

```
rpois(n = 20, lambda = 2) # Poisson
```

```
[1] 2 2 2 1 3 2 3 0 3 2 3 2 3 2 2 3 0 2 3 3
```

```
rbinom(n = 20, size = 1, prob = 0.5) # Binomial
```

```
[1] 0 1 0 0 0 0 0 1 1 0 1 0 0 0 1 0 0 1 0 1
```

The set.seed() function allows you to set the "starting point" for the randomization. You give an integer value as the single parameter. The upshot is that you can reproduce seemingly random results.

Note: Distribution types

Type help(Distributions) from your R console to see the range of distribution types that are inbuilt. Note that other command packages may add other distributions.

Example:

Random seed and repeatability

```
set.seed(123)
runif(n = 5)
```

```
[1]  0.2875775 0.7883051 0.4089769 0.8830174 0.9404673
```

```
runif(n = 5)
```

```
[1]  0.0455565 0.5281055 0.8924190 0.5514350 0.4566147
```

```
set.seed(123)
runif(n = 5)
```

```
[1]  0.2875775 0.7883051 0.4089769 0.8830174 0.9404673
```

```
runif(n = 5)
```

```
[1]  0.0455565 0.5281055 0.8924190 0.5514350 0.4566147
```

The random seed is set by the system when you undertake a process that requires it. You can "reset" the seed to a quasi-random state with set.seed(NULL). You can also tinker with the underlying algorithms that generate random values with the RNGkind() function.

There are other distribution functions, see Chapter 14 *Analyze data: Statistical analyses* for more details about those.

8.2 Manipulating `vector` objects

A `vector` is a one-dimensional object, which you can think of as analogous to a single column in a spreadsheet. R displays `vector` objects in rows, to save screen space.

8.2.1 Making `vector` objects

A `vector` can hold a single value or many. The contents of a `vector` must all be of the same type, which can be `integer`, `numeric`, `complex`, `character`, `logical` or `raw`. A `factor` variable is a special kind of `vector` that holds category (grouping) information (Table 8.1).

Table 8.1 Types of vector.

Type	Description
integer	Integer values, that is whole numbers.
numeric	Numbers that may have decimal portions, `double` is a synonym for `numeric`.
complex	Complex numbers, that is with a real and imaginary part.
character	Text values. These are displayed in "quotes".
logical	Logical values: TRUE or FALSE. When entering `logical` values you can use 0 or F for FALSE, 1 or T for TRUE. They are always displayed with the full name.
raw	Raw bytes (hexadecimal).
factor	A `factor` is a grouping `vector`. The data are stored as `integer` values but you can give identifying labels.

You can make an empty `vector` in two general ways:

- Use `vector(mode, length)`
- Use the mode-type as a function e.g. `character(length)`

```
vector(mode, length)
numeric(length)
character(length)
```

Note: Making `factor` variables

You cannot make a `factor` variable with the `vector()` function. See section 8.3 *Manipulating* `factor` *objects* for details.

The `vector()` function allows you to specify the mode of the resulting object as well as the desired `length`. You may also use the name of the mode as a function in its own right, when you need only specify the `length`.

Example:

Making empty vector objects

```
vector(mode = "integer", length = 10)

[1] 0 0 0 0 0 0 0 0 0 0
```

```
vector(mode = "character", length = 10)

 [1] "" "" "" "" "" "" "" "" "" ""

numeric(length = 10)

 [1] 0 0 0 0 0 0 0 0 0 0

logical(length = 10)

 [1] FALSE FALSE FALSE FALSE FALSE FALSE FALSE FALSE FALSE FALSE
```

Many functions return `vector` objects as a result, such as `c()` for example:

```
c(2, 4, 4, 3, 5, 1)
[1] 2 4 4 3 5 1
c("a", "c", "eg")
[1] "a" "c" "eg"
```

8.2.2   Altering vector objects

There are many functions that will alter `vector` objects. You've seen various examples in previous chapters.

Altering vector size

The `length()` function is generally used to return the number of elements in an object. You can also use it to alter `vector` length.

```
length(x) <- value
```

If the `value` you set is smaller than the current length the object is trimmed to that. If it is larger, extra elements are appended. The additional elements are assigned NA values.

Example:

Alter `vector` length

```
x <- 1:20
length(x)
[1] 20
length(x) <- 10
x

 [1] 1 2 3 4 5 6 7 8 9 10

length(x) <- 15
x

 [1] 1 2 3 4 5 6 7 8 9 10 NA NA NA NA NA
```

Altering vector contents

You can use the [] to extract or alter any one or more elements of a `vector`.

Example:

Alter vector contents

```
x <- 1:20
x[1] <- 99
x
```

```
 [1] 99 2 3 4 5 6 7 8 9 10 11 12 13 14 15 16 17 18 19 20
```

```
x[11:15] <- 1:5
x
```

```
 [1] 99 2 3 4 5 6 7 8 9 10 1 2 3 4 5 16 17 18 19 20
```

See Chapter 7 *Working with data objects* for a reminder about using [].

Joining vector *objects*

The c() function will combine vector objects.

Example:

Joining vector objects

```
x <- LETTERS[1:13]
y <- letters[14:26]
c(y, x)
```

```
 [1] "n" "o" "p" "q" "r" "s" "t" "u" "v"  "w" "x" "y" "z" "A" "B" "C" "D" "E" "F"
[20] "G" "H" "I" "J" "K" "L" "M"
```

See Chapter 4 *Making and importing data objects* for a reminder about the c() function.

8.3   Manipulating factor objects

A factor variable is a special kind of vector that holds grouping information. The data are essentially stored as integers with optional identifying labels. The different values are known as levels.

Generally a factor is unordered, that is the levels are just groups (categories) and not in any particular arrangement. They are usually displayed in alphabetic order for convenience. It *is* possible to have ordered factor variables, where the labels/levels have an explicit order. Factors are used to structure analyses, most often in Analysis of Variance and its extensions.

8.3.1   Making factor objects

There are three main ways to make a factor object:

- Use factor() to create a variable and assign labels.
- Use gl() for generating repeated sequences for use as a factor.
- Use as.factor() to coerce an existing vector to a factor.

Use the factor() function to make factor objects (Table 8.2).

```
factor(x, levels, labels, ordered, ...)
```

The data you specify in x will be coerced to a character, then assigned labels corresponding to the different values of x, unless you specify new labels explicitly.

Table 8.2 Some parameters of the factor() function.

Parameter	Description
x	A vector of data.
levels	A character vector giving the levels of x. The values must match x but can be in a different order.
labels	A vector of character labels to assign to the data. The default is to use the original values of x coerced via as.character().
ordered	If TRUE the levels of the factor are ordered (in the order given). The default is FALSE.
...	Other parameters are possible.

The levels parameter can be used to specify an explicit order to the levels. The values you specify must match those in x or you'll end up with <NA> values.

Example:

Make factor objects

```
set.seed(1)
# Make a vector of letters
(x <- sample(letters[1:4], size = 12, replace = TRUE))

 [1] "a" "d" "c" "a" "b" "a" "c" "c" "b" "b" "c" "c"

# Make a factor from the data
f <- factor(x) # labels taken from data
f

 [1] a d c a b a c c b b c c
Levels: a b c d

# Make factor but give new labels
f <- factor(x, labels = LETTERS[1:4])
f

 [1] A D C A B A C C B B C C
Levels: A B C D

# Factor with explicit levels
factor(x, levels = c("d", "c", "b", "a"))
 [1] a d c a b a c c b b c c
Levels: d c b a
```

You can use the ordered = TRUE parameter to flag the factor as being ordered. The order of the factor levels is set to the same as the levels. You can set the order afterwards, using any arrangement of levels, using the order() function.

Example:

Ordered factor objects

```
x # data

 [1] "a" "d" "c" "a" "b" "a" "c" "c" "b" "b" "c" "c"
```

```
# Ordered in default order
factor(x, labels = letters[1:4], ordered = TRUE)

 [1] a d c a b a c c b b c c
Levels: a < b < c < d

# Unordered factor
f <- factor(x, labels = letters[1:4])

# Explicit order afterwards
ordered(f, levels = c("b", "a", "d", "c"))

 [1] a d c a b a c c b b c c
Levels: b < a < d < c

# Explicit order de novo
fo <- factor(x, levels = c("d", "c", "b", "a"), ordered = TRUE)
fo
 [1] a d c a b a c c b b c c
Levels: d < c < b < a
```

The gl() function is another way to make a factor object, which uses a pattern (of numbers) to build the levels and assigns labels that you provide (Table 8.3).

```
gl(n, k, length = n * k, labels, ordered = FALSE)
```

Table 8.3 Parameters of the gl() function.

Parameter	Description
n	The number of levels required, as an integer.
k	The number of replications, as an integer.
length	The number of elements required, the default is n*k.
labels	An optional vector of labels. The default uses 1:n.
ordered	If TRUE the resulting factor is ordered (default FALSE).

Use simple integer values to make regular factor objects.

Example:

Using gl() to make factor objects

```
gl(n = 3, k = 5) # blocks of 5

 [1] 1 1 1 1 1 2 2 2 2 2 3 3 3 3 3
Levels: 1 2 3
gl(n = 3, k = 1, length = 15) # sequential repeating

 [1] 1 2 3 1 2 3 1 2 3 1 2 3 1 2 3
Levels: 1 2 3

# blocks of 3 but 'cut short'
gl(n = 3, k = 3, length = 11, labels = month.abb[1:3])
 [1] Jan Jan Jan Feb Feb Feb Mar Mar Mar Jan Jan
Levels: Jan Feb Mar
```

Note that it is possible to specify a shorter `length` than n*k, in which case you can end up with levels that don't have any data.

```
gl(n = 3, k = 3, length = 5, labels = month.abb[1:3])

[1] Jan Jan Jan Feb Feb
Levels: Jan Feb Mar
```

The `gl()` function is particularly helpful in creating `factor` objects that are "nicely balanced". The `as.factor()` can also be used to make `factor` objects but you'd generally use `factor()` instead. The `as.factor()` command is probably more useful as a transitory function (that is, when you want to make a `factor` but not keep it), or when you want to convert an existing object to a `factor`.

Tip: Convert `character` columns in a mixed `data.frame`

If you have a `data.frame` object and need to convert just the `character` columns to `factor`, you can use `rapply()` like so:

```
rapply(x, f = as.factor, classes = "character", how = "replace")
```

8.3.2   Properties of `factor` objects

A `factor` is essentially a `vector` but with some additional properties. You can get information about a `factor` object in various ways (Table 8.4).

Table 8.4 Functions to help explore factor objects.

Function	Description/Result
length	Returns the number of elements in the `factor`.
nlevels	The number of levels.
levels	The names of the levels as a `character` vector.
str	The structure of the `factor`.
class	The object class. An ordered `factor` holds two classes, "factor" and "ordered".
as.integer	Returns the `factor` as an `integer` vector.
summary	Returns the level of replication for each level as a named `vector`.

These functions (Table 8.4) are useful in helping you understand the nature of your `factor` objects.

Example:

Properties of `factor` objects

```
f # an unordered factor

[1] a d c a b a c c b b c c
Levels: a b c d

length(f)
```

```
[1]  12
levels(f)

[1]  "a" "b" "c" "d"

fo  # an ordered factor

 [1]  a d c a b a c c b b c c
Levels:  d < c < b < a

nlevels(fo)
[1]  4
class(fo)
[1]  "ordered"  "factor"
str(fo)

 Ord.factor w/ 4 levels "d"<"c"<"b"<"a":  4 1 2 4 3 4 2 2 3 3 ...

as.integer(fo)

 [1]  4 1 2 4 3 4 2 2 3 3 2 2

summary(fo)

d c b a
1 5 3 3
```

Note: NA in `factor` objects

Any NA elements are retained when you make a `factor`; they are displayed as <NA> but are not a level. You can use addNA() to allow the <NA> elements to be treated as a level.

8.3.3 Altering `factor` objects

You can alter `factor` objects using various functions (Table 8.5).

Table 8.5 Functions that alter factor objects.

Function	Description/Result
levels	View or alter the levels. Use levels(f) <- value to alter levels.
droplevels	Remove unused levels from a `factor`.
ordered	Change to an `ordered` `factor` or alter the order.
addNA	Add NA as a level.
xtfrm	Returns the `factor` as an `integer` vector. This is similar to as. integer() or as.numeric().

Use levels() to view the current names of the levels or to assign new values.

```
levels(f) <- value
```

If you assign two levels to the same value you effectively merge them.

```
f
```
```
 [1] a d c a b a c c b b c c
Levels: a b c d
```
```
levels(f)
```
```
[1] "a" "b" "c" "d"
levels(f) <- c("x", "x", "c", "d")
```
```
f
 [1] x d c x x x c c x x c c
Levels: x c d
```

> **Tip: Set a single level of a `factor`**
>
> You can use [ ] to subset levels, this allows you to alter a single level.

It is possible to have more levels than exist in the data. This can happen of you assign extra levels or if you extract a subset. Use `droplevels()` to remove unused levels from a `factor`.

Example:

Unused `factor` levels

```
x
 [1] "a" "d" "c" "a" "b" "a" "c" "c" "b" "b" "c" "c"
```
```
f <- factor(x, levels = letters)
f
```
```
 [1] a d c a b a c c b b c c
Levels: a b c d e f g h i j k l m n o p q r s t u v w x y z
```
```
f <- droplevels(f)
f
```
```
 [1] a d c a b a c c b b c c
Levels: a b c d
```

> **Tip: `droplevels()` on an entire `data.frame`**
>
> If you execute `droplevels()` on a `data.frame` you will remove any unused levels from *all* factor variables.

The `ordered()` function can set or alter the ordering of a `factor`, as you saw earlier.

In a `factor` missing values are shown as <NA>, which is itself not treated as a level. You can use `addNA()` to incorporate NA as a level.

```
nad # data containing NA
```
```
 [1] NA 20 30 60 50 40 60 80 110 90 NA NA
```
```
naf <- factor(nad)
```

```
naf

 [1] <NA> 20  30  60  50  40  60  80  110 90  <NA> <NA>
Levels: 20 30 40 50 60 80 90 110

addNA(naf)

 [1] <NA> 20  30  60  50  40  60  80  110 90  <NA> <NA>
Levels: 20 30 40 50 60 80 90 110 <NA>
```

The xtfrm() function is similar to as.integer() or as.numeric() in that it returns the data as a numeric coding (an integer vector). It is useful when you need to sort or order your data, see section 7.3 *Rearranging data* in Chapter 7 *Working with data objects* for a reminder.

```
fo # An ordered factor

 [1] a d c a b a c c b b c c
Levels: d < c < b < a

xtfrm(fo)

 [1] 4 1 2 4 3 4 2 2 3 3 2 2
```

You can use as.xxxx() functions to coerce a factor into another type (where xxxx is the type). Examples include as.character(), as.numeric(), and as.integer().

8.4 Manipulating data.frame objects

A data.frame is a two-dimensional object, where each column is a variable. Columns can be different kinds (but only one dimensional) but must be the same length. Short columns are padded with NA.

8.4.1 Making data.frame objects

There are various ways to make a data.frame object, the main ones are:

- Use read.table() or read.csv() to import data from disk (or from clipboard for Windows users).
- Use data.frame() to assemble a data.frame from existing objects.

The read.table() and read.csv() functions will import tabular (that is, spreadsheet-like two-dimensional) data from a file. The result is a data.frame. See Chapter 4 *Making and importing data objects* for a review.

If you need to make a data.frame *de novo* you'll need the data.frame() function, which assembles a data.frame from other component objects (Table 8.6).

```
data.frame(name _ value, row.names, stringsAsFactors, ...)
```

Essentially, you use data.frame() to assemble objects into a data.frame layout. You supply name = value pairs, where the name part will be the name of the resulting column and value is the object you want to "insert" into the data.frame. If you miss out the name part, the columns assume their name from the value (the object name).

Objects (usually vector objects) *must* be the same length, so that the result is a rectangular layout. Any "short" objects can be padded with NA but this is not done automatically. The simplest method is to use length(x) <- size, where size is the required length. Objects that are longer will be truncated, shorter ones will be padded with NA.

Table 8.6 Some parameters of the data.frame() function.

Parameter	Description
name _ value	Name=Value pairs, giving the name for a column and the variable associated with it. Multiple name=value pairs can be used, separated by commas. If the name part is omitted the name is taken from the object.
row.names	An integer value giving a column, or a character vector to use as row names for the resulting data.frame.
stringsAsFactors	Should character vector objects be converted to factor objects. Set to FALSE to retain character objects.
...	Other parameters are possible.

Example:

Making data.frame objects

```
d1 <- 1:5
d2 <- letters[1:5]
d3 <- month.abb[1:5]
# Names from original data but with row.names
data.frame(d1, d2, d3, row.names = 2)

     d1    d3
a    1    Jan
b    2    Feb
c    3    Mar
d    4    Apr
e    5    May

# Name = Value pairs
data.frame(nos = d1, alpha = d2, month = d3)

   nos alpha   month
1    1    a     Jan
2    2    b     Feb
3    3    c     Mar
4    4    d     Apr
5    5    e     May

# Retain character variables
dat3 <- data.frame(nos = d1, mnth = d3, stringsAsFactors = FALSE)
sapply(dat3, FUN = class)

    nos      mnth
"integer" "character"
```

Tip: stringsAsFactors in data.frame objects

The default behavior since R version 4 is to leave character variables as-is. You can set stringsAsFactors = TRUE to convert to factor on import. If you leave text columns as character you can alter them later in one of several ways:

- Use factor() to change a single variable.
- Use as.factor() to convert a single variable.
- Use rapply(x, f = factor, classes = "character", how = "replace") to alter all character columns in x to factors.

8.4.2 Properties of `data.frame` objects

There are various ways in which you can explore or tinker with the properties of `data.frame` objects (Table 8.7).

See Chapter 6 *R object types and their properties* for a review.

Table 8.7 Some functions dealing with the properties of `data.frame` objects.

Function	Result/Action
names	View the column names. Use `names(x) <- value` to alter.
colnames	View or set column names, much like `names()`.
rownames	View or set row names. Use `rownames(x) <- value` to alter.
row.names	More or less the same as `rownames()`.
ncol	The number of columns in a `data.frame`.
nrow	The number of rows in a `data.frame`.
dim	The number of rows and columns in a `data.frame`. The result is a `vector` giving rows then columns.

8.4.3 Altering columns of `data.frame` objects

There are several ways you can alter the columns of a `data.frame` object:

- Add new columns
- Alter the contents of a column
- Remove columns

Adding new columns to a `data.frame`

You can add new columns to a `data.frame` in four main ways (Table 8.8).

Table 8.8 Methods of adding new columns to a `data.frame` object

Method	Description
$	Use `frame$column` to assign `column` to `frame` (and existing `data.frame`).
[, column]	Use `frame[, column] <- object` to assign the `object` to the `column` of an existing `data.frame`. You can use a quoted "name" or an index position in the `[]`.
data.frame()	Use `data.frame(x, name = value)` to add the `name` column to `x`.
cbind()	Use `cbind(x, name = value)` to add the `name` column to `x`.

In all the methods (Table 8.8) the new column must be the same length as the existing columns.

The simplest methods use $ and `[, column]` sub-setting syntax, see Chapter 7 *Working with data objects* for a reminder.

Example:

Using $ and `[, column]` to add new columns to a `data.frame`

```
hrs <- BOD$Time * 24
mins <- hrs * 60
secs <- mins * 60
```

```
bod <- BOD # Make a copy to work on
bod

    Time   demand
1     1      8.3
2     2     10.3
3     3     19.0
4     4     16.0
5     5     15.6
6     7     19.8
bod$hour <- hrs
bod[, "minute"] <- mins
bod[, 5] <- secs
bod

    Time   demand   hour   minute        V5
1     1      8.3      24     1440     86400
2     2     10.3      48     2880    172800
3     3     19.0      72     4320    259200
4     4     16.0      96     5760    345600
5     5     15.6     120     7200    432000
6     7     19.8     168    10080    604800
```

Note that if you use a column index value it will be un-named. R will assign something "sensible" (which you can alter later). Also, the index value must be the "next" in line to be created – you cannot leave "gaps".

The preceding methods allow you to alter existing columns of course, see section 8.12 *Transforming elements* for other ways to transform existing variables (and potentially add the result to the object).

The data.frame() and cbind() functions also allow you to add new columns. The commands are similar in that you specify the items to join together. The main difference is that cbind() will preferentially create matrix objects as the result unless one of the items to bind is a data.frame to begin with.

Example:

Add columns to a data.frame with data.frame() and cbind() functions

```
data.frame(BOD, hours = hrs)

    Time   demand   hours
1     1      8.3      24
2     2     10.3      48
3     3     19.0      72
4     4     16.0      96
5     5     15.6     120
6     7     19.8     168

cbind(bod, minutes = mins, seconds = secs)

    Time   demand   hour   minute       V5   minutes   seconds
1     1      8.3      24     1440    86400      1440     86400
2     2     10.3      48     2880   172800      2880    172800
3     3     19.0      72     4320   259200      4320    259200
4     4     16.0      96     5760   345600      5760    345600
5     5     15.6     120     7200   432000      7200    432000
6     7     19.8     168    10080   604800     10080    604800
```

As before, the new variables need to be the same length as the existing variables. See section 8.11 *Merging items* for details about merging two data.frame objects using a "common" key variable.

Removing columns of a *data.frame*

You can assign a single column to NULL to "remove" it from a data.frame.

Example:

Use NULL to remove a column of a data.frame

```
bod <- cbind(BOD, minutes = mins, seconds = secs)
names(bod)

[1] "Time"  "demand" "minutes" "seconds"

bod$minutes <- NULL
names(bod)

[1] "Time"  "demand" "seconds"
```

You can also use [] square brackets to select (or deselect) columns, effectively making a subset.

Example:

Use square brackets [] to select (and so remove) columns

```
bod <- cbind(BOD, minutes = mins, seconds = secs)
names(bod)

[1] "Time"  "demand" "minutes" "seconds"

bod[, 1:3]

    Time demand  minutes
1      1    8.3     1440
2      2   10.3     2880
3      3   19.0     4320
4      4   16.0     5760
5      5   15.6     7200
6      7   19.8    10080

bod[, -1]

   demand minutes  seconds
1     8.3    1440    86400
2    10.3    2880   172800
3    19.0    4320   259200
4    16.0    5760   345600
5    15.6    7200   432000
6    19.8   10080   604800
```

The subset() function can also be used with the select parameter, see section 7.2 *Subsets and selecting elements* for a reminder.

8.4.4 Altering rows of `data.frame` objects

In a `data.frame` columns are "independent" of each other and can contain different types of data. This means that altering the rows of a `data.frame` is potentially more "awkward" than columns.

You can always use `[row, column]` syntax to change individual elements but more generally when it comes to dealing with rows you are likely to want to add or remove entire rows. Practically, it is often easier to do this externally and (re)import the data. The `edit()` function has some use but is clunky.

Adding rows to a `data.frame`

The `rbind()` command can add one or more rows to an existing `data.frame`. In most situations you'll need to have the new rows laid out in a `data.frame` where the columns match the types of the existing `data.frame`.

Example:

Adding new rows to a `data.frame`

```
dat1 <- data.frame(nos = 1:3, let = letters[1:3])
dat2 <- data.frame(nos = 98:99, let = LETTERS[4:5])

# Join two data.frames..
rbind(dat1, dat2)

    nos   let
1    1     a
2    2     b
3    3     c
4   98     D
5   99     E
```

See section 8.11 *Merging items* for details about merging two `data.frame` objects using a "common" key variable, which can result in extra rows being added.

Removing rows from a `data.frame`

You cannot assign a row to `NULL` to remove it, as you can with a column. Instead, the simplest method is to use `[rows, columns]`. You either define the rows you want to keep, or the rows you want to eliminate.

Example:

Remove rows from a `data.frame`

```
BOD

    Time    demand
1    1       8.3
2    2      10.3
3    3      19.0
4    4      16.0
5    5      15.6
6    7      19.8
```

```
BOD[1:3, ] # Select rows to keep

    Time   demand
1      1      8.3
2      2     10.3
3      3     19.0

BOD[-1:-3, ] # Select rows to drop

    Time   demand
4      4     16.0
5      5     15.6
6      7     19.8
```

A subset will of course generally contain fewer rows than the original data, see section 7.2 *Subsets and selecting elements* for a reminder.

8.5 Manipulating `matrix` objects

A `matrix` is a two-dimensional data object. All data must be of the same type (e.g. numbers or text). A `matrix` is stored as a `vector`, with additional attributes that define how the data are split into rows and columns.

You can check that an object is a `matrix` using the `class()` command. The `str()` function can give you some information about the `matrix` "structure".

```
class(VADeaths)

[1] "matrix" "array"

str(VADeaths)

 num [1:5, 1:4] 11.7 18.1 26.9 41 66 8.7 11.7 20.3 30.9 54.3 ...
 - attr(*, "dimnames")=List of 2
 ..$ : chr [1:5] "50-54" "55-59" "60-64" "65-69" ...
 ..$ : chr [1:4] "Rural Male" "Rural Female" "Urban Male" "Urban Female"
```

8.5.1 Making `matrix` objects

There are three main ways to assemble/construct a `matrix`:

- `matrix()` – split a `vector` into rows and columns as you direct.
- `cbind()` – bind elements column-wise.
- `rbind()` – bind elements row-wise.

You can also attempt to coerce a two-dimensional object into a `matrix` with as. `matrix()` or `data.matrix()` commands.

The `matrix()` function allows you to split a `vector` into rows and columns, forming a `matrix` (Table 8.9).

```
matrix(data = NA, nrow = 1, ncol = 1, byrow = FALSE, dimnames = NULL)
```

You need to ensure that the number of rows and columns will produce a rectangular `matrix`. Elements can be recycled but you will get an error if you cannot form a "proper" rectangular `matrix`.

By default the rows and columns will be un-named. You can do this afterwards (recall Chapter 6 *R object types and their properties*) or you can use the `dimnames` parameter. You **must**

Table 8.9 Parameters of the matrix() function

Parameter	Description
data	The data to use to form the matrix, coercible to a vector.
nrow	The number of rows to form (default = 1).
ncol	The number of columns to form (default = 1). Note: nrow * ncol must equal the total length of the data
byrow	Should the data be assembled row by row? The default is FALSE, meaning that the matrix is assembled column-wise.
dimnames	Row and column names, usually a list of two (the first element being the rows).

give both row and column names (using a list()) but you may allocate one (or both) dimensions to NULL.

Example:

Make a matrix using the matrix() function

```
matrix(1:12, ncol = 4)

     [,1]  [,2]  [,3]  [,4]
[1,]   1     4     7    10
[2,]   2     5     8    11
[3,]   3     6     9    12

# Build row-wise
matrix(1:12, ncol = 4, byrow = TRUE)

     [,1]  [,2]  [,3]  [,4]
[1,]   1     2     3     4
[2,]   5     6     7     8
[3,]   9    10    11    12

# Use dimnames to set row/col names must be as a list()
matrix(1:12, ncol = 4, dimnames = list(letters[1:3], LETTERS[1:4]))

    A   B   C    D
a   1   4   7   10
b   2   5   8   11
c   3   6   9   12

# name the names
matrix(1:12, ncol = 4, dimnames = list(rows = letters[1:3],
                                       cols = LETTERS[1:4]))

     cols
rows  A  B   C    D
   a  1  4   7   10
   b  2  5   8   11
   c  3  6   9   12
```

You can also bind together objects to form a matrix. You can do this row-by-row or column-by-column. Usually the objects you bind are vector objects but they may be other matrix objects.

Example:

Bind objects to make a matrix

```
hrs <- BOD$Time * 24 # A vector
mins <- hrs * 60    # A vector
secs <- mins * 60   # A vector

# Bind vectors by row
mat <- rbind(hrs, mins, secs)
mat

         [,1]    [,2]    [,3]     [,4]     [,5]     [,6]
hrs        24      48      72       96      120      168
mins     1440    2880    4320     5760     7200    10080
secs    86400  172800  259200   345600   432000   604800

# Bind a vector and a matrix by column
cbind(1:3, mat)

       [,1]    [,2]    [,3]     [,4]     [,5]     [,6]     [,7]
hrs       1      24      48       72       96      120      168
mins      2    1440    2880     4320     5760     7200    10080
secs      3   86400  172800   259200   345600   432000   604800
```

Remember that all the elements must be the same length when using rbind() or cbind() functions.

Note: Changing objects into matrix form

You can "convert" some objects into a matrix. The as.matrix() function will attempt to coerce an object to a matrix. The data.matrix() function does a similar job but is intended to be applied to numeric data.frame objects.

8.5.2   Altering matrix objects

You can alter the contents of a matrix using [row, column] syntax. Using this method allows you to change any number of elements, including entire rows or columns. You can also alter the various names attributes:

- colnames() – note that names() does not work.
- rownames() or row.names().
- dimnames().

See Chapter 6 *R object types and their properties* for a reminder.

Tip: Transpose a matrix

Use the t() function to transpose a matrix, that is switch the rows/columns.

Adding columns to *matrix* objects

Use the cbind() function to add one or more columns to a matrix. The new data can be vector or matrix objects. New data should be the same length as the existing columns; short data will be recycled and long data truncated.

Adding rows to *matrix* objects

Use the rbind() function to add one or more rows to a matrix. The new data can be vector or matrix objects. New data should be the same length as the existing rows; short data will be recycled and long data truncated.

Note: Binding matrix and data.frame objects

You can use cbind() or rbind() to bind a data.frame and matrix, but the result will always be a data.frame.

8.6   Manipulating *array* objects

An array is very much like a matrix but can have more than two dimensions. Use the array() function to create an array from vector data.

```
array(data = NA, dim, dimnames = NULL)
```

In the array() function you specify the dim parameter as a vector, where each value gives the length of the (rows, columns, ...) dimensions of the array. You can also assign names to the dimensions with the dimnames parameter, you must use a list. Note that unlike matrix() you cannot specify the order that the dimensions are "filled" and the array is always constructed column-by-column.

Example:

Make an array

```
array(1:24, dim = c(2,6,2),
            dimnames = list(row = letters[1:2],
                            col = LETTERS[1:6],
                            D3 = c("first", "second")
            ))

, , D3 = first

   col
row  A  B  C  D   E   F
  a  1  3  5  7   9  11
  b  2  4  6  8  10  12

, , D3 = second

   col
row  A   B   C   D   E   F
  a 13  15  17  19  21  23
  b 14  16  18  20  22  24
```

> ### Note: `array` dimensions and source data
>
> The number of items you specify as `data` do not have to match the number of elements in the `dim` parameter. If there are too few `data` items will be recycled to "fill" the dimensions you specified. If there are too many `data` they will be truncated.

You can also treat an `array` somewhat like a `table` object, see Chapter 10 *Tabulation* for more details about tabulation.

8.6.1 Altering `array` objects

An `array` object is usually harder to handle than a `matrix`, not least because it can have more than two dimensions. Effectively, an `array` is stored internally as a `vector` with attributes for the dimension names. You can alter any of the elements using the `[]` in the same manner as for a `matrix` but adding or removing entire rows/columns is harder.

There are some operations that are relatively easy to accomplish, such as:

- Alter the names of the rows, columns and other dimensions.
- Rearrange the data into a new "shape", i.e. change the dimensions.
- Combine `array` objects of the same shape into one `array`.
- Adding new data to an existing `array`.

You can also use `as.vector()` to return an `array` to a `vector` and re-build from there.

Altering `array` name attributes

You can use the `dimnames()` function to alter the names of the dimensions of an `array` in much the same manner as for a `matrix`.

```
dimnames(object) <- list(name = value, ...)
```

You supply the names you want in a `list`, with an entry for each dimension as a `name = value` pair. If you set a name to `NULL` this effectively removes the name.

The `dimnames()` function is primarily used for setting/resetting *all* the dimensions. If you want to alter a single dimension you can use `rownames()` or `colnames()`, this will set the first and second dimensions respectively. You can also use `[[]]`, which allows you to set any dimension name. The `$` can also be used if there is an existing named element.

Example:

Altering `array` name elements

```
x <- array(1:24, dim = c(2,6,2))
dimnames(x)

NULL

# Set all names at once
dimnames(x) <- list(row = letters[1:2],
                    col = LETTERS[1:6],
                    D3 = c("First", "Second"))
dimnames(x)

$row
[1] "a" "b"
```

```
$col
[1] "A" "B" "C" "D" "E" "F"

$D3
[1] "First" "Second"

# [[n]] a single dimension
dimnames(x)[[3]] <- c("1st", "2nd")

# $name for existing element name
dimnames(x)$col <- LETTERS[21:26]

# rownames()
rownames(x) <- c("R1", "R2")
dimnames(x)

$row
[1] "R1" "R2"

$col
[1] "U" "V" "W" "X" "Y" "Z"

$D3
[1] "1st" "2nd"
```

Note that you *must* use double [[]] if you are setting a dimension name, single [] does not work and gives an error.

Altering *array* shape

An array has dimensions, you can see the size of them with dim(). The dim() function also allows you to alter the dimensions. Essentially it "unpacks" the array back to a vector and re-builds the array using the new dimensions. You must therefore ensure that the new dimensions match the size of the data.

Example:

Reshape an array

```
x <- array(1:24, dim = c(2, 6, 2))
x

, , 1

     [,1] [,2] [,3] [,4] [,5]   [,6]
[1,]    1    3    5    7    9     11
[2,]    2    4    6    8   10     12

, , 2

     [,1] [,2] [,3] [,4] [,5]   [,6]
[1,]   13   15   17   19   21     23
[2,]   14   16   18   20   22     24

dim(x) <- c(3, 8)
x
```

```
      [,1]  [,2]  [,3]  [,4]  [,5]   [,6]   [,7]   [,8]
[1,]    1     4     7    10    13     16     19     22
[2,]    2     5     8    11    14     17     20     23
[3,]    3     6     9    12    15     18     21     24
```

You can also change the "shape" of an array using aperm(), which is analogous to t() for matrix objects.

```
aperm(x, perm, ...)
```

In the function you give the "new order" to construct the dimensions. Note that the perm parameter requires the order that you want the array to be re-constructed.

Example:

Use aperm() to reshape an array

```
x <- array(1:12, dim = c(3, 2, 2))
x

, , 1

      [,1]  [,2]
[1,]    1     4
[2,]    2     5
[3,]    3     6

, , 2

      [,1]  [,2]
[1,]    7    10
[2,]    8    11
[3,]    9    12

# Switch rows/columns
aperm(x, perm = c(2, 1, 3))

, , 1

      [,1]  [,2]  [,3]
[1,]    1     2     3
[2,]    4     5     6

, , 2

      [,1]  [,2]  [,3]
[1,]    7     8     9
[2,]   10    11    12
```

Remember that you can "extract" the values from an array with as.vector(), which returns a vector object.

Combine *array* objects

You can combine array objects into one array in two main ways:

- Combine two or more array objects then re-build with array().
- Use sapply() to "add" one array to another.

The first method doesn't need the array objects to match in shape but the number of elements in total needs to "fit" the new dimensions.

Example:

Combine two array objects to one

```
a <- array(1:24, dim = c(2, 3, 2))
b <- array(25:36, dim = c(2, 3))
dimnames(a) <- list(row = letters[1:2],
                    col = LETTERS[1:3],
                    D3 = c("1st", "2nd"))
dimnames(b) <- list(row = letters[1:2], col = LETTERS[1:3])

# We need 36 "cells" in total
array(c(a, b), dim = c(3, 12))

      [,1] [,2] [,3] [,4] [,5] [,6]  [,7] [,8] [,9] [,10] [,11] [,12]
[1,]    1    4    7   10   25   28     1    4    7   10    25    28
[2,]    2    5    8   11   26   29     2    5    8   11    26    29
[3,]    3    6    9   12   27   30     3    6    9   12    27    30
```

Note that any dimnames are "lost" when the array is reconstructed.
   The second method works when you have array objects of the same shape.

Example:

Combine two array objects of the same shape

```
a <- array(1:12, dim = c(2, 3, 2))
b <- array(13:24, dim = c(2, 3, 2))

dimnames(a) <- list(row = letters[1:2],
                    col = LETTERS[1:3],
                    D3 = c("1st", "2nd"))
dimnames(b) <- list(row = letters[1:2],
                    col = LETTERS[1:3],
                    D3 = c("1st", "2nd"))

sapply(list(a,b), FUN = identity, simplify = "array")
, , D3 = 1st, 1

   col
row  A   B   C
  a  1   3   5
  b  2   4   6

, , D3 = 2nd, 1

   col
row  A   B   C
  a  7   9  11
  b  8  10  12

, , D3 = 1st, 2
```

```
    col
row    A    B    C
  a   13   15   17
  b   14   16   18

, , D3 = 2nd, 2

    col
row    A    B    C
  a   19   21   23
  b   20   22   24
```

In this case the dimnames are retained.

The sapply() function allows you to apply a function to each element of an object, see Chapter 9 *Summarizing data* for more information.

Adding new data to an `array`

Adding new data to an array is potentially complicated and not for the faint-hearted. A good starting point is to convert the array to a data.frame using the as.data.frame.table() function. You'll end up with a column for each dimension plus one for the "contents", which will be named Freq. You can then add new data to your data.frame and rebuild your array from there.

8.7   Manipulating `list` objects

A list is a loose collection of objects. Each element can be "anything". This feature can be handy but also potentially awkward. R has various ways to handle list objects.

8.7.1   Making `list` objects

The list() function is used to form a list object.

```
list(name = value, ...)
```

In the function you give the names of the objects you want to form the list. You *may* use name = value pairs, in which case each element is named as you like. If you just give the objects, their names are a simple numeric index value.

Example:

Constructing list objects

```
require(MASS) # for the datasets
# Elements un-named
list(DDT, abbey)

[[1]]
 [1]  2.79 2.93 3.22 3.78 3.22 3.38 3.18 3.33 3.34 3.06 3.07 3.56 3.08
4.64 3.34

[[2]]
 [1]  5.2  6.5  6.9  7.0  7.0  7.0  7.4  8.0  8.0  8.0  8.0  8.5
[13]  9.0  9.0 10.0 11.0 11.0 12.0 12.0  13.7 14.0 14.0 14.0 16.0
[25] 17.0 17.0 18.0 24.0 28.0 34.0 125.0

# Named elements
list(ddt = DDT, nickel = abbey)
```

```
$ddt
 [1] 2.79 2.93 3.22 3.78 3.22 3.38 3.18 3.33 3.34 3.06 3.07 3.56 3.08
4.64 3.34

$nickel
 [1]  5.2  6.5  6.9   7.0   7.0   7.0    7.4   8.0  8.0  8.0  8.0   8.5
[13]  9.0  9.0 10.0  11.0  11.0 12.0   12.0  13.7 14.0 14.0 14.0  16.0
[25] 17.0 17.0 18.0  24.0  28.0 34.0 125.0
```

> **Note: Empty `list` objects**
>
> You can make an empty `list` by assigning NULL multiple times (once for each element you want). More easily use `vector(mode = list, length = n)`, where n is the number of elements you want.

8.7.2 Altering `list` objects

You can alter a `list` in various ways:

- View or change the element names.
- Add elements.
- Remove elements.
- Change one or more elements.

A `list` object has a `names` attribute, which you can return or alter using the `names()` function (see Chapter 6 *R object types and their properties* for a review).

The key to `list` elements is to use the square brackets [] (or [[]]). you can also use $ if your `list` has named elements. The different syntax provides subtly different results (Table 8.10).

Table 8.10 Extracting elements of `list` objects

Syntax	Result
x$name	Returns the name element of the `list` called x. The result includes the $name component.
x[n]	Returns element n of `list` x. The result includes the $name component. You can also give the name as long as it is quoted: x["name"].
x[[n]]	Returns element n of `list` x. The result does *not* include the $name component. You can also give the name as long as it is quoted: x[["name"]].

As you can see from Table 8.10, the main difference between single [] and double [[]] square brackets is that with [] you see the $name component, whilst with [[]] you do not.

Example:

View `list` components

```
ml <- list(ddt = DDT, prawn = shrimp)
names(ml)

[1] "ddt"  "prawn"
```

```
ml$prawn
```

```
 [1] 32.2 33.0 30.8 33.8 32.2 33.3 31.7 35.7 32.4 31.2 26.6 30.7 32.5
30.7 31.2
[16] 30.3 32.3 31.7
```

```
ml[1]
```

```
$ddt
```

```
 [1]  2.79 2.93 3.22 3.78 3.22 3.38 3.18 3.33 3.34 3.06 3.07 3.56 3.08
4.64 3.34
```

```
ml[[1]] # element name not shown
```

```
 [1]  2.79 2.93 3.22 3.78 3.22 3.38 3.18 3.33 3.34 3.06 3.07 3.56 3.08
4.64 3.34
```

Note that you can "daisy-chain" the $ and/or [] **but** you can only use $ or [[]] for the first "level".

Example:

Daisy-chain elements of a list

```
names(ml)
```

```
[1] "ddt"  "prawn"
```

```
ml$ddt[3]
```

```
[1] 3.22
```

```
ml[2][4] # Gives error
```

```
$<NA>
NULL
```

```
# You must use [[]] for 'top' level
ml[[2]][4]
```

```
[1] 33.8
```

Addling list elements

Use $ or [[]] to add an element to an existing list. In fact the same syntax can replace an element. Note that you *must* use double [[]].

Removing list elements

Use $ or [] and set the value to NULL to remove an element from a list. Note that you *can* use single [].

Example:

Adding and removing list elements

```
ml <- list(ddt = DDT, prawn = shrimp)
names(ml)
```

```
[1] "ddt"  "prawn"
```

```
# Use $ to give explicit name
ml$copper <- chem
names(ml)

[1] "ddt"   "prawn" "copper"

# Use [n] or [[n]] to remove element
ml[3] <- NULL
names(ml)

[1] "ddt"   "prawn"

# Must use [[n]] to add element
ml[[3]] <- abbey
names(ml) # Note added element is un-named

[1] "ddt"   "prawn" ""
```

There are other functions that will "tinker" with list data, see Chapter 9 *Summarizing data* for example.

8.8   Time-series objects

The ts object class is connected to time-series data, that is, data which has a time element. A time series is effectively a vector with additional information about the time intervals.

You can create ts objects using the ts() function (Table 8.11).

```
ts(data, start = 1, end, frequency = 1, deltat = 1,
        ts.jpg = getOption("ts.jpg"), class, names)
```

There is also a as.ts() function that attempts to coerce an object to a ts time series. You can make two kinds of time series:

- **Single** – a single time series holds the ts object class.
- **Multiple** – a matrix can be used where the columns are different series. The result has multiple class labels: matrix, ts and mts.

Table 8.11 Parameters of the ts() function

Parameter	Description
data	The observations, a vector for a single time series or a matrix for a multiple time series. You can use a data.frame, which will be coerced to a matrix.
start	The time of the first observation. Give either a single integer or a vector of two.
end	The time of the last observation. If you do not specify the end it is determined from the length of the data and the start.
frequency	The number of observations per unit time (the default, 1, is annual). See also deltat.
deltat	The fraction of the sampling period between observations. So 1/12 would be monthly data. You should specify frequency or deltat but not both.
ts.jpg	A tolerance for time comparison, the default uses getOption("ts.jpg").
class	You can specify a class, the default is ts for single and c("mts", "ts", "matrix") for multiple series.
names	For a multiple series, you can give a vector of names for the columns.

Generally you will only need to specify the start and frequency parameters. The start can be a vector of two elements giving the start point and the position in the period.

Example:

Make single time series

```
# Default is annual (frequency = 1)
ts(1:12, start = 1970)

Time Series:
Start = 1970
End = 1981
Frequency = 1
 [1] 1 2 3 4 5 6 7 8 9 10 11 12

# Monthly
ts(1:12, start = 1970, frequency = 12)

     Jan Feb Mar Apr May  Jun Jul Aug Sep Oct  Nov Dec
1970   1   2   3   4   5    6   7   8   9  10   11  12

# Quarterly, with start at Qtr2
ts(1:12, start = c(1970, 2), frequency = 4)

     Qtr1  Qtr2  Qtr3  Qtr4
1970          1     2     3
1971    4     5     6     7
1972    8     9    10    11
1973   12
```

Note: ts and data type

In general you will be using numeric data. However, you can also make time series with other types. Note, however, that factor variables are coerced to an integer based on the levels.

To make a multiple time series you need a matrix or a data.frame that can be coerced to such. The names of the columns are taken from the data by default, but you can use names to create new ones.

Example:

Make a multiple time series

```
USPersonalExpenditure
```

	1940	1945	1950	1955	1960
Food and Tobacco	22.200	44.500	59.60	73.2	86.80
Household Operation	10.500	15.500	29.00	36.5	46.20
Medical and Health	3.530	5.760	9.71	14.0	21.10
Personal Care	1.040	1.980	2.45	3.4	5.40
Private Education	0.341	0.974	1.80	2.6	3.64

```
# Transpose matrix and make into multi-ts
ts(t(USPersonalExpenditure), start = 1940, freq = 1/5,
        names = c("Food/Tobacco", "Household",
                  "Medical", "Personal Care",
                  "Education"))

Time Series:
Start = 1940
End = 1960
Frequency = 0.2
       Food/Tobacco  Household  Medical  Personal Care   Education
1940           22.2       10.5     3.53           1.04       0.341
1945           44.5       15.5     5.76           1.98       0.974
1950           59.6       29.0     9.71           2.45       1.800
1955           73.2       36.5    14.00           3.40       2.600
1960           86.8       46.2    21.10           5.40       3.640
```

Tip: Multiple time series from existing ts

You can use cbind() to join together existing single ts to make a multiple series. The cbind() function makes a matrix but also retains the original time properties of the component objects.

```
deaths <- ts(cbind(fdeaths, mdeaths, ldeaths),
          start = 1974, freq = 12)
```

8.8.1 Properties of ts objects

You can view some of the properties of time-series objects using a variety of functions (Table 8.12).

A single time series is essentially a vector that has additional attributes regarding the time component of the data. A multiple time series is similar but is "built" on a matrix.

Table 8.12 Functions to explore properties of time-series objects

Function	Description
start	The starting time.
end	The ending time.
time	The times of all the observations.
cycle	The cycle intervals – positions of each item.
frequency	The frequency (number of samples per unit time).
deltat	The interval (essentially 1/frequency).
tsp	The time attributes (start, end, frequency).
window	A kind of subset – extract a "window" into the series.
class	Returns the object class.

Example:

Some properties of `ts` objects

```
# A portion (window) of a larger time series
ld <- window(ldeaths, start = 1974, end = c(1975, 12))
ld
```

```
     Jan  Feb  Mar  Apr  May   Jun  Jul  Aug  Sep Oct   Nov  Dec
1974 3035 2552 2704 2554 2014  1655 1721 1524 1596 2074  2199 2512
1975 2933 2889 2938 2497 1870  1726 1607 1545 1396 1787  2076 2837
```

```
start(ld)
```

```
[1] 1974   1
```

```
tsp(ld)
```

```
[1]  1974.000 1975.917   12.000
```

```
time(ld)
```

```
            Jan        Feb        Mar        Apr        May      Jun        Jul        Aug
1974 1974.000   1974.083   1974.167   1974.250   1974.333 1974.417   1974.500  1974.583
1975 1975.000   1975.083   1975.167   1975.250   1975.333 1975.417   1975.500  1975.583
            Sep        Oct        Nov        Dec
1974 1974.667   1974.750   1974.833   1974.917
1975 1975.667   1975.750   1975.833   1975.917
```

```
cycle(ld)
```

```
     Jan Feb Mar Apr May  Jun Jul Aug Sep Oct  Nov Dec
1974   1   2   3   4   5    6   7   8   9  10   11  12
1975   1   2   3   4   5    6   7   8   9  10   11  12
```

8.9   Dates and times in R

Many data are time-sensitive and have dates and/or times associated with them. There are various functions in R that allow you to deal with dates and times.

Dates are handled in two main ways, each associated with one or more object `class`:

- Number of days since 1970-01-01 – "Date".
- Number of seconds since 1970-01-01 – "POSIXlt" and "POSIXct".

The main different between the "POSIX" class types is that "lt" includes various components, whilst "ct" does not – think of the former as "long type" and the latter "concise type".

8.9.1   Date and time formats

You can see what the date `class` types look like by getting the current system date and/or time.

```
Sys.Date()
```

```
[1] "2022-06-22"
```

```
Sys.time()
```

```
[1] "2022-06-22 12:57:47 GMT"

class(Sys.time())

[1] "POSIXct" "POSIXt"
```

Tip: Current date/time

Use the date() function to get a "friendly" version of the current date/time in your locale.

```
date()
[1] "Wed Jun 22 12:57:47 2022"
```

The Sys.time() result is in POSIxct format but note that it also has class POSIXt, which is a *virtual* class that helps R "manage" date/time.

Note: Timezone

The Sys.time() function returns a timezone as well as a date and time. The timezone is usually set by your operating system. This can sometimes be set to "NA" and you may get a warning message. You can "force" your system to set a timezone using something like: Sys .setenv(TZ = "GMT"). See the database of timezones with OlsonNames().

Usually your first task when dealing with date/time data is to convert the data you have into an appropriate class. In the following example you'll see some simple data, which needs to be converted.

Example:

Date needing to be converted to date/time format

```
dtt <- data.frame(Id = LETTERS[1:3],
                  dat = c("12/06/2015", "04/11/2015", "03/05/2016"),
                  tim = c("10:25", "13:45", "19:45"))

dtt

  Id       dat   tim
1  A 12/06/2015 10:25
2  B 04/11/2015 13:45
3  C 03/05/2016 19:45
```

Once you have dates and/or times in some kind of dataset you can "re-format" them into the appropriate class type.

Set Date class

The Date is the simplest of the class types. Use the as.Date() function to coerce a vector into a date.

```
as.Date(x, format, origin, tz, ...)
```

The function can deal with vector data of character or factor class. You can also handle numeric data, in which case you need to specify the origin parameter. The tz parameter is only used if you are converting from POSIXct data.

The format parameter is used to describe the format of the data you have. To do this you use tokens of the form %x, where x is some date format (Table 8.13). You put together a character string that includes the tokens and separators, e.g. "%d/%m/%Y" for day month and year with / separators.

There are more tokens; use ?strptime to see the full range.

Example:

Making Date class from vector data

```
mydat <- as.Date(dtt$dat, format = "%d/%m/%Y")
mydat
```

```
[1] "2015-06-12" "2015-11-04" "2016-05-03"
```

```
class(mydat)
```

```
[1] "Date"
```

Table 8.13 **Some date tokens**

Token	Description
a	Abbreviated weekday name.
A	Full weekday name.
b	Abbreviated month name.
B	Full month name.
d	Day of the month as a number (01–31).
e	Day of the month as a number but with leading space for single digits (1–31).
m	Month as a decimal number (01–12).
u	Weekday as a decimal number (1–7) with Monday as 1.
w	Weekday as a decimal number (0–6) with Sunday as 0.
y	Year without century (00–99). Values 00–68 should be prefixed with 20, others with 19 (this is the current standard).
Y	Year with century.

Once you have your dates safely stored in a date/time class you can display them in other layouts – sometimes retaining the original class and sometimes not.

Note: Dates from numbers

You can convert a "raw" number into a date with as.Date() as long as you know the origin (that is, what day = 0 would be).

```
as.Date(18100, origin = "1970-01-01")
```

```
[1] "2019-07-23"
```

You *must* specify an origin or you get an error.

Set *POSIXt* class

The POSIXt class is a *virtual* class that covers POSIXct and POSIXlt formats. In general the *concise* format is the most useful. Use the as.POSIX*() functions to convert data into the appropriate POSIX format.

```
as.POSIXct(x, tz = "", ...)
as.POSIXlt(x, tz = "", ...)
```

The default tz takes the current system timezone; you can specify a different one (see OlsonNames() for a list of appropriate names). You also need to specify a format, which must match the input data. Note that you cannot give a time alone, you *must* include a date. The date and time components need to be specified using tokens (as in Table 8.13). See Table 8.14 for examples of some time tokens.

Table 8.14 Some time tokens

Token	Description
H	Hours as a decimal (00–23).
I	Hours as a decimal (01–12).
M	Minute as a decimal (00–59).
p	AM/PM indicator (use with %I).
S	Seconds (00–61).

Note that %S can be 61, which allows for use of leap seconds.

If your dates and times are in separate locations, you'll need to use paste() make a single date-time variable for conversion.

Example:

Making POSIXt class from vector data.

```
# Specify date only
as.POSIXct(dtt$dat, format = "%d/%m/%Y")

[1] "2015-06-12 GMT" "2015-11-04 GMT" "2016-05-03 GMT"

# Paste date and time variables
mytime <- as.POSIXlt(paste(dtt$dat, dtt$tim), format = "%d/%m/
%Y %H:%M")
mytime

[1] "2015-06-12 10:25:00 GMT" "2015-11-04 13:45:00 GMT"
[3] "2016-05-03 19:45:00 GMT"

class(mytime)

[1] "POSIXlt" "POSIXt"

# Specify timezone
 as.POSIXct(paste(dtt$dat, dtt$tim),
          format = "%d/%m/%Y %H:%M", tz = "UTC")
```

```
[1] "2015-06-12 10:25:00 UTC" "2015-11-04 13:45:00 UTC"
[3] "2016-05-03 19:45:00 UTC"
```

> **Tip: Time-stamp**
>
> Use the `timestamp()` function to produce the current date and time in a "friendly" layout. The result is sent to the console as a comment.
>
> ```
> timestamp()
> ##------ Wed May 25 07:45:18 2022 ------##
> ```

8.9.2 Working with date and time objects

There are various ways you can "tinker" with dates and times:

- Change format, e.g.:
  - Display layout.
  - Timezone.
- Extract components, e.g.:
  - View time-only.
  - Weekdays, months, quarters etc.
- Maths, e.g.:
  - Date sequences.
  - Differences between date elements.

There is something of an overlap between these methods; for example, changing the format to display only the year is essentially the same as extracting the year.

Convert date/time formats

There are two main `class` types when it comes to dates:

- `"Date"`
- `"POSIXt"`

The `as.Date()`, `as.POSIXct()` and `as.POSIXlt()` functions are the "main" ways to "convert" data from one form to the specific `class` you require. However, there are other functions that can produce a conversion:

```
strptime(x, format, tz)
strftime(x, format, tz, usetz)
format(x, format, ...)
```

The parameters of these functions are shown in Table 8.15.

- `strptime()` **Converts:** `character` → `POSIXlt`.
- `strftime()` **Converts:** `POSIXt` → `character`.
- `format()` **Converts:** `POSIXt` → `character`.

The `format()` and `strftime()` functions can also handle the `"Date"` object `class`.

Table 8.15 Parameters of date/time conversion functions

Parameter	Description
x	The data (a vector) to be converted.
format	A character string describing the date/time format. For strptime() this will be the format of the input, for the others it will be the desired format of the output.
tz	The timezone to be used as a character string.
usetz	If TRUE the timezone stamp is appended to the output, the default is FALSE.
...	Other parameters may be used.

Note:

- the tz parameter only works with POSIXct date class.
- strptime() can be used instead of as.POSIXlt().

Example:

Changing date formats

```
mytime

[1] "2015-06-12 10:25:00 GMT" "2015-11-04 13:45:00 GMT"
[3] "2016-05-03 19:45:00 GMT"

class(mytime)

[1] "POSIXlt" "POSIXt"

# Change timezone
format(as.POSIXct(mytime), usetz = TRUE, tz = "America/New_York")

[1] "2015-06-12 06:25:00 EDT" "2015-11-04 08:45:00 EST"
[3] "2016-05-03 15:45:00 EDT"

# Alter format - result is character
strftime(mytime, format = "%d/%m/%Y %H:%M:%S")

[1] "12/06/2015 10:25:00" "04/11/2015 13:45:00" "03/05/2016 19:45:00"
```

Extract components from date/time objects

The format() function can alter the way a date/time is presented. This also means that you can "extract" elements of date/time data objects by using the appropriate % tokens in the format parameter. There are also several convenience functions that you can use:

```
format(x, format, ...)
julian(x, origin, ...)
weekdays(x, abbreviate = FALSE)
months(x, abbreviate = FALSE)
quarters(x, ...)
```

For julian() the origin parameter should be a date/time class. The function gives the number of days from the origin.

Example:

Components of dates/times

```
weekdays(mydat)

[1] "Friday"  "Wednesday" "Tuesday"

months(mytime, abbreviate = TRUE)

[1] "Jun" "Nov" "May"

julian(mydat, origin = as.Date("2015-01-01"))

[1] 162 307 488

attr(,"origin")

[1] "2015-01-01"

quarters(mydat)

[1] "Q2" "Q4" "Q2"
```

Tip: Use `format()` on `date/time`

There is no convenience function for the year so you'll need to use `format()`. The same applies to times.

```
format(mytime, format = "%Y")

[1] "2015" "2015" "2016"

format(mytime, format = "%H:%M")

[1] "10:25" "13:45" "19:45"
```

The `POSIXlt()` format contains several elements. However, you cannot "view" them using `names()`, you need to use `attributes()` instead. The individual elements can still be "extracted" using $name.

Example:

Attributes of `POSIXlt` objects

```
attributes(mytime)

$names

[1] "sec"  "min"  "hour" "mday" "mon"  "year" "wday" "yday" "isdst"

$class

[1] "POSIXlt" "POSIXt"

$tzone

[1] "GMT"
```

See `?POSIXt` for the help entry and details of these attributes. In the main you'll use `format()` or the convenience functions.

Make date/time sequences

You can make sequences of dates in several ways. Two potential methods are:

- `seq.POSIXt()`
- `ISOdate()` and `ISOdatetime()`

The `seq.POSIXt()` function is a special method of `seq()` that operates on `POSIXt class`. The `ISOdate*()` functions are convenience methods that allow you to specify elements of date/time using simple numbers (Table 8.16).

```
seq.POSIXt(from, to, by, length.out, along.with, ...)
ISOdate(year, month, day, hour = 12, min = 0, sec = 0, tz = "GMT")
ISOdatetime(year, month, day, hour, min, sec, tz = "")
```

The main difference between the `ISO*()` functions is in their parameter defaults (Table 8.16).

Table 8.16 Parameters of date sequence functions

Parameter	Description
`from`	Starting date in a date/time `class`. This is required.
`to`	End date (optional).
`by`	Increment: a number of seconds or a `character` string. The string can be: "sec", "min", "hour", "day", "week", "month", "quarter" or "year". Optionally you can include an integer and space at the start of the string.
`length.out`	The desired length.
`along.with`	Take the length from the length of this argument.
`...`	Other parameters can be used.
`year, month, day, hour, min, sec`	Numerical values for date/time components. For `ISOdate()` there are default values for `hour`, `min` and `sec`.
`tz`	A timezone as a `character` string.

Note that for `seq.POSIXt()` you must give at least two of the parameters `to, by, length.out` and `along.with`.

The functions are often used in conjunction to create date sequences.

Example:

Date/time sequences

```
seq(from = as.POSIXct("2019-01-01"), by = "2 day", len = 4)

[1] "2019-01-01 GMT" "2019-01-03 GMT" "2019-01-05 GMT" "2019-01-07 GMT"

ISOdate(year = 2010:2013, month = 1, day = 1)

[1] "2010-01-01 12:00:00 GMT" "2011-01-01 12:00:00 GMT"
[3] "2012-01-01 12:00:00 GMT" "2013-01-01 12:00:00 GMT"

ISOdate(year = 2010:2013, month = 1, day = 1, hour = 0)

[1] "2010-01-01 GMT" "2011-01-01 GMT" "2012-01-01 GMT" "2013-01-01 GMT"
```

Math with date/times

It is possible to do some primitive mathematics on date/time data. The main function to use, difftime(), compares the difference between two date/times (Table 8.17). The function creates a difftime data class and there are some limited math functions that can be used on those.

```
difftime(time1, time2, tz, units)
as.difftime(tim, format, units)
format(x, ...)
units(x)
```

Use difftime() to get a result that contains information about time differences.

Example:

Table 8.17 Parameters of difftime() functions

Parameter	Description
time1	Date/time class object.
time2	Date/time class object.
tz	Timezone specification.
units	Units for the result, a character string: "auto", "secs", "mins", "hours", "days", or "weeks".
tim	A character string or numeric value specifying a time interval.
format	A character string giving the format of tim, using % tokens. The default is "%X" a locale-specific date/time.
x	A difftime object.
...	Other parameters are possible.

Time differences

```
mytime

[1] "2015-06-12 10:25:00 GMT" "2015-11-04 13:45:00 GMT"
[3] "2016-05-03 19:45:00 GMT"

difftime(mytime[1], mytime[2])

Time difference of -145.1389 days

difftime(mytime[1], mytime[2], units = "weeks")

Time difference of -20.73413 weeks

dift <- as.difftime(1:12, units = "days")
dift

Time differences in days

 [1]  1  2  3  4  5  6  7  8  9 10 11 12
```

Once you have a difftime object you can alter the units.

Example:

Alter time difference units

```
units(dift)

[1] "days"

units(dift) <- "weeks"
dift

Time differences in weeks
 [1]  0.1428571 0.2857143 0.4285714 0.5714286 0.7142857 0.8571429 1.0000000
 [8]  1.1428571 1.2857143 1.4285714 1.5714286 1.7142857
```

Use as.numeric() to get a plain numeric result. The format() function allows you to produce a "printable" output as a character vector.

Example:

Time different units as numeric

```
z <- as.difftime(c(0, 30, 60), units = "mins")
z

Time differences in mins

[1] 0 30 60

as.numeric(z, units = "secs")

[1]    0 1800 3600

as.numeric(z, units = "hours")

[1] 0.0 0.5 1.0

format(z)

[1] " 0 mins" "30 mins" "60 mins"
```

You can carry out some basic math operations on difftime objects (Table 8.18).

Table 8.18 Some math functions for difftime objects

Function	Result/Description
+ - * /	Regular math operations: addition, subtraction, multiplication and division.
sum	The total differences.
mean	The arithmetic mean of the differences.
median	Median.
trunc	Truncate to leave integer portion of values.
ceiling	Round up to next integer.
floor	Round down to lowest integer.
round	Round to digits number of decimals.
abs	Absolute values (– signs removed).

You can of course convert all your data to POSIXct and use as.numeric() to get the date/time value in seconds. Use of difftime() is essentially a convenience to avoid this.

Example:

Math on difftime objects

```
dift

Time differences in weeks
 [1] 0.1428571 0.2857143 0.4285714 0.5714286 0.7142857 0.8571429 1.0000000
 [8] 1.1428571 1.2857143 1.4285714 1.5714286 1.7142857

sum(dift)

Time difference of 11.14286 weeks

mean(dift)

Time difference of 0.9285714 weeks

round(dift, digits = 2)

Time differences in weeks

 [1] 0.14 0.29 0.43 0.57 0.71 0.86 1.00 1.14 1.29 1.43 1.57 1.71
```

> ### Note: Time-series graphics
>
> There are dedicated plotting routines for ts and mts objects, see Chapter 11 *Graphics* and section 11.8 for more details.

8.10 Adding elements

You can add elements to objects using a range of functions. You've seen these functions in operation in the previous sections, in relation to each kind of object class. Table 8.19 shows a summary of the principal functions and the object classes they operate upon.

The table is not exhaustive, but should serve as a general reminder.

8.10.1 Removing elements

You've already seen how to alter various objects, including removal of elements, in previous sections. Here's a quick reminder of the key points (Table 8.20).

The table is not exhaustive, but should serve as a general reminder. You can also use some kind of sub-setting function, e.g. which() or subset(), see section 7.2 *Subsets and selecting elements* for a reminder.

Table 8.19 Some functions and syntax for adding to objects

Function	Target(s)
c()	vector
$	list, data.frame
[], [[]]	list, matrix, array
cbind()	matrix, data.frame
data.frame()	data.frame
rbind()	matrix, data.frame
levels()	factor

Table 8.20 Methods for removing elements from objects

Method	Object
x$y <- NULL	Set y to NULL, where y is an element of a data.frame (a column), or list.
z <- x[-y]	Remove element(s) y from x and save object as z, where x is a vector or similar one-dimensional object. Also, y can be a column of a data.frame.
x[, col] <- NULL	Set col of x to NULL, where x is a column of a matrix or data.frame.
x[row,] <- NULL	Set row of x to NULL, where x is a row of a matrix or data.frame.

8.11 Merging items

Sometimes you have data in one place that you need to merge with data in another. You can use the merge() command to "mingle" two datasets (Table 8.21). This is a bit like the lookup table in a spreadsheet or database joining using the SQL language.

```
merge(x, y, by.x, by.y, all.x, all.y, sort, ...)
```

In merge() you specify the two datasets (x and y) and how they are to be merged. The by and all parameters allow you to specify "key" columns and how the JOIN process is to be carried out (Table 8.21).

If you do not specify by.x and by.y the function will look for columns with matching names. It is probably "safest" to specify the columns explicitly.

The all.x and all.y parameters enable you to specify all the possibilities for the merge operation (Table 8.22).

Any unmatched data are represented with NA in the final result.

Example:

Joining data using merge()

```
# Some simple data
x <- data.frame(input = letters[c(1, 3, 4, 2, 1, 3)])
x
    input
1       a
2       c
3       d
4       b
5       a
6       c
```

Table 8.21 Some parameters of the merge() function

Parameter	Description
x	The "left" dataset, usually a data.frame. This is the one that is merged into using information from y.
y	The "right" dataset. This contains the information to be merged into x.
by.x	The name ("quoted") of the key column of x.
by.y	The name ("quoted") of the key column of y.
all.x	If TRUE all the data in x are kept, even if there is no corresponding data in y. If FALSE (the default), unmatched data are dropped.
all.y	If TRUE all the data in y are kept, even if there is no corresponding data in x. If FALSE (the default), unmatched data are dropped.
sort	If TRUE (the default) the resulting columns are sorted.
...	Other parameters are possible.

Table 8.22 Types of join in merge()

Join type	all.x	all.y	Result
INNER (natural)	FALSE	FALSE	Returns records that have matching values in both tables.
LEFT (outer)	TRUE	FALSE	Return all records from the left table, and the matched records from the right table.
RIGHT (outer)	FALSE	TRUE	Return all records from the right table, and the matched records from the left table.
FULL (outer)	TRUE	TRUE	Return all records when there is a match in either left or right table.

```
# lookup table
y <- data.frame(lower = letters[1:3], upper = LETTERS[1:3])
y

  lower   upper
1   a       A
2   b       B
3   c       C

# LEFT join - unmatched entries give NA
merge(x, y, by.x = "input", by.y = "lower", all.x = TRUE, all.y = FALSE)

  input   upper
1   a       A
2   a       A
3   b       B
4   c       C
5   c       C
6   d      <NA>
```

Tip: merge() and sort

By default sort = TRUE in the merge() function. Use sort = FALSE to prevent sorting as this can occasionally lead to problems.

8.12   Transforming elements

You've already seen examples of transforming elements in the previous sections. If you want to alter the values in a column of a data.frame, for instance, then you "set" the column to new values.

```
BOD

      Time    demand
1       1        8.3
2       2       10.3
3       3       19.0
4       4       16.0
5       5       15.6
6       7       19.8
bod <- BOD
bod$Time <- bod$Time * 24
bod

      Time   demand
1       24      8.3
2       48     10.3
3       72     19.0
4       96     16.0
5      120     15.6
6      168     19.8
```

In the preceding example the Time column is a numeric variable that you multiply by 24 to give a new result. You might also make a new column containing the same result. You have to "point" explicitly at the Time variable using the $. You can also use [] or the with() function (see Chapter 7 *Working with data objects* for a review).

There are a couple of R functions that allow you to evaluate expressions without having to resort to the $ or [] syntax:

```
transform(data, name = value, ...)
within(data, expr, ...)
```

The transform() command allows you to alter an element within a data.frame and possibly make a copy of it. The within() function is similar in that you can evaluate an expression "within" a data.frame (or list).

The transform() function requires one or more name = value pairs, any variables within the parent data.frame can be names "as-is", you don't need $.

```
transform(BOD, hrs = Time * 24, log = log(demand))

      Time   demand    hrs        log
1       1       8.3     24    2.116256
2       2      10.3     48    2.332144
3       3      19.0     72    2.944439
4       4      16.0     96    2.772589
5       5      15.6    120    2.747271
6       7      19.8    168    2.985682
```

The within() function allows you to evaluate an expression "inside" a parent data.frame. You *can* evaluate multiple expressions, in which case you need to use { and } to put the expressions on separate lines.

```
within(BOD, {
      hrs <- Time * 24
      min <- hrs * 60
      sec <- min * 60
})
    Time  demand      sec     min    hrs
1     1     8.3    86400    1440     24
2     2    10.3   172800    2880     48
3     3    19.0   259200    4320     72
4     4    16.0   345600    5760     96
5     5    15.6   432000    7200    120
6     7    19.8   604800   10080    168
```

Note that you *must* use <- in the expressions (not =).

See section 7.4 *Working with text and strings* in Chapter 7 *Working with data objects* for details about transforming character (text) variables.

Note: with () and within ()

The with () function is superficially similar to within (). However with () only "sees" variables that exist in the parent data, whilst within () can create a new variable that is then "available" in further expressions.

8.13   Altering data layout or form

Sometimes you need to alter the layout or "shape" of your data. It may be that you want to present your data in a more "compact" layout for printing/display. Some analytical and graphical functions require your data to be in a particular layout, so you may need to alter the data before running the analysis or plotting the graphic.

In the following sections you'll see examples of altering the data layout in four broad ways:

- Transpose – switching rows and columns.
- Stacking – using grouping variables to reduce number of columns.
- Reshape – for repeated measurements on individuals you can have data in "wide" or "long" format.
- Un-list – simplifying list objects.

Altering the layout of your data is an important skill.

8.13.1   Transpose rows and columns

One of the simplest ways to alter your data layout is to switch the rows and columns. There are two functions that can do this:

```
t(x)
aperm(a, perm, ...)
```

The t() function will transpose a matrix or data.frame; the result is always a matrix. Remember that for a matrix all the data must be of the same kind, but for a data.frame each column can be different (although within each column the data should be the same kind).

Example:

Transpose rows/columns

```
VADeaths
```

	Rural Male	Rural Female	Urban Male	Urban Female
50-54	11.7	8.7	15.4	8.4
55-59	18.1	11.7	24.3	13.6
60-64	26.9	20.3	37.0	19.3
65-69	41.0	30.9	54.6	35.1
70-74	66.0	54.3	71.1	50.0

```
t(VADeaths)
```

	50-54	55-59	60-64	65-69	70-74
Rural Male	11.7	18.1	26.9	41.0	66.0
Rural Female	8.7	11.7	20.3	30.9	54.3
Urban Male	15.4	24.3	37.0	54.6	71.1
Urban Female	8.4	13.6	19.3	35.1	50.0

```
# data.frame ends up as matrix
t(BOD)
```

	[,1]	[,2]	[,3]	[,4]	[,5]	[,6]
Time	1.0	2.0	3	4	5.0	7.0
demand	8.3	10.3	19	16	15.6	19.8

The `aperm()` function will work on objects that have two or more dimensions (such as `table` or `array` objects). You use the `perm` parameter to state the new order of the dimensions.

Example:

Use `aperm()` to transpose multidimensional objects

```
# Use dimension numbers
aperm(USPersonalExpenditure, perm = 2:1)
```

	Food and Tobacco	Household Operation	Medical and Health	Personal Care
1940	22.2	10.5	3.53	1.04
1945	44.5	15.5	5.76	1.98
1950	59.6	29.0	9.71	2.45
1955	73.2	36.5	14.00	3.40
1960	86.8	46.2	21.10	5.40

	Private Education
1940	0.341
1945	0.974
1950	1.800
1955	2.600
1960	3.640

```
# Use dimension names
aperm(HairEyeColour, perm = c("Eye", "Hair", "Sex"))
, , Sex = Male
```

```
       Hair
```

Eye	Black	Brown	Red	Blond
Brown	32	53	10	3
Blue	11	50	10	30
Hazel	10	25	7	5
Green	3	15	7	8

```
, , Sex = Female
```

```
      Hair
Eye        Black   Brown   Red   Blond
   Brown     36      66     16     4
   Blue       9      34      7     64
   Hazel      5      29      7      5
   Green      2      14      7      8
```

Note: Dimension specification

You can specify the `perm` parameter of `aperm()` using `integer` values or "quoted" names (if the dimensions are named). You must give all the dimensions, in the required order.

8.13.2 Stack and unstack variables

When you have data in multiple samples you can arrange them in different ways.

- Each sample as a separate column ("wide" format).
- A column for the values, and one for the grouping ("long" format).

These basic arrangements are sometimes known as "wide" and "long" format. The `stack()` and `unstack()` functions potentially enable you to switch between these layouts.

```
unstack(x, form, ...)
stack(x, ...)
```

A limitation is that your data can only utilize one grouping variable. You'll see more about this shortly.

Unstack variables

In general the "long" layout, where you have a *response* variable and a *grouping* variable (a *predictor*) is the most "robust" layout. In this layout the different sample values are stacked upon one another to form a single *response* variable. The labels for the different samples form the *predictor* or *grouping* column.

Example:

Data in stacked ("long") format

```
summary(PlantGrowth)
```

```
      weight        group
Min.:     3.590    ctrl:10
1st Qu.:  4.550    trt1:10
Median:   5.155    trt2:10
Mean:     5.073
3rd Qu.:  5.530
Max.:     6.310
```

In the preceding example the `PlantGrowth` data are shown in two columns: `weight` are the values collected during an experiment (the *response*), `group` shows the experimental treatment (the *predictor*) for each corresponding `weight`.

You can use unstack() to rearrange the data into a sample layout (e.g. "wide") where each group has its own column:

Example:

Unstack data

```
PG <- unstack(PlantGrowth)
head(PG, n = 4)

    ctrl   trt1   trt2
1   4.17   4.81   6.31
2   5.58   4.17   5.12
3   5.18   4.41   5.54
4   6.11   3.59   5.50
```

You can see that you now have three columns, one for each of the original grouping levels.

The unstack() function can only "deal" with a single grouping variable; if you have more you'll need to specify which one to use via the form parameter. The form parameter requires a formula of the form response ~ predictor.

Example:

Unstack a selected variable

```
head(warpbreaks, n = 4)

    breaks   wool   tension
1       26      A         L
2       30      A         L
3       54      A         L
4       25      A         L

WB <- unstack(warpbreaks, form = breaks ~ tension)
head(WB, n = 4)

     L    M    H
1   26   18   36
2   30   21   21
3   54   29   24
4   25   17   18
```

The unstack() process will result in a list where each sample is an element. If the elements are all the same length they will be coerced into a data.frame, if not they remain as a list.

Example:

Unstacking data with unequal replication

```
CW <- unstack(chickwts)
str(CW)

List of 6
 $ casein:   num [1:12]   368 390 379 260 404 318 352 359 216 222 ...
 $ horsebean: num [1:10]  179 160 136 227 217 168 108 124 143 140
 $ linseed:  num [1:12]   309 229 181 141 260 203 148 169 213 257 ...
 $ meatmeal: num [1:11]   325 257 303 315 380 153 263 242 206 344 ...
```

```
 $ soybean:   num [1:14]   243 230 248  327 329 250 193 271  316  267 ...
 $ sunflower: num [1:12]   423 340 392  339 341 226 320 295  334  322 ...
```

> ## Tip: Unstacking multivariable data
>
> If you have multiple *predictor* variables you can combine them with paste(), then unstack() using the new variable.
>
> ```
> wb <- transform(warpbreaks, WT = paste0(wool, tension))
> WB <- unstack(wb, form = breaks ~ WT)
> head(WB)
> ```
>
> ```
>     AH  AL  AM  BH  BL   BM
> 1   36  26  18  20  27   42
> 2   21  30  21  21  14   26
> 3   24  54  29  24  29   19
> 4   18  25  17  17  19   16
> 5   10  70  12  13  29   39
> 6   43  52  18  15  31   28
> ```

Stack variables

If you have data in multi-column layout you can use stack() to combine the data into a "long" format, with columns for the *response* and *predictor*. You can optionally use the select parameter *if* the data are in a data.frame (not a list).

The result is a data.frame with columns labelled values and ind.

Example:

Stacking data

```
cw <- stack(CW)
summary(cw)
```

```
      values              ind
   Min.:    108.0      casein:12
1st Qu.:    204.5   horsebean:10
 Median:    258.0      linseed:12
   Mean:    261.3    meatmeal:11
3rd Qu.:    323.5     soybean:14
   Max.:    423.0   sunflower:12
```

```
# Omit one (grouping) variable
pg <- stack(PG, select = -ctrl)
summary(pg)
```

```
      values          ind
   Min.:    3.590   trt1:10
1st Qu.:    4.620   trt2:10
 Median:    5.190
   Mean:    5.093
3rd Qu.:    5.605
   Max.:    6.310
```

You can alter the column names afterwards, using `names()` or `colnames()` functions (see Chapter 6 *R object types and their properties* for a reminder).

8.13.3 Reshape data

A special case of stacking and unstacking data is where you have "identifiable" replicates. A common scenario is where you have individuals who are "measured" at different time intervals. This kind of thing is sometimes known as *repeated measures,* where you record information repeatedly on various individuals.

Your data can be set out in "wide" or "long" format. It is common for the "wide" format to be used to display the data, as it is more compact. However, many analytical functions require the data to be in "long" format, with *response* and *predictor* variables.

The `reshape()` function allows you to convert your data between "wide" and "long" formats. The various parameters allow you to specify how the variables relate to one another (Table 8.23).

```
reshape(data, varying, v.names, timevar, idvar, drop, direction,
    ...)
```

Table 8.23 Some parameters of the `reshape()` function

Parameter	Description
data	The data for reshaping, must be a `data.frame`.
varying	Names of variables in "wide" layout that correspond to variables in "long" layout. This should be given as a `list`.
v.names	Names of variables in "long" layout that correspond to variables in "wide" layout.
timevar	The variable in "long" layout that differentiates multiple replicates from the same group/individual.
idvar	Names of variables in "long" layout that identify multiple replicates from the same group/individual.
drop	A `vector` of names to drop before reshape takes place.
direction	A `character` string `"wide"` or `"long"`, that determines the ultimate shape of the result.
...	Other parameters are possible.

In the "wide" layout each row contains complete data for a single individual/group. In the "long" layout there are multiple rows, but fewer columns.

Example:

Reshape data from "wide" to "long" layout

```
summary(anorexia)

  Treat         Prewt            Postwt
 CBT:29    Min.  :70.00      Min.  :71.30
 Cont:26   1st Qu.:79.60     1st Qu.:79.33
 FT:17     Median:82.30      Median:84.05
           Mean  :82.41      Mean  :85.17
           3rd Qu.:86.00     3rd Qu.:91.55
           Max.  :94.90      Max.  :103.60
```

```
an.long <- reshape(anorexia,
                   varying = list(2:3),
                   direction = "long",
                   v.names = "wt")

summary(an.long)
```

```
 Treat        time             wt              id
  CBT:58     Min.:1.0      Min.:70.00      Min.:1.00
 Cont:52     1st Qu.:1.0   1st Qu.:79.50   1st Qu.:18.75
  FT:34      Median:1.5    Median:82.85    Median:36.50
             Mean:1.5      Mean:83.79      Mean:36.50
             3rd Qu.:2.0   3rd Qu.:87.72   3rd Qu.:54.25
             Max.:2.0      Max.:103.60     Max.:72.00
```

Note that if there is no "ID" variable in the "wide" layout one will be created using simple integer values.

The result contains attributes pertaining to the reshaping process, so once you have "converted" a dataset it is easy to reshape it in the other direction.

```
an.wide <- reshape(an.long, direction = "wide")
head(an.wide)
```

```
      Treat  id  Prewt   Postwt
1.1   Cont   1   80.7    80.2
2.1   Cont   2   89.4    80.1
3.1   Cont   3   91.8    86.4
4.1   Cont   4   74.0    86.3
5.1   Cont   5   78.1    76.1
6.1   Cont   6   88.3    78.1
```

When reshaping to "wide" layout you use slightly different parameters.

Example:

Reshape data from "long" to "wide" layout

```
summary(Sitka)
```

```
      size             Time             tree           treat
  Min.:2.230       Min.:152.0        Min.:1      control:125
 1st Qu.:4.345    1st Qu.:174.0    1st Qu.:20       ozone:270
 Median:4.900     Median:201.0     Median:40
 Mean:4.841       Mean:202.4       Mean:40
 3rd Qu.:5.400    3rd Qu.:227.0    3rd Qu.:60
  Max.:6.630       Max.:258.0       Max.:79
```

```
sitka <- reshape(Sitka, v.names = "size",
                        idvar = "tree",
                        timevar = "Time",
                        direction = "wide")
```

```
head(sitka)
```

```
     tree  treat  size.152  size.174  size.201  size.227  size.258
1     1    ozone    4.51      4.98      5.41      5.90      6.15
6     2    ozone    4.24      4.20      4.68      4.92      4.96
11    3    ozone    3.98      4.36      4.79      4.99      5.03
```

16	4	ozone	4.36	4.77	5.10	5.30	5.36
21	5	ozone	4.34	4.95	5.42	5.97	6.28
26	6	ozone	4.59	5.08	5.36	5.76	6.00

Notice that the column names are a combination of the v.names and timevar. It *is* possible to alter the names using other parameters of reshape() (see ?reshape for details).

8.13.4   Unlist and relist data

The unlist() function changes the shape of a list, making it into a vector. The relist() function does more or less the opposite, allowing you to re-construct an unlisted object back to the original form.

```
unlist(x, use.names = TRUE, ...)
relist(flesh, skeleton)
```

Although the functions are primarily concerned with list objects they will work with other types.

Unlist objects

The unlist() function attempts to de-construct an object and represent it as a vector.

```
require(MASS)
shoes
$A
 [1] 13.2 8.2 10.9 14.3 10.7 6.6 9.5 10.8 8.8 13.3

$B
 [1] 14.0 8.8 11.2 14.2 11.8 6.4 9.8 11.3 9.3 13.6

unlist(shoes)

  A1   A2   A3   A4   A5   A6   A7   A8  A9 A10   B1   B2   B3   B4   B5   B6
13.2 8.2 10.9 14.3 10.7 6.6 9.5 10.8 8.8 13.3 14.0 8.8 11.2 14.2 11.8 6.4
  B7   B8   B9  B10
 9.8 11.3  9.3  13.6
```

In general the names of the vector elements are a combination of the element name and an integer. You can suppress the names with the parameter use.names = FALSE.

You can also unlist() other objects (with varying degrees of success). A factor object will be represented as an integer using the levels of the factor. If you have a data.fra me with a mix of numeric and character, the entire result will be a character vector.

Example:

Un-list a data.frame

```
# Add a factor variable
bod <- transform(BOD,
                 day = c("Mon", "Tue", "Wed", "Thu", "Fri", "Sat"))
bod

  Time demand  day
1    1    8.3  Mon
2    2   10.3  Tue
3    3   19.0  Wed
4    4   16.0  Thu
```

```
5    5    15.6    Fri
6    7    19.8    Sat
```

```
unlist(bod)
```

```
Time1  Time2  Time3  Time4  Time5  Time6 demand1 demand2
demand3 demand4
 "1"    "2"    "3"    "4"    "5"    "7"   "8.3" "10.3"   "19"   "16"
demand5 demand6 day1  day2   day3   day4  day5  day6
"15.6" "19.8"  "Mon"  "Tue"  "Wed"  "Thu"  "Fri"  "Sat"
```

```
# Note how the result matches the factor levels
levels(bod$day)
```

```
NULL
```

The unlist() function can be used with character objects too.

Example:

Un-list character objects

```
x <- "a character string I want to split into pieces"

# Split by the spaces
y <- strsplit(x, split = " ")
y
```

```
[[1]]
[1]     "a" "character"  "string"     "I"    "want"       "to"
[7] "split"            "into"   "pieces"
```

```
unlist(y)
```

```
[1]     "a" "character"  "string"     "I"    "want"       "to"
[7] "split"            "into"   "pieces"
```

See section 8.7 *Manipulating* list *objects* for a reminder of how to deal with list objects.

Relist objects

The relist() function attempts to re-construct a vector into a list or other structure that you define. You start with the flesh (your unlisted object, usually a vector) and specify the skeleton, which is the structure you require (this *must* be a list).

The skeleton can be an object, such as a data.frame, that holds existing data, or you can define an "empty" object.

Example:

Re-list an object

```
skel <- list(X = numeric(10), Y = numeric(10))
socks <- unlist(shoes)
skel
```

```
$X
 [1] 0 0 0 0 0 0 0 0 0 0
```

```
$Y
 [1] 0 0 0 0 0 0 0 0 0 0

socks
 A1   A2   A3   A4   A5   A6   A7   A8   A9  A10   B1   B2   B3   B4   B5   B6
13.2 8.2 10.9 14.3 10.7 6.6 9.5 10.8 8.8 13.3 14.0 8.8 11.2 14.2 11.8 6.4
 B7   B8   B9  B10
9.8 11.3 9.3 13.6

# Note how names are taken from skeleton
relist(socks, skeleton = skel)

$X
 [1] 13.2 8.2 10.9 14.3 10.7 6.6 9.5 10.8 8.8 13.3

$Y
 [1] 14.0 8.8 11.2 14.2 11.8 6.4 9.8 11.3 9.3 13.6
```

Note that you *must* use a `list` structure for your `skeleton`. If you need to re-form a `data.fra me` you need to convert the re-listed result afterwards.

Example:

Re-list a `data.frame`

```
BOD

   Time   demand
1    1      8.3
2    2     10.3
3    3     19.0
4    4     16.0
5    5     15.6
6    7     19.8

skel <- list(day = numeric(6), bod = numeric(6))
o2 <- unlist(BOD)
o2

 Time1  Time2  Time3  Time4  Time5  Time6 demand1 demand2
demand3 demand4
  1.0    2.0    3.0    4.0    5.0    7.0    8.3   10.3   19.0   16.0
demand5 demand6
 15.6   19.8

# relist() forms a list
relist(o2, skeleton = skel)

$day
[1] 1 2 3 4 5 7

$bod
[1] 8.3 10.3 19.0 16.0 15.6 19.8

# convert the list to a data.frame
data.frame(relist(o2, skeleton = skel))
```

```
    day   bod
1    1    8.3
2    2   10.3
3    3   19.0
4    4   16.0
5    5   15.6
6    7   19.8
```

Note: Fleshing out a skeleton

You need to get the `length` correct when using `relist()` as the elements are filled left → *right* along the `vector` and padded with NA if necessary. Skeletons that are too short end up with truncated data.

You'll see more about dealing with `list` objects (and others) in the next chapter, 9 *Summarizing data.*

EXERCISES:

Self-Assessment for Manipulating data objects

1. To get 25 random values from the uniform distribution, between 0 and 100, type ____.
2. Use row parameter in the `matrix()` function to build a `matrix` row-by-row, rather than columnwise. TRUE or FALSE?
3. Which of the following commands *cannot* add a column to a `data.frame`:
   a. `data.frame()`
   b. `cbind()`
   c. `x[, "data"]`
   d. `x$variable`
4. To convert a character `vector` to POSIX date you use the `format()` function. TRUE or FALSE?
5. To switch data between "wide" and "long" layouts you might use ____ or ____ functions.

Answers to exercises are in the *Appendix*.

8.14 Chapter Summary: Manipulating data objects

Topic	Key Points
Random numbers	Generate random numbers from various underlying distributions with `rxxxx()`, where `xxxx` is the distribution e.g.: `rnorm()`, `runif()`, `rpois()`. Use `set.seed()` to "fix" a starting point. Use `help(Distributions)` to see available distribution families.
Vector objects	Make empty `vector()` objects with `vector(mode, length)`. Alter size of `vector` using `length() <- value`, this will either add empty elements or truncate the `vector`. Combine `vector` objects with `c()`.

(Continued)

(Continued)

Topic	Key Points
Factor objects	Make a factor with: factor(), gl(), or coerce an existing object with as.factor(). A factor has levels, which can have labels and be ordered. Use levels to see or alter levels. Use droplevels() to remove unused levels.
Data.Frame objects	Use read.table() or read.csv() to import data from disk as a data.frame. Use data.frame() to build an object, or add to an existing data.frame. You can convert character columns to factor variables on import using the stringsAsFactors parameter.
Properties of data.frame	View or set name elements with: names(), colnames(), rownames(), and row.names() functions.
Add rows/cols	Use $ or square brackets [] to add column data to a data.frame. Also use data.frame(), or cbind(). Use rbind() to add new rows.
Matrix objects	Make a matrix using matrix(), cbind(), or rbind() functions. To view/alter names use colnaqmes(), rownames(), or dimnames(). Add more columns/rows with cbind() or rbind(). Transpose rows/cols using t().
Array objects	An array is a multidimensional object like a matrix. Use array() to build an array. Use dimnames() to view/set name elements. Change array dimensions using array(), or aperm(). Combine array objects with sapply().
List objects	A list is a loose collection of objects. Use list() to build a list. Add elements using $, or square brackets [] (or [[]] doubled). Add elements using list(), remove by assigning elements to NULL.
Time series	Use ts() to make a time-series object. A single vector will form a ts object, but multiple data from a matrix can make a mts, multiple time series. Use cbind() to join several ts objects to form mts. View ts properties using e.g.: start(), end(), time(), and frequency() functions.
Date and Time	Use Sys.Date(), Sys.time(), and date() to get date and time fro the current system. Use as.Date() to format a vector as a Date object. POSIX dates can be formatted using as.POSIXct() or as.POSIXlt() functions.
Date/time conversion	Use strptime() to convert character to POSIX, use strftime() or format() to convert POSIX to character. See also: julian(), weekdays(), months(), and quarters() functions.
Merge data	Use merge() to carry out data merging, analogous to SQL join operations (or Excel LOOKUP).
Transform elements	Use transform(), or within() functions to carry out operations "inside" an object (usually data.frame).
Transpose rows and columns	Use t() to transpose a matrix or data.frame, switching rows/cols to make a new matrix result. The equivalent for an array is aperm().
Reshape data	Use stack() and unstack() for simple operations. Use reshape() for more complicated data objects that need converting between "wide" and "long" layout. Use unlist() and relist() with list objects (this may also work with other kinds).

9. Summarizing data

This chapter is concerned with data summary, that is ways to simplify data and make them more easily understandable. Classic methods of summarizing data include averages and measures of the spread of values around the average. However, there are other ways of summarizing data, such as group proportions and percentages. In this chapter you'll see how to carry out a variety of summarizing functions that will help you deal with data in various ways.

What's in this chapter

» Summary functions.
» Cumulative functions.
» Functions on entire elements (e.g. rows/columns) of data.
» Functions on groups in your data.
» Custom data summary routines.

Note: Support material

See the ↘ for links to material on the support website.

9.1 General summary statistics

Many of the functions that compute summary statistics are designed to operate on one-dimensional objects, that is `vector` objects (Table 9.1). There are also various "helper" functions that allow you to compute summary statistics in different ways:

- cumulatively.
- for all the elements of an object (e.g. all columns).
- use a grouping variable to split data into chunks, and return the summary for each chunk.
- for entire tables (e.g. to return marginal totals or proportions).

In this section the focus is on the general summary functions that operate on `vector` objects (Table 9.1).

All of the functions in Table 9.1 return single values except `range()` and `nchar()`.

Example:

Simple summary functions on `vector` objects

```
shrimp
```

```
 [1] 32.2 33.0 30.8 33.8 32.2 33.3 31.7 35.7 32.4 31.2 26.6 30.7 32.5 30.7 31.2
[16] 30.3 32.3 31.7
```

Table 9.1 Some summary functions

Function	Result
sum	The sum of all the values.
mean	The arithmetic mean.
median	The median value.
sd	The standard deviation.
var	Variance.
mad	Median Absolute Deviation.
max	Maximum value.
min	Minimum.
range	Range, the result is a vector giving the min and max.
IQR	Inter Quartile Range, that is the 0.75 quantile - 0.25 quantile.
length	The number of elements.
nchar	The number of characters in elements of a character vector.

```
mean(shrimp)

[1]  31.79444

sd(shrimp)

[1]  1.843421

range(shrimp)

[1]  26.6 35.7

length(shrimp)

[1]  18
```

Note: Non-zero elements of a character vector

The nzchar() function returns TRUE for each element of a character vector that is non-zero. Empty elements (i.e. "") return FALSE.

Note that there is no function for mode in Table 9.1. If you try mode() you get the "storage mode" of an object:

```
mode(shrimp)

[1]  "numeric"
```

Modal value is not a commonly used statistic. If you want the mode, you'll have to dip into tabulation (see Chapter 10 *Tabulation*) and undertake a bit of programming. Here is an example function that will compute the mode.

Example:

Function to compute modal values

```
# A function to calculate mode
Mode <- function(x) {
    tx <- table(x)
    mx <- which(tx == max(tx))
    fx <- as.vector(tx[mx])
    mv <- as.numeric(names(mx))
    result <- list(mode = mv, freq = fx)
    invisible(result)
}
```

The Mode() function returns a list giving the modal values and their frequencies. If there are two or more values tied for the highest frequency, the result shows them all. If all values are unique their frequencies will all be 1 and the result will reflect that. Note that R has a mode() function, which returns the storage mode of an object (we use Mode() here to differentiate, as R is case-sensitive).

Example:

Using a custom function for modal values

```
x <- Mode(chem)

# There is one mode (3.7) with frequency = 4
unlist(x)

mode freq
 3.7  4.0

# DDT has two modal values
(Mode(DDT))

$mode
[1] 3.22 3.34

$freq
[1] 2 2
```

You'll see other examples of simple custom functions through the text. See Chapter 15 *Programming tools* for details about creating custom function objects.

The summary() function will give you some basic statistics if your data are a numeric vector:

```
summary(shrimp)

Min.  1st Qu. Median   Mean 3rd Qu.   Max.
26.60    30.90  31.95  31.79   32.48  35.70
```

The quantile() function returns the quantiles you specify, the default being the quartiles.

```
quantile(x, probs = seq(0, 1, 0.25), na.rm = FALSE, ...)
```

You specify the probs you require and the result shows those quantiles.

Example:

The `quantile()` function

```
quantile(shrimp)
```

```
    0%     25%     50%     75%     100%
26.600  30.900  31.950  32.475   35.700
```

```
quantile(abbey, probs = c(0.33, 0.67))
```

```
33%   67%
 8    14
```

Note that the `quantile()` function has other parameters, the most important is `na.rm`, which details what happens if the are `NA` elements in the data. Missing values, `NA` will generally cause a result of `NA` but setting `na.rm = TRUE` will "overcome" this.

Example:

Summary functions on data with `NA`

```
# Data with NA
summary(airquality$Ozone)
```

```
Min.  1st Qu.  Median  Mean  3rd Qu.   Max.   NA's
1.00   18.00    31.50  42.13  63.25  168.00    37
```

```
max(airquality$Ozone)
```

```
[1] NA
```

```
max(airquality$Ozone, na.rm = TRUE)
```

```
[1] 168
```

Tip: Missing values

You can use `na.omit()` to remove `NA` elements before carrying out a summary function if `na.rm` is not an accepted parameter.

```
length(na.omit(airquality$Ozone))
[1] 116
```

See more about `NA` elements in section 7.2.5 *Dealing with missing values* of Chapter 7 *Working with data objects*.

9.1.1   Cumulative statistics

Some statistics calculate cumulative values. There are four basic functions:

- `cumsum(x)` – cumulative sum (a running total).
- `cummax(x)` – cumulative maximum.

- `cummin(x)` – cumulative minimum.
- `cumprod(x)` – cumulative product.

The functions all return a `numeric vector`, which is the same length as the input (which should be a `vector`).

Example:

Cumulative functions

```
x <- c(1:3, 2:0, 4:1)
x

  [1] 1 2 3 2 1 0 4 3 2 1

cumsum(x)

  [1] 1 3 6 8 9 9 13 16 18 19

cummax(x)

  [1] 1 2 3 3 3 3 4 4 4 4
```

Any NA elements will result in NA for that and subsequent elements.

Note: Parallel max/min

The `pmax()` and `pmin()` functions compute parallel maxima and minima respectively. You specify the `vector` objects to compare (there can be more than two) and may use `na.rm = TRUE` as a parameter (the default is `FALSE`).

```
pmax(1:5, pi)

  [1] 3.141593 3.141593 3.141593 4.000000 5.000000

pmin(1:5, pi)

  [1] 1.000000 2.000000 3.000000 3.141593 3.141593
```

Define your own cumulative function

It is possible to define your own cumulative function. To do this you need to create a custom `function`.

Example:

Custom cumulative function

```
cumfun <- function(x, FUN = median, ...) {
   tmp <- numeric(length = length(x))
   for (i in 1:length(tmp)) tmp[i] <- FUN(x[1:i], ...)
   print(tmp)
}
```

In the cumfun() function the ... allows the user to input other parameters (such as na.rm = TRUE) without being defined. The parameter has to be "correct" for the FUN being used (the default function is median. In the function:

1. tmp is a vector that starts off with zeroes, this will be filled in as the function proceeds.
2. The for line is a loop, this fills in each successive element of tmp.
3. The print line sends the final result to the console.

Example:

Using a custom cumulative function

```
cumfun(shrimp, FUN = mean, na.rm = TRUE)

[1] 32.20000 32.60000 32.00000 32.45000 32.40000 32.55000 32.42857  32.83750
[9] 32.78889 32.63000 32.08182 31.96667 32.00769 31.91429 31.86667  31.76875
[17] 31.80000 31.79444
```

You'll encounter other examples of simple custom functions through the text. See Chapter 15 *Programming tools* for details about creating custom function objects.

9.2 Statistics on elements of an object

Most commands that calculate summary statistics are designed to operate on vector objects. Various "helper" functions allow you to perform a summary statistic over elements of a dataset, such as the columns of a data.frame or elements of a list.

* colSums() – sum of all columns for a data.frame or matrix.
* colMeans() – mean values for all columns of a data.frame or matrix.
* rowSums() rowMeans() – for rows.
* apply() – apply a function over all the rows or columns of a data.frame or matrix object.
* lapply() – apply a function over the elements of a list (or vector). The result is a list.
* sapply() – same as lapply() but the result is a vector or matrix.

See also the functions in the section 9.5 *Statistics over an entire data table.*

Tip: Statistics on selective elements

The rapply() function allows you to apply a function to elements of your data based on their class. See section 9.3 *Apply a function over elements of an object selectively* for more details.

9.2.1 Simple sums or means

The colSums() and colMeans() functions, and their row equivalents, give sums and mean values for all columns (or rows) in a data.frame or matrix object.

```
colSums(x, na.rm = FALSE, ...)
rowSums(x, na.rm = FALSE, ...)
```

```
colMeans(x, na.rm = FALSE, ...)
rowMeans(x, na.rm = FALSE, ...)
```

If there are NA elements in the data, you may consider using na.rm = TRUE to eliminate them before the sum or mean is applied.

Example:

Simple row and column sums or means

```
VADeaths
```

	Rural Male	Rural Female	Urban Male	Urban Female
50-54	11.7	8.7	15.4	8.4
55-59	18.1	11.7	24.3	13.6
60-64	26.9	20.3	37.0	19.3
65-69	41.0	30.9	54.6	35.1
70-74	66.0	54.3	71.1	50.0

```
colSums(VADeaths)
```

Rural Male	Rural Female	Urban Male	Urban Female
163.7	125.9	202.4	126.4

```
rowMeans(VADeaths)
```

50-54	55-59	60-64	65-69	70-74
11.050	16.925	25.875	40.400	60.350

Note: Multidimensional objects

In the col* and row* functions x is usually a data.frame or a matrix; however, multi-dimensional array objects can be used. In this case you use the dims parameter to specify the dimension(s) to be regarded as the rows (or columns). Use ?colSums to see the help entry and further explanation.

These functions are faster than some of the other "helper" functions you'll encounter, but of course they only return the sum or mean values. In the next section you'll see more generalized functions that can use *any* function.

9.2.2 Apply any function over elements of an object

If you want a simple sum or mean, then the functions in the previous section are a good choice. However, if you want something else you need a different approach. There are several functions that permit you to apply a function over every element in an object.

The apply() function

The apply() function allows you to run more or less any function over the rows or columns of a data.frame or matrix.

```
apply(X, MARGIN, FUN, ...)
```

In the function, X is the object you want to look at, MARGIN is the dimension you want to apply the function, FUN to. The MARGIN relates directly to the result of the dim() function; thus MARGIN = 1 is for rows, MARGIN = 2 is for columns, and so on. You can also give additional parameters, such as may relate to the FUN you are using, na.rm for example.

Example:

Use apply() for summary statistics

```
head(attitude, n = 3)

  rating  complaints  privileges  learning  raises  critical  advance
1     43          51          30        39      61        92       45
2     63          64          51        54      63        73       47
3     71          70          68        69      76        86       48

# Median for columns
apply(attitude, MARGIN = 2, FUN = median, na.rm = TRUE)

  rating  complaints  privileges  learning  raises  critical  advance
    65.5        65.0        51.5      56.5    63.5      77.5     41.0

# Standard deviation for rows
apply(attitude, MARGIN = 1, FUN = sd)

 [1]  20.263737  8.994707 11.412191 15.830952 13.458932  7.244045  12.948616
 [8]  12.641579 17.471065 13.950593 10.734901 13.300555 15.063358  18.856602
[15]  13.259318 18.803495  8.300889  8.864053 14.683972 10.047506  11.385036
[22]  12.088956 13.756384  8.223080 14.638501  8.638232 11.926361  14.784161
[29]  10.246951 18.776885
```

If your function returns a single result, then apply() will produce a vector. If your function produces multiple results, you get a matrix.

```
apply(attitude, MARGIN = 2, FUN = quantile, probs = 1:3/4)

     rating complaints privileges  learning raises critical  advance
25%   58.75       58.5       45.0     47.00  58.25    69.25    35.00
50%   65.50       65.0       51.5     56.50  63.50    77.50    41.00
75%   71.75       77.0       62.5     66.75  71.00    80.00    47.75
```

> ## Note: Multidimensional objects and apply()
>
> The apply() function can be used on objects with more than two dimensions; you specify the MARGIN you want to operate over.
>
> ```
> dim(HairEyeColour)
>
> [1] 4 4 2
>
> apply(HairEyeColour, MARGIN = 3, FUN = sum)
>
>   Male  Female
>    279     313
> ```

Generally speaking you use apply() on data.frame or matrix-like objects. The examples shown here show numeric data but you can use apply() on other data types.

> ## Note: Simple sums for matrix and array objects
>
> The `margin.table()` and `marginSums()` functions compute row and/or column sums for `matrix` or `array` objects. The `marginSums()` function is a newer version of `margin.table()`.
>
> ```
> margin.table(x, margin = NULL)
> marginSums(x, margin = NULL)
> ```
>
> You specify the `margin` as for `apply()` except that `margin = NULL` (the default) returns the grand total.

The *lapply()* and *sapply()* functions

The `apply()` function works generally with objects that have a non-NULL result with `dim()`. If you have a `list` object (or a `vector`) you need a different approach.

```
lapply(X, FUN, ...)
sapply(X, FUN, ...)
```

The `lapply()` function allows you to apply a function to each element in a `list`. The result is a `list`. The `sapply()` function is similar except that it will produce a `vector` as the result (or a `matrix`). As with `apply()`, you provide a function (FUN) and may give additional parameters that are relevant to that function.

Example:

Use `lapply()` and `sapply()` on a `list`

```
# Make a list
CW <- unstack(chickwts)
str(CW, vec.len = 3)

List of 6
$ casein:    num[1:12] 368  390   379 260   404   318 352 359  ...
$ horsebean: num[1:10] 179  160   136 227   217   168 108 124  ...
$ linseed:   num[1:12] 309  229   181 141   260   203 148 169  ...
$ meatmeal:  num[1:11] 325  257   303 315   380   153 263 242  ...
$ soybean:   num[1:14] 243  230   248 327   329   250 193 271  ...
$ sunflower: num[1:12] 423  340   392 339   341   226 320 295  ...

# Median for each element as a list
lapply(CW, FUN = median)

$casein
[1] 342

$horsebean
[1] 151.5

$linseed
[1] 221
```

```
$meatmeal
[1] 263

$soybean
[1] 248

$sunflower
[1] 328

# Mean value as a vector
sapply(CW, FUN = mean)
  casein horsebean  linseed meatmeal  soybean sunflower
323.5833  160.2000 218.7500  276.9091 246.4286  328.9167

# Multiple results make a matrix with sapply()
sapply(CW, FUN = quantile, probs = 1:3/4)

 casein  horsebean  linseed  meatmeal soybean sunflower
25% 277.25    137.00   178.00    249.5  206.75    312.75
50% 342.00    151.50   221.00    263.0  248.00    328.00
75% 370.75    176.25   257.75    320.0  270.00    340.25
```

> **Note: `lapply()` and `sapply()` with `data.frame` objects**
>
> You can use these functions with non-`list` objects but generally only get "sensible" results with `data.frame` objects (the columns). Sometimes `sapply()` is preferable!
>
> ```
> str(chickwts)
>
> 'data.frame':   71 obs. of 2 variables:
>  $ weight: num 179 160 136 227 217 168 108 124 143 140 ...
>  $ feed : Factor w/ 6 levels "casein","horsebean",..: 2 2 2 2 2 2
> 2 2 2 2 ...
>
> apply(chickwts, MARGIN = 2, FUN = class)
>
>     weight           _feed
> "character" "character"
>
> sapply(chickwts, FUN = class)
>
>   weight       feed
> "numeric" "factor"
> ```

9.3 Apply a function over elements of an object selectively

The `rapply()` function is a recursive form of `lapply()` that allows you to apply a function to elements of an object in a selective manner. In short, you can choose the `class` of the elements to which you want to execute a function (Table 9.2).

```
rapply(object, f, classes = "ANY", deflt = NULL, how, ...)
```

Essentially `rapply()` works on objects that have $ components. Each of these components has the function f applied. The result depends on the how parameter.

Table 9.2 Parameters of the `rapply()` function

Parameter	Description
object	An R object, generally a `list` but a `data.frame` is also acceptable.
f	A function, this must have only a single argument.
classes	A character vector of class names, the default (`"ANY"`) uses all `classes`.
deflt	A default result, this is not used if `how = "replace"`.
how	How to process the result. There are three options: `"replace"`, `"unlist"` (the default) or `"list"`.
...	Other parameters can be passed to the function f.

Example:

Apply a function over selected classes with `rapply()`

```
head(cabbages, n = 2)

  Cult  Date HeadWt   VitC
1  c39   d16    2.5     51
2  c39   d16    2.2     55

sapply(cabbages, FUN = class)

    Cult     Date   HeadWt    VitC
"factor" "factor" "numeric" "integer"

# Get mean for columns with numbers
rapply(cabbages, f = mean, classes = c("integer", "numeric"),
       how = "unlist")

  HeadWt         VitC
2.593333    57.950000

# list the levels for factor variables
rapply(cabbages, f = levels, classes = "factor", how = "list",
      deflt = "Not applicable")

$Cult
[1] "c39" "c52"

$Date
[1] "d16" "d20" "d21"

$HeadWt
[1] "Not applicable"

$VitC
[1] "Not applicable"
```

The `rapply()` function is especially useful if you have a `data.frame` with multiple columns of mixed type.

Tip: Using `rapply()` to convert character to `factor`

Since version 4 the default behavior of `read.table()` is *not* to convert `character` data into `factor` variables. You can set the `stringsAsFactors` argument to `TRUE` or use `rapply()` afterwards:

```
rapply(x, f = as.factor, classes = "character", how = "replace")
```

9.4   Statistics based on a grouping variable

Some helper functions allow you to perform a summary statistical function on a variable that is split into smaller units using a grouping variable.

* `rowsum()` – use a grouping variable to get a simple sum for each group.
* `tapply()` – use a grouping variable with any function.
* `aggregate()` – ditto.

The first of these is quite simple, and only gives group sums. The other two functions allow more or less any function to be applied to groups. The differences between the two are due to the different syntax required by the functions and in their output, as you'll see shortly.

Tip: Add summary information to your dataset

Most summary functions return a result giving a result that is "separate" from the original data. See section 9.6 *Adding group information to your data* for notes on how to add group summary statistics to your original data.

9.4.1   Group sums with `rowsum()`

The `rowsum()` function computes column sums for `vector`, `matrix` or `data.frame` objects, where each row is assigned to a group.

```
rowsum(x, group, reorder = TRUE, na.rm = FALSE, ...)
```

The default is to `reorder` the results according to the `group`.

Example:

Group sums with `rowsum()`

```
head(airquality, n = 3)

  Ozone  Solar.R  Wind  Temp  Month  Day
1    41      190   7.4    67      5    1
2    36      118   8.0    72      5    2
3    12      149  12.6    74      5    3
```

```
rowsum(airquality[, 1:4], group = airquality$Month, na.rm = TRUE)

    Ozone  Solar.R  Wind   Temp
5    614     4895  360.3   2032
6    265     5705  308.0   2373
7   1537     6711  277.2   2601
8   1559     4812  272.6   2603
9    912     5023  305.4   2307
```

This function is designed only for group sums, if that is all you want then this is faster than alternatives, especially for large data objects.

See also section 9.6 *Adding group information* for details of the ave() function, which can add a summary statistic over groups in your dataset.

9.4.2 Apply a function to groups using `tapply()`

The tapply() function allows you to apply more or less any function to a vector using a grouping variable.

```
tapply(X, INDEX, FUN, ...)
```

In the function X is the data you want to operate on, usually a vector. The INDEX is the grouping variable and FUN is the function to apply.

Example:

Use tapply() to apply a function with a grouping variable

```
str(chickwts)

'data.frame':   71 obs. of 2 variables:
 $ weight: num 179 160 136 227 217 168 108 124 143 140 ...
 $ feed : Factor w/ 6 levels "casein","horsebean",..: 2 2 2 2 2 2
 2 2 2 2 ...

tapply(chickwts$weight, INDEX = chickwts$feed, FUN = mean)

   casein  horsebean   linseed   meatmeal   soybean  sunflower
  323.5833   160.2000  218.7500   276.9091  246.4286   328.9167
```

You can give the INDEX as a list, allowing you to give multiple grouping variables.

Example:

Multiple grouping variables and tapply()

```
with(warpbreaks, tapply(breaks, INDEX = list(wool, tension),
    FUN = median))

    L    M    H
A  51   21   24
B  29   28   17
```

Note that the result is a matrix when you use multiple grouping variables.

> **Note: Get a list result with `tapply()`**
>
> If you use the parameter `simplify = FALSE` the result of `tapply()` is a `list` rather than a `vector` or `matrix`.

See section 9.6 *Adding group information to your data* for notes on how to add group summary statistics to your original data using a combination of the `ave()` and `within()` functions.

9.4.3 Aggregating data with `aggregate()`

The `aggregate()` command is similar to `tapply()` in that you can apply any function to groups in your data.

```
aggregate(x, by, FUN, ...)
aggregate(formula, data, FUN, ...)
```

There are two main ways to specify the data to use in the function (Table 9.3).

Table 9.3 Some parameters of the `aggregate()` function

Parameter	Description
x	The data to be aggregated. Usually a `vector`, `matrix`, or `data.frame`. There is also a method for `ts` (time-series) objects.
by	A `list` of the grouping variable(s).
formula	A `formula` giving the `response ~ predictor`. Multiple `predictor` variables can be specified (separated with +). Multiple `response` variables can be given using `cbind()`.
data	The `data` object where the variables in `formula` are found.
FUN	The function to apply to each group/subset.
...	Other parameters are possible.

The `aggregate()` function gives a result that is generally a `data.frame`, however, there is a time-series method that will result in an object of class `ts`.

Use `aggregate()` *for single response*

When you have a single `response` variable you refer to it as if it were a `vector`. The two main methods of specifying the `predictor` vary, if you use `by` you'll need a `list`, even if there is only one `predictor` (grouping) variable.

Example:

`aggregate()` with a single response variable

```
# Comparison of two forms of syntax
str(PlantGrowth)

'data.frame':   30 obs. of 2 variables:
```

```
$ weight: num 4.17 5.58 5.18 6.11 4.5 4.61 5.17 4.53 5.33 5.14 ...
$ group : Factor w/ 3 levels "ctrl","trt1",..: 1 1 1 1 1 1 1 1 1
1 ...

aggregate(PlantGrowth$weight, by = list(PlantGrowth$group),
FUN = mean)

   Group.1       x
1     ctrl    5.032
2     trt1    4.661
3     trt2    5.526

aggregate(weight ~ group, data = PlantGrowth, FUN = mean)

    group   weight
1    ctrl    5.032
2    trt1    4.661
3    trt2    5.526
```

Note that the result is a data.frame, furthermore, the columns are named more appropriately if you use the formula method.

Multiple predictors can be specified using either syntax:

Example:

Multiple predictor variables and aggregate()

```
str(warpbreaks)
'data.frame':   54 obs. of 3 variables:

$ breaks : num 26 30 54 25 70 52 51 26 67 18 ...
$ wool    : Factor w/ 2 levels "A","B": 1 1 1 1 1 1 1 1 1 1 ...
$ tension: Factor w/ 3 levels "L","M","H": 1 1 1 1 1 1 1 1 1 2 ...

with(warpbreaks, aggregate(breaks, by = list(tension, wool),
    FUN = mean))

   Group.1  Group.2        x
1      L        A     44.55556
2      M        A     24.00000
3      H        A     24.55556
4      L        B     28.22222
5      M        B     28.77778
6      H        B     18.77778

aggregate(breaks ~ wool + tension, data = warpbreaks, FUN = median)

   wool  tension    breaks
1    A       L        51
2    B       L        29
3    A       M        21
4    B       M        28
5    A       H        24
6    B       H        17
```

The order you specify the predictor variables merely affects the order they appear in the result.

> **Tip: `aggregate()` and named results**
>
> Specify the `predictor` variable(s) using `name = value` pairs in the `list` when using the `by` syntax, to get result columns with the names you specified.

Use aggregate() for multiple response

You can specify multiple `response` variables using either syntax. The `response` variables must be a `data.frame` or `matrix`.

Example:

Multiple response variables and `aggregate()`

```
head(fgl, n = 3)

      RI    Na    Mg   Al    Si      K   Ca Ba  Fe   type
1   3.01 13.64  4.49 1.10 71.78  0.06 8.75  0   0   WinF
2  -0.39 13.89  3.60 1.36 72.73  0.48 7.83  0   0   WinF
3  -1.82 13.53  3.55 1.54 72.99  0.39 7.78  0   0   WinF

aggregate(fgl[, 2:5], by = list(type = fgl$type), FUN = mean)

   type        Na         Mg        Al        Si
1  WinF  13.24229  3.5524286  1.163857  72.61914
2  WinNF 13.11171  3.0021053  1.408158  72.59803
3   Veh  13.43706  3.5435294  1.201176  72.40471
4   Con  12.82769  0.7738462  2.033846  72.36615
5  Tabl  14.64667  1.3055556  1.366667  73.20667
6  Head  14.44207  0.5382759  2.122759  72.96586

aggregate(cbind(Ca, K, Al) ~ type, data = fgl, FUN = median)

   type     Ca    K    Al
1  WinF   8.675 0.56  1.23
2  WinNF  8.275 0.58  1.46
3   Veh   8.790 0.56  1.28
4   Con  11.270 0.58  1.76
5  Tabl   9.570 0.00  1.56
6  Head   8.670 0.00  2.06
```

Note that `cbind()` produces a `matrix` result, which is acceptable. You cannot use `list` for specifying the `response` variable(s).

Use aggregate() for time series

It is possible to use `aggregate()` on `ts` (time-series) objects. Essentially, you specify a period over which you want the `FUN` to be applied. This period is given with the `nfrequency` parameter, which must be exactly divisible into the original frequency.

```
tsp(Nile) # Frequency 1 (year)

[1] 1871 1970  1
```

```
aggregate(Nile, nfrequency = 1/4, FUN = mean)

Time Series:
Start = 1871
End = 1967

Frequency = 0.25
 [1]  1113.25 1090.75 1110.00 1021.00 1019.25 1177.50 1152.50  795.50  847.50
[10]   932.75  709.25  938.50  799.50  817.25  834.75  858.75  928.25  735.50
[19]   848.75  868.00  845.25  906.00  929.00  932.25  772.75
```

Note that the result is not a "rolling" statistic (e.g. a running mean) but is based on the original data being split into smaller chunks.

9.5   Statistics over an entire data table

Although most summary statistics operate on `vector` objects, there are some functions that are designed to operate on an entire data table (*see also section 10.3: Table Summary*). There are two main ways to proceed:

- Add to a table: add one or more margins (containing a statistic).
- Alter a table: use a statistic on an entire table.

In the first case, you add some kind of summary statistic to the rows and/or columns of an existing dataset, e.g. sum totals. In the second case you replace the entire table using a function, e.g. proportions.

9.5.1   Any statistic in a margin

The `addmargins()` command allows you to add one or more margins to a `matrix` or `array` object, using a function.

```
addmargins(A, margin, FUN = sum, quiet = FALSE)
```

You must specify the data table A and the `margin` over which you want the `FUN` to be returned. The result is the original data with the marginal data you requested.

The `margin` parameter is different to `MARGIN` in the `apply()` function in that you get an extra row when `margin = 1` and a column with `margin = 2`. The function (`FUN`) you use must only produce a single result.

```
# A column of mean values
addmargins(VADeaths, margin = 2, FUN = mean)
```

	Rural Male	Rural Female	Urban Male	Urban Female	mean
50-54	11.7	8.7	15.4	8.4	11.050
55-59	18.1	11.7	24.3	13.6	16.925
60-64	26.9	20.3	37.0	19.3	25.875
65-69	41.0	30.9	54.6	35.1	40.400
70-74	66.0	54.3	71.1	50.0	60.350

If you specify multiple margins the function gives a message telling which statistic was computed first.

```
# Different functions over different margins
addmargins(USPersonalExpenditure, margin = 2:1, FUN = c(sd, mean))
```

```
Margins computed over dimensions
in the following order:
1:

2:

                         1940      1945     1950   1955    1960           sd
Food and Tobacco       22.2000   44.5000   59.600  73.20  86.800    25.120669
Household Operation    10.5000   15.5000   29.000  36.50  46.200    14.713361
Medical and Health      3.5300    5.7600    9.710  14.00  21.100     6.995902
Personal Care           1.0400    1.9800    2.450   3.40   5.400     1.658156
Private Education        0.3410    0.9740    1.800   2.60   3.640     1.304928
mean                     7.5222   13.7428   20.512  25.94  32.628     9.958603
```

If you have an object with multiple dimensions, you can specify any of the dimensions to use
as the margin.

```
# A three-dimensional table
dim(HairEyeColour)

[1] 4 4 2

addmargins(HairEyeColour, margin = 1:3, FUN = sum)
Margins computed over dimensions
in the following order:
1: Hair
2: Eye
3: Sex

, , Sex = Male

          Eye
Hair     Brown  Blue  Hazel  Green    sum
  Black     32    11     10      3     56
  Brown     53    50     25     15    143
  Red       10    10      7      7     34
  Blond      3    30      5      8     46
  sum       98   101     47     33    279

, , Sex = Female

          Eye
Hair     Brown  Blue  Hazel  Green    sum
  Black     36     9      5      2     52
  Brown     66    34     29     14    143
  Red       16     7      7      7     37
  Blond      4    64      5      8     81
  sum      122   114     46     31    313

, , Sex = sum

          Eye
Hair     Brown  Blue  Hazel  Green    sum
  Black     68    20     15      5    108
  Brown    119    84     54     29    286
  Red       26    17     14     14     71
  Blond      7    94     10     16    127
  sum      220   215     93     64    592
```

> **Tip: Suppress information message in `addmargins ()`**
>
> Use `quiet = TRUE` to suppress the information message you get if you compute over more than one `margin`.

9.5.2 Table proportions

The `prop.table()` and `proportions()` functions return the data as proportions, where the proportions are computed for rows/columns or the grand total, as you require. The two functions are equivalent, with the latter being new since R version 4.

```
prop.table(x, margin = NULL)
proportions(x, margin = NULL)
```

In the function `x` is a `matrix`-like object. The `margin` specifies how the proportions should be computed, `NULL` gives the proportion of each element of the table relative to the grand total. Use `margin = 1` to get proportions row by row. Use `margin = 2` to get column by column proportions.

```
# Proportions overall
prop.table(VADeaths, margin = NULL)
```

	Rural Male	Rural Female	Urban Male	Urban Female
50–54	0.01891979	0.01406856	0.02490298	0.01358344
55–59	0.02926908	0.01891979	0.03929495	0.02199224
60–64	0.04349935	0.03282665	0.05983182	0.03120957
65–69	0.06630013	0.04996766	0.08829237	0.05675938
70–74	0.10672704	0.08780724	0.11497413	0.08085382

```
# Proportions column-wise
round(prop.table(USPersonalExpenditure, margin = 2), digits = 3)
```

	1940	1945	1950	1955	1960
Food and Tobacco	0.590	0.648	0.581	0.564	0.532
Household Operation	0.279	0.226	0.283	0.281	0.283
Medical and Health	0.094	0.084	0.095	0.108	0.129
Personal Care	0.028	0.029	0.024	0.026	0.033
Private Education	0.009	0.014	0.018	0.020	0.022

If you have an object with more than two dimensions, you can specify any of the dimensions to use as the `margin`. Remember that the sum of the proportions will equal unity for each element of the chosen dimension.

```
# A three-dimensional table
dim(HairEyeColour)
```

```
[1] 4 4 2
```

```
prop.table(HairEyeColour, margin = 3)
```

```
, , Sex = Male
```

```
     Eye
Hair           Brown          Blue         Hazel          Green
 Black     0.114695341    0.039426523   0.035842294    0.010752688
 Brown     0.189964158    0.179211470   0.089605735    0.053763441
   Red     0.035842294    0.035842294   0.025089606    0.025089606
 Blond     0.010752688    0.107526882   0.017921147    0.028673835

, , Sex = Female

     Eye
Hair           Brown          Blue         Hazel          Green
 Black     0.115015974    0.028753994   0.015974441    0.006389776
 Brown     0.210862620    0.108626198   0.092651757    0.044728435
   Red     0.051118211    0.022364217   0.022364217    0.022364217
 Blond     0.012779553    0.204472843   0.015974441    0.025559105
```

9.5.3   Scale and center (standardization)

You can carry out standardization on a dataset using the scale() function. This function operates on matrix-like numeric objects, that is, objects with rows and columns.

```
scale(x, center = TRUE, scale = TRUE)
```
The function can carry out two processes:

* center – a value is subtracted from each column of x.
* scale – values are divided by the scale.

The default center = TRUE subtracts the column mean from each column element. The default scale = TRUE divides each column element by the column standard deviation if center = TRUE or the root mean square if not.

You can set either parameter to FALSE, allowing you to center or scale. If you want to use a function other than mean or sd you must provide a function that gives a result for each column.

```
scale(VADeaths)
          Rural Male  Rural Female   Urban Male    Urban Female
50-54     -0.9742485    -0.8944746   -1.1105970      -0.9892563
55-59     -0.6778991    -0.7316455   -0.7164856      -0.6845091
60-64     -0.2704188    -0.2648687   -0.1541020      -0.3504593
65-69      0.3824759     0.3104609    0.6252643       0.5755034
70-74      1.5400905     1.5805280    1.3559203       1.4487213
attr(,"scaled:center")
          Rural Male  Rural Female   Urban Male    Urban Female
              32.74         25.18        40.48           25.28
attr(,"scaled:scale")
Rural MaleRural FemaleUrban MaleUrban Female
21.59613    18.42422      22.58245       17.06332

# Center only using column median
scale(VADeaths, center = apply(VADeaths, MARGIN = 2, FUN = median),
      scale = FALSE)

          Rural Male  Rural Female   Urban Male    Urban Female
50-54         -15.2         -11.6        -21.6           -10.9
55-59          -8.8          -8.6        -12.7            -5.7
60-64           0.0           0.0          0.0             0.0
65-69          14.1          10.6         17.6            15.8
70-74          39.1          34.0         34.1            30.7
```

```
attr(,"scaled:center")
       Rural Male   Rural Female   Urban Male   Urban Female
              26.9           20.3         37.0           19.3
```

Note that the result contains additional attributes, showing the scale and/or center parameters used.

> ### Tip: Standardize by row
>
> Use t(object) to transpose a matrix, allowing you to standardize row-wise.

Scaling with *sweep()*

The sweep() function is used to "sweep out" a summary statistic from a data table. You can use it in standardization as an alternative to scale().

```
sweep(x, MARGIN, STATS, FUN = "-", ...)
```

In the function x is a data array of some kind. You specify a value via the STATS parameter, this value will be then operated on by the FUN you specify, the default being "-", which carries out subtraction. The MARGIN parameter is used to set the margin over which you want to operate.

Example:

Use sweep() to sweep out a statistic

```
# Get column means
x <- colMeans(USPersonalExpenditure)

# Subtract column means
sweep(USPersonalExpenditure, MARGIN = 2, STATS = x, FUN = "-")
```

	1940	1945	1950	1955	1960
Food and Tobacco	14.6778	30.7572	39.088	47.26	54.172
Household Operation	2.9778	1.7572	8.488	10.56	13.572
Medical and Health	-3.9922	-7.9828	-10.802	-11.94	-11.528
Personal Care	-6.4822	-11.7628	-18.062	-22.54	-27.228
Private Education	-7.1812	-12.7688	-18.712	-23.34	-28.988

In many cases you can find an alternative to using sweep()!

9.6   Adding group information to your data

The ave() function allows you to apply a function over combinations of factor (grouping) variables. The result is a vector that is the same length as your data; this makes it especially useful if you want to add group statistics to your data. The default function is the mean.

```
ave(x, ..., FUN = mean)
```

In the ave() function x is the data you want to apply the function FUN to. You also specify the grouping variables ... as variables names, separated by commas.

Example:

Apply a function to groups with `ave()`

```
str(warpbreaks)

'data.frame':   54 obs. of 3 variables:
 $ breaks : num 26 30 54 25 70 52 51 26 67 18 ...
 $ wool   : Factor w/ 2 levels "A","B": 1 1 1 1 1 1 1 1 1 1 ...
 $ tension: Factor w/ 3 levels "L","M","H": 1 1 1 1 1 1 1 1 1 2 ...

# Sum of breaks for combinations of wool and tension
with(warpbreaks, ave(breaks, wool, tension, FUN = sum))

 [1] 401 401 401 401 401 401 401 401 401 216 216 216 216 216 216 216 216 216 221
[20] 221 221 221 221 221 221 221 221 254 254 254 254 254 254 254 254 254 259 259
[39] 259 259 259 259 259 259 259 169 169 169 169 169 169 169 169 169
```

To add the group statistic to the data you can use a combination of `within()` and `ave()`.

Example:

add group statistics to a dataset

```
# Add median for each combination wool:tension
WB <- within(warpbreaks, MV <- ave(breaks, wool, tension, FUN =
median))
WB[seq(1, 54, len = 6), ]

   breaks wool tension   MV
1      26    A       L    51
11     21    A       M    21
22     18    A       H    24
32     29    B       L    29
43     21    B       M    28
54     28    B       H    17
```

So, the `ave()` function operates differently from `tapply()` or `aggregate()` in that the result doesn't merely give the group statistic but "ties" the statistic to the original data.

EXERCISES:

Self-Assessment for Summarizing data

1. You can use `cumSum()` to get a cumulative sum.. TRUE or FALSE?
2. To get column means for a numeric `matrix` you could use ____, or ____ functions.
3. Which of these options will allow you to summarize data by a grouping variable:
   a. `apply()`
   b. `sapply()`
   c. `tapply()`
   d. `lapply()`
4. To get a marginal statistic for a table-like object, you can use ____.
5. You can use `sweep()` in standardization instead of `scale()`. TRUE or FALSE?

Answers to exercises are in the *Appendix*.

9.7 Chapter Summary: Summarizing data

Topic	Key Points
Summary functions	Some common summary functions are: `sum()`, `mean()`, `median()`, `sd()`, `var()`, `mad()`, `max()`, `min()`, `range()`, `IQR()`, `quantile()`, `length()`, and `nchar()`.
Missing values	Objects with `NA` elements will often result in `NA` when using summary functions. Many will accept `na.rm = TRUE` as a parameter. Alternatively use `na.omit()` to remove `NA` before calculation.
Cumulative stats	Four basic cumulative statistics: `cumsum()`, `cummax()`, `cummin()`, and `cumproduct()`. Use `pmax()` and `pmin()` for parallel max/min. With a simple function you can define your own cumulative statistic.
Summarize columns or rows	Get simple row/column sums/means with: `rowSums()`, `colSums()`, `rowMeans()`, and `colMeans()` functions. Use `apply(x, MARGIN, FUN)` to use other functions for rows (`MARGIN = 1`) or columns (`MARGIN = 2`). Use `sapply()` as a simple alternative for `data.frame` columns.
Summary for `matrix` or `array`	Use `margin.table()` or `marginSums()` to get marginal (or overall) statistics.
Summary for `list` objects	Use `lapply()` or `sapply()` to summarize `list` (or `vector`) objects.
Selective summary	Use `rapply()` to apply a function over selected elements, based on their class.
Summarize by group	Use `rowsum()` to get a `sum` based on a grouping variable. Use `tapply()`, or `aggregate()` to apply a function over groups of `data.frame` objects. The `aggregate()` functions allows use of a `formula`. Use `ave()` to return a group statistic for a `vector`, that is the same length as the original `vector`.
Summarize tables	Use `addmargins()` to apply a statistic over margins of a table-like object (e.g. `matrix` or `array`). Use `prop.table()` or `proportions()` to return proportions from `matrix`-like objects.
Standardization	Use `scale()` and `center()` for standardization of `matrix`-like objects (that are `numeric`). Use `sweep()` as an alternative approach, where you "sweep" a statistic from an object using an operator.
Add group summary statistic	Use `ave()` in concert with `within()` to *add* a group statistic to an object.

10. Tabulation

This is a chapter about data tables, that is, frequency tables (also known as contingency tables). Frequency tables are a useful way of summarizing categorical data and have many uses. R contains a range of functions for creating and manipulating table data.

What's in this chapter

Major types of tabulation:

»   `table()` – basic tabulation.
»   `ftable()` – flat tables.
»   `xtabs()` – cross tabulation.

Also:

»   Convert other R objects into `table` format.
»   Manipulate and alter tables.
»   Summary functions for table objects.

Note: Support material

See the ➘ for links to material on the support website.

10.1   Creating table objects

There are various methods to construct a `table` object. You can cross-tabulate data using one of the main tabulation functions:

* `table()`
* `ftable()`
* `xtabs()`

You can also coerce another object to act like a `table` with `as.table()`.

10.1.1   The `table` function

In general parlance a table is merely a way of laying out any kind of data. In R, a `table` is a special `class` of object that summarizes cross-classification of categorical data to form a contingency table (frequency table). You can make a table with the `table()` command.

The `table()` command is quite general.

```
table(..., exclude, useNA)
```

In the function, ... are variables to be cross-classified, usually `factor` variables (other types are coerced to `factor` where possible). You can also `exclude` levels and control the tabulation of NA items with the useNA parameter. Other parameters are also available.

The simplest `table` is one dimensional, where you tabulate the frequency of a single variable.

Example:

Tabulate a single `factor` variable

```
require(MASS)
head(farms, n = 4)

    Mois   Manag    Use   Manure
1    M1      SF     U2      C4
2    M1      BF     U2      C2
3    M2      SF     U2      C4
4    M2      SF     U2      C4

table(farms$Mois)

M1 M2 M4    M5
 7  4  2     7
```

If you specify more variables, you get more dimensions (in the order you specify). You can help the "readability" of the table by using `print()` and setting the zero.print parameter.

Example:

Multidimensional `table` data and "sparse" printing

```
# Two-dimensional table
tb <- with(farms, table(Mois, Manag))
print(tb, zero.print = ".")

   Manag
Mois  BF HF NM  SF
  M1   2  3  1   1
  M2   1  .  1   2
  M4   .  1  .   1
  M5   .  1  4   2

# Three dimensions
tb <- with(farms, table(Mois, Manag, Use))
print(tb, zero.print = ".")

, , Use = U1

   Manag
Mois   BF   HF   NM   SF
  M1    .    1    1    .
  M2    1    .    1    .
  M4    .    1    .    .
  M5    .    .    2    .

, , Use = U2
```

```
   Manag
Mois    BF   HF   NM    SF
  M1     1    1    .     1
  M2     .    .    .     2
  M4     .    .    .     1
  M5     .    .    1     1

, ,  Use = U3

   Manag
Mois    BF   HF   NM    SF
  M1     1    1    .     .
  M2     .    .    .     .
  M4     .    .    .     .
  M5     .    1    1     1
```

It is also possible to include a conditional expression in a table. You simply include the expression and "assign" it a name.

Example:

Conditional expression in a `table`

```
require(MASS)
head(crabs, n = 2)

  sp   sex   index    FL     RW      CL      CW    BD
1  B     M      1    8.1    6.7    16.1    19.0   7.0
2  B     M      2    8.8    7.7    18.1    20.8   7.4

with(crabs, table(sp, Big = CL > 40))

    Big
sp     FALSE      TRUE
 B       92        8
 O       81        19
```

You can exclude certain levels from the resulting table, using `exclude`. This is a `vector` of levels from one or more of the component variables.

Example:

Exclude levels from a `table`

```
with(farms, table(Manag, Manure, exclude = c("C0", "C1", "BF")))

       Manure
Manag   C2   C3   C4
   HF    2    2    0
   NM    0    0    0
   SF    1    2    3
```

If there are NA elements, they will not be included by default. To force NA to appear in the table use useNA = "always" as a parameter.

The `as.table()` function can be used to coerce an existing table-like object to a `table`. The function is most sensibly used on count data (i.e. `integer` values), as part of a `matrix` (or `array`). If you have a `data.frame` you'll need to use `as.matrix()` first.

Example:

Convert objects to a `table`

```
# Convert vector
as.table(1:12)
```

```
 A  B  C  D  E  F  G  H  I  J  K  L
 1  2  3  4  5  6  7  8  9 10 11 12
```

```
# Convert array
x <- array(1:3, c(2, 4))
as.table(x)
```

```
    A   B   C   D
A   1   3   2   1
B   2   1   3   2
```

```
# data.frame needs to be matrix first
require(MASS)
class(caith)
```

```
[1] "data.frame"
```

```
as.table(as.matrix(caith))
```

```
         fair   red   medium   dark   black
blue      326    38      241    110       3
light     688   116      584    188       4
medium    343    84      909    412      26
dark       98    48      403    681      85
```

Note that if there are no element names, `as.table()` will use upper-case letters.

10.1.2 Making flat Tables

A "flat" table is one where dimensions are combined to reduce the table, keeping a 2-D look. The `ftable()` function can make this kind of table. There are two "versions" of the function:

```
ftable(x, ..., exclude, row.vars = NULL, col.vars = NULL)
ftable(formula, data)
```

The two versions allow you to specify the data in subtly different ways (Table 10.1).

Table 10.1 Some parameters of the `ftable()` function

Parameter	Description
x, ...	R object(s) that form the contents of the table. These can also be other `table` objects.
exclude	Levels of variables to exclude from the final table, as a `character` vector.
row.vars	Which of the variables to use for the rows. A `vector` giving the name or "position" of the variable.
col.vars	Which of the variables to use for the columns. A `vector` as above.
formula	A `formula` of the form `col.items ~ row.items`.
data	An optional `data.frame` where the elements in `formula` are found.

The two forms of ftable() allow you some flexibility in how you specify the data to be used in the construction of the final table.

In the "basic" version you specify the variables you want to use, separated by commas. By default the last variable you specify forms the columns of the final table, with the others forming the row items. You can change the way the variables are presented using the row.vars and/or col.vars parameters.

Example:

Specify variables to form a flat table

```
with(farms, ftable(Mois, Use, Manag, exclude = "U1"))

          Manag BF   HF   NM   SF
Mois  Use
M1    U2          1    1    0    1
      U3          1    1    0    0
M2    U2          0    0    0    2
      U3          0    0    0    0
M4    U2          0    0    0    1
      U3          0    0    0    0
M5    U2          0    0    1    1
      U3          0    1    1    1

with(farms, ftable(Mois, Use, Manag, col.vars = 1:2))
          Mois M1              M2          M4          M5
          Use U1 U2   U3   U1   U2   U3 U1   U2 U3 U1   U2 U3
Manag
BF            0  1    1    1    0    0  0    0  0  0    0  0
HF            1  1    1    0    0    0  1    0  0  0    0  1
NM            1  0    0    1    0    0  0    0  0  2    1  1
SF            0  1    0    0    2    0  0    1  0  0    1  1
```

The formula version of the function allows you to specify the variables in an alternative fashion. Your formula should give the columns variables on the left of the ~ (separated by +), with the row variables on the right of the ~ (also separated by +).

Example:

Flat table using formula interface

```
ft <- ftable(Manag + Manure ~ Mois + Use, data = farms,
             exclude = c("BF", "U1"))
print(ft, zero.print = ".")

          Manag  HF NM SF
          Manure CO C1 C2 C3 C4 CO C1 C2 C3 C4 CO  C1 C2 C3 C4
Mois   Use
M1     U2         .  .  1  .  .  .  .  .  .  .  .   .  .  .  1
       U3         .  .  .  1  .  .  .  .  .  .  .   .  .  .  .
M2     U2         .  .  .  .  .  .  .  .  .  .  .   .  .  .  2
       U3         .  .  .  .  .  .  .  .  .  .  .   .  .  .  .
M4     U2         .  .  .  .  .  .  .  .  .  .  .   1  .  .  .
       U3         .  .  .  .  .  .  .  .  .  .  .   .  .  .  .
M5     U2         .  .  .  .  1  .  .  .  .  .  .   .  1  .  .
       U3         .  .  .  1  .  1  .  .  .  .  .   .  1  .  .
```

> ### Tip: Wildcard for names
>
> In a `formula` you can use the `.` to indicate "all other variables". You can only use this once in a `formula`.

You can also specify an existing R object, such as a `data.frame`, `list`, `matrix` or `table`. The `ftable()` function is especially useful for re-shaping a multidimensional `table`.

Example:

Reshaping an existing table with `ftable`

```
ftable(Titanic, row.vars = "Class", col.vars = 2:3)

          Sex   Male   Female
          Age  Child   Adult   Child  Adult
Class
1st               5     175      1     144
2nd              11     168     13      93
3rd              48     462     31     165
Crew              0     862      0      23
```

> ### Tip: Changing displayed names in flat tables
>
> You can use name-value pairs to alter the names in a basic `ftable` (i.e. not `formula`). You can also use `dnn` as a parameter, giving a `character vector` of names in the same order you specified them in the function.

10.1.3 Cross tabulation

The `xtabs()` command carries out cross-classification using count data and grouping variables. Unlike `table()` or `ftable()`, the `xtabs()` function can use a variable of counts (e.g. frequencies).

```
xtabs(formula, data, exclude, ...)
```

The main "driver" for `xtabs()` is the `formula`, but there are other parameters you can include (Table 10.2).

Table 10.2 Some parameters of the `xtabs()` function

Parameter	Description
formula	A formula of the form: `freq ~ x + y + z + ....` Where `freq` is a `numeric` variable. The `freq` can be omitted, in which case `xtabs()` acts like `table()`.
data	An optional `data.frame` where the variables in `formula` are to be found.
exclude	A `character vector` of levels to exclude.
...	Other parameters are available.

The most sensible use for xtabs() is when you have a variable with count data (i.e. frequency).

Example:

Using xtabs() for cross-classification

```
# One-dimensional table
xtabs(count ~ spray, data = InsectSprays)

spray
  A    B    C    D    E    F
174  184   25   59   42  200

# Two-dimensional
xtabs(breaks ~ wool + tension, data = warpbreaks)

       tension
wool    L    M    H
   A  401  216  221
   B  254  259  169
```

If you do not have a frequency variable you can use xtabs() as an alternative to table(). This means that you can produce "regular" tables using the formula interface.

Example:

Using xtabs() without a frequency variable

```
xtabs(~Use + Manag, data = farms)

      Manag
Use   BF   HF   NM   SF
  U1   1    2    4    0
  U2   1    1    1    5
  U3   1    2    1    1
```

10.1.4 Binning data

Some data do not tabulate "neatly". This tends to happen when you are attempting to tabulate a numeric variable to produce a frequency table. The table() function will treat the numeric variable like a factor. This can produce two undesirable results:

- Too many "bins" and an overly long table.
- Unequal intervals between "bins".

Example:

Using table() on a numeric variable

```
require(MASS)
table(shrimp)

shrimp
26.6 30.3 30.7 30.8 31.2  31.7  32.2 32.3 32.4 32.5  33 33.3 33.8 35.7
1       1    2    1    2     2     2    1    1    1    1    1    1    1
```

The example shows that the `shrimp` data has been tabulated perfectly, but most of the entries are 1 and the "intervals" between the "bins" (that is, the size class) are not equal. You might find this acceptable for some purposes, but in order to get a better sense of the frequency distribution you can control the splitting of the original variable.

The `cut()` function takes a `numeric` variable and splits it into "bins" according to various parameters, which you specify.

```
cut(x, breaks, labels, dig.lab, ...)
```

There are various parameters you can use (Table 10.3). The most basic parameter is simply to give the number of "bins" you want via the `breaks` parameter.

Table 10.3 Some parameters of the `cut()` function

Parameter	Description
x	A `numeric vector` to be cut into bins.
breaks	The number of breaks. Give either an `integer` (the number of required bins), or a `numeric vector`, with the explicit breakpoints.
labels	A `vector` of labels. The default produces labels along the lines of: `"(a,b]"`. Set `labels = FALSE` to have simple index values.
dig.lab	The number of decimals to use for regular numeric labels (unless you specified explicit labels).
...	Other parameters are possible.

The result of `cut()` is a `factor` variable the same length as the original, where the levels correspond to the "bins". You can use `cut()` to "bin" any `numeric` variable, and so reduce the number of entries (and equalize the spacing).

Example:

```
Using cut() to "bin" numeric data in a table()

# One variable
table(cut(shrimp, breaks = 6, dig.lab = 0))

 (27,28]  (28,30]  (30,31]  (31,33]   (33,34]   (34,36]
    1        0        4        9         3         1

# Two variables
with(airquality, table(Ozone = cut(Ozone, breaks = 4, dig.lab = 4),
        Temp = cut(Temp, breaks = 6, dig.lab = 0)))

                 Temp
Ozone            (56,63]   (63,70]  (70,76]  (76,83]  (83,90]  (90,97]
 (0.833,42.75]      9        17       22       21        3        0
 (42.75,84.5]       0         0        0       11       15        4
 (84.5,126.2]       0         0        0        1        5        6
 (126.2,168.2]      0         0        0        1        1        0
```

The `cut()` function is particularly useful if you want/need to split a variable into equal-spaced intervals. However, it is not the only way to achieve this result. You can use the `hist()` function to produce a histogram (a frequency plot) instead. You'll see more about hist() in the coming chapter on Graphics.

```
hist(x, breaks, plot = FALSE)
```

The result is an object that includes $counts and $breaks elements. The number of breaks may not be exactly the number you requested, as the function makes "pretty" intervals.

Example:

Use hist() to split a variable into "bins"

```
hist(galaxies, br = 8, plot = FALSE)[1:2]

$breaks
[1] 5000 10000 15000 20000 25000 30000 35000

$counts
[1] 5 2 24 45 3 3
```

You can see that there are more breaks than counts, because you need two breaks for each bin (a lower and an upper limit for each bin). In the preceding example we only show the first two elements as the others are not required.

Tip: Make a dedicated function for histogram binning

You can "extract" the counts element from a hist() function. You could then easily make names for the data from the breaks component. If you bundle the commands into a custom function the process becomes a bit more automated.

```
hgt <- function(x, ...) {
  hd <- hist(x, plot = FALSE, ...)
  cd <- hd$counts
  br <- hd$breaks
  lb <- vector(mode = "numeric", length = length(cd))
  for (i in 1:length(cd)) {
    lb[i] <- paste(br[i], br[i + 1], sep = "-")
  }
  names(cd) <- lb
  invisible(cd)
}
x <- hgt(galaxies, breaks = 6)
x
```

5000-10000	10000-15000	15000-20000	20000-25000	25000-30000	30000-35000
5	2	24	45	3	3

10.2 Manipulating table objects

Frequency tables are potentially useful for many purposes, not least of which is showing data in a compact manner. Rearranging and generally manipulating frequency tables can be accomplished using a variety of functions.

10.2.1 Properties of table objects

The frequency tables produced by the main table-making functions (table, ftable and xtabs) have various attributes, including element names, that you can interrogate and potentially alter.

When you make a frequency table using table() or xtabs(), the result will have one, two or more dimensions. These will be labelled with names taken from the levels of the variables. There also extra names/labels that correspond to the major variables used to construct the frequency table. Flat tables are slightly different in that they are always only two dimensional, but they do include this "extra" level of names/labels.

You can see the structure of a frequency table using the str() function. Using str() will help you see what "components" there are in a frequency table, so you can interrogate or alter them more easily.

Example:

Use str() to view structure of frequency table objects

```
# Make frequency tables
require(MASS)
tb <- with(farms, table(Use, Manag))
ft <- ftable(Manag ~ Use, data = farms)
xt <- xtabs(breaks ~ wool + tension, data = warpbreaks)

str(tb)
 'table' int [1:3, 1:4] 1 1 1 2 1 2 4 1 1 0 ...
 - attr(*, "dimnames")=List of 2
 ..$ Use : chr [1:3] "U1" "U2" "U3"
 ..$ Manag: chr [1:4] "BF" "HF" "NM" "SF"

str(ft)
 'ftable' int [1:3, 1:4] 1 1 1 2 1 2 4 1 1 0 ...
 - attr(*, "row.vars")=List of 1
 ..$ Use: chr [1:3] "U1" "U2" "U3"
 - attr(*, "col.vars")=List of 1
 ..$ Manag: chr [1:4] "BF" "HF" "NM" "SF"

str(xt)
 'xtabs' num [1:2, 1:3] 401 254 216 259 221 169
 - attr(*, "dimnames")=List of 2
 ..$ wool   : chr [1:2] "A" "B"
 ..$ tension: chr [1:3] "L" "M" "H"
 - attr(*, "call")= language xtabs(formula = breaks ~ wool + ten-
sion, data = warpbreaks)
```

You can see from the example that the table and xtabs objects have dimnames components (attr(*, "dimnames")). The ftable object is slightly different, with "row.vars" and "col.vars" components, but no mention of "dimnames".

Change properties for *table* and *xtabs* objects

You can change the basic names labels for rows and columns in table or xtabs objects in the same manner as for matrix objects, using rownames() and colnames() functions. However, you may have more than two dimensions, so it is a good habit to use the dimnames() function.

The dimnames() function returns a list, which you can subset using square brackets []. If you want to subset a subset, you'll need double brackets [[]] for the first level. The following example shows this.

Example:

Use dimnames() for table names

```
dimnames(xt)

$wool
[1] "A" "B"

$tension
[1] "L" "M" "H"

dimnames(xt)[2]

$tension
[1] "L" "M" "H"

dimnames(xt)[[2]]
[1] "L" "M" "H"

dimnames(xt)[[2]][1]
[1] "L"
```

Notice the subtle difference with the double [[]]; single brackets return the $label and its elements, whilst double brackets return the elements only.

If you want to alter the row/column "title", you need to use names() with dimnames() nested inside.

Example:

Alter dimension name labels for a table object

```
names(dimnames(xt))

[1] "wool"  "tension"

names(dimnames(xt))[2]

[1] "tension"
```

Now you know how to access the labels you can easily alter one or more by assigning new values to them in the "usual" manner.

Example:

Alter label components of table objects

```
xt

   tension
wool   L    M    H
   A  401  216  221
   B  254  259  169
names(dimnames(xt)) <- c("Yarn", "Tightness")
dimnames(xt)[["Tightness"]] <- c("Low", "Mid", "Hi")
xt
```

```
   Tightness
Yarn   Low   Mid    Hi
   A    401   216   221
   B    254   259   169
```

Change properties for ftable objects

An ftable object doesn't have *names() attributes, so you need a different approach to alter the "labels". You need to use the attr() function to access the "row.vars" and "col.vars" attributes.

```
attr(x, which, exact = FALSE)
attr(x, which) <- new _ value
```

The which parameter is the name (in quotes) of the attribute you wish to return. You can also set new values by assigning them to the attribute.

Example:

Viewing "labels" of ftable objects using attr()

```
ft <- ftable(Manag ~ Mois + Use, data = farms)
attr(ft, which = "row.vars")

$Mois
[1] "M1" "M2" "M4" "M5"

$Use
[1] "U1" "U2" "U3"

# Double [[]] needed for sub-setting
attr(ft, which = "row.vars")[[1]][2:3]

[1] "M2" "M4"

# Use names to see the top-level labels
names(attr(ft, which = "row.vars"))

[1] "Mois" "Use"
```

You can easily set new values by assigning them to the attr(x) or names(attr(x)) functions.

Example:

Alter ftable "labels"

```
str(ft)
 'ftable' int [1:12, 1:4] 0 1 1 1 0 0 0 0 0 0 ...
 - attr(*, "row.vars")=List of 2
 ..$ Mois: chr [1:4] "M1" "M2" "M4" "M5"
 ..$ Use : chr [1:3] "U1" "U2" "U3"
 - attr(*, "col.vars")=List of 1
 ..$ Manag: chr [1:4] "BF" "HF" "NM" "SF"
names(attr(ft, which = "row.vars"))[[1]] <- "H2O"
attr(ft, which = "row.vars")[[1]] <- c("Dry", "Moist", "Wet",
"Swampy")
```

```
ft
           Manag BF    HF    NM      SF
H2O     Use
Dry     U1        0     1     1       0
        U2        1     1     0       1
        U3        1     1     0       0
Moist   U1        1     0     1       0
        U2        0     0     0       2
        U3        0     0     0       0
Wet     U1        0     1     0       0
        U2        0     0     0       1
        U3        0     0     0       0
Swampy  U1        0     0     2       0
        U2        0     0     1       1
        U3        0     1     1       1
```

Note that you need double [[]] in the subset.

> ### Note: Frequency table dimensions
>
> You can see the dimensions of a table object using dim(). This works for objects created by table(), xtabs() and ftable(). Remember though, that ftable objects are always two dimensional and that the rows (the 1st dimension) are a combination of the row variable names.

10.2.2   Reshaping table objects

You can alter the shape/construction of frequency tables in a number of ways. If you have the "original" data, you can simply make a new table that matches your requirements. If you only have the frequency table, you'll have to rearrange that.

Your general options are:

- Use t() to transpose a 2D object.
- Use ftable() to rearrange an existing table object.
- Return a table to frequency-factor layout and rebuild from that.

The following sections show these options.

Transpose a 2D table

The t() function rotates a table-like object, so that rows become columns and vice versa. Note that this only works for two-dimensional objects. It also fails on ftable objects. However, it is a quick and dirty way to rotate a 2D object.

Example:

Rotate or transpose 2D objects with t()

```
require(MASS)
tb <- with(farms, table(Use, Manag))
tb

   Manag
Use    BF   HF   NM   SF
   U1    1    2    4    0
   U2    1    1    1    5
   U3    1    2    1    1
```

```
t(tb)

     Use
Manag   U1  U2  U3
   BF    1   1   1
   HF    2   1   2
   NM    4   1   1
   SF    0   5   1

# Also works on matrix
t(VADeaths)

             50-54   55-59   60-64   65-69   70-74
Rural Male    11.7    18.1    26.9    41.0    66.0
Rural Female   8.7    11.7    20.3    30.9    54.3
Urban Male    15.4    24.3    37.0    54.6    71.1
Urban Female   8.4    13.6    19.3    35.1    50.0
```

The result of t() is to produce a matrix, so it is most useful on all-numeric data. It will operate on a data.frame but the result might be "awkward".

Use *ftable()* to reshape a table

The ftable() function can reshape an existing table, xtabs or ftable object. Of course the result is an ftable result so can only be two dimensional. You need to specify the "row.vars", and/or "col.vars" parameters to get the result you want.

The "row.vars" and "col.vars" parameters can accept values as integer or character. Use str() on the original object to see the variables. **Note** that your original data do not necessarily have to have a class "table". The ftable() function will operate on a matrix object too (but not on a data.frame).

Example:

Use ftable() to reshape an existing frequency table

```
# Alter a table
str(HairEyeColour)
 'table' num [1:4, 1:4, 1:2] 32 53 10 3 11 50 10 30 10 25 ...
 - attr(*, "dimnames")=List of 3
 ..$ Hair: chr [1:4] "Black" "Brown" "Red" "Blond"
 ..$ Eye : chr [1:4] "Brown" "Blue" "Hazel" "Green"
 ..$ Sex : chr [1:2] "Male" "Female"

ftable(HairEyeColour, row.vars = 3:2)
```

		Hair	Black	Brown	Red	Blond
Sex	Eye					
Male	Brown		32	53	10	3
	Blue		11	50	10	30
	Hazel		10	25	7	5
	Green		3	15	7	8
Female	Brown		36	66	16	4
	Blue		9	34	7	64
	Hazel		5	29	7	5
	Green		2	14	7	8

```
# Alter a matrix
str(VADeaths)
```

```
num [1:5, 1:4] 11.7 18.1 26.9 41 66 8.7 11.7 20.3 30.9 54.3 ...
- attr(*, "dimnames")=List of 2
..$ : chr [1:5] "50-54" "55-59" "60-64" "65-69" ...
..$ : chr [1:4] "Rural Male" "Rural Female" "Urban Male" "Urban
Female"

ftable(VADeaths, row.vars = 2)

                   50-54   55-59   60-64   65-69   70-74

Rural     Male     11.7    18.1    26.9    41.0    66.0
Rural    Female     8.7    11.7    20.3    30.9    54.3
Urban     Male     15.4    24.3    37.0    54.6    71.1
Urban    Female     8.4    13.6    19.3    35.1    50.0
```

Undo a table

If you have a table object you can "undo" the table; effectively reversing the tabulation and returning to a column-wise data object. The result is a data.frame with columns relating to each of the original dimensions. A final column gives the frequency data.

This may be the most effective way to "restore" the data to a "long" layout, and allows you to re-make the frequency table from a fresh starting point. The function as.data.frame() carries out the transformation, which is more or less the opposite of xtabs().

```
as.data.frame(x, ...)
```

The main parameter is x, the object you want to transform. Other parameters are possible, depending on the class of the object to be transformed.

Example:

Transform frequency table data to a data frame layout

```
ut <- as.data.frame(HairEyeColour)
summary(ut)

     Hair           Eye            Sex           Freq
  Black:8       Brown:8       Male:16      Min.    :2.00
  Brown:8       Blue:8        Female:16    1st Qu. :7.00
  Red:8         Hazel:8                    Median :10.00
  Blond:8       Green:8                    Mean    :18.50
                                           3rd Qu. :29.25
                                           Max.    :66.00

# Rename Freq column directly
ut <- as.data.frame(Titanic, responseName = "Number")
head(ut)

   Class     Sex      Age   Survived   Number
1   1st     Male     Child        No        0
2   2nd     Male     Child        No        0
3   3rd     Male     Child        No       35
4  Crew     Male     Child        No        0
5   1st   Female     Child        No        0
6   2nd   Female     Child        No        0
```

If your starting point has the class "table" you can use the responseName parameter to alter the Freq column heading. So, this works for table or xtabs objects but not ftable.

If your starting point is a matrix you'll have to make the object into a table first. The easiest way is to use as.data.frame.table(), which converts the object via as.table() and then transforms it.

Example:

Transform a matrix to a table and then to frequency layout

```
class(VADeaths)

[1] "matrix" "array"

ut <- as.data.frame.table(VADeaths, responseName = "Count")
head(ut)

       Var1              Var2    Count
1     50-54      Rural Male      11.7
2     55-59      Rural Male      18.1
3     60-64      Rural Male      26.9
4     65-69      Rural Male      41.0
5     70-74      Rural Male      66.0
6     50-54    Rural Female       8.7
```

You can only alter the column name that related to Freq, with the responseName parameter. Since a matrix does not have upper tier labels (like a table), the columns are headed "Var1", "Var2" and so on. Use colnames() to change them to something more suitable.

Once you have your data rearranged into the "long" format you can use one of the cross tabulation functions to create a new frequency table.

Tip: Frequency tables as data.frame objects

Occasionally you may encounter a frequency table that is a data.frame. You cannot use as.data.frame.table() directly! You must convert the object to a matrix first.

```
require(MASS)
caith

          fair   red   medium   dark   black
blue       326    38      241    110       3
light      688   116      584    188       4
medium     343    84      909    412      26
dark        98    48      403    681      85

class(caith)

[1] "data.frame"

ut <- as.data.frame.table(as.matrix(caith))
head(ut)

         Var1    Var2    Freq
1       blue    fair     326
2      light    fair     688
3     medium    fair     343
4       dark    fair      98
5       blue     red      38
6      light     red     116
```

Note: `array` objects

an `array` is essentially a `vector` with attributes that specify how the data are split. There can be 1-many dimensions. Many functions that act on `table`, or `matrix` objects will also work with `array` objects.

Convert Frequency data to Records

The `as.data.frame()` function will transform a frequency table into a `data.frame` that includes a "Freq" column. Each row of the `data.frame` will be a unique combination of factors, with the frequency at the end.

It is possible to remove the frequency column and have your `data.frame` display only factor data. In other words, each row will be a single observation, with a combination of the various `factor` variables. There is no in-built function that will do this, and so you'll have to make your own function to do it. Programming is covered in Chapter 13, but here is a preview of what you need for this task.

Example:

Remove frequency data and create factor-only records

```
# function to convert frequency records to factor:
countsToCases <- function(x, countcol = "Freq") {
    # Get the row indices to pull from x
    idx <- rep.int(seq_len(nrow(x)), x[[countcol]])
    # Drop count column
    x[[countcol]] <- NULL
    # Get the rows from x
    x[idx, ]
}
```

Once you have the custom function ready to go, it can be used on any `data.frame` object. In other words, you need to "undo" a `table` beforehand (but see the following example). You need to tell the function the name of the column that contains the frequencies via the count-col parameter. The default is "Freq", which is what you get by default from `as.data.frame()`.

Example:

Using a custom function to transform frequency data to single records

```
hec <- countsToCases(as.data.frame(HairEyeColour))
head(hec)
```

```
      Hair    Eye     Sex
1     Black   Brown   Male
1.1   Black   Brown   Male
1.2   Black   Brown   Male
1.3   Black   Brown   Male
1.4   Black   Brown   Male
1.5   Black   Brown   Male
```

```
summary(hec)

     Hair          Eye          Sex
Black:  108    Brown:220      Male:279
Brown:  286    Blue:215     Female:313
  Red:   71    Hazel:93
Blond:  127    Green:64

titanic <- countsToCases(as.data.frame(Titanic))
head(titanic)

      Class    Sex      Age    Survived
3       3rd   Male    Child          No
3.1     3rd   Male    Child          No
3.2     3rd   Male    Child          No
3.3     3rd   Male    Child          No
3.4     3rd   Male    Child          No
3.5     3rd   Male    Child          No

str(titanic)

'data.frame':   2201 obs. of 4 variables:
 $ Class    : Factor w/ 4 levels "1st","2nd","3rd",..: 3 3 3 3 3 3 3 3 3 3 ...
 $ Sex      : Factor w/ 2 levels "Male","Female": 1 1 1 1 1 1 1 1 1 1 ...
 $ Age      : Factor w/ 2 levels "Child","Adult": 1 1 1 1 1 1 1 1 1 1 ...
 $ Survived : Factor w/ 2 levels "No","Yes": 1 1 1 1 1 1 1 1 1 1 ...
```

You can see from the preceding examples that all numeric data have been stripped out and the resulting data.frame objects are columns containing factor variables only. The row names look a bit "odd", if you want to restore a simple index number use rownames(x) <- NULL.

10.3 Table summary commands

Once you have a frequency table you can use various commands to execute summary statistics. Examples include:

- colMeans()
- apply()
- margin.table() or marginSums()
- prop.table() or proportions()
- addmargins()

An object with the class "table" will act much like a matrix or array. Summary functions that operate on an array or matrix will also usually work on a table. See *Chapter 9: Summarizing data* for a review of summary functions.

Flat tables, made with ftable(), can also be summarized with the same functions but you need to remember that the row label are combinations of the levels of the component variables.

Example:

Using summary functions on ftable objects

```
require(MASS)
ft <- ftable(Manag ~ Mois + Use, data = farms)
```

```
# Columns sums
apply(ft, MARGIN = 2, FUN = sum)
```

```
BF  HF  NM   SF
 3   5   6    6
```

```
# Row sums
apply(ft, MARGIN = 1, FUN = sum)
```

M1_U1	M1_U2	M1_U3	M2_U1	M2_U2	M2_U3	M4_U1	M4_U2	M4_U3	M5_U1	M5_U2	M5_U3
2	3	2	2	2	0	1	1	0	2	2	3

One potential by-product of summarizing a table is that you may be able to "collapse" and combine dimensions, and reshape your table.

Example:

Summarize a table over multiple dimensions to reshape it

```
# Collapse a table and combine dimensions
addmargins(HairEyeColour, margin = 3, FUN = sum)[, , 3]
margin.table(HairEyeColour, margin = 1:2)
apply(HairEyeColour, MARGIN = 1:2, FUN = sum)
```

```
These three functions all produce the same result.
```

```
      Eye
Hair      Brown   Blue   Hazel   Green
  Black      68     20      15       5
  Brown     119     84      54      29
  Red        26     17      14      14
  Blond       7     94      10      16
```

So if you use any two dimensions, you'll "collapse" the table to two dimensions and sum the frequencies across the chosen dimensions. This is of course *not* the same as making a "flat" table.

EXERCISES:

Self-Assessment for Tabulation

1. To make a table more readable you can change 0 to something else via the _____ argument.
2. You can use ftable() to reshape an existing table.. TRUE or FALSE?
3. The xtabs() function can only be used with a formula.. TRUE or FALSE?
4. Which of the following functions can return name attributes for ftable objects?
   a. names()
   b. colnames()
   c. attr()
   d. dimnames()
5. If you "un-pivot" a table object using as.data.frame() you can rename the frequency column using the _____ argument.

Answers to exercises are in the *Appendix*.

10.4 Chapter Summary: Tabulation

Topic	Key Points
Basic tables	Use `table()` for simple Cross tabulation. Variables that are `numeric` are treated like a `factor`. Coerce an object with `as.table()`.
Flat tables	Use `ftable()` to make "flat" tables, which remain two dimensional. The function can use a `formula` interface.
Cross tabulation	Use `xtabs()` for cross tabulation via a `formula`. You can use a frequency variable (unlike `table()` or `ftable()` functions).
Binning data	Use `cut()` to split a `vector` into bins. Specify number of bins with the `breaks` argument.
Table names	Use `dimnames()` to view or set name attributes for table objects. Use `attr()` to help manage names attributes as an alternative to `dimnames()`.
Reshape table	Use `t()` to transpose rows/columns of 2D `table`. Use `ftable()` to reshape a `table` or `matrix` object. Use `as.data.frame()` to un-pivot a `table`. You can alter a `matrix` by first making it into a `table`. Use `as.matrix()` to convert a `data.frame` to a `matrix`.
Summarize tables	Various summary functions operate on `table` objects. `addmargins()`, `apply()`, `prop.table()`, `proportions()`, and `addmargins()`. Get simple marginal sums with `margin.table()` or `marginSums()` functions.

11. Graphics: basic charts

R has powerful and flexible graphical capabilities, and using R you can produce a wide range of graphs and charts. In this chapter you will see how to produce a variety of graphs and charts for various purposes. You will also see how to customize your plots, allowing you to visualize data in different ways.

What's in this chapter

» Making various graphs and charts.
» Commonly used and useful graphical parameters.
» Visualizing data distribution.
  » Histogram.
  » Density plot.
  » QQ plots.
» Visualizing sample differences.
  » Box-whisker plots.
  » Bar charts.
» Visualizing relationships.
  » Scatter plots.
  » Line charts.
» Compositional data.
  » Pie charts.
  » Mosaic plots.
  » Dot charts.

Note: Support material

See the ↘ for links to material on the support website.

11.1   Types of graphical function

You can think of the graphical functions as being in one of three camps, those that:

- Make a new plot window.
- Add to an existing plot window.
- Modify graphical parameters.

In this chapter the focus is on the first of these, and you'll see how to produce various useful types of graphic. Once you have a graph/plot you can add things to it (such as more data, text, lines, or legend), this is the focus of *Chapter 12*.

There are many ways to alter the appearance of your graphics and you'll see these illustrated throughout the text. There are also particular functions that alter the graphical system itself (think of them as the system defaults). You can alter these to change things such as the margin sizes or how to deal with colours. This aspect of the graphical system is dealt with in *Chapter 13*. In that chapter you'll also encounter some slightly more advanced kinds of graphic.

Graphs can be used for different purposes (Table 11.1).

Table 11.1 Some common types of graph and their uses.

Chart type	R function	Uses
Histogram	hist	Data distribution.
Density plot	density	Data distribution.
QQ-plot	qqnorm	Assessing normal distribution.
Bar chart	barplot	Differences between groups, compositional data.
Box-whisker	boxplot	Differences between groups.
Scatter plot	plot	Relationships between variables.
Pie chart	pie	Compositional data.
Mosaic plot	mosaic	Compositional data.
Dot chart	dotchart	Compositional data.
Strip chart	stripchart	Data overview.

There are many types of graph and each one may be suitable for visualizing more than one "kind" of data. Table 11.1 shows just a few of the options available in R.

11.2 Histogram

A histogram is the go-to tool to visualize data distribution, use the hist() function to make one. A histogram is a sort of bar chart, showing the frequency of observations. Unlike a regular bar chart though, the x-axis is not categorical. Instead, the axis represents a continuous numerical range, with breaks here and there to split the axis into chunks (called bins). Each bar shows the frequency of observations in a single bin.

```
hist(x, breaks, freq, ...)
```

The hist() function has various potential parameters (Table 11.2).

Table 11.2 Some parameters of the hist() function.

Parameter	Description
x	A vector of numeric values.
breaks	A specification for the locations of the breakpoints. The default is "Sturges". Other options are "Scott" or "FD". Alternatively you can give a single number or specify the positions of the breakpoints as a vector.
freq	Should the bars show frequency? Use freq = FALSE to "force" the bars to display density.
...	Other parameters are possible.

The minimum you need to specify is x, the data, which should be a numeric vector. The defaults will produce a basic histogram. the other parameters can be split into two camps:

- Altering the way the bars are produced.
- Altering the general appearance.

Many of the potential graphical parameters can be used in other types of R graphic, you'll see many examples throughout the text. You can also alter the way the bars are produced, most commonly by altering the breakpoints. The breaks parameter allows you to alter the break-points; the default setting is "Sturges".

Example:

A histogram using default breakpoints

```
require(MASS)
shrimp
 [1] 32.2 33.0 30.8 33.8 32.2 33.3 31.7 35.7 32.4 31.2 26.6 30.7 32.5 30.7 31.2
[16] 30.3 32.3 31.7

hist(shrimp, las = 1, col = "salmon", main = "")
```

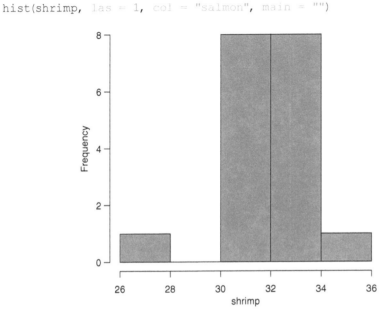

Figure 11.1 A histogram with default breakpoints.

In the preceding example the default breaks = "Sturges" parameter used a standard algo-rithm to split the data and form the breakpoints. The las, col and main parameters were used to alter the general appearance of the graphic:

las: Axis label orientation.

col: Bar colour.

main: Main title.

Tip: Default titles

Some graphics set a default title, for hist() this is: "Histogram of "data. If you want no title then set main = "" (an empty string).

As already noted, many graphical parameters are common to other types of graphic (see Table 11.11 in the chapter summary).

11.2.1   Histogram breakpoints

You can alter the breakpoints using the `breaks` parameter. The default is to use a named algorithm. You can also specify breaks numerically:

* A single `integer` value, the (approximate) number of breakpoints.
* A numeric `vector`, giving the exact position of the breakpoints (note that values need to span the range of values in x, the data.).

These options give you a good deal of flexibility for specifying breakpoints.

Example:

Specifying breakpoints for `hist()`

```
# Approx number of breaks
hist(shrimp, col = "pink", breaks = 9, xlab = "Data: shrimp")
```

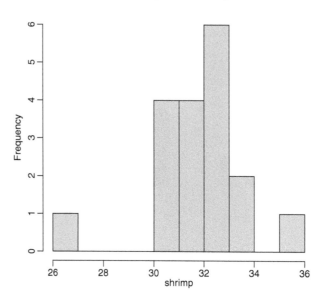

Figure 11.2 Specified number of breakpoints.

```
# Exact breakpoints
hist(shrimp, col = "bisque", breaks = c(26, 28, 32, 34, 36))
```

Note that you don't always get the exact number of breaks you ask for, as the function makes the x-axis "pretty". If you specify the exact breakpoints you need to span the entire range of x or you'll get an error.

> **Note: Histogram density**
>
> In the preceding example the breaks are unequal. The result is that the y-axis is changed to display density, and the area under the bars sums to unity. You can choose to plot either frequency or density using `freq = TRUE` (or `FALSE`). However, if you attempt to use `freq = TRUE` with unequal breakpoints you'll get a warning.

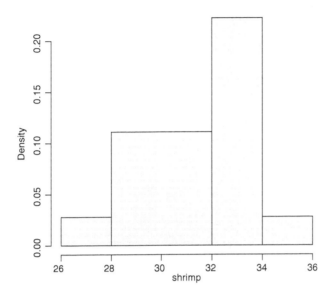

Histogram of shrimp

Figure 11.3 Exact positions for breakpoints.

11.2.2 Histogram data

You can use the `hist()` function without plotting an actual graphic. Use `plot = FALSE` and you will return an object with components that include, `$breaks $counts $mids` and `$density`. This can be an efficient way to split a large `numeric vector` into equal-sized chunks. See Chapter 10 and section 10.1.4 *Binning data* for an example.

Note: Stem-leaf plots

The `stem()` function produces an output that is a primitive form of histogram. It is not a graphic at all but a text representation of the frequency distribution of a `numeric vector`.

```
stem(x, scale = 1, width = 80)
require(MASS)
DDT
 [1] 2.79 2.93 3.22 3.78 3.22 3.38 3.18 3.33 3.34 3.06 3.07 3.56 3.08 4.64 3.34

stem(DDT)

 The decimal point is at the |

 2 | 89
 3 | 1112223334
 3 | 68
 4 |
 4 | 6
```

11.3   Density plot

An alternative to a histogram is a *density plot*. This allows you to visualize distribution of a sample with a smooth line, rather than a series of bars.

The density() function computes the x,y coordinates that you need. You can then draw these as a line by itself or add it to an existing histogram.

- To draw a density plot use plot().
- To add a density line use lines().

Regardless of which option you choose, the plotted line can itself be modified using various graphical parameters (see Table 11.11), such as:

- col colour.
- lwd width.
- lty type.

Example:

Density plot instead of a histogram

```
require(MASS)
DDT
```
```
[1] 2.79 2.93 3.22 3.78 3.22 3.38 3.18 3.33 3.34 3.06 3.07 3.56 3.08 4.64 3.34
```
```
plot(density(DDT), col = "darkgreen", lwd = 2, lty = "dashed")
```

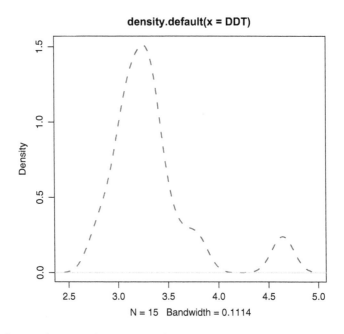

Figure 11.4 A density plot as an alternative to a histogram.

11.3.1   Add density line to a histogram

Use `lines()` to add a density line to an existing histogram. Start by making your histogram with `hist()`, be sure to use `freq = FALSE` to ensure the y-axis shows density. Then use `lines()` to add the density to the graphic.

Example:

Adding a density line to an existing histogram

```
# Histogram first
hist(DDT, freq = FALSE, col = "lightgreen", ylim = c(0, 1.5))

# Add density
lines(density(DDT), lwd = 2, lty = 2, col = "brown")
```

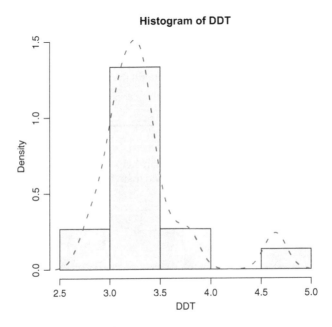

Figure 11.5 Plotting density lines on a histogram.

In the preceding example the histogram and density line incorporated some graphical parameters:

col:	colour.	ylim:	Limits for y-axis (both min & max).
lwd:	Line width.	lty:	Line type.

Tip: Fitting lines and histogram together

If you add a density line to a histogram the y-axis may not be large enough to accommodate all the data, resulting in some clipping. You'll need to set the `ylim` parameter in the `hist()` function. Compute the `density()` before plotting the `hist()` and you'll see the maximum value required for the y-axis. Note that `ylim` always needs both min and max values as a `vector`.

11.4 Quantile-Quantile plot

A quantile-quantile plot (QQ plot) draws the quantiles of your data against theoretical quantiles based on normal (Gaussian) distribution. It is usually easier to spot departures from normality using a QQ-plot than using a histogram. You can fit a QQ-line to the plot to help the visualization.

The qqnorm() function draws the graphic.

```
qqnorm(y, plot.it = TRUE, datax = FALSE, ...)
```

The qqnorm() function requires a numeric vector to operate on, other parameters are concerned mainly with altering the general appearance, and are common to many other plot types (Table 11.3).

Table 11.3 Some parameters of the qqnorm() function.

Parameter	Description
y	A vector of numeric values.
plot.it	A logical, if TRUE (the default) the graphic is plotted.
datax	If TRUE plot the sample on the x axis instead of the y.
...	Other graphical parameters.

You can add a line to the QQ-plot, which can help you assess departure from normality, using qqline(). The line can be customized using various graphical parameters (see Table 11.11).

Example:

Quantile plot and line

```
require(MASS)
DDT
```

```
[1] 2.79 2.93 3.22 3.78 3.22 3.38 3.18 3.33 3.34 3.06 3.07 3.56 3.08 4.64 3.34
```

```
qqnorm(DDT, pch = 21, bg = "skyblue", las = 1, cex = 2)

# Add qq-line to help visualization
qqline(DDT, lty = "dotted", lwd = 2, col = "blue")
```

In the preceding example, various graphical parameters were used:

pch: Plotting symbol.

las: Axis label orientation.

lty: Line type.

col: colour of line.

bg: Background colour of symbol.

cex: Character expansion.

lwd: Line width.

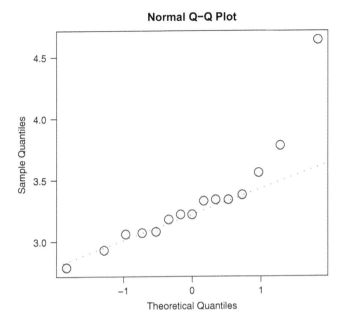

Figure 11.6 A quantile-quantile plot (qqnorm) and line (qqline) are helpful in assessing departure from the normal distribution.

Note: QQ-plots and non-Gaussian distribution

The qqline() function *can* use distributions other than Gaussian. However, you would need to use qqplot(), where you have to compute the appropriate x values.

11.5   Box & Whisker plot

A box-whisker plot conveys a lot of information in a concise manner. You use a box-whisker plot to visualize differences between samples (groups of numeric values) using the boxplot() function.

```
boxplot(x, range = 1.5, names, horizontal = FALSE, ...)
```

A box-whisker plot incorporates several elements; as the name suggests, there is a box and some whiskers! There is also a stripe (which can be shown as a different symbol). These elements "describe" the sample like so:

- **Stripe** shows median.
- **Box** shows inter-quartiles.
- **Whiskers** Extend to the min and max.

The samples are described using non-parametric statistics. If your data are Gaussian, the mean and median will be co-incidental, and the inter-quartiles will be similar to the standard error. Thus, regardless of the underlying distribution of the data, the box-whisker plot is a robust visualization.

The `boxplot()` function has many potential parameters (Table 11.4), many of which are graphical tweaks (see Table 11.11 for a summary).

Table 11.4 Some parameters of the `boxplot()` function.

Parameter	Description
x	The data. You can give as multiple `vector` objects (separate names with commas), or as a single object (i.e. a `list`, `matrix` or `data.frame`) that can be decomposed to multiple `vector`. Alternatively give a `formula` of form y ~ x where y is the response variable and x is a grouping variable. If you give a `formula` you can also use `data` = to "point" to the object containing the variables.
range	The extent of the whiskers. By default this is 3/2, which results potentially with some points marked as outliers. Use `range` = 0 to "suppress" outliers and have whiskers always as max-min.
names	The names to appear on the axis by each sample. Names are automatically taken from objects (e.g. `list`, `data.frame` or `formula`) but *not* if you use separate `vector` objects.
horizontal	Set to `TRUE` to draw bars horizontally.
...	Other parameters are possible, many of these are standard graphical parameters.

The `boxplot()` function is quite flexible in how you supply the input, as you will see in the following examples. The `boxplot()` function does not actually draw the plot, but rather computes the required statistics, which are passed to the `bxp()` function. You can use many "standard" graphical parameters as well as some extra ones that are explicit to `bxp()`.

Example:

A `boxplot()` from a `list` containing multiple `vector` objects

```
# Make a list
CW <- unstack(chickwts)

# Use range = 0.5 to show more outliers
boxplot(CW, col = "yellow", las = 1, range = 0.5, cex.axis = 0.7,
            xlab = "Feed Type", ylab = "Final weight (g)")
```

In the preceding example the `range` parameter was used to reduce the threshold for outliers, which results in shorter whiskers and more points. Several graphical parameters were also deployed:

col: colour.

xyalb: x-axis label.

cex.axis: Expansion for axis annotations.

las: axis label orientation.

ylab: y-axis label.

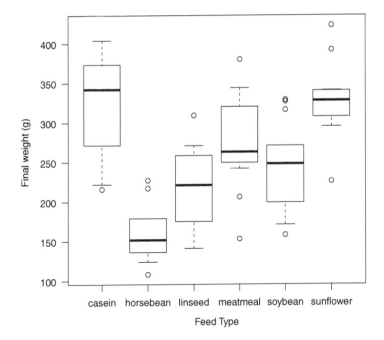

Figure 11.7 Box-whisker plot from a list of vectors. Parameter range = 0.5 has been used to reduce threshold for outlier detection.

Example:

A boxplot() using a formula

```
head(InsectSprays, n = 3)

     count    spray
1      10        A
2       7        A
3      20        A

# Use range = 0 for max-min whiskers
boxplot(count ~ spray, data = InsectSprays, las = 1, range = 0,
        col = "yellowgreen", xlab = "Spray Type", ylab = "Number
killed")
```

In the preceding example the range parameter was set to range = 0, forcing the whiskers to extend to the max-min of the data range for each sample. Several graphical parameters were also used:

col:	colour.	las:	axis label orientation.
xyalb:	x-axis label.	ylab:	y-axis label.

The formula method allows you to visualize data with multiple predictors (grouping variables). You simply "add" them to the formula.

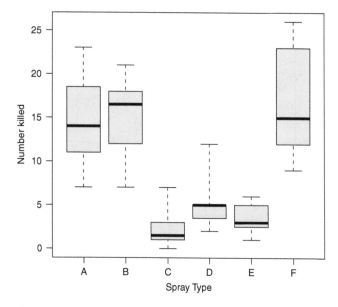

Figure 11.8 Box-whisker plot from a formula, using response and predictor (grouping) variables. Use range = 0 to ensure whiskers extend to max-min values.

Example:

A boxplot() with two grouping variables

```
head(warpbreaks, n = 3)

    breaks    wool    tension
1       26    A             L
2       30    A             L
3       54    A             L

boxplot(breaks ~ wool + tension, data = warpbreaks,
    col = c("pink", "skyblue"), las = 1,
    xlab = "Wool type . Tension", ylab = "Breaks per run")
```

Note that in the preceding example two colours were used. colours are used cyclically, in this case pink and skyblue alternately. This "works" in the example because the samples are plotted alternately. Try breaks ~ tension + wool and you get a mess! Several other graphical parameters were also used:

col:	colour(s).	las:	axis label orientation.
xyalb:	x-axis label.	ylab:	y-axis label.

See more about colours in section 13.1 *Working with colour.*

Note: Horizontal boxplot() and axes

If you use horizontal = TRUE the bars are drawn horizontally rather than vertically. However, the bottom axis is still the x-axis and the left side the y-axis. So, xlab and ylab arguments will annotate the bottom and left axes respectively.

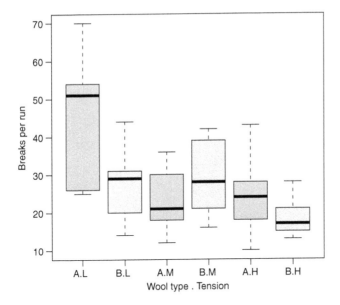

Figure 11.9 A box-whisker plot can use multiple colours, which can be helpful with multiple predictor variables.

11.6 Bar charts

Bar charts are used for showing values of elements in groups. Use `barplot()` to make various bar charts in R.

```
barplot(height, names.arg, legend.text, beside, horiz, ...)
```

You can produce different kinds of bar chart using the `barplot()` function and there are many potential parameters (Table 11.5).

Table 11.5 Some parameters of the `barplot()` function.

Parameter	Description
height	The data, usually a `vector` or `matrix` of numeric values. If you want a multi-series bar chart then your data *must* be a `matrix`.
names.arg	A `vector` of names to label the bars.
legend.text	Text to use for a legend. Use `TRUE` to have "automatic" legend entries.
beside	If `FALSE` (the default) a multi-series bar chart will be stacked. If `TRUE` the series are presented side-by-side in clusters.
horiz	If `horiz = TRUE` the bars are drawn horizontally. **Note:** that in this case the bottom axis is still the x-axis.
...	Other parameters are available, many of these are "standard" graphical parameters.

There are three main kinds of bar chart and you can produce all these with `barplot()` using the appropriate data and parameters:

- Single-series chart: data as a `vector`.
- Multi-series chart: data as a `matrix`.
  - Stacked bars: `beside = FALSE` (the default).
  - Clustered bars: `beside = TRUE`.

The simplest bar chart involves a single series of data, as a `numeric vector`. If your data have names as an attribute this will be used for labels, or you can supply your own labels with the `names.arg` parameter.

Example:

Single-series bar chart from a `vector`

```
# Temperature data in Fahrenheit
nottem[1:12]
```

```
[1] 40.6 40.8 44.4 46.7 54.1 58.5 57.7 56.4 54.3 50.5 42.9 39.8
```

```
# Convert data to Centigrade
temp <- (nottem[1:12] -32) *5/9
```

```
barplot(temp, col = "lightblue3", names = month.abb, cex.names = 0.7,
        ylab = "Mean temperature Centigrade", las = 1)
```

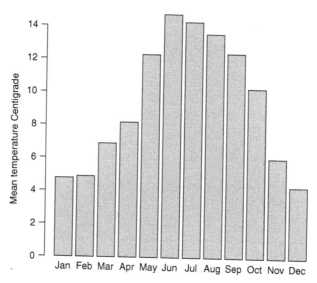

Figure 11.10 A single-series bar chart requires a numeric vector of data.

In the preceding example the `names` parameter was used to produce the labels for the bars, since the `vector` did not have any names of its own. Various "standard" graphical parameters were also used:

`col:` colour.

`las:` Axis label orientation.

`cex.names:` size of names labels.

`ylab:` y-axis label.

Tip: Data names and bar charts

If you are plotting a `vector` of data, which does not have its own names attribute, it may be best to assign names to the data with the `names ()` function before running `barplot ()`.

Multi-series bar charts require your data to be in the form of a matrix (see sections 3.5 and 8.5). Each column of your matrix will form a "bar". The rows form the series, with each row making up either a section of a stacked bar (default, beside = FALSE) or a separate bar in a cluster (beside = TRUE). The default colours are fairly boring so you'll generally want to specify the colours to use explicitly (see section 13.1).

Example:

Multiple series bar chart as a stacked chart

```
VADeaths
```

	Rural Male	Rural Female	Urban Male	Urban Female
50-54	11.7	8.7	15.4	8.4
55-59	18.1	11.7	24.3	13.6
60-64	26.9	20.3	37.0	19.3
65-69	41.0	30.9	54.6	35.1
70-74	66.0	54.3	71.1	50.0

```
class(VADeaths)

[1] "matrix" "array"

mycol <- c("seagreen", "sienna", "slategray", "tan", "wheat")
barplot(VADeaths, beside = FALSE, col = mycol, las = 1,
    ylab = "Road deaths per 1000", xlab = "Area:Gender",
    cex.names = 0.8, cex.axis = 0.8)
```

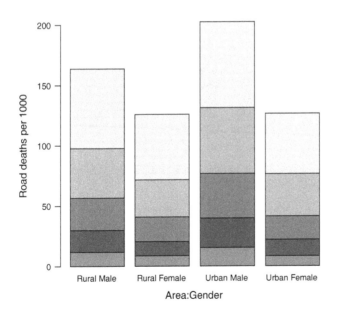

Figure 11.11 The barplot() default is beside = FALSE, which produces stacked charts.

In the preceding example the mycol variable was set-up in advance, but you can give the vector of colours explicitly in the barplot() function if you prefer. The parameter beside = FALSE is the default, producing a stacked chart, so could be omitted. The other arguments are "standard" graphical parameters:

col:	colour.	las:	axis label orientation.
cex.names:	Size of names labels.	cex.axis:	Size of axis labels.
ylab:	y-axis label.	xlab:	x-axis label.

Example:

Multiple series bar chart as a clustered chart

```
mycol <- c("seagreen", "sienna", "slategray", "tan", "wheat")
barplot(VADeaths, beside = TRUE, col = mycol, las = 1,
        ylab = "Road deaths per 1000", xlab = "Area:Gender",
        cex.names = 0.8, cex.axis = 0.8)
```

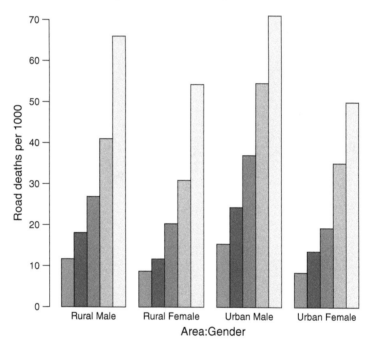

Figure 11.12 Use beside = TRUE in barplot() to draw a clustered bar chart.

In the preceding example the only change of parameter from the earlier bar chart is that beside = TRUE was used to create the clustered bars, instead of stacked.

Tip: Multiple data series as columns

The barplot() function "reads" multiple series from a matrix row by row, so each row is a series (and the columns are the categories). If you want to read the columns as series transpose the matrix with t() and plot that.

There are various other parameters not discussed here, but the ones illustrated will cover the most useful options. You can add various elements to your bar charts (and other plot types), such as:

- Grid lines.
- Error bars.
- Legends.

See Chapter 12 *Graphics: Adding to plots* for more details and examples.

11.7   Scatter plots

A scatter plot draws points (and possibly connecting lines) for numeric x,y data, thus provides a visual summary of the relationship between two sets of values. The plot() function will produce scatter plots.

```
plot(x, y, ...)
```

The plot() command is very flexible, and *can* produce graphics other than scatter plots. However, the emphasis will be on scatter plots in this section. You may see plot() used in other contexts at other places in the text.

To make a scatter plot you need x,y values, which you can specify in various ways:

- As separate x and y vector objects.
- An object with x,y components, such as a matrix, list or data.frame.
- A formula of the form y ~ x. You can also specify data = z, where z is the object that contains the variables.

There are many other arguments you can pass to the plot() function. A lot of these are "standard" graphical parameters, but there are some that are more "useful" for scatter plots (Table 11.6).

Table 11.6 Some useful graphical parameters for the plot() function.

Parameter	Description
pch	The plotting symbol. Either an integer value or a character (in quotes). Standard symbols are 0:25. Values 26:31 are unused. Values 31:127 are ASCII values.
col	The colour for the symbols. For open symbols this will affect the border only.
bg	Background colour for symbols. This affects open symbols (21:25) only.
cex	Symbol size (character expansion). Values > 1 make points larger.

The plot() function will "fill" the plot area as fully as possible, so that the points are more spread out. You can alter the axis limits using the xlim and ylim parameters.

> ### Note: The log parameter
>
> Many graphics functions have a log parameter. This allows you to specify axes to be drawn on a log scale. You give a character vector with the axis(es) required to be on the log scale, e.g. log = "xy" draws both on a log scale.

Example:

Scatter plot from an object containing x,y data

```
head(cars, n = 3)

  speed   dist
1     4      2
2     4     10
3     7      4

plot(cars, cex = 0.8, pch = 19, col = "steelblue", las = 1,
     ylab = "Distance Ft.", xlab = "Speed mph")
```

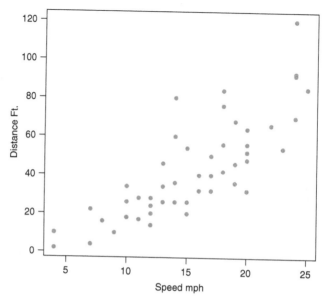

Figure 11.13 The plot() function creates scatter plots.

In the preceding example a "closed" plotting symbol was used (pch = 19); the colour of the symbol was altered using col = "steelblue". The graphical parameters used were:

cex: symbol size.   pch: plotting symbol.
col: colour.   las: Axis label orientation.
xlab: x-axis label.   ylab: y-axis label.

You can specify the variables to plot using a formula. This can be helpful:

- The formula syntax is used extensively in statistical analysis functions.
- You can "point" to the location of the variables using the data = argument.

Example:

Scatter plot using a formula.

```
head(trees, n = 3)

    Girth  Height  Volume
1    8.3      70    10.3
2    8.6      65    10.3
3    8.8      63    10.2

plot(Girth ~ Height, data = trees, pch = 21,
     bg = "green", col = "brown4", cex = 2, las = 1)
```

In preceding example an "open" plotting symbol was used (pch = 21); the col argument altered the border of the symbol ("brown4"), whilst the bg argument set the background colour (to "green"). The various "standard" graphical parameters used were:

cex:	symbol size.	pch:	plotting symbol.
col:	colour.	bg:	Background colour for symbol.
xlab:	x-axis label.	ylab:	y-axis label.
las:	Axis label orientation.		

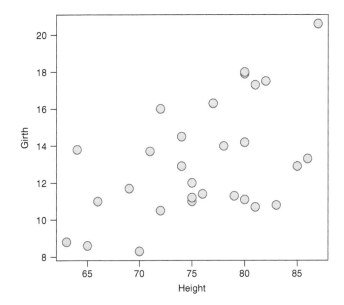

Figure 11.14 A formula can be used in plot() to specify the data for a scatter plot.

Tip: Scatter plot axis labels/titles

The plot() function will produce default labels for the x and y axes. If you want to add axis titles later (using title()), set titles to an empty string: xlab = " " and ylab = " ".

The pch argument allows you to specify a symbol (or more than one) for the plotting. In most cases one of the "standard" symbols should be sufficient (pch = 0:25).

Note: UniCode characters

You can specify UniCode characters in the form -0xnnnnL where nnnn is the Unicode value. However, this is very machine dependent and may not always work. For example codes 0x2660L, 0x2663, 0x2665L and 0x2666L produce the card suit symbols (spades ♠, clubs ♣, hearts ♥, diamonds ♦) on most machines.

There are plenty of ways to customize and tinker with scatter plots. See Chapter 12 *Graphics: Adding to plots* for examples of adding things like: more data series, best-fit lines, grid lines, error bars, titles and text, and custom axes.

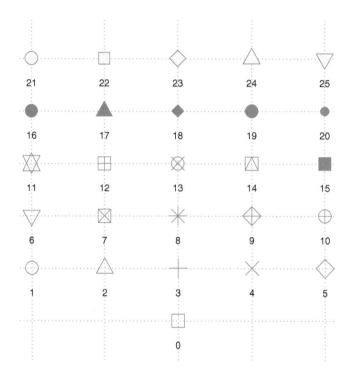

Figure 11.15 Standard R plotting symbols pch 0–25. In this example symbols are plotted with col = 'red' and bg = 'gray90' to help differentiate 'open' and 'closed' symbols.

11.7.1 Plotting multiple data series

The general `plot()` function allows you to plot a single data series, that is one y value (response), and one x value (predictor). If you need to plot multiple data series there are several ways you might proceed:

- Use `plot()` to visualize the first data series, then add more data using `points()` (see Chapter 12).
- Use the `matplot()` function to plot one `matrix` against another (see Chapter 13).
- Use some multivariate plotting function, e.g. `pairs()` or `coplot()` (see Chapter 13).

The choice you make ultimately depends on the exact nature of the visualization you require.

11.8 Line charts

Line charts are intended to help visualize variables that change between set (and equal) intervals. There is no dedicated function to draw line charts in R but the `plot()` function can be used with a `type` argument. Here are some of the options:

- `type = "p"` – Plot points only (the usual default).
- `type = "l"` – Plot lines only.
- `type = "b"` – Points with segments of line between them ("both").
- `type = "o"` – Lines and points "over-plotted".
- `type = "n"` – Nothing!

You can format the style of the lines and or points using "standard" graphical parameters (e.g. `lwd`, `lty`, `pch`).

Because a line chart is essentially a scatter plot at heart, you need to pay careful attention to the data that will form the x-axis. If your data are annual (i.e. year values on the x-axis) these are easily handled with "regular" numeric values. If you have some other sort of time interval (e.g. monthly), you will probably need to convert the x-data to a time format of some kind (see section 8.7 *et seq.*).

Example:

Line chart of values over yearly intervals

```
# New Haven temp by year (start, end, frequency)
tsp(nhtemp)

[1] 1912 1971   1

# First 10 years
nh <- nhtemp[1:10]
names(nh) <- 1912:1921
nh

1912 1913 1914 1915 1916 1917 1918 1919 1920 1921
49.9 52.3 49.4 51.1 49.4 47.9 49.8 50.9 49.3 51.9

plot(1912:1921, nh, type = "o", pch = 19, lwd = 2, lty = "dashed",
    col = "blue", las = 1, ylab = "New Haven mean temperature (F)",
    xlab = "Year")
```

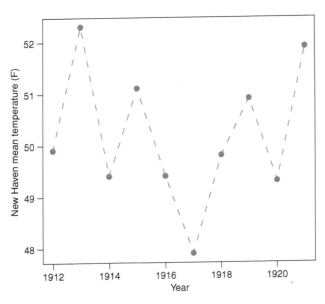

Figure 11.16 A line chart is a kind of scatter plot. If x-axis data are annual, the year values form the x-axis data.

In the preceding example the x data were year values, so plot(x, y, ...) was used to draw the data. The type = "o" set the plot to produce both lines and points, but with the points "over" the line. Other parameters used were:

pch:	Plot character.	lwd:	Line width.
lty:	Line type.	col:	Colour (of line and points).
las:	Axis label orientation.	xlab:	x-axis label.
ylab:	y-axis label.		

If your x-axis data are not plain `numeric` values, you have a bit more work to do. If you can coerce the data into some sort of date format this is usually the best way forward (see sections 8.7 and 8.8). In the following example the data are monthly.

Example:

Line chart of values over monthly intervals.

```
# Extract 1st 12 months and convert F to C
temp <- (nottem[1:12] -32) *5/9

# Add names
names(temp) <- month.abb
temp
```

```
      Jan       Feb       Mar       Apr       May       Jun       Jul       Aug
 4.777778  4.888889  6.888889  8.166667 12.277778 14.722222 14.277778 13.555556
      Sep       Oct       Nov       Dec
12.388889 10.277778  6.055556  4.333333
```

```
# Make a date object
dv <- ISOdate(year = 1920, month = 1:12, day = 1)

# Now plot
plot(temp ~ dv, type = "b", las = 1, cex.axis = 0.8, col = "blue",
pch = 21,
    bg = "pink", xlab = "Month",
    ylab = "Mean monthly temperature (C)")
```

In the preceding example the x data were month names. These had to be incorporated into a date structure; the `ISOdate()` function is a convenient way to do this. An alternative would be:

```
as.Date(paste(1920, month.abb, 1, sep = "-"), format = "%Y-%b-%d")
```

In the plot the `type = "b"` argument produced both lines and points, but with the points "between" segments of line. Other parameters used were:

las:	Axis label orientation.	xlab:	x-axis label.
ylab:	y-axis label.	col:	colour (for line and symbol border).
pch:	Plotting character.	bg:	Background colour for open symbol.
cex.axis:	Size of axis labels.		

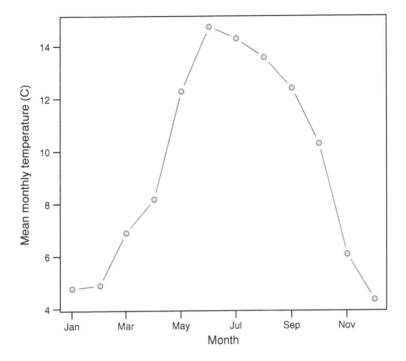

Figure 11.17 If x-axis data are in a date format, the line chart automatically formats the x-axis.

Note: Time-series plotting

An object with the class `ts`, that is a time-series object, will automatically plot as a line chart, and with the x-axis appropriately formatted. However, sometimes the time axis labels don't appear as you'd like. In such cases you'll need to plot the chart without an axis and add one explicitly using the `axis()` function. See Chapter 12 *Adding to plots* for more details.

There are other functions that can help you draw line charts, such as `matplot()` for example (see section 13.9 *Matrix plots*). However, you'll often want/need to alter the x-axis; see section 12.8 *Custom axes* for more details.

11.8.1   Time-series plots

R has "dedicated" functions for dealing with time series. If your data hold the class `ts` or `mts` (see section 8.7) you can use the `plot.ts()` function to present your data (see section 13.6 for details).

11.9   Pie charts

Pie charts are used to view compositional data; the `pie()` function will do this.

```
pie(x, labels, clockwise, col, border, lty, init.angle, ...)
```

Pie charts aren't a good way to display data, which is probably why your options are somewhat limited in base R. However, you can produce quite adequate pie charts using the parameters available (Table 11.7).

Table 11.7 Some parameters of the pie() functions.

Parameter	Description
x	The data, a numeric vector.
labels	Optional labels, as a character vector.
clockwise	If TRUE the slices are drawn clockwise. The default is FALSE.
col	colour for the slices, colours are recycled if necessary. The default colours are 6 pastel shades.
border	The colour for the border of the slices.
lty	Line type for the borders.
init.angle	The starting angle for the slices. A value of 90 equates to "noon", whilst 0 equates to 3 o'clock.
...	Additional parameters are possible.

You can only draw one data series (a single vector) at a time with pie(). The defaults produce an anti-clockwise pie with labels taken from the names attribute of the data, and with a starting angle of 0.

Example:

Pie chart

```
temp <- (nottem[1:12] - 32) * 5/9
pie(temp, labels = month.abb, clockwise = TRUE, init.angle = 180,
    cex = 1.3, col = c("white", "lightblue", "steelbluel",
    "lightgreen",
    "springgreen", "mistyrose", "lightcyan", "lavender",
    "turquoise", "cornsilk", "palegoldenrod", "yellowgreen"),
    border = "darkblue")
```

In the preceding example the data were a simple vector without any names attribute, so the labels argument was used along with cex (to make them slightly larger). The slices were drawn clockwise = TRUE with the starting point init.angle = 180 at 9 o'clock.

> ### Note: Pie starting angle
>
> The init.angle has a default that starts at 0 if clockwise = FALSE and 90 if clockwise = TRUE. It's a good habit to specify the starting angle explicitly, so you can always be sure of the result.

The pie() function is one of the few plotting commands that does not "link" so closely with the "standard" graphical parameters: you can only sensibly affect the titles. It *is* possible to tinker with pie charts but this involves modifying the pie() function itself, which is something for more advanced users.

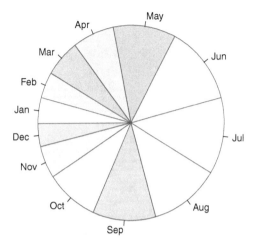

Figure 11.18 A pie chart is a poor way to present data.

In the example pie chart the colours were given as part of the command, in a `character` `vector`. There are more efficient ways to deal with colour, see section 13.1 *Working with colour* for more details.

In general the pie chart is not the most useful plot-type. The kinds of data you represent can be better represented with bar charts and Cleveland dot charts.

11.10 Mosaic plots

A mosaic plot is a way to visualize compositional data. Use `mosaicplot()` to draw mosaic plots.

```
mosaicplot(x, data, off, colour, dir, ...)
```

Your data (in the form of a contingency table) are split into blocks where the size of the block represents the proportion that element contributes to the total. There are a number of parameters you can use (Table 11.8).

Table 11.8 Some parameters of the `mosaicplot()` function.

Parameter	Description
x	The data. This is usually a contingency table (e.g. `table`, `array` or `matrix`) but can be a `formula` of the form `y ~ x`.
data	If x is a `formula` this gives the `data.frame` that holds the variables.
off	Offset between blocks; you can tinker with values in the range 0--20 if the default is not what you want.
colour	colours for the blocks. If `TRUE` then a grey palette is used.
dir	The direction of the splits. Provide a `character vector` with a direction for each dimension of the contingency table ("v", "h").
...	Other parameters are possible.

There are other arguments that can be used, some of these are "standard" graphical parameters and others relate to the production of log-linear model (extended mosaic plots).

A mosaic plot helps you visualize proportions, this is simplest when the data are two dimensional.

Example:

Mosaic plot from two-dimensional data

```
mosaicplot(VADeaths,
           colour = c("skyblue", "mistyrose", "slateblue4", "violetred"))
```

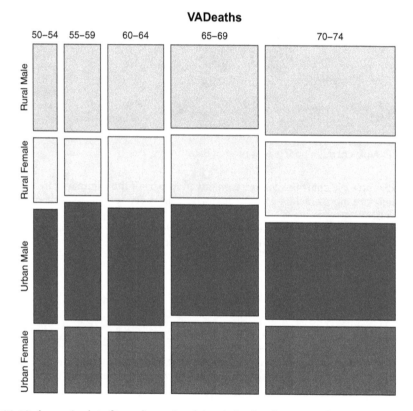

Figure 11.19 A mosaic plot of two-dimensional data help visualize proportions.

In the preceding example the data are in a `matrix`, and so are two dimensional. The `colour` parameter was given to use four colours for the blocks (the columns of the `matrix` formed the "rows", which get the different colours applied to them).

Note: Arguments and abbreviations

It is usually possible to give an argument name in an abbreviated form; as long as it is uniquely "recognized", it will be used appropriately. In the `mosaicplot()` function for example, the `colour` argument could be abbreviated to `col`. It's a good habit to *not* use abbreviations but to use the full names.

If you have more than two dimensions, it becomes more of a challenge to present the data in the "best" layout. Using a `formula` and the `dir` argument are helpful in getting your data arranged "nicely".

Example:

Mosaic plot from three-dimensional data

```
mosaicplot(~ Hair + Sex + Eye, data = HairEyeColour,
           dir = c("v","h", "h"), las = 1,
           colour = c("sienna", "blue", "tan", "green"))
```

Figure 11.20 Data with more than two dimensions usually need to be presented by altering the order of the variables and the dir argument, to produce a readable plot.

In the preceding example the data (a three-dimensional `table`) were plotted using a `formula`, which allowed the variables to be arranged in the "best" manner. The `dir` argument controls how the data are "split", and was used to make the plot "readable". The `colour` argument was used to specify four colours (corresponding to the "rows", the last variable). The "standard" graphical parameter `las` was also used to alter the orientation of the axis labels.

Tip: Mosaic plot colours

Use of colour can help a good deal in the readability of a mosaic plot. To help you manage the colours, start by using `colour = TRUE` in your plot. This produces a set of grey colours, and will help you to determine how many colours you'll need to specify. Rather than put all the colours in the `mosaicplot()` function (like the examples), make a `character vector` and alter the `colour` argument to point to that.

11.11   Dot charts

A Cleveland Dot Chart is useful for visualizing compositional data. A dot chart makes a good alternative to a pie chart (or a bar chart). The dotchart() function can produce dot charts, which can handle multiple data series and also incorporate a summary statistic (such as a group mean).

```
dotchart(x, labels, groups, gdata, pt.cex, gpch, colour, gcolour,
    lcolour, ...)
```

The dotchart() function has a few more arguments than some other plotting functions (Table 11.9).

Table 11.9 Some parameters of the dotchart() function.

Parameter	Description
x	The data, usually a vector or a matrix.
labels	Labels for the points, the default uses the names attribute.
groups	A grouping variable. If x is a matrix the default is to use the columns as the groups.
gdata	Data values for the group summary.
pt.cex	The size of the points (note that cex affects the labels).
gpch	The plotting symbol for the grouping variable (if used).
colour	The colours for points and labels.
gcolour	A single colour to use for the group label.
lcolour	colour of the lines.
...	Other parameters are possible.

Part of the reason for the large number of potential parameters is that you can plot two kinds of points: the data, and a grouping variable. Other "standard" graphical parameters can be used, such as pch, lty and cex.

Example:

A Cleveland dot chart with a grouping variable (mean)

```
dotchart(VADeaths, gdata = colMeans(VADeaths), pch = 21, bg = "pink",
    pt.cex = 1.5, gpch = 16, gcolour = "blue", lcolour = "gray70",
    cex = 0.8, xlab = "Deaths per 1000 population")
```

In the preceding example the gdata parameter was set to the colMeans of the data, to give mean values for each group (columns of the matrix). Two different plotting symbols were employed: pch = 21 for the main points and gpch = 16 for the mean statistic. The cex parameter was used to "shrink" the labels slightly, whilst pt.cex was used to make the plotted points slightly larger.

Tip: Plotting symbols and dot charts

It is useful to use an open symbol for the regular data (pch 21 or 23 are ideal), and a closed one for any grouping variable (e.g. 16). This allows you to specify the bg for the plotted points without affecting the label colour.

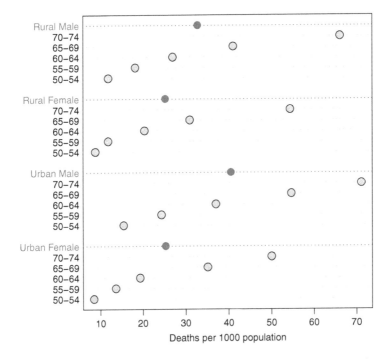

Figure 11.21 A dot chart makes a concise summary of multiple data series. You can also add a group variable (in this case the mean).

11.12   Strip charts

Strip charts show vectors of values in a one-dimensional scatter plot. The stripchart() function can produce strip charts, which can be useful as a general overview of data samples.

```
stripchart(x, method, jitter, offset, vertical, group.names,
    log, ...)
```

The stripchart() function has various parameters to help you customize the output (Table 11.10).

Table 11.10 Some parameters of the stripchart() function.

Parameter	Description
x	The data. Can be a numeric vector or an object that can be decomposed to such (e.g. list or data.frame). Alternatively use a formula of form y ~ g where g is the grouping variable. If you use a formula you can also give data = z where z is the object that contains the variables.
method	A character string that controls how coincident points are drawn. Options are: "jitter" (points are given random "tweak"), "stack" (points are stacked), or "overplot" (the default, points remain coincident).
jitter	If method = "jitter" this sets the amount of "wobble".
offset	If method = "stack" this sets the amount of separation.
vertical	If TRUE the samples are drawn vertically (default = FALSE).
group.names	A character vector of labels to use for the groups, the default uses the levels of the grouping variable.
log	A character string giving the axes to plot on a log scale (e.g. log = "x").
...	Other parameters are possible.

The method parameter is especially helpful, as it allows you to "deal" with coincident points; generally method = "jitter" is the best option. Other arguments are possible and many "standard" graphical parameters can be used. A strip chart can be a useful tool in data exploration or data mining, and can make a good alternative or addendum to a box-whisker plot.

Example:

Strip chart using a formula interface

```
stripchart(weight ~ feed, data = chickwts, method = "jitter",
    bg = "gold3", pch = 23, cex.axis = 0.7, las = 1, xlab = "Final Weight")
```

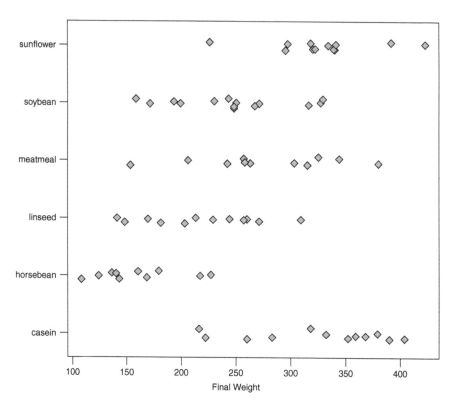

Figure 11.22 A strip chart can be a useful overview of a dataset.

In the preceding example a formula was used to specify the response and grouping variables. The method = "jitter" argument added a random vertical element to the plotted points, to help pick out coincident (or close) data. Various "standard" graphical parameters were also used:

bg:	background colour for plot symbol.	pch:	plot symbol (open diamond).
cex.axis:	Size for axis labels.	las:	Axis label orientation.
xlab:	x-axis title.		

Tip: Coincident points and jitter

Open symbols work best when you have coincident (or close) data points. The open diamond (pch = 23) is particularly useful. The method = "jitter" argument will result in some random "wobble" of your points, to help separate and visualize them. If you want to repeat a plot *exactly* then use set.seed(n) before plotting (where n is an integer).

Note: Chart types

There are other chart types available in R. This chapter illustrates the most common and useful ones. See *Chapter 13* for a few other examples of plotting functions.

EXERCISES:

Self-Assessment for Graphics

1. The classic method for visualizing sample distribution is a ____, which you can plot using the ____ function.
2. To make a bar chart your data must be a matrix.. TRUE or FALSE?
3. Which of the following plot functions can help visualize compositional data?
   a. dotchart()
   b. barplot()
   c. boxplot()
   d. stripchart()
4. You can use the outliers parameter to control outliers in boxplot().. TRUE or FALSE?
5. To alter the rotation of the axis annotations you need the ____ parameter.

Answers to exercises are in the *Appendix*.

11.13   Chapter Summary: Graphics – basic charts

Topic	Key Points
Histogram	Use hist() to make a basic histogram to visualize sample distribution. Control the data bins with the breaks parameter. You can specify freq = FALSE to ensure data is plotted as density rather than frequency.
Density plot	Use density() to get x and y coordinates for a density plot. The actual visualization uses plot(). You can add a density line to a histogram: use hist(x, freq = FALSE) to ensure y-axis is density, then plot(density(x)).
QQ plots	Use qqnorm() to plot a quantile-quantile plot of your sample quantiles against theoretical normal quantiles. Use qqline() to add an isocline to help visualize departure from normality.

(Continued)

(Continued)

Topic	Key Points
Box-whisker plot	Use boxplot() to create a box-whisker plot. Data can be expressed as multiple vector objects, a single numeric object (list, matrix or data.frame), or a formula of form response ~ groups. The result shows median and inter-quartile box. The range parameter controls how the whiskers extend: range = 0 gives max-min, whilst other positive values shorten the whiskers and potentially show outlier points.
Bar chart	Use barplot() to make a column chart from either a single vector or a matrix. If you use a matrix you get a multiple series chart. Control the bars with the beside parameter (TRUE = clustered, FALSE = stacked).
Scatter plot	Use plot() for a basic scatter plot. Specify the data as x and y coordinates, a single object containing x and y components, or a formula of form response ~ predictor. The pch parameter determines the plotting character(s) used. You can add more data series using points().
Line chart	Use plot() to make a line chart but specify type = "l" as a parameter. Other options allow you to add points between sections of line (type = "b"), or overplotted points and line (type = "b").
Pie chart	Use pie() to draw pie charts (if you must). You can control the direction the slices are drawn as well as the starting position.
Mosaic plot	Use mosaicplot() to help visualize compositional data. You can specify the data as a single object (usually a matrix), or via a formula. Other parameters help alter the colour, direction, and gaps between blocks.
Dot chart	Use dotchart() to create Cleveland dot charts, a good alternative to pie or mosaic plots for matrix objects. You can add a group statistic to the chart with the gdata parameter.
Strip chart	Use stripchart() to make a strip chart, to show one or more samples along a single axis. You can specify the data as a vector, list, or data.frame and optionally can use a formula of form response ~ group.

Table 11.11 Graphical graphical parameters common to many plot functions.

Parameter	Explanation
col	colour. Usually as a `character vector` but other options are possible.
	Other `col` variants include: `col.axis` (axis annotations), `col.lab` (labels for x/y titles), `col.main` (main title), `col.sub` (subtitle).
bg	Background colour for open plotting symbols.
border	Border colour on plots where a border is drawn (e.g. `barplot`, `pie`, `boxplot`).
pch	Plotting character/symbol. Standard symbols are 0–25 but there are other options.
lty	Line type. Specify an `integer` or a `character` e.g.: 0/"blank, 1/"solid", 2/"dashed", 3/"dotted". There are also other options.
lwd	Line width; values >1 make lines wider.
cex	Character expansion. Values >1 make things larger.
	Other `cex` variants include: `cex.axis` (axis annotations), `cex.lab` (labels for x/y titles), `cex.main` (main title), `cex.sub` (subtitle).
las	Axis label orientation (0–3): 0: labels parallel to axes (default), 1: all horizontal, 2: all perpendicular to axes, 3: all vertical.
log	Use a log scale for axes as a `character vector`, e.g. "x", "y" or "xy".
xlab	Label for x-axis as a `character vector`.
ylab	Label for y-axis as a `character vector`.
main	Main title as a `character vector`. Drawn at top of plot window.
sub	Subtitle as a `character vector`. Drawn at bottom of plot window.
xlim	Limits for x-axis as a `numeric vector` giving both min and max values, e.g `xlim = c(0, 10)`.
ylim	Limits for y-axis as a `numeric vector` giving both min and max values e.g. `ylim = c(0, 10)`.

12. Graphics: adding to plots

In the preceding chapter you learnt how to create a range of graphical objects. This chapter is about how to add extra content to those graphics. There are many ways to add to existing plot windows, and various functions dedicated for that purpose.

What's in this chapter

Adding elements to existing plots:

» Adding more data.
  » as points.
  » as lines.
» Adding grid-lines.
» Adding best-fit lines.
» Adding error bars.
» Adding titles.
» Adding text.
  » to the plot.
  » in the margin.
  » text formatting.
» Adding legends.
» Adding axes.

Note: Support material

See the ↘ for links to material on the support website.

12.1   Adding more data

There are various ways to add additional data series to an existing plot. Some functions allow additional data to be added via an argument add = TRUE, such as boxplot() or barplot(). However, these functions also permit the plotting of multiple data series from the outset. In this section the focus will be on adding scatter-plot data to an existing chart (which might not be a scatter plot).

Note: Multiple data series scatter plots

You *can* use the matplot() function to draw multiple series scatter plots. The function plots the columns of one matrix against the columns of another matrix. See section 13.1 *Matrix plots* for more details.

12.1.1 Data as points

The points() function will add x,y data to any existing plot window.

```
points(x, y = NULL, type = "p", ...)
```

Essentially points() works just like plot(), and you specify the data in a similar manner. The data can be separate vector objects, a single object with x and y components (e.g. list or data.frame), or a formula of the form y ~ x. You can specify many "standard" graphical parameters to alter the appearance of the points (e.g. pch, col, bg, cex) but obviously you cannot alter the axis, as you are adding to an already existing plot.

Example:

A multi-series scatter plot using points() to add data series

```
# The data
head(iris, n = 3)

  Sepal.Length Sepal.Width Petal.Length Petal.Width Species
1          5.1         3.5          1.4         0.2  setosa
2          4.9         3.0          1.4         0.2  setosa
3          4.7         3.2          1.3         0.2  setosa

# Three data series
levels(iris$Species)

[1] "setosa"    "versicolour" "virginica"

# Basic plot window without data
plot(Sepal.Length ~ Sepal.Width, data = iris, type = "n", las = 1)

# Plot each dataset with different symbol/colour
points(Sepal.Length ~ Sepal.Width, data = iris,
       subset = Species == "setosa", col = "black", pch = 15)
points(Sepal.Length ~ Sepal.Width, data = iris,
       subset = Species == "versicolour", col = "deeppink", pch = 16)
points(Sepal.Length ~ Sepal.Width, data = iris,
       subset = Species == "virginica", col = "blue", pch = 17)
```

In the preceding example the first plot() function used type = "n" so that no data were drawn, but the axis limits were set. This ensured that the succeeding points would "fit" in the chart area. Note that the other parameters in plot() were used to set the axis titles and label orientation (las = 1).

The points() commands each plotted a data series, using subset to select the data, and alter the appearance: pch (plotting symbol) and col (symbol colour). The final plot would benefit from a legend (see section 12.7 *Legends* for notes about that).

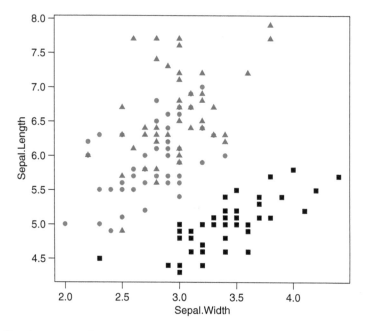

Figure 12.1 Morphometrics of three Iris species (*setosa* = squares, *versicolor* = circles, *virginica* = triangles). Data series can be added to an existing plot using the points() function. A legend would help the readability of the plot.

Tip: Differentiating colours and symbols in plots

It can sometimes be helpful to assign a variable to "point" to a colour or plotting symbol. To do this make a copy of the grouping variable but use labels to re-label the levels as the colours you want, or the plotting symbols.

Then you can point to the new variables for col or pch. However, your variables will be factor so you need to convert them:

- For col use: as.character(x)
- For pch use: as.numeric(as.character(x))

Note that for the pch you need the two steps.

The command lines needed to re-create the example would now become:

```
plocol <- factor(iris$Species,
    labels = c("black", "deeppink", "blue"))
ploch <- factor(iris$Species, labels = c(15:17))
plot(Sepal.Length ~ Sepal.Width, data = iris, col = as.character(plocol),
    pch = as.numeric(as.character(ploch)), las = 1)
```

Notice that the points() function has a type = "p" parameter. This is effectively the same as for plot(), and allows you to use points() to add lines. However, there is a dedicated function lines() that does just that.

12.1.2   Data as lines

The lines() function is essentially the same as points(), but with type = "l" as a default argument.

```
lines(x, y = NULL, type = "l", ...)
```

As with points(), you can specify the data in several ways. You can also use various graphical parameters to alter the appearance of the lines (and symbols if you choose).

Example:

Using lines() to add data to a plot window

```
# Temperature data for Nottingham & New Haven
Not <- rowMeans(matrix(nottem, ncol = 12))[1:10]
NH <- as.numeric(window(nhtemp, start = 1920, end = 1929))
Yr <- 1920:1929
Td <- data.frame(Yr, Not, NH)

# Get range to help set axis limits
range(c(Not, NH))

[1]  47.84167 51.90000

plot(Not ~ Yr, data = Td, type = "o", ylim = c(47.5, 52), lty = "dashed",
     lwd = 2, col = "blue", ylab = "Temperature (F)", xlab = "Year",
     las = 1, pch = 16)
lines(NH ~ Yr, data = Td, type = "o", lwd = 2, lty = "dotted",
      col = "red", pch = 16)
```

In the preceding example two sets of temperature data were added to a data.frame. The data did not have to be in a data.frame but it is generally convenient to "tie" data together. The range() function was used to determine the limits for the y-axis. The plot() function drew the first data series (Nottingham: Not), with type = "o" to give lines and over-plotted points, and the ylim parameter setting the y-axis (to allow room for the 2nd data series). The lines() function was then used to add the second data series (New Haven: NH).

Various "standard" graphical parameters were also used:

lty:	Line type.	lwd:	Line width.
col:	colour for line/symbol.	pch:	Plotting character.
las:	Axis label orientation.		

The lines() function will add any x,y data to a graphic.

The points() and lines() functions are especially suitable for adding xy data series to plots. Adding bars or box-whiskers is more of a challenge. However, many plot types have an add argument, which allows you to add to an existing chart. In practice the most useful application for this is to re-draw data over the top of grid lines, see the following section for an example.

Tip: Find coordinates for lines or points on a bar chart

If you want to add points or lines to a barplot you need to determine the coordinates along the x axis for the center of each bar. Re-draw your barplot but assign it to a named object. The chart will plot and if you open the object you'll see the appropriate coordinates. See section 12.8 *Custom axes* for more details.

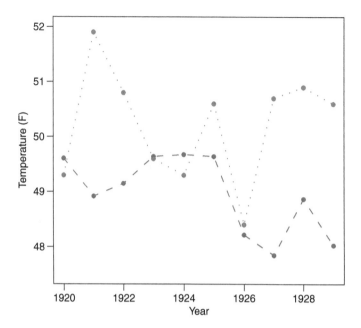

Figure 12.2 Mean annual temperature of two cities (Nottingham: blue, New Haven: red). The lines() function is used to add additional data to an existing plot window.

Mathematical curves

It is possible to draw mathematical functions using the `curve()` function.

> ### ↘ Online: Mathematical curves
>
> See the online support pages for examples of drawing mathematical expressions using `curve()`.

12.2 Grid lines

Grid lines can be a useful addition to a chart, although they can also be a distraction so should be used with caution. There are a couple of ways to add grids to an R graphic:

- Horizontal and/or Vertical lines: `abline()`.
- Complete grid: `grid()`.

12.2.1 Horizontal and vertical lines

The most common kinds of grid-lines are horizontal, and can be useful on various types of plot (e.g. bar charts). Vertical lines are slightly less useful. Both kinds of line can be added using the `abline()` function.

```
abline(h = NULL, v = NULL, ...)
```

In the `abline()` function you can specify h or v, which will become the horizontal or vertical position(s) of drawn lines. You can also use some "standard" graphical parameters to alter the appearance of the lines, such as `lty`, `lwd` and `col`.

You can specify a single value, or some kind of expression that creates multiple values.

Example:

Adding horizontal grid lines to a graphic with `abline()`

```
plot(Nile)
abline(h = seq(from = 600, to = 1200, by = 200), lty = "dashed",
       col = "skyblue", lwd = 2)
```

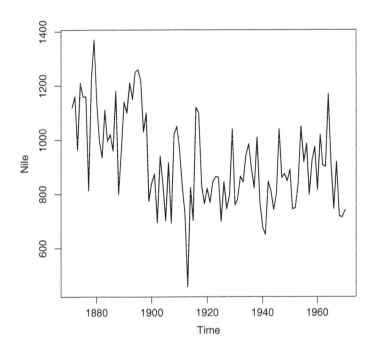

Figure 12.3 The abline() function can add horizontal and vertical lines to an existing plot.

In the preceding example the `Nile` data were plotted (the data are a `ts` object and plots by default as a line), using `plot()`. The `abline()` function was used to add horizontal lines at intervals of 200 (using the `seq()` function). Various "standard" graphical parameters were also used:

`lty`:	line type.	`lwd`:	line width.
`col`:	colour of line.		

You can use `abline()` repeatedly, should you wish, to add lines as you require.

12.2.2 Grids

You can add grid-lines quickly using the `grid()` function.

```
grid(nx = NULL, ny = nx, ...)
```

Using `grid()` is an alternative to `abline()` but with less fine control over their placement. In `grid()` you specify nx as the number of "cells" (gaps between grid-lines) you want along the x-axis. The default `NULL` uses the placement of the tick-marks on the axis. For the y-axis you specify ny, which defaults to whatever you use for nx. You can also format the lines, the default is lty = "dotted" and col = "lightgray". Other parameters are possible (e.g. lwd).

This means that you can make a "quick and dirty" grid simply by using grid() after any plot.

Place grid-lines behind graphic data

Typically the grid() or abline() commands will be the last to be typed, resulting in grid-lines that over-top your points/bars/boxes. With a little ingenuity you can get the grid-lines to be placed behind the main plot.

- For plot(): Use type = "n" then add the grid(). Now use points() or lines() to add your data.
- For barplot() or boxplot(): Create your plot as usual, then add your grid(). Now redraw the chart but use arguments, axes = FALSE, add = TRUE.

The axes parameter allows you to draw a plot without axes (if FALSE). The add parameter allows the data to be added to the current plot.

Example:

Adding a grid in the background

```
boxplot(weight ~ group, data = PlantGrowth, col = "lightgreen")
grid()
boxplot(weight ~ group, data = PlantGrowth, col = "lightgreen",
        axes = FALSE, add = TRUE)
```

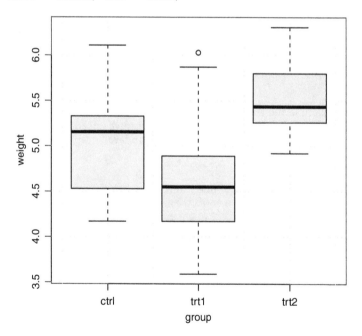

Figure 12.4 Grid-lines can be added using grid(). If the plot is redrawn with axes = FALSE, add = TRUE, the grid appears in the background.

In the preceding example the boxplot() function was used to draw the data. Unlike plot() there is no equivalent to type = "n", so the grid() was added to overlay the boxes. However, the `boxplot()` function was re-run using `axes = FALSE, add = TRUE` to re-draw the boxes and add them, thus overlaying the grid-lines. The example used `grid()` but `abline()` would have been suitable.

Note: Arguments add and axes

Many plot types use the `add` and `axes` arguments, allowing you to redraw data over various "decorations". Check the help entry for the plotting function you want to use, or simply give it a go.

12.3 Best-fit lines

A best-fit line can help to summarize the relationship between two numeric variables in a scatter plot. You can think of best-fit lines as falling into one of two camps:

- Based on a mathematical model.
- Based on a "local-fit".

Best-fit lines are often based on some mathematical relationship, defined by an equation. If you know the equation you can draw the line. Other kinds of best-fit take a different approach, using a "local" method. Such methods are often called *scatter plot smoothers*.

12.3.1 Best-fit from equation

If you can represent the relationship between two numeric variables with an equation some kind, you can take known values of one variable to "predict" values of the other. The commonest relationship is a straight line, given by $y = mx + c$. Where m is the slope and c is the intercept. You can use the `abline()` function to add a straight line to a plot window if you know the slope and intercept.

```
abline(a = NULL, b = NULL, ...)
```

You saw `abline()` in a previous section, used with arguments h and v, to draw gridlines. The straight-line equation is sometimes written as: $y = a + bx$, So if you specify a (the intercept) and b (slope) your line assumes those properties.

You do not necessarily need to specify a and b directly; if a is the result of a regression it will contain the coefficients (i.e. slope and intercept).

The `lm()` function will carry out linear regression, see section 14.3.2 *Regression* for more details.

Example:

Add a best-fit line from a linear equation

```
head(trees, n = 3)

  Girth  Height   Volume
1   8.3      70     10.3
2   8.6      65     10.3
3   8.8      63     10.2

plot(Girth ~ Height, data = trees, pch = 21, bg = "green", cex = 2)
```

```
# Regression
fit <- lm(Girth ~ Height, data = trees)

# The coefficients
coef(fit)

(Intercept)      Height
-6.1883945    0.2557471

# Add the fit-line
abline(a = fit, col = "darkgreen", lty = "dashed", lwd = 1.5)
```

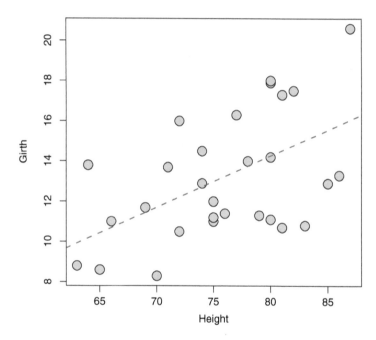

Figure 12.5 A linear best-fit line can be added using the abline() function to 'read' the intercept and slope from a regression result.

In the preceding example the data were visualized using plot() with a formula giving the variables to use. The lm() function used the same formula to determine the regression between the variables. The abline() function was used to draw the best-fit line, using the result of the lm() command. Various "standard" graphical parameters were also used:

pch:	Plot character.	bg:	Background colour (of plot symbol).
cex:	Character size (for plot symbol).	col:	colour (of line).
lty:	Line type.	lwd:	Line width.

The abline() function is quite flexible but it can *only* draw straight lines. If you require curved lines then you'll need to use the lines() function. See more about regression and best-fit lines in section 14.3.2 *Regression*.

12.3.2 Scatter plot smoothers

You can make a best-fit line without needing to carry out a regular regression. The lowess() function uses a locally weighted polynomial regression to find the "best path" through the data. This is often called a scatter plot smoother.

```
lowess(x, y = NULL, ...)
```

The lowess() function returns x and y co-ordinates, which allow you to draw a scatter plot smoother. You can use lines() to add this to an existing graphic. In the lowess() function you need to supply the x and y data, but y may be omitted if x is an object with the appropriate data (e.g. data.frame or list).

Note that lowess() cannot use a formula, so you need to specify the x and y data explicitly.

Example:

A locally weighted scatter plot smoother (lowess()) compared to a linear best-fit line (abline())

```
head(cars, n = 3)

   speed    dist
1     4       2
2     4      10
3     7       4

with(cars, plot(speed, dist, pch = 19, col = "steelblue"))
lines(lowess(cars$speed, cars$dist), col = "rosybrown",
      lwd = 3, lty = 4)
abline(lm(dist~speed,cars), col = "gray")
```

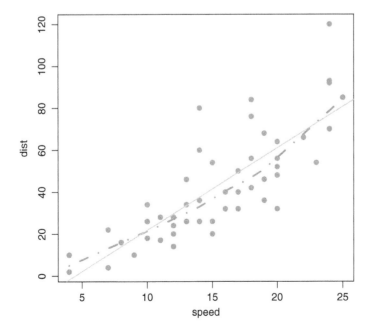

Figure 12.6 The lowess() function computes a locally weighted scatter plot smoother, which is added using the lines() function. Compare to the straight line from a linear fit.

In the preceding example the `cars` data were plotted as a scatter plot. The `lines()` function added the scatter plot smoother, which was generated via the `lowess()` function. Finally the `abline()` function was used to add a regular straight line for comparison. Various "standard" graphical parameters were also used:

pch:	Plotting character.	col:	colour (of symbol and line).
lwd:	Line width.	lty:	Line type.

You can also use the `loess()` function to produce a local polynomial regression (i.e. a scatter plot smoother).

```
loess(formula, data, ...)
```

The `loess()` function uses a `formula` to "describe" the data, rather than the x,y input for `lowess()`. The result contains different components, including:

- x the original predictor variable.
- y the original response variable.
- fitted the locally weighted response.

So, the draw the best-fit line you need to use `lines()` with the x and fitted components.

Tip: Data order and curved lines

Your data do not have to be in numerical order to generate the co-ordinates for a scatter plot smoother **but...** if they aren't in order the `lines()` function will produce a mess. The `lowess()` function produces results that are in the correct order, but `loess()` does not. So, either re-order the original data or your `loess()` result (the former is usually easiest).

The fewer the data points you have the more "angular" any curved scatter plot smoother will be. You can "bend" lines using the `spline()` function.

```
spline(x, y = NULL, ...)
```

You need to give x and y values, although if x is an object that has x,y components you can supply x only.

Example:

Using `spline()` to curve a best-fit line

```
head(BOD, n = 3)

     Time    demand
1      1       8.3
2      2      10.3
3      3      19.0

plot(demand ~ Time, data = BOD, pch = 21, bg = "tan")

# Use lowess
lo <- with(BOD, lowess(Time, demand))
```

```
# Simple line
lines(lo, col = "red")

# Interpolated/curved line
lines(spline(lo), col = "blue", lwd = 2)
```

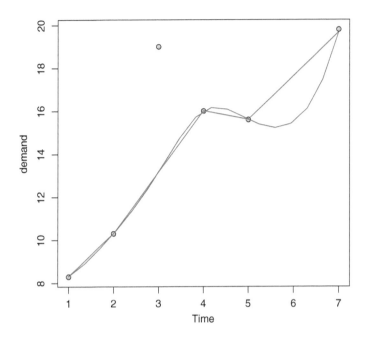

Figure 12.7 The spline() function can interpolate and produce curved lines. Compare the two lowess() scatter-plot smoothers (blue = with spline, red = plain).

In the preceding example the lowess() function was used to generate the coordinates for the smoother. The "basic" smoother was drawn using lines(), whilst the spline() function was introduced to interpolate and "bend" the line. Various "standard" graphical parameters were also used:

pch:	Plotting character.	bg:	Background colour for symbols.
col:	colour for line.	lwd:	Line width.

> **Tip: Missing data and scatter plot smoothers**
>
> If you have NA elements in one of your variables you may end up with gaps in your smoother line, which will also not give a proper result. You need to use na.omit() to "take out" the NA elements.

12.4   Error bars

Error bars are a way of showing data variability for data that are based on some kind of group average. Typically you would use error bars on a bar chart that showed group means. The error bars could convey any "statistic" but standard deviation or standard error are the most common. It is less common to use error bars on a scatter plot, because these usually show individual data points. However, you can add some kind of error bar to more or less any kind of plot, if appropriate for the data.

There are two main functions that you can press into service for drawing error bars:

- `segments()` – adds sections of straight line to an existing plot.
- `arrows()` – adds arrows to an existing plot.

The two functions operate in a very similar way, with the latter differing only in allowing arrowheads (and/or tails).

12.4.1 Segments

The `segments()` function allows you to add bits of straight line to any plot.

```
segments(x0, y0, x1, y1, ...)
```

You need to supply the xy co-ordinates for the starting points (x0, y0) and the equivalent for the end points (x1, y1). You can also use various "standard" graphical parameters to alter the appearance of the line segments.

You'll need to decide on the statistic you want to display as the error measurement. Then follow these steps:

1. Calculate the value of the error statistic.
2. Get or calculate the data values to plot.
3. Determine the maximum value for the y-axis.
4. Plot the main data.
5. Add the error bars using the data values ± the error statistic.

For a scatter plot you are usually going for error bars based solely on the y values. So your segments of line need to be drawn vertically from "just above" to "just below" each datum. It is easiest to see using an example.

Example:

Add error bars to a scatter plot using `segments()`

First off the data need to be prepared, you need the values to plot, the error values and the maximum value (so the y-axis can accommodate the data plus the bars). For this example the `nottem` data will be used, a time series of mean monthly temperatures over several years.

```
# Convert data from ts to a matrix
nt <- matrix(nottem, ncol = 12, byrow = TRUE)
dimnames(nt) <- list(1920:1939, month.abb[1:12])

# Fahrenheit to Centigrade
nt <- (nt - 32) * 5/9

# Monthly (column) means
nmt <- colMeans(nt)

# Standard Dev. for each month (column)
nsd <- apply(nt, MARGIN = 2, FUN = sd)

# The maximum the y-axis needs to fit
maxv <- max(nmt + nsd)
```

The first step was to make the data into a `matrix` and then to add appropriate names to the rows and columns. The data were then converted to Centigrade. The mean values and the standard deviations were then calculated. The last step is to determine how "tall" the y-axis needs to be to fit the data points plus the error bars.

```
# Convert x-axis to a date value for the axis
dv <- ISOdate(year = 1920, month = 1:12, day = 1)
plot(dv, nmt, type = "b", ylim = c(0, maxv + 0.5), xlab = "Month",
    ylab = "Mean monthly temperature (C)")

# add error bars
segments(dv, nmt + nsd, dv, nmt - nsd)
```

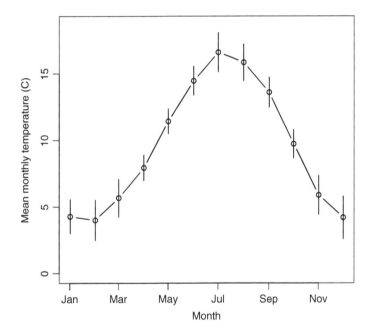

Figure 12.8 The segments() function can add error bars. In this case standard deviation on mean monthly temperature (Celsius) for Nottingham.

In the preceding example the `ISOdate()` function was used to make the x-axis into a date format (allowing values 1–12 to be automatically converted to a month). The `plot()` function simply drew the points and `type = "b"` was used to draw points with sections of line "between". The `segments()` function added the error bars by drawing from "top to bottom". In this case the error bars were left "plain", but additional "standard" graphical parameters could be used to alter their appearance.

Tip: Cross-bars on error bars

You *can* add cross-bars to your error bars. You need to use `segments()` once more but add and subtract a small amount from the x values. In practice this is tedious, and it is a lot easier to use the `arrows()` function instead.

12.4.2 Arrows

The arrows() function is similar to segments() but it allows you to add arrowheads (and/or tails) to the sections of line. This means that you can easily add cross-bars to your error bars.

```
arrows(x0, y0, x1, y1, length, angle, code, ...)
```

The arrows() function is very similar to segments() in that you require the xy co-ordinates for the start and ending points. However, there are some additional parameters that allow you to include heads/tails (Table 12.1).

Table 12.1 Some parameters of the arrows() function.

Parameter	Description
x0,y0	Co-ordinates for the start of an arrow.
x1,y1	Co-ordinates for the end of an arrow.
length	The length of any arrowhead/tail (inches). Use length = 0 to suppress all arrowheads.
angle	The angle of the arrowhead (default = 30).
code	The type of arrowheads: 1 = at tail, 2 = at end (default), 3 = both ends.
...	Additional graphical parameters.

Although you *can* use segments() to draw cross-bars it is a lot easier to use arrows(). A common use for error bars is to add a measure of variability to a bar chart. However, this is slightly problematic, as you do not have any x values. The bars in a barplot() do not center on simple integer positions. However, a simple "trick" makes it quite easy to get the appropriate x values to use, as you'll see in the following example.

Example:

Error bars on a bar chart using arrows()
    The example uses the same nottem data as before.

```
# Draw a barplot and save the x-values
bp <- barplot(nmt, col = "paleturquoise2", cex.names = 0.7, las = 1,
    ylim = c(0, maxv + 0.5), ylab = "Mean temperature Centigrade")

# The bar centers
as.numeric(bp)

[1] 0.7 1.9 3.1 4.3 5.5 6.7 7.9 9.1 10.3 11.5 12.7 13.9

# Error bars with crossbars
arrows(bp, nmt + nsd, bp, nmt - nsd, length = 0.05, angle = 90,
    code = 3, col = "darkblue", lwd = 1.5)
```

In the preceding example the "trick" was to assign the barplot() to a named object. This bp object contains the x co-ordinates for each bar. These values can now be used in the arrows() function. In this case code = 3 forms arrowheads at both ends, length = 0.05 set the size of the crossbars, and angle = 90 created the flat-ends. Various "standard" graphical parameters were also used:

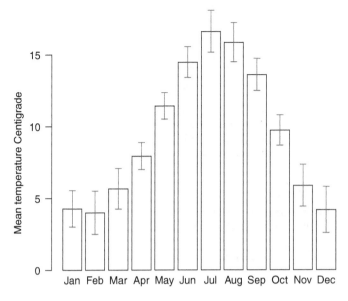

Figure 12.9 The arrows() function can add crossbars to error bars. In this case standard deviation on mean monthly temperature.

col:	colour (for bars and then error bars).	lwd:	line width.
cex.names:	axis label size.	las:	axis label orientation.
ylim:	extent of the y-axis.	ylab:	y-axis title.

Note that the plot() function will try to make the axes "pretty", and attempts to make nice intervals.

Tip: Axis limits

The various plotting functions attempt to make the intervals "pretty". If you want to ensure that your "top-value" gets incorporated use the ylim parameter to resize the y-axis limits.

12.5   Adding titles

Most plotting functions allow you to specify text to add to the y-axis and/or x-axis, as well as for regular "titles" at the top or bottom. The usual parameters are:

- xlab label the bottom axis.
- ylab label the left axis.
- main label at the top of the plot window.
- sub label at the very bottom of the plot window.

You can also add titles to an existing plot window; there are two main options:

- title() adds regular titles (x, y, main, sub).
- mtext() adds text into any of the four margins.

In general `title()` gives better control over "regular" titles than using the parameters `xlab`, `ylab` and so on. The `mtext()` function is more general and allows you to place text in any of the four margins.

Tip: Empty titles

Some graphical functions have "default" titles. You can suppress these by setting them to `""`. You can then use `title()` to add the titles afterwards. Alternatively just specify the text you want directly, as part of the graphical function.

12.5.1 Regular titles

You can add general titles to your plots directly from the plotting functions. However, sometimes it is better to add the titles separately. You can do this using the `title()` function.

```
title(main, sub, xlab, ylab, line, outer, ...)
```

The `title()` function allows you additional control over the text that you cannot achieve when using the parameters `xlab`, `ylab`, `main` or `sub` in a regular plotting command (Table 12.2).

Table 12.2 **Parameters of the `title()` function.**

Parameter	Description
main	The main title. The default makes a title in the middle of the top margin.
sub	A subtitle. The default makes a title in the middle of the lower edge of the graphical window.
xlab	Title for the bottom axis.
ylab	Title for the left axis.
line	Placement of the title n lines from the plot edge. The default is NA.
outer	If TRUE the titles are placed in the outer margin (default is FALSE).
...	Additional parameters to alter the title appearance.

Additional parameters can be passed to the `title()` function that allow you to alter the appearance and position of the text. Some of the parameters affect *all* the titles in the command at the same time:

- `line` the number of lines from the plot edge.
- `adj` the position along each side, 0 being the "start" and 1 being the "end" of a side. So, `adj = 0.5` is centered.

Other parameters are more specific:

Parameter	Effect
col.main col.sub col.lab	The colour for the titles. Note that xlab and ylab are both encompassed by col.lab.
cex.main cex.sub cex.lab	The size of the title relative to "normal". So values >1 make text larger, whilst c=values<1 make text smaller.
font.main font.sub font.lab	The font style as a simple integer. Where 1 = plain, 2 = bold, 3 = italic, 4 = bold + italic.

12.5.2 Marginal titles

The `mtext()` command is broadly similar to `title()` but allows you to add text to any of the four marginal areas (see also *section 12.6*).

```
mtext(text, side, line, outer, adj, padj, ...)
```

The various parameters allow you to specify how the text is positioned and formatted (Table 12.3).

Table 12.3 **Some parameters of the `mtext()` function.**

Parameter	Description
text	The text, specified as a `character vector` or `expression`.
side	The side of the plot to use: 1, = bottom, 2 = left, 3 = top (default), 4 = right.
line	The line of the margin to plot into (default = 0).
outer	If `TRUE` use the outer margin.
adj	Position along the side: 0 is the "start" and 1 is the "end" of a side.
padj	Adjustment perpendicular to the reading direction: 0 = right/top, 1 = left/bottom. Essentially, this "tweaks" the vertical position by n lines down or up (-^{ve} values are "up").
...	Other parameters are possible.

You can control the formatting of the text using various graphical parameters, such as: `cex` (text size), `col` (colour), `font` (typeface: 1 = plain, 2 = bold, 3 = italic, 4 = bold+italic). This is similar to the `title()` function.

Unlike `title()`, you can use the `las` parameter to alter the "reading direction" of the text relative to the plot axes:

- 0: all parallel to the axis (default)
- 1: all horizontal,
- 2: all perpendicular to the axis,
- 3: all vertical.

The `las` parameter interacts with `padj`, which shifts the text relative to the reading direction.

Tip: Multiple line text

You can "split" text over more than one line using `\n` as a `newline` character. The `"\"` is an `"escape character"`. If you want to display a `"\"` use `"\\"`.

12.6 Adding text

There are several ways to add text to a plot window:

- `title()` for general titles.
- `mtext()` for marginal text.
- `text()` for text in the plot region.
- `legend()` for legends.

The title() and mtext() functions were described in the previous sections, and deal with text around the "edge" of a plot. In the following sections you'll see how to add text into the main plotting region of graphics windows.

12.6.1   General text

The text() function is a general command that allows you to place text at specific co-ordinates in a plot window.

```
text(x, y, labels, adj, pos, offset, cex, col, font, ...)
```

The text() function allows you a great deal of control over the position and appearance of the text with its various parameters (Table 12.4).

Table 12.4 **Some parameters of the** text() **function.**

Parameter	Description
x, y	The co-ordinates in the plotting area where the text will be placed. If x has a plotting structure, y can be omitted.
labels	The text to be placed, usually a character vector or an expression.
adj	An adjustment to the text position relative to the xy co-ordinates. Values in the range 0–1 are used (but larger values often work). You give one or two values to alter the x and/or y positions. Positive values shift text left/down.
pos	The position of the text relative to the co-ordinates. If specified this overrides adj. Values 1–4 place text: below, left, above, or right of the co-ordinates. The default (pos = NULL) centers text on the co-ordinates.
offset	An offset from the pos value as fractions of a character width (default = 0.5). The offset is in the direction of pos.
cex	The text size, values >1 make text larger.
col	The colour of text.
font	The font format, where 1 = plain, 2 = bold, 3 = italic, 4 = bold + italic.
...	Other parameters are possible.

The argument defaults result in text centered on the co-ordinates. Use pos for a general "shift", along with offset. The adj parameter is best used for small adjustments. A value of adj = c(0.5, 0.5) will result in the text being centered on the co-ordinates. You can shift text to the left/down using larger values, or right/up with smaller values (including negative).

> ### Note: Text outside the plotting region
>
> The text() function will place text at the specified co-ordinates in the plotting region. If any text "spills over" to the margin it will be "clipped". Use xpd = TRUE to allow text to extend over the margins.

The text is usually placed with a standard reading direction but you can use the srt parameter to alter the "string rotation". Give a value in degrees. **Note:** the adj argument shifts the text in the x and y directions relative to the "reading direction".

You can use the font parameter to alter the entire text (e.g. bold, italic), but if you want more complicated formatting (e.g. superscript) you need to use the expression() function to make your text.

12.6.2 Title text

It *is* possible to use title() to place text in the plotting region. To do this you need to use the line parameter. If you use a negative value you can get the text to appear inside the plot instead of the margin.

12.6.3 Marginal text

The mtext() function is mostly used for text "around the edge" of plots. However, you can use the line and padj parameters to shift the text to the inside of the plotting region.

12.6.4 Fancy text and scientific symbols

You can alter the general appearance of text using cex, col and font parameters. However, these affect the entire text. If you want more complicated formatting, such as superscript or scientific symbols, you need to use the expression() function.

An expression object can be used in any function that uses text, such as text(), mtext() and title().

The expression() function is very flexible. You can see many examples by using help(plotmath) in R. Here you'll see a few useful examples (Table 12.5). Try also typing demo(plotmath) in R, for many graphical examples direct in R.

An expression() consists of a string of characters that are evaluated to produce the graphical output when plotted. The miscellaneous characters in Table 12.5 are very important, as they help you construct a complicated expression. In an expression spaces are ignored, and certain other characters or words have special meanings. If you want to use these words/characters you need to put them in quotes. The ~ character is used as a space and the * is a "join", which is allows you to mix elements.

Examples:

Constructing expression() objects.
   Put text in quotes to have it represented "as-is". The * allows you to mix elements.

```
expression("The value of pi, " *pi* ", is roughly " *frac(22, 7))
```

The value of pi, π, is roughly $\dfrac{22}{7}$

   The * symbol is also useful in that it "turns off" superscript.

```
expression(2^3*~is~exactly~8)
```

2^3 is exactly 8.
   Use bold(...) to get **bold** text. The * allows you to place the emboldened text.

```
expression("Infinity, " *infinity* ", is a" *bold(big)* " number")
```

Infinity, ∞, is a **big** number.
   The ~ symbol acts as a space, but not in mathematical statements.

```
expression(The~value~of~ sqrt(2)  == 1.414)
```

The value of $\sqrt{2}$ = 1.414.

Table 12.5 **Some examples of** `expression()` **syntax.**

Syntax	Effect
Typeface	
^	Text following ^ is^{superscript}, e.g. 2^3 2^3.
[]	Text inside [] is$_{subscript}$, e.g. H[2]O H_2O.
plain()	Text in () is plain, e.g. plain(text) text.
italic()	Text in () is *italic*, e.g. italic(text) *text*.
bold()	Text in () is **bold**, e.g bold(text) **text**..
Maths, Symbols and operators	
+	Plus sign +, e.g. a + b a + b.
-	Minus sign -, e.g. a - b a - b.
==	Equals sign =, e,g, x == 44 x = 44.
%/%	Division sign, e.g. 21 %/% 3 21 ÷ 3.
%*%	Multiplication sign, e.g. y %*% z y × z.
%+-%	Plus/Minus sign, e.g. 33 %+- 4 33 ± 4.
%up%	Up arrow ↑.
%down%	Down arrow ↓.
bar()	Over-bar, e.g. bar(x) $\bar{x}$.
frac(x, y)	Fraction, e.g. frac(2, 3) $\frac{2}{3}$.
sqrt(x, y)	Root of x (optional base y), e.g. sqrt(8, 3) $\sqrt[3]{8}$.
sum(x, y, z)	Sigma x (optional y, z range), e.g. sum(x, 1, 100) $\sum_{1}^{100}x$.
infinity	Infinity symbol ∞.
degree	Degree symbol °.
alpha	Greek letter alpha lower case α.
Gamma	Greek latter alpha upper case Γ.
Miscellaneous	
*	A connector.
~	A space.
\n	A newline character.
""	Text in "" is treated as-is.

Example:

Using `expression()` to create "special" text

```
plot(1:8, 1:8, type = "n")
grid()
text(1, 1, pos = 4, expression(x + y))
text(2, 1, pos = 4, expression(x - y))
text(3, 1, pos = 4, expression(x == y))
text(4, 1, pos = 4, expression(x %+-% y))
text(5, 1, pos = 4, expression(x%/%y))
text(1, 2, pos = 4, expression(bar(x)))
text(2, 2, pos = 4, expression(hat(x)))
text(3, 2, pos = 4, expression(180 * degree))
```

```
text(1, 3, pos = 4, expression(frac(x, y)))
text(2, 3, pos = 4, expression(x %up% y))
text(3, 3, pos = 4, expression(x %down% y))
text(1, 4, pos = 4, expression("To" * ~infinity))
text(2, 4, pos = 4, expression(To ~ "infinity" ~ and ~ beyond))
text(1, 5, pos = 4, expression(italic(Italics)))
text(2, 5, pos = 4, expression(bold(Bold)))
text(3, 5, pos = 4, expression(plain(Plain)))
text(1, 6, pos = 4, expression("Greek: " * alpha ~ beta ~ gamma ~
  delta))
text(4, 6, pos = 4, expression("GREEK: " * Alpha ~ Beta ~ Gamma ~
  Delta))
text(1, 7, pos = 4, expression(sqrt(x)))
text(2, 7, pos = 4, expression(sqrt(x, y)))
text(3, 7, pos = 4, expression(sum(x^2)))
text(4, 7, pos = 4, expression(sum(x, 1, 2)))
text(5, 7, pos = 4, expression(sum(x, 0, infinity)))
text(6, 7, pos = 4, expression(bar(x) == sum(frac(x[i], n), i ==
  1, n)))
```

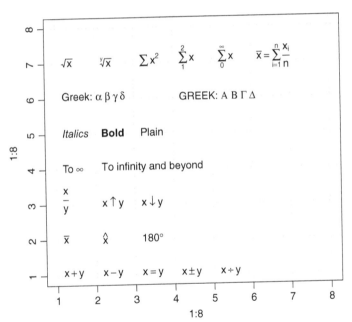

Figure 12.10 Adding expression() text to a plot.

In the preceding example the plot() command was used to make a simple plot-space, whilst the grid() command added gird-lines to help see how the following text matches up to the co-ordinates.

Note: Multiple `expression` statements

An `expression()` can be made up of several parts, separated by commas. If you want to display a comma, place it in "quotes".

An `expression()` can be made with several elements, named or un-named. These elements can be accessed using $, [] or [[]].

```
# expression with 3 named elements
myexp <- expression(a = x + y, b = x %*% y, c = x%/%y)
myexp

expression(a = x + y, b = x %*% y, c = x%/%y)

myexp$a

x + y

myexp[2]

expression(b = x %*% y)

myexp[["c"]]

x%/%y
```

You can name the elements using `name = value` pairs or simply use a comma to separate un-named elements. **Note** that if you use the entire `expression()` each element will be plotted one after the other (thus they'll all occupy the same space).

12.7 Legends

You can add a legend to any graphical window using `legend()`. The `barplot()` command is the only one that allows you to add a legend direct from the plot command; all other plot commands you need to add the legend afterwards.

The `legend()` function has a lot of potential parameters (Table 12.6)! You need to be able to match colours, line style, plotting characters and so on.

```
legend(x, y = NULL, legend, fill = NULL, col, border = "black",
    lty, lwd, pch, bty = "o", bg, box.lwd, box.lty, box.col,
    pt.bg = NA, cex = 1, pt.cex = cex, y.intersp = 1, text.col,
    ncol = 1, title = NULL, ...)
```

The *key* thing is to make sure that your legend matches all the arguments you used in the plotting command.

Example:

Add a legend to an existing plot

```
matplot(t(USPersonalExpenditure),
        type = "b", pch = 19:15, lty = 1:5,
        axes = FALSE, ylab = "Expenditure")
axis(side = 2)
axis(side = 1, at = 1:ncol(USPersonalExpenditure),
        labels = colnames(USPersonalExpenditure))
legend(x = "topleft",
        legend = rownames(USPersonalExpenditure),
        bty = "n",
        pch = 19:15,
```

```
col = 1:5,
lty = 1:5,
cex = 0.8,
title = "Expenditure categories")
```

Table 12.6 Some parameters of the legend() function.

Parameter	Explanation
x, y	Position of the legend. Give x,y coordinates or use x = "location", where "location" is one of: "top", "left", "right", "bottom" or a combination e.g. "topright".
legend	Text for the legend.
fill	Vector of colours to fill boxes in the legend.
col	colours for points or lines appearing in the legend.
border	If fill is specified border gives the colours for the border(s) of the boxes.
lty	Type(s) of lines in the legend, use a number or dotted, dashed, solid.
lwd	Widths of lines in the legend values >1 make lines wider.
pch	Plotting symbols in the legend.
bty	The box type surrounding the legend. Default: bty = "o". Use bty = "n" to suppress a box.
bg	If there is a legend box, this specifies the background colour for the legend.
box.lwd	The width of the legend box.
box.lty	The style of the legend box.
box.col	The colour of the legend box.
pt.bg	Background (fill) colour for points in the legend.
cex	Expansion factor for text.
pt.cex	Expansion factor for points in the legend.
y.intersp	Sets the vertical spacing of legend lines, values >1 space out more.
text.col	colour for text in the legend.
ncol	The number of columns the legend should occupy (default ncol =1).
title	A text title to appear above the legend.
...	Other parameters may be used!

In the preceding example the matplot() command was used to draw lines of different styles and colours, with different plotting symbols too. The legend() command needs to match all the arguments.

If you are using barplot() with the parameter: legend = TRUE you can pass additional parameters to the legend() command with: args.legend = list() and use name = value pairs in the list.

Example:

Pass additional legend parameters from a barplot() command

```
VADeaths

        Rural Male  Rural Female  Urban Male  Urban Female
50-54        11.7           8.7        15.4           8.4
55-59        18.1          11.7        24.3          13.6
60-64        26.9          20.3        37.0          19.3
65-69        41.0          30.9        54.6          35.1
70-74        66.0          54.3        71.1          50.0
```

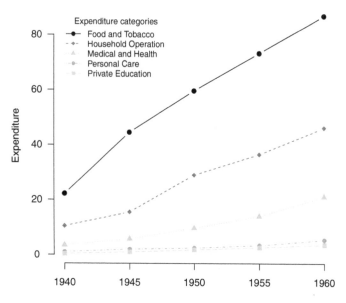

Figure 12.11 When adding a legend you need to match all the parameters used in the plotting command.

```
barplot(VADeaths, beside = TRUE,
                  las = 1,
                  ylim = c(0, 80),
                  legend = TRUE,
                  col = 1:5,
                  args.legend = list(bty = "n",
                                     x = "top",
                                     ncol = 2)
       )
```

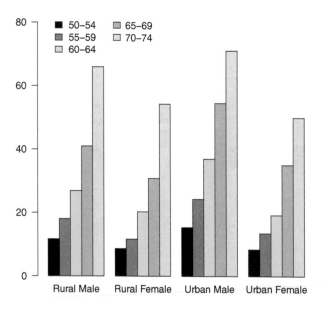

Figure 12.12 You can add a legend to a barplot but need to use args.legend to pass parameters to the legend.

In the preceding example the legend was added directly from within the barplot(). Arguments passed to the legend() function are via the args.legend parameter and then given as a list.

Tip: Legend placement

The x and y coordinates can be used to place the legend. You need to choose the position for the top-left point of the legend box. If you use locator(1) you can click a point in a graphic window and the x-y coordinates are returned to screen.

You can also use ylim as a parameter in the plotting command to give a bit more room for the legend.

It is possible to place the legend in the marginal area (Figure 12.13), but this needs a bit of tweaking of the graphical parameters.

Example:

Legend in the plot margin

```
# Set outer margins
opar <- par(oma = c(0,0,0,4)) # Large right margin for plot
barplot(VADeaths, beside = TRUE, col = terrain.colours(5))
par(opar) # Reset par

# Now reset the margins for the legend
opar <- par(oma = c(0,0,0,0),
            mar = c(0,0,0,0),
            new = TRUE)
legend(x = "right",
       legend = rownames(VADeaths),
       fill = terrain.colours(5),
       bty = "n",
       y.intersp = 2)
par(opar) # Reset par
```

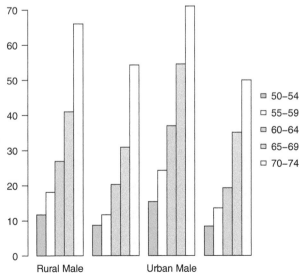

Figure 12.13 Placing a legend in the margin requires some manipulation of the graphical parameters.

In the preceding example the first `par()` command sets the outer margin sizes; you need to give room for the legend. After the main plot has been produced you need to reset the graphical parameters (the `par(opar)` part) and then alter the margins once more. You need to set the outer and plot margins all to 0. After the legend is drawn you need to reset the graphical parameters once again (just to be tidy).

12.8   Custom axes

When you execute a plotting command in R it will generate the axes automatically. However, there are occasions when you want/need to over-ride the default axes and produce your own. The `axis()` function allows you to construct and add custom axes to an existing graphical window.

```
axis(side, at, labels, tick, line, lty, lwd, lwd.ticks, col,
    col.ticks, ...)
```

There are various parameters you can use to alter the position and appearance of your customized axis (Table 12.7).

Table 12.7 **Some parameters of the** `axis()` **command.**

Parameter	Description
side	The side to place the axis, where `side` = 1 is the bottom, 2 = left, 3 = top and 4 = right.
at	Positions for the tick-marks along the axis. Usually a `numeric vector`. The default `NULL` takes the positions as computed by the graphical command you used to draw the plot.
labels	The labels to add to the axis.
tick	The default `TRUE` adds an axis line and tick-marks.
line	Which line to add the axis to in the margin, the default is `NA`. Positive values move the axis outwards, negative values move it inwards.
lty	Line type for axis line *and* tick-marks.
lwd	The width of the axis line. Use `lwd.ticks` to affect the ticks. Use 0 to suppress the line or ticks.
col	The colour of the axis line. Use `col.ticks` to affect the ticks.
...	Other parameters are available.

Most plotting functions will allow you to suppress the in-built axes, using the argument `axes = FALSE`. Once you have your plot without any default axes, you can build your own using `axis()`. If you want to place an axis using the default values just give the `side` argument, the `axis()` function will then fill in the rest using the defaults.

When you have a `boxplot` the positions of the box-whiskers are easily determined, as they are simple `integer` values. The first box-whisker is at position 1, the 2nd at 2 and so on (Figure 12.14).

Example:

Add custom axis to a `boxplot()`

```
# Draw plot but suppress axes (and titles)
boxplot(breaks ~ wool + tension, data = warpbreaks,
    ylab = "", xlab = "",
    axes = FALSE, col = c("skyblue", "pink"))
```

```
# Bottom axis for tension with ticks
axis(side = 1, line = 0, at = seq(1.5,5.5,2),
     labels = c("L","M","H"), tick = TRUE)

# Bottom axis for wool type
axis(side = 1, line = 1, at = 1:6,
     labels = rep(c("A","B"),3), tick = FALSE)

# Default y-axis but rotate annotations
axis(side = 2, las = 1)

# Frame the plot
box(bty = "L")

# Add titles
title(xlab = "Tension and Wool Type", line = 3.5)
title(ylab = "No. Breaks")
```

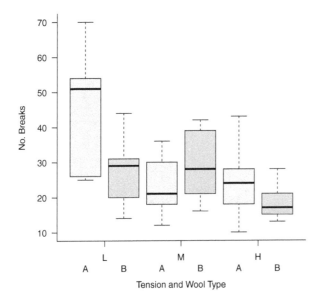

Custom axis added to a boxplot.

In the preceding example the first axis() command makes the axis at line = 0 and adds tick marks for the Tension variable. The 2nd axis() command is placed slightly further outwards and without ticks. The 3rd axis() makes the default y-axis but las was added to rotate the annotations. The box() command adds a frame (see next section). Note that the xlab title was placed so as not to overlap the axis.

Tip: Suppress a single axis

Use the parameters xaxt = "n", or yaxt = "n" to suppress a single axis. These parameters are general and should work for most R plotting functions.

If you have a barplot it is slightly more difficult to determine the positions of the bars, as they are not placed at integer "distances". What you must do is to assign your barplot to a named object. This will result in your plot and the named object, which is a matrix (or numeric vector) holding the positions of the centres of the bars (or bar stacks) along the axis (Figure 12.15).

Example:

Add custom axis to a `barplot()`

```r
# Numeric vector of data
temp <- (nottem[1:12] -32) *5/9

# Make plot and assign to object
bp <- barplot(temp, col = "steelblue1", axes = FALSE)

# Object holds bar axis positions
as.numeric(bp)

[1] 0.7 1.9 3.1 4.3 5.5 6.7 7.9 9.1 10.3 11.5 12.7 13.9

# Add month labels close to plot without ticks
axis(side = 1, line = -1, at = bp[1:12],
     labels = month.abb, cex.axis = 0.7, tick = FALSE)

# Add "quarter" labels further out, with tick but no line
axis(side = 1, line = 1.5, at = bp[1:4*3-1],
     labels = paste0("Q", 1:4), cex.axis = 0.7, tick = TRUE,
     lwd = 0, lwd.tick = 1)

# Default y-axis but rotate annotations
axis(2, las = 1)

# Frame the plot
box(bty = "L")

# Add axis titles
title(ylab = "Mean monthly temperature (C)")
title(xlab = "Month and Quarter", line = 3.5)
```

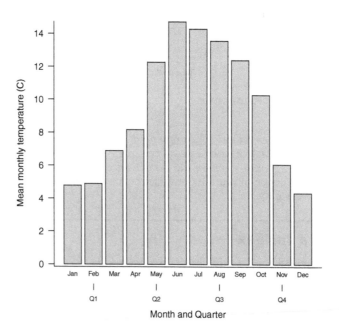

Figure 12.15 Custom axis added to a barplot.

In the preceding example you can see that the bp object holds the bar positions. For the month names we use these 12 values (bp[1:12]) in the axis() command. The "quarter" labels need a bit of work to get the positioning, which is done via bp[1:4 * 3 - 1] in the 2nd axis() command. Here too the tick marks are shown but the line is suppressed.

Tip: Nice breakpoints using "pretty" positioning

The pretty() command can split a numeric vector into "pretty" intervals.

It can take a little bit of fiddling around to get the "perfect" axis!

12.9 Framing plots

You can add a bounding box around a graphic using the box() function.

```
box(which = "plot", lty = "solid", ...)
```

The box() command is useful for those occasions when your axes "don't join up" and when you want to present a neater result. There are various arguments you can add to the command to alter the framing (Table 12.8).

Table 12.8 Some parameters of the box() function.

Parameter	Description
which	A character giving the region you wish to frame. The default is "plot", other options are "figure", "inner", and "outer".
lty	The line type for the frame (default = "solid").
...	Other graphical parameters such as col and bty.

The bty parameter controls the "type" of box used in the framing. You use a character that "resembles" the shape you require: "L", "U", "C", "7", "]", and the default "O". Use bty = "n" to suppress the box. Note that this means you cannot have a frame that is a "single line".

EXERCISES:

Self-Assessment for Graphics – Adding to plots

1. You can add lines to an existing plot window using points().. TRUE or FALSE?
2. You need to use the abline() command to draw best-fit lines.. TRUE or FALSE?
3. You can use the ____ function to add text in the plot margin areas. Justify text using the ____ argument.
4. Suppress axes using ____ argument from most graphical functions. Alternatively you can suppress a single axis with ____ or ____ arguments.
5. Which of the following is/are used to add "special" text to plots?
   a. italic()
   b. sqrt()
   c. mean()
   d. expression()

Answers to exercises are in the *Appendix*.

12.10　Chapter Summary: Graphics – adding to plots

Topic	Key Points
Add points	Use `points()` to add points to a plot window.
Add lines	Use `lines()` to add lines to a plot window.
Grid lines	Use `abline()` with arguments h or v to add horizontal or vertical lines. Use `grid()` to add a grid (both horizontal and vertical lines).
Best-fit lines	Use `abline()` to add a best-fit line using a and b arguments (intercept and slope). Alternatively, the function can "read" the values from certain objects (e.g. regression results). Use `lowess()` to add scatter-plot smoothers using a locally weighted polynomial fit, which means you do not need to run a regression separately.
Error bars	Use `segments()` to add error bars (vertical or horizontal). You can also use `arrows()`, which allows you to more easily add end-caps.
Titles	Use `title()` to add various titles (e.g. `xlab`, `ylab`). Use `mtext()` to add marginal titles based on one of the four sides. Arguments `adj` and `line` allow you to alter the positioning.
Add text	Use `text()` to add general text to co-ordinates in a plot window. The `expression()` function allows you to use "fancy" text (e.g. superscript, italic) and symbols (e.g. Greek letters).
Legends	Use `legend()` to add a legend to any plot window. There are many arguments, which allow you to match elements of the original plot.
Custom axes	Use `axis()` to draw a custom axis on any `side`. You can suppress axes in regular plots with `axes = FALSE`, or just one axis with `xaxt` (or `yaxt = "n"`).

13. Graphics: advanced methods

The graphical capabilities of R are extensive. In previous chapters you have seen examples of various "basic" charts, and methods for adding various useful elements (e.g. axis titles, error bars, legends). In this chapter you'll see various "advanced" graphical topics, things that simply don't fit neatly into the "basic" category.

What's in this chapter

» Working with colour
» Tweaking the graphical system
» Split plot windows
» Exporting graphics to disk
» Time-series plots
» Multivariate plots:
  » scatter plot matrix
  » interaction plots
  » conditional plots
  » matrix plots
  » multivariate time series

Note: Support material

See the ⟍ for links to material on the support website.

13.1   Working with colour

Colour is a very important aspect of visually presenting data and results. There are various ways you can use and manipulate colours in R.

In the main, R refers to colours by "name". You can see all the standard built-in colours by using the `colours()` command. This will show you the names of all 657 colours generally available. These are all `character` names, and you can use these names in graphics, usually via the `col` argument. You can specify several colours if necessary by using the `c()` function to create a `character vector`.

> ## Tip: Colour names
>
> You can view colour names that contain a particular "colour" by utilizing the grep function.
>
> ```
> colours()[grep(pattern = "red", colours())]
> ```
>
> ```
>  [1] "darkred"          "indianred"        "indianred1"       "indianred2"
>  [5] "indianred3"       "indianred4"       "mediumvioletred"  "orangered"
>  [9] "orangered1"       "orangered2"       "orangered3"       "orangered4"
> [13] "palevioletred"    "palevioletred1"   "palevioletred2"   "palevioletred3"
> [17] "palevioletred4"   "red"              "red1"             "red2"
> [21] "red3"             "red4"             "violetred"        "violetred1"
> [25] "violetred2"       "violetred3"       "violetred4"
> ```
>
> Try typing demo("colours") for a good look at the range of colours.

You can type a colour directly as a hex code by specifying the name of the colour as "#rrggb-baa", where rr, gg, bb, aa are the hex code (2 digits) for red, green, blue and alpha (note: alpha is optional). For example:

```
boxplot(attitude, col = "#0b41dc40")
```

Each named colour has rgb values, which you can extract via the col2rgb() command:

```
col2rgb("indianred")
```

```
       [,1]
red     205
green    92
blue     92
```

Note that the result of rgb() comes out as integer values in the range 0–255.

13.1.1   Custom colours

You can make "custom" colours using the rgb() function:

```
rgb(red, green, blue, alpha, names = NULL, maxColourValue = 1)
```

In rgb() you specify the values for the components and end up with your own colour (Table 13.1).

Table 13.1 Parameters of the rgb() function.

Parameter	Description
red	A numeric integer value for the red component.
green	Value for green.
blue	Value for blue.
alpha	Value for transparency (low values are more transparent).
names	You can give names to your custom colour(s).
maxColourValue	The maximum value for the red, green, blue and alpha values.

The main values are scaled by maxColourValue, and you will get an error if any single value is higher than this. Note that the col2rgb() function returns values with a maximum of 255.

You may provide the values as a matrix or data.frame, in which case the columns are regarded as: red, green, and blue. Other columns are ignored, and you must specify alpha separately.

Example:

Custom colours from a matrix using rgb()

```
mcol <- matrix(c(12, 11, 45, 62, 65, 100, 200, 220, 230), ncol = 3)
mcol

      [,1]   [,2]   [,3]
[1,]    12     62    200
[2,]    11     65    220
[3,]    45    100    230

rgb(mcol, max = 255, names = c("Mcol_1", "Mcol_2", "Mcol_3"))

   Mcol_1      Mcol_2       Mcol_3
"#0C3EC8"   "#0B41DC"    "#2D64E6"
```

Tip: Hex code colours

You can get named colour values directly in hex using the following "trick":

```
paste("#", paste0(as.hexmode(col2rgb("cornsilk")), collapse = ""),
      sep = "", collapse = "")

[1]  "#fff8dc"
```

13.1.2   Colour gradient

If you need multiple colours, you can create a character vector of names to use. Alternatively you can create a gradient, where the starting and ending colours are specified by you, with the intermediates interpolated by R.

Use colourRampPalette() for this:

```
colourRampPalette(colours,  ...)
```

In the function you specify at least two colours; these will form the end-points for your final gradient. You can specify additional intermediate colours as part of the gradient. There are additional parameters you might include but colours is generally sufficient.

You can specify the colours in several ways, such as by name, #RGB, or the rgb() function.

The colourRampPalette() command returns a function, which will "make" a gradient when called. You simply specify how many colours you want and the vector of colours will include the specific colours you specified, with intermediate values between them.

Example:

Colour Gradient with colourRampPalette()

```
# Colour gradient function
pal <- colourRampPalette(colours = c("cornsilk", "darkgreen"))

# Make gradient with six colours
pal(6)


[1] "#FFF8DC" "#CCDAB0" "#99BC83" "#659F58" "#32812B" "#006400"
```

The colourRampPalette() function is useful for generating simple colour gradients. There are other ways to produce gradient colours, such as hsv() and hcl(), check out their help entries in R for more details.

13.1.3 Colour palette

Named colours are the general way you specify what you need when making graphics. However, it can be helpful to specify colours by number, rather than a character. The palette() command allows you to specify a "default" set of colours, which will be used whenever a graphical output is required.

The default palette can be viewed like so:

```
# Re-set palette to default
palette("default")

# View current palette
palette()
[1] "black"   "#DF536B" "#61D04F" "#2297E6" "#28E2E5" "#CD0BBC" "#F5C710"
[8] "gray62"
```

These 8 colours form the default palette and thus if you were to specify col = 6 in a graphical command, the result would be "magenta".

You can set the palette to any vector of colours, and then simply refer to the colours you want by their position in the palette.

There are various in-built colour palettes, which you can access:

- rainbow
- heat.colours
- terrain.colours
- topo.colours
- cm.colours

In general you specify n, being the number of colours you with to return. There are additional parameters for some of these functions, see the help entry for any of these for more information.

> ### Note: gray() colour palette
>
> There is also a gray palette. The values for this are specified differently from the the other palette functions. You need to give a numeric vector of values between 0 and 1, where 0 is "black" and 1 is "white".
>
> ```
> gray(0:10/10)
>
>
> [1] "#000000" "#1A1A1A" "#333333" "#4D4D4D" "#666666" "#808080" "#999999"
> [8] "#B3B3B3" "#CCCCCC" "#E6E6E6" "#FFFFFF"
> ```

You can use the built-in colour palettes or specify your own values. In any event, the colours you specify will end up on the palette. You can always return to the default with: palette("default").

> **Tip: Colour wheel**
>
> You can view a colour palette (or any set of colours you define) using a pie chart, via the pie() command (Figure 13.1).
>
> ```
> pal <- topo.colours(8)
> pie(x = rep(1, length(pal)),
>     col = pal,
>     labels = as.character(pal))
> ```
>
>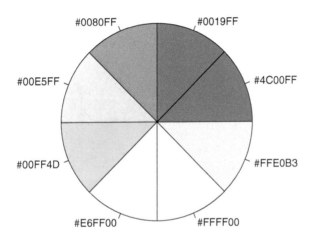
>
> Figure 13.1 A pie chart used for a colour wheel.
>
> Note that the vector of colours does not have a name attribute so you need to use as. character for the labels in the pie function.

13.2 Tweaking the graphical system

There are various way to tinker with the graphical system in R. Most of the time you simply alter appropriate parameters in the graphical command you are using. Other times you may need to change a "setting" before making a new plot. The command par() is a general function that allows you to change many graphical settings.

In general you use par() to:

- Query one or more current settings.
- Alter one or more settings to new value(s).

To view one or more settings you give the name (in quotes) of the settings you wish to view. If you omit any names you'll get all the settings.

```
# The graphical parameter names
names(par())
```

```
 [1] "xlog"      "ylog"       "adj"       "ann"       "ask"       "bg"
 [7] "bty"       "cex"        "cex.axis"  "cex.lab"   "cex.main"  "cex.sub"
[13] "cin"       "col"        "col.axis"  "col.lab"   "col.main"  "col.sub"
[19] "cra"       "crt"        "csi"       "cxy"       "din"       "err"
[25] "family"    "fg"         "fig"       "fin"       "font"      "font.axis"
[31] "font.lab"  "font.main"  "font.sub"  "lab"       "las"       "lend"
[37] "lheight"   "ljoin"      "lmitre"    "lty"       "lwd"       "mai"
[43] "mar"       "mex"        "mfcol"     "mfg"       "mfrow"     "mgp"
[49] "mkh"       "new"        "oma"       "omd"       "omi"       "page"
[55] "pch"       "pin"        "plt"       "ps"        "pty"       "smo"
[61] "srt"       "tck"        "tcl"       "usr"       "xaxp"      "xaxs"
[67] "xaxt"      "xpd"        "yaxp"      "yaxs"      "yaxt"      "ylbias"
```

```
# Get current margin sizes
par("mar")
```

```
[1] 5.1 4.1 4.1 2.1
```

```
# View two settings
par("mar", "bg")
```

```
$mar
[1] 5.1 4.1 4.1 2.1
```

```
$bg
[1] "white"
```

To alter one or more settings you call par and give the settings as name = value pairs.

```
# Alter margin and plot background
par(mar = c(1, 1, 1, 1), bg = "gray80")
```

```
# See the new values
par("mar", "bg")
```

The new settings remain in force until you change them, close the graphical window, or reset them.

Note: Commonly used graphical parameters

See (Table 11-11) for a list of common graphical parameters.

13.2.1 Reset graphical parameters

The simplest way to restore graphical parameters to their default values is to close all graphical windows. You can also "save" the current parameter settings, and use them to restore later.

```
# Get current margin sizes
par("mar")
```

```
[1] 5.1 4.1 4.1 2.1
```

```
# Set new values
opar <- par(mar = c(0.1, 0.1, 0.1, 0.1))
par("mar")
```

```
[1] 0.1 0.1 0.1 0.1
```

```
# Reset to original values
par(opar)
par("mar")
```

```
[1] 5.1 4.1 4.1 2.1
```

When you save one or more graphical parameters to a named object the result is not what you expect. The named object holds the *original* parameter(s). If you aren't sure that you've reset parameters properly you can always close all the plot windows!

Use help(par) to bring up the help entry for par, this has comprehensive details about all the graphical parameters.

13.3 Split plot windows

In most cases you'll want a plot to be in a window of its own, but occasionally you might need to have several plots in one graphical window. This means you will have to split the plot window into multiple sections. There are 3 main ways to do this is base R:

- Use par(mfrow = c(row, col)) or par(mfcol = c(row, col)).
- Use split.screen().
- Use layout().

These three methods are *incompatible* with one another. The first is the simplest, and the last is the most "complicated".

13.3.1 Split screen with par()

You can use the graphical parameters mfrow or mfcol to split the graphics window into equal portions.

```
par(mfrow = c(rows, cols))
par(mfcol = c(rows, cols))
```

Note that you always specify the number of rows and columns (in that order) you require. The difference between the two is that with mfrow the plots are "filled in" row by row, whilst for mfcol they are drawn column by column.

Tip: Skip a plot panel section

If your plot window is split with mfrow or mfcol each plotting function is drawn into the "next" panel. You can use plot.new() to skip a panel.

When you run the par() command a new graphical window will be opened if none are already in place, otherwise the parameters are applied to the currently active graphic window. When you "turn off" the window the parameter(s) are reset.

Note: Panel recycling

Each plotting command will draw into a new panel. When all panels are "full" the next plotting command will start at the beginning *but* this will also wipe the existing drawings. So, it is important to complete a plot with additional text, legend and so on, before moving to the next.

13.3.2   Split screen with `split.screen()`

The `split.screen()` command allows you to split a graphical window. Unlike `par()` you can subdivide each section. There are several related functions:

- `split.screen()` splits a window (or previously created panel) into rows/columns.
- `screen()` selects a partition/panel as "active" (or tells you which is).
- `erase.screen()` "paints" the background colour over a partition/panel.
- `close.screen()` closes one or more partition/panels *or* returns a `vector` of available screens.

The `split.screen()` function starts the splitting process, the other functions are only "available" once you are in split-screen mode, and return `FALSE` if you try to call them when the screen is not split (Table 13.2).

```
split.screen(figs = c(rows, cols), screen, erase = TRUE)
screen(n = , new = TRUE)
erase.screen(n)
close.screen(n = , all.screens = FALSE)
```

Table 13.2 Functions and parameters for `split.screen()`.

Parameter	Description
figs	The number of rows and columns required as a two-element `vector`.
screen	Which screen to split. If the screen is already split this defaults to the current (active) portion, otherwise the default is the entire plot window.
erase	If `TRUE` (the default) the selected screen is cleared.
n	The screen "number" to be used, `close.screen` will accept a `vector` of values. If omitted you get the "active" screen (with `screen`), or a `vector` of available partitions (with `close.screen`), or nothing happens (with `erase.screen`).
new	If `TRUE` (the default) the selected screen is cleared/erased.
all.screens	If `TRUE` this closes all screens, effectively closing split-screen mode.

> **Tip: Erasing a screen**
>
> When you use `erase.screen()` on a panel/partition the background colour is drawn over the plot. Your system might be set to `bg = "transparent"`, in which case nothing will apparently happen!
>   You may need to use `par(bg = "white")` to get the default background to match.

The `split.screen()` function is useful in that you can select directly which partition to plot into.

13.3.3   Split screen with `layout()`

The `layout()` function lets you split a graphical window into multiple sections using a `matrix` as a kind of map.

- `layout()` splits the graphical window into portions using a `matrix` as a map.
- `layout.show()` shows (in the graphical window) the layout.
- `lcm()` a helper function that allows explicit partition sizing in centimeters.

The layout() command has various parameters (Table 13.3) and a couple of related functions:

```
layout(mat, widths, heights, respect)
layout.show(n)
lcm(x)
```

The layout() function is useful as it allows you to visualize how your plot window is partitioned.

Table 13.3 Functions and parameters for layout().

Parameter	Description
mat	A matrix whose rows and columns show which plots are associated with each section. The matrix thus acts like a map.
widths	The widths of the columns as a vector. These are relative to the heights. You can use lcm() to give absolute values in centimeters.
heights	The heights of the rows.
respect	if TRUE the relationship between widths and heights is maintained.
n	The number of figures to "show" (default is all).
x	A numerical value in centimeters.

13.4   Managing graphics windows

When you first run a graphical command a new plot window is opened, and the results go into that window. Your system will be setup to open graphical windows with certain dimensions. You can use a variety of functions to open and manage graphical windows. In this way you can have plot windows of various sizes and send graphical commands to any of the windows you want.

To open a "blank" plot window you can use one of the following, according to your operating system:

- windows() opens a graphic window on Windows machines.
- quartz() for Macintosh machines.
- x11() for Linux and machines with X Window server.

```
windows(title, width, height, bg, canvas, family, ...)
```

These functions allow you to open a graphic window and set various parameters (Table 13.4).

Table 13.4 Some parameters for graphics windows functions.

Parameter	Description
title	A title for the graphics window as a "character". This is only used as a label for the window itself.
width	The window width in inches (a common default is 7).
height	Window height in inches.
bg	Background colour for the window (default is usually "transparent").
canvas	The canvas colour to use when bg = "transparent" (default = "white").
family	The font family to use (default = "Arial"). In practice it is easier/better to use par(family = "") to set the plotting font family.
...	Other parameters are possible.

In practice you'll mainly want to open a graphical window with specific dimensions, so the width and height parameters are the most likely to be used.

There are various functions that allow you to manage the open graphics windows (Table 13.5):

Table 13.5 Functions for managing graphics windows.

Function	Description
dev.list()	returns a vector showing the open graphics devices.
dev.cur()	shows the current (active) device window.
dev.off(which)	closes a device window.
dev.set(which)	selects a particular graphics device to be current (active).
dev.next(which)	shows which is the next graphic device (window).
dev.prev()	shows which is the previous graphics device.
dev.new(...)	creates a new graphics window.
graphics.off()	closes all graphics windows.

The which parameter selects the device, the default is dev.cur(). For dev.new() you can use parameters such as height and width.

NOTE: the graphics device number 1 is always reserved for NULL. In practice this means your device "numbers" start from 2.

```
# Shut down all existing graphics device windows
graphics.off()
x11(width = 6, height = 4)
x11(width = 4, height = 2)

dev.list()

X11 X11
  2   3

dev.cur()

X11
  3

dev.set(which = dev.prev())

X11
  2

graphics.off()
```

Note: Graphics windows in RStudio

If you use the RStudio IDE to "run" R then the dev... functions will work with the exception of dev.new(), which may report NULL unless you use the argument noRStudioGD = TRUE. Setting this argument to TRUE also allows you to pass parameters to the device window. The device will use your system default. In practice it is probably best to use an explicit windows(), quartz() or x11() command whenever possible.

13.5 Exporting graphics to disk

Usually you'll send your graphical commands to plot windows on screen. If you want to create graphics on disk (e.g. png, jpeg) you need to use a special device type. In brief, you open a device of the type you want, send the graphical commands (which go to the disk file), close the device (which writes the graphical file to disk).

There are several basic types:

```
bmp(filename, width, height, units, bg, res, ...)
png(filename, width, height, units, bg, res, ...)
jpeg(filename, width, height, units, quality, bg, res, ...)
tiff(filename, width, height, units, compression, bg, res, ...)
pdf(filename, width, height, onefile, family, title, bg, colourmodel,
    ...)
```

There are various parameters you might pass to the graphics devices (Table 13.6):

Table 13.6 **Some parameters for on-disk graphics devices.**

Parameter	Description
filename	A filename (in "quotes"). File names are relative to the current working directory, folder separators are *always* /. If omitted, a "sensible" default is used.
width	The plot window width (default 480 for all except pdf, which is 7).
height	The plot height (default 480 for all except 1, which is 7).
units	The units for width and height; "in", "cm", "mm", or "px" (the default for all non-pdf). Not applicable for pdf.
bg	The plot background colour.
res	The ppi resolution.
quality	The quality of jpeg image as a percentage (default = 75). Smaller values give more compression and smaller file size.
compression	Type of compression to use for tiff; "none" (the default), "rle", "lzw", "jpeg", "zip", "lzw+p", "zip+p".
onefile	If TRUE (the default), then multiple graphics will be stored on a single file. If FALSE multiple files have a number appended.
family	The font family to use (default = "Helvetica").
title	A title embedded in the pdf metadata.
colourmodel	Colour to be used; "srgb" (the default), "gray" or "cmyk".
...	Other parameters can be used.

The general running order is:

1. Open a device type with the parameters you want, and enter a filename as the target on disk.
2. Issue graphical commands, which will be sent directly to the target file.
3. Add extra graphical commands as required.
4. Close the device (with dev.off(), which "writes" the graphic file on disk.

As long as the graphical device is "open" and current, any graphical commands will be sent to the target disk file. The file is "finalized" by using dev.off() on the device.

> ### Note: GUI and graphics export
>
> If you run R through a GUI or IDE (such as RStudio) you'll have options to save a graphic plot window directly to disk.

13.5.1   Copy an on-screen graphic to disk

You may have a situation where you've created a graphic to an on-screen plot window and you want to save this to disk. There are three main options, depending on how you are running R:

- Copy the plot window to the clipboard.
- Use the GUI to save the plot to disk.
- Use `dev.print()` and "copy" the on-screen plot window to a disk-based device.

You can copy a graphic window to the clipboard. The clipboard can be pasted to many targets, such as a word processor, presentation software, or a graphics program. This may be sufficient for many needs but you have less control over things like resolution.

If you use a GUI or IDE (e.g. RStudio), you will be able to use this to save graphics windows. You will still be limited to some extent but the process is generally easy.

Using `dev.print()` gives you the greatest control over the final graphic. The process is:

1. Make sure the current device is the one you want to copy (use dev.set() if needed.
2. Use dev.print(device = , ...) which sends to device and closes it.

Example:

Use `dev.print()` to send on-screen graphics to disk

```
# Plot opens on-screen
boxplot(attitude, col = "tan", las = 2)

# Send on-screen plot to PNG file at 150 dpi
dev.print(device = png, width = 6 * 150, height = 4 * 150, res = 150,
    filename = "boxplot.png")
```

13.6   Time series

Data that have a time element can be stored as time-series objects (see section 8.7). There are two main kinds of time series: those with class `ts` have a single data series, whilst `mts` objects are multiple time series.

The classes `ts` and `mts` have their own plotting method (Table 13.7):

```
plot.ts(x, y, plot.type, xy.labels, xy.lines, yax.flip, nc, mar.multi,
    ...)
```

The function allows you to draw three main kinds of plot:

- a line chart of a single series;
- multiple line charts (one for each series in a multivariate dataset);
- a scatter plot of two time series (where you give both x and y).

Table 13.7 Some parameters for the `plot.ts()` function.

Parameter	Description
x	A time-series object `ts` or `mts`.
y	An optional time series. If x and y are both given they must both be univariate (`ts`), in which case a scatter plot is drawn.
plot.type	For multivariate objects (`mts`) specify `"multiple"` to have each series drawn in a separate panel, or `"single"` to plot all series in one window.
xy.labels	If x and y are plotted (as a scatter plot) you can specify explicit labels for the data points.
xy.lines	If x and y are plotted (as a scatter plot), you can specify `FALSE` to suppress joining lines.
yax.flip	Specify `TRUE` to flip y-axis annotations left and right on alternate plots. This can help readability when `plot.type = multiple"`.
nc	The number of columns for multivariate plots.
mar.multi	Margin sizes (as a `numeric vector`) for the 4 margins of each panel in a multivariate plot.
...	Other parameters may be used.

Note: Plot function name

You do not need to type `plot.ts` to "run" the `ts` plotting function. Simply using `plot(x)` will work as long as your data are a time series. When you type `plot`, R will check the `class` of your data and find the appropriate `plot.xxx` function (where `xxx` matches the `class` of your data).

13.6.1 Single time series

Use `plot()` to visualize a single time-series (`ts`) object.

Example:

A single time series as a line plot

```
class(AirPassengers)

[1] "ts"

plot(AirPassengers, las = 1, lwd = 2, ylab = "Monthly totals (1000s)")
```

In the example (Figure 13.2), the main data are `AirPassengers`. The other arguments are basic graphical parameters (see Table 11-11 for a reminder summary).

13.6.2 Multivariate time series

A multivariate time series contains several data items. The `class mts` is a kind of matrix where each column is a time series, and each row shares a time period.

When you have a `mts` you have various options for visualizing the data:

- draw all the series in one window.
- draw the series in separate panels.

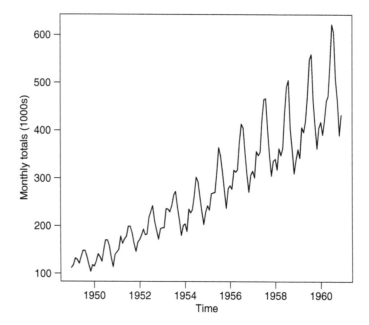

Figure 13.2 Time-series plot.

Example:

Plot multiple time series in a single window

```
ld <- cbind(mdeaths, fdeaths)
class(ld)

[1] "mts"  "ts"   "matrix"

plot(ld, plot.type = "single", col = 1:2, lty = 1:2, type = "b",
     pch = 16, cex = 0.6, lwd = 1.5, ylab = "Monthly Deaths")

# Add legend
legend(x = "topright", legend = c("Male", "Female"), col = 1:2,
     lty = 1:2, pch = 16, bty = "n")
```

In the example for the single window plot (Figure 13.3) a `legend` was added to differentiate the traces. This is not needed when you use a "multi" plot, as each panel has its own axis label (Figure 13.4).

Example:

Plot multiple time series in separate panels

```
plot(ld, plot.type = "multiple", col = "darkblue", lwd = 1.5,
     yax.flip = TRUE, main = "Lung Deaths")
```

In the example of a multi-panel time-series plot (Figure 13.4), the `yax.flip` parameter was set to TRUE so that the y-axis labels alternated sides.

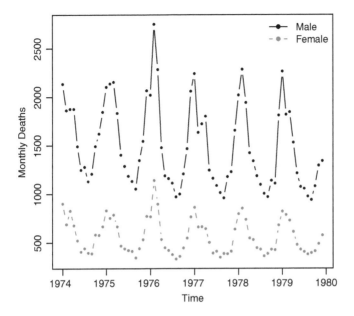

Figure 13.3 Multivariate time series plotted in one window.

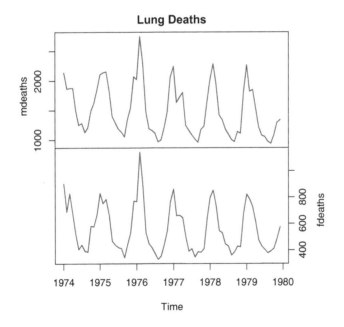

Figure 13.4 Multivariate time series plotted in separate panels.

Tip: Y-axis names with multivariate time series

The `plot.ts()` function takes the names for the y-axes from the column names in your `mts` object. The `ylab` parameter will *not* override these names. The easiest way to use "custom" axis labels is to alter the column names (e.g. with the `colnames()` function).

13.7   Scatter plot matrix

A scatter plot matrix is an example of a *multivariate plot*. Such plots are sometimes called pairs plots, because they visualize pairs of numeric variables in multiple panels, with each panel showing a particular pair of variables. A pairs plot can be very useful in data exploration, to give an overview of multiple relationships in your data.

To make a scatter plot matrix, you use the `pairs()` function to plot several variables in a matrix that shows bi-variate scatter plots of all combinations of variables.

```
pairs(x, labels, panel = points, upper.panel = panel, lower
      .panel = panel,
          cex.labels = NULL, ...)
```

The `pairs()` function has various parameters, which allow you to determine the data and how they are displayed (Table 13.8).

Table 13.8 **Some parameters of the `pairs()` command.**

Parameter	Explanation
x	The data to plot. If x is a data.frame or matrix then the columns are treated as the samples to plot. Alternatively use a formula of the form: ~ a + b + c where items following ~ are variables.
labels	Optional labels for the variables. The default uses the colnames of the data.
panel	Optional function to plot the panels.
upper.panel	Optional function to plot the upper triangle of plots.
lower.panel	Optional function to plot the lower triangle of plots.
cex.labels	Size of text labels, <1 makes labels smaller.
...	Other graphical parameters can be used.

The default is to plot a basic scatter plot of all the variables described in x, which may result in many (small) panels being displayed. You can use a formula, or square brackets [] to choose which variables are presented.

Example:

A basic `pairs()` plot using a selection of variables from the dataset

```
pairs(~Ozone + Solar.R + Wind + Temp, data = airquality)
```

The preceding graph used a formula to select the variables for display. However, you can also use the square brackets to give the index position of the variables like so:

```
pairs(airquality[1:4])
```

This can be quicker/easier to type, especially if you have many variables.

An important feature of `pairs()` plots are the `panel` parameters. These allow you to create your own functions that will be plotted. This gives great flexibility, and allows you to create customized plots. Once you have created customized panel functions, they can be used over and over again on different datasets.

The base version of R comes with one built-in panel function, `panel.smooth`, which adds a locally weighted scatter plot smoother to a scatter plot. You can add the `panel.smooth` to the upper or lower "triangles", or both (using the `panel` parameter).

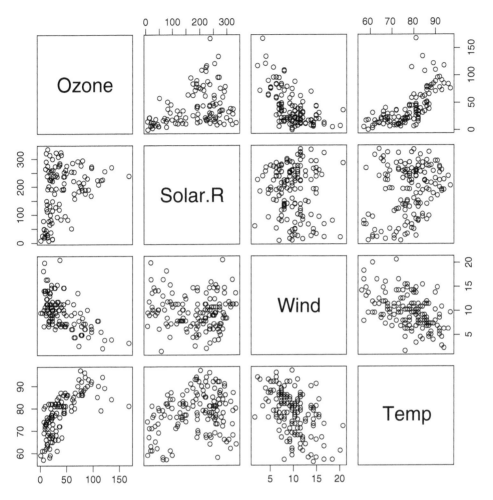

Figure 13.5 Selected variables as a scatter plot matrix via the pairs() function.

Example:

A basic pairs() plot using a selection of variables from the dataset.

```
pairs(~Fertility + Agriculture + Education + Catholic, data = swiss,
    upper.panel = panel.smooth, col = "gray50", bg = "pink",
    pch = 21)
```

In the preceding example, additional graphical parameters were used to alter the appearance of the points. You can use various standard parameters but it is often best to do this using your custom panel function.

13.7.1 Custom panel functions

The panel.smooth function is the only built-in panel function. You can create your own functions but you must ensure that these do not attempt to *draw* a plot, you can only add to a panel window.

To make a panel function you use the function() command:

```
fn.name <- function(params) {body}
```

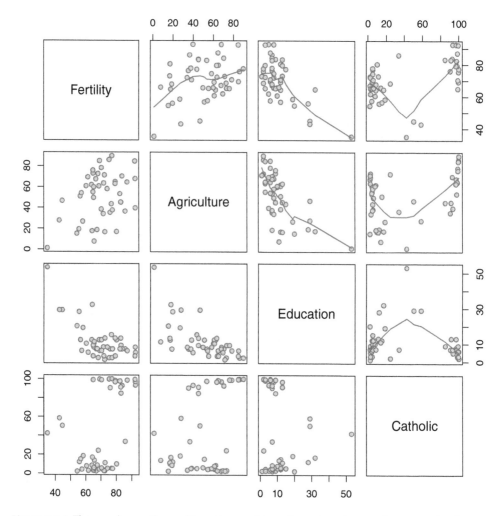

Figure 13.6 The panel.smooth panel function used to add a scatter plot smoother to a pairs plot.

There are three parts to a function, the name, the parameters, and the body. The name is what you will use to "call" the function. The parameters are the basic inputs. The body is the series of R commands that will be executed. You can have multiple lines, but the entire body should be "enclosed" between curly brackets.

Example:

Simple panel function to add a linear regression line to a pairs plot

```
panel.lm <- function(x, y, ...)
{
points(x, y, ...)     # Draw points
abline(lm(y ~ x), ...) # Add best-fit line
}
```

In our panel.lm function there are two lines to the body:

- The points part adds the basic scatter of points, using x and y coordinates.
- The abline part adds the linear regression line, using the lm function.

Note that there is a parameter … that allows you to pass additional graphical parameters to the function. See Chapter 15 for more information about programming using R.

13.8 Interaction plot

Interaction plots show differences in a response variable across logical groups. An interaction plot is used to help visualize potential *interactions*, which are important in analysis of variance (see *Chapter 14*). Use the `interaction.plot()` command:

```
interaction.plot(x.factor, trace.factor, response,
                 fun = mean, type, legend = TRUE, ...)
```

The `interaction.plot()` function has various parameters, used to select the variables you want to display, and to alter the appearance of the plot (Table 13.9).

Table 13.9 Some parameters of the `interaction.plot()` function.

Parameter	Description
x.factor	The factor variable to plot on the x-axis.
trace.factor	The factor variable to show as separate traces.
response	THe factor variable to show on the y-axis.
fun	The summary statistic (default = mean).
type	The type of plot, e.g.: "l" for lines, "p" for points, "b" for both.
legend	Use TRUE to incorporate a legend (this is the default).
trace.label	A character label to use for the legend title (defaults to the name of the trace.factor).
leg.bty	The box-type to pass to the legend. **Note** this is the only parameter that will pass "correctly" to legend().
…	Other graphical parameters may be used.

You can customize the general appearance of the plot using the parameters, and can add a basic legend too (Figure 13.7).

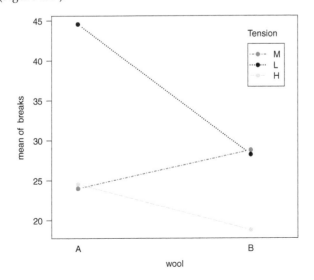

Figure 13.7 An interaction plot with basic legend.

Example:

An interaction plot with customized appearance

```
with(warpbreaks,
    interaction.plot(x.factor = wool,
            trace.factor = tension,
            response = breaks,
            fun = mean,
            las = 1,
            col = 1:3,
            type = "b",
            lty = 3:5,
            pch = c(19,19,19),
            leg.bty = "l",
            trace.label = "Tension"))
```

In the preceding example various "standard" graphical parameters were used to alter the general appearance:

`col`	the colour of the points and lines.	`las`	orientation of the axis labels.
`lty`	the line styles.	`pch`	plotting symbol(s).

Other parameters included: `leg.bty` to add a box surrounding the legend, and `trace.label` for the legend title.

> ### Tip: Legends and `interaction.plot()`
>
> If you use the `legend` parameter with the `interaction.plot` some elements may not "transfer" to the legend. You'll need to ensure that you specify separate elements for each trace (even if they are the same, as for pch in the example). It may be easiest to add a legend separately via the `legend()` function, where you can specify the elements you want more explicitly.

The interaction plot can be useful to explore potential interactions between variables in analysis of variance (see *Chapter 14*). The `interaction.plot()` function actually calls upon `matplot()` to draw the results, which you'll see shortly.

13.9 Matrix plots

The `matplot()` function plots the columns of one `matrix` against the columns of another `matrix`. There are also `matpoints()` and `matlines()` functions, which add point or lines to an existing plot.

These functions are useful for plotting multiple series of data. There are various parameters you can utilize (Table 13.10).

```
matplot(x, y, type, lty, lwd, pch, col, add, ...)
matpoints(x, y, type = "p", ...)
matlines(x, y, type = "l", ...)
```

If you plot a single `matrix`, each column will be plotted against an x-axis that is a `vector` 1:n, where n is the number of columns. You can use `numeric` values of your own for x. If your x-axis is formed from categorical data you'll need to suppress the axes and use `axis()`, as categorical data will give an error. The next example shows this (Figure 13.8).

Table 13.10 Some parameters of the `matplot()` function.

Parameter	Description
x, y	The data as a `matrix` or `vector`. If both x and y are given the first column of y is plotted against the first of x, then the second column of y is plotted against the second of y. If either x or y is a `vector` it will be re-cycled.
type	The type of plot as a `character vector` as for `plot()`, e.g. use "p" for points (the default), "l" for lines, "b" for both.
lty	The line type (default = 1:5).
lwd	Line width (default = 1).
pch	Plotting symbol, the default uses a sequence starting with digits 1 to 9, then 0 followed by lowercase letters then uppercase.
col	Colours for points and/or lines (default 1:6).
add	If TRUE the plot is added to the existing plot window (default = FALSE).
...	Other parameters can be used.

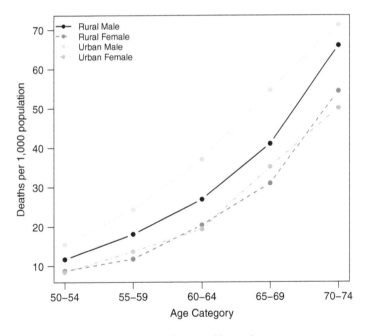

Figure 13.8 Matrix plot with custom categorical axis and legend.

Tip: Matrix plot legends

If you are plotting multiple data series you'll probably need a legend; use the `legend()` function separately.

Example:

Matrix plot and legend using categorical x-axis

```
VADeaths
```

	Rural Male	Rural Female	Urban Male	Urban Female
50–54	11.7	8.7	15.4	8.4
55–59	18.1	11.7	24.3	13.6
60–64	26.9	20.3	37.0	19.3
65–69	41.0	30.9	54.6	35.1
70–74	66.0	54.3	71.1	50.0

```
# Plot the columns against 1:5 but suppress the axes
matplot(VADeaths, type = "b", axes = FALSE, pch = 16, ylab = "")

# Add the x-axis using the category labels
axis(side = 1, at = 1:nrow(VADeaths), labels = rownames(VADeaths))

# The y-axis is 'standard'
axis(side = 2, las = 1)

# Add bounding box then axis titles
box()
title(xlab = "Age Category", ylab = "Deaths per 1,000 population")

# Add legend
legend(x = "topleft", legend = colnames(VADeaths), lty = 1:nrow(VADeaths),
       col = 1:nrow(VADeaths), pch = 16, bty = "n", cex = 0.8)
```

Tip: Axis titles and `matplot()`

The `matplot()` function usually makes axis titles of some sort. You can suppress a title using `xlab = ""`.

13.10 Conditioning plot

A conditioning plot is one where the main plot is "split" into panels using one or more grouping variables. In other words you visualize sections of your data, where each section is conditional upon other variables.

Use the `coplot()` command to draw conditioning plots.

```
coplot(formula, data, panel, given.values, rows, columns, show.given,
       col, pch, bar.bg, number, overlap, ...)
```

There are quite a lot of potential parameters (Table 13.11).

You specify the data using a `formula`, and can use one or two conditioning variables to split your visualization. Your conditioning variables can be `numeric` or `factor`. Your plotted variables can also be categorical but the default `panel` function that draws the panel is `points()`, so you would need to use a custom panel function to cope.

Note: Co-plot splits

It is possible to define splits using other methods, for example the `co.intervals()` function. You can also use a `matrix` with `given.values` to define the splits.

Table 13.11 Some parameters of the `coplot()` function.

Parameter	Explanation
formula	A formula describing how the variables should be displayed: y ~ x | a * b where a and b are the conditioning variables.
data	A data.frame that contains the variables in the formula.
panel	A function that draws the main plot – of the form function(x, y, col, pch, ...). The default is a scatter plot. Panel function should only add points, lines or text (i.e. not draw a new plot window).
given.values	A value or list of two values that determine how the conditioning takes place.
rows	The number of rows (of panels) to display.
columns	The number of columns (of panels) to display.
show.given	Set to FALSE to disable the shingle bars for either/both conditioning variables (default = TRUE).
col	The colour(s) of the points.
pch	The plotting symbol(s) to use.
bar.bg	Background colours for the shingle bars. Use a named vector with two elements: "num" and "fac" for numeric and factor variables.
number	The number of conditioning intervals (default = 6).
overlap	The fraction (must be <1) of overlap of the conditioning variable(s) (default = 0.5). Set overlap = -1 to have gaps.
...	Other parameters can be used (usually these are passed to the panel function).

13.10.1 Single conditioning variable

Using a single conditioning variable means your `formula` will be of the form y ~ x | a, where a is your conditioning variable. If a is a `factor` the data will be split accordingly. If a is numeric the values will be split to give several "slices", where you can control the `number` and `overlap` of the slices.

The following example shows a `factor` conditioning variable (Figure 13.9).

Example:

Single conditioning variable in `coplot()`

```
head(iris, n = 3)

  Sepal.Length Sepal.Width Petal.Length Petal.Width Species
1          5.1         3.5          1.4         0.2  setosa
2          4.9         3.0          1.4         0.2  setosa
3          4.7         3.2          1.3         0.2  setosa

coplot(Sepal.Length ~ Sepal.Width | Species, data = iris, rows = 1,
    pch = 16)
```

In the preceding example (Figure 13.9), the `rows` parameter was used to set the number of rows in the display to 1. The upper part of the plot shows "shingles" that form a kind of map/legend for the main plot window. Panels are always plotted from "bottom-left" to "top-right".

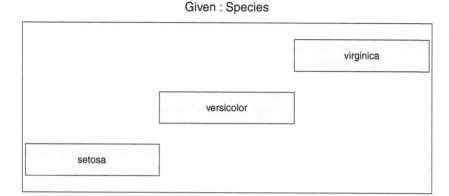

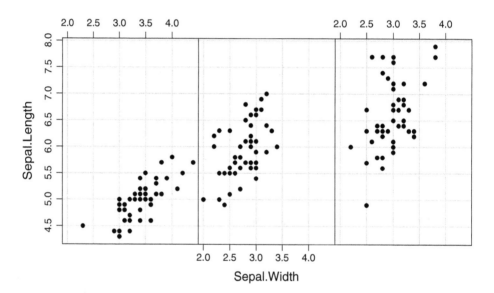

Figure 13.9 Conditioning Plot with a single (factor) conditioning variable.

13.10.2 Two conditioning variables

Using two conditioning variables means your formula will be of the form y ~ x | a * b, where a and b are the conditioning variables. The a conditional will "split" along the x-axis with the given values shown at the top of the plot. The b conditional will split along the y-axis with given values shown at the right edge of the plot.

With numeric conditioning variables you can use the number and overlap parameters to help control how the variables are split (Figure 13.10).

Example:

Controlling the split and overlap of two numeric conditioning variables

```
coplot(mpg ~ disp | carb * cyl, data = mtcars,
       bg = "steelblue", pch = 21,
       ylab = "Miles per Gallon (US)",
       xlab = "Displacement (cubic in.)",
       bar.bg = c(num = "rosybrown"),
       number = c(2, 4), overlap = c(0.5, 0))
```

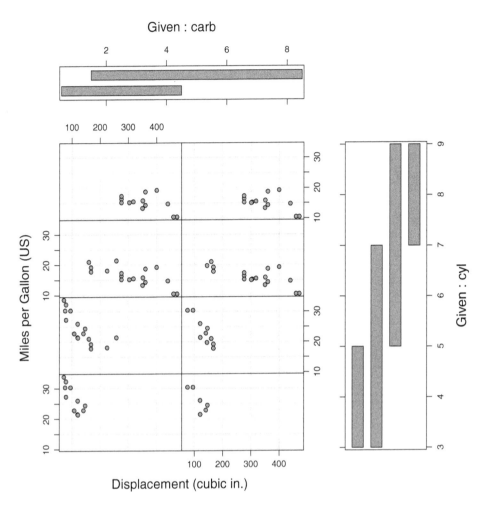

Figure 13.10 Two numeric conditioning variables with customized splits.

Tip: Default for factor conditioning variables with overlap and number

Use NULL to pass the default for a factor variable to the number and overlap argument.

In the example (Figure 13.10) several additional parameters were used to alter the appearance. The bg argument alters the plotting symbol background colour, but only if you explicitly specify an open symbol with pch. The bar.bg argument alters the colour of the shingles, note how the argument requires num = colour as a vector.

Tip: Conditioning plot titles

You can give two values to x/y axes (as a character vector), the 1st is the axis title and the 2nd is the title of the "Given" box. In this way you can make your own custom titles.

13.10.3 Custom panel functions

You can make a custom function for plotting in the panels. The functions should *not* make a new plot but only add points, lines or text. The default panel function uses `points()` to plot your x and y data. The conditioning variables are dealt with by the main `coplot()` function itself.

> #### Note: Built-in panel functions
>
> The only pre-built panel function is `panel.smooth`, which adds a locally weighted polynomial scatter plot smoother (in red) to a scatter plot.

The following example shows how to add a linear regression "best-fit" line to a scatter plot (Figure 13.11). This is essentially the same function that was used in section 13.7 to add to scatter plot matrices.

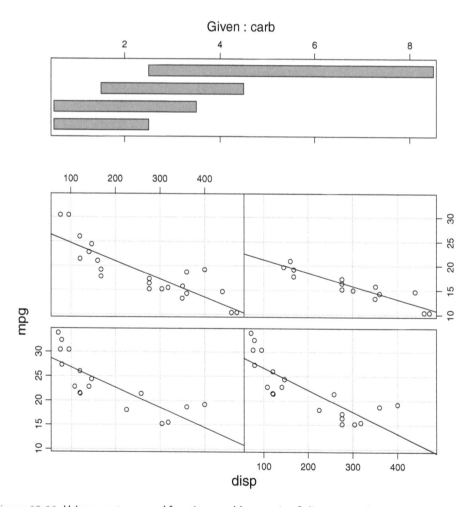

Figure 13.11 Using a custom panel function to add regression fit line to a coplot.

Example:

Adding a custom panel function to a `coplot()` to draw linear best-fit lines

```
panel.lm <- function(x, y, ...)
  {
  points(x, y, ...)       # Draw points
  abline(lm(y ~ x), ...)    # Add best-fit line
  }
head(mtcars, n = 3)
```

```
                 mpg  cyl disp   hp drat   wt   qsec vs am gear carb
Mazda RX4        21.0   6  160  110 3.90 2.620 16.46  0  1    4    4
Mazda RX4 Wag    21.0   6  160  110 3.90 2.875 17.02  0  1    4    4
Datsun 710       22.8   4  108   93 3.85 2.320 18.61  1  1    4    1
```

```
coplot(mpg ~ disp | carb, data = mtcars, panel = panel.lm, number = 4,
   bar.bg = c(num = "steelblue3"))
```

Tip: Custom panel functions for `coplot()`

Your custom panel function needs two parts:

- The fist is a name `<- function(x,y,...)` part. This sets the name and parameters. Note that `...` is a general "anything" placeholder.
- The second part is a pair of curly brackets { and }, between which you put the R commands to run.

In the `panel.lm` example you see x and y as the variables. The `...` part allows you to add suitable parameters, e.g. `lty`, `lwd`, or `pch`, without needing to write them in the function explicitly.

Note: Lattice graphics

R "contains" an entirely separate graphical system, which can be accessed from the `lattice` package. This comes bundled with R but is not enabled by default; use `library(lattice)` to enable the functions. The `lattice` package has the ability to make multivariate plots (and others) quite easily. However, it is a big system in its own right and it was not possible to give it justice in these pages.

EXERCISES:

Self-Assessment for Graphics: Advanced methods

1. You always have to refer to a colour by name, either as a `character` string or a hex-triplet ("`#rrggbb`").. TRUE or FALSE?
2. You can split a plot window with ____, ____, or ____ functions.
3. Which of the following functions allow you to export graphics?
    a. `dev.cur()`
    b. `dev.off()`
    c. `x11()`
    d. `wmf()`
4. You can plot a multiple time series using separate panels using the ____ function with ____ argument.
5. You can restore all the graphical defaults using `graphics.off()`.. TRUE or FALSE?

Answers to exercises are in the *Appendix*.

13.11   Chapter Summary: Graphics – advanced methods

Topic	Key Points
Using colour	See all colours with `colours()` function. Use `col` and `bg` as parameters to set foreground and background colours. Colours are specified by name but hex values can be used if character string prepended with #. Use `col2rgb()` to get rgb values from a named colour. Use `rgb()` to make custom colours. Use `colourRampPalette()` to make gradients of colours. Use `palette()` to control default colours (which can be referred to by position on palette). There are some default palettes, e.g. `topo.colours()`.
Graphical system	Access graphical system using `par()` function. Get settings with `par("name")`, and change setting with `par(name = value)`.
Split plot windows	Create split plot windows using: `par()` and `mfrow` or `mfcol`. Functions `split.screen()` and `layout()` can split into unequal sections. **Note** that the 3 methods are incompatible with one another.
Graphic windows	Open empty plot windows with OS-specific functions: `windows()`, `quartz()`, and `x11()`. Close all windows using `graphics.off()`. Other functions help manage the windows, e.g. `dev.cur()`, `dev.next()`, `dev.off()`.
Export graphics	Send graphics commands direct to disk by first opening a *device* e.g. `png()`, `pdf()`, `jpeg()`. Finish the export process with `dev.off()`. Use arguments `width`, `height`, and others (e.g. `res`) to control size, resolution etc. Use `dev.print()` to send on-screen graphic to a *device*.
Time series	Time series have their own `plot.ts()` function, which is automatically used if the class is `ts` or `mts`. With multiple time series use argument `plot.type` to show series in "`single`" or "`multiple`" panels.
Scatter plot matrix	Use `pairs()` to draw a scatter plot matrix of combinations of variables in a numeric `data.frame`. Use arguments `upper.panel` and `lower.panel` to create different displays in upper/lower "triangles". Specify input as an entire `data.frame` or `matrix`, or use formula of form ~ a + b + ... Use `function()` to make custom panel functions that alter graphical appearance. **Note** that panel functions should only *add* to a plot window, not draw a chart de-novo.

(Continued)

(Continued)

Topic	Key Points
Interaction plot	Use `interaction.plot()` for visualizing interactions between two variables. Especially helpful in 2-way ANOVA.
Matrix plot	Use `matplot()` to plot columns of one `matrix` against columns of another. Useful for multiple series scatter or line charts. Use `matpoints()` and `matlines()` functions to add points/lines to existing matrix plot. It is often necessary to customize the axes using `axis()`, and to require a `legend()`.
Conditioning plot	Use `coplot()` for conditioning plots, where the response variable is split into panels using one (or two) conditioning variables. Input is via a `formula` of form `y ~ x	a * b`, where a and b are conditioning variables.

14. Analyze data: statistical analyses

R has a wide range of statistical capabilities. The base distribution of R includes functions that can carry out many different kinds of analysis. In this chapter you'll see some of the more widely used analytical methods.

The functions you see here will give you a flavor of the capabilities of R.

> ## What's in this chapter
> » Tests of data distribution
> > » Distribution families
> » Tests for differences
> > » T-test
> > » U-test
> > » Analysis of variance (ANOVA)
> > » Kruskal-Wallis
> » Test of relationships
> > » Correlation
> > » Regression
> » Tests of association
> > » Chi-Squared
> > » Goodness of Fit

The analyses described here are shown without any accompanying graphics. It is always important to visualize your data, which you ought to do before attempting anything much in the way of analysis. For additional practice you could visualize the data examples for yourself.

> ## Note: Support material
> See the ↘ for links to material on the support website.

14.1 Test of distribution and normality

The distribution of your data is an important consideration, as this will affect the analytical methods available to you. Most often you are interested in knowing if your data are likely to be from the normal (Gaussian) distribution.

It is common to use graphical methods to help assess the "shape" of your data. Such tools as histogram, density plot, and QQ-plot can be useful. See *Chapter 11* for details about `hist()`, `density()` and `qqnorm()`.

There are statistical tests that can assess your data, with respect to the normal distribution (and potentially others). Here, you'll see Shapiro-Wilk, and Kolmogorov-Smirnov tests.

14.1.1 Shapiro-Wilk test for normality

The `shapiro.test()` command carries out a test for departure from normality.

```
shapiro.test(x)
```

There is only one required parameter, x, which should be a numeric vector.

Example:

The Shapiro-Wilk test for normality

```
shapiro.test(shrimp)

  Shapiro-Wilk normality test

data: shrimp
W = 0.91057, p-value = 0.08804

shapiro.test(airquality$Ozone)

    Shapiro-Wilk normality test

data: airquality$Ozone
W = 0.87867, p-value = 2.79e-08
```

The result comes in two parts: the test statistic W and the p-value. The latter gives the probability that the sample departs from normality. The usual value for the threshold is 0.05, but some statisticians prefer a slightly more conservative 0.1.

So, in the first example (shrimp) the sample can be considered to be normally distributed. In the second example (airquality) the sample appears to be significantly different from normal.

14.1.2 Distribution families

Data distribution is not simply "normal" or non-normal, there are many other well-described distribution types (often called distribution families). You saw some of these in Chapter 8, when looking at *Random numbers*. There are four main kinds of distribution function:

- rxxx Random variates
- dxxx Density/Mass function
- pxxx Cumulative Probability function
- qxxx Quantile function

Each distribution has one or more parameters that enable it to be "described", for example:

- Normal: mean, standard deviation
- Poisson: lambda

Random variates can be produced using rxxx functions (as seen in Section 8.1 *Random numbers*). You need to state how many values you want, as well as the distribution parameters.

Example:

Random variates from different distributions

```
set.seed(10)
rnorm(n = 10, mean = 10, sd = 1)

[1] 10.018746   9.815747   8.628669   9.400832 10.294545 10.389794 8.791924
[8]  9.636324   8.373327   9.743522

rpois(n = 10, lambda = 3)

[1] 5 3 4 2 2 4 5 2 4 2
```

The density/mass function (dxxx) requires one or more quantiles, the return gives the density at those quantiles.

Example:

Density/mass functions

```
dnorm(x = seq(from = -2, to = 2, by = 0.5), mean = 0, sd = 1)
```

```
[1] 0.05399097 0.12951760 0.24197072 0.35206533 0.39894228 0.35206533 0.24197072
[8]  0.12951760  0.05399097
```

```
dpois(x = 1:6, lambda = 2)
```

```
[1]  0.27067057  0.27067057  0.18044704  0.09022352  0.03608941  0.01202980
```

The cumulative probability function (pxxx) requires one or more quantiles, the return gives the probabilities at those values.

Example:

Cumulative probability functions

```
pnorm(q = seq(from = -2, to = 2, by = 0.5), mean = 0, sd = 1)
```

```
[1] 0.02275013 0.06680720 0.15865525 0.30853754 0.50000000 0.69146246 0.84134475
[8]  0.93319280  0.97724987
```

```
ppois(q = 0:5, lambda = 3)
```

```
[1]  0.04978707  0.19914827  0.42319008  0.64723189  0.81526324  0.91608206
```

The quantile function (qxxx) requires one or more probabilities, the return gives the quantiles at those probabilities.

Example:

Quantile functions

```
qnorm(p = c(0.01, 0.05, 0.5, 0.95, 0.99), mean = 0, sd = 1)
```

```
[1] -2.326348 -1.644854 0.000000 1.644854 2.326348
```

```
qpois(p = c(0.01, 0.05, 0.5, 0.95, 0.99), lambda = 3)
[1] 0 1 3 6 8
```

> ## Note: Distribution functions, critical values and test statistics
>
> You can use qxxx to get critical values for various stats tests. You can use pxxx to get the statistical significance (probability) if you have a test statistic. See the following sections for examples.

14.1.3 Kolmogorov-Smirnov goodness of fit test

The Kolmogorov-Smirnov test can be used as a test of distribution. You can use the ks.test() function to do this. Essentially it is a goodness of fit test, where you compare your sample to a "known" distribution.

```
ks.test(x, y, ...)
```

You need to supply two samples, x is usually your data. The y parameter can be another sample (presumably of known distribution), or a character giving the probability function for a distribution family. You can add other parameters to describe the known distribution.

Example:

Kolmogorov-Smirnov test

```
mean(shrimp)

[1]  31.79444

sd(shrimp)

[1]  1.843421

ks.test(shrimp, "pnorm", mean = 32, sd = 1.8)

Warning in ks.test(shrimp, "pnorm", mean = 32, sd = 1.8): ties
should not be

present for the Kolmogorov-Smirnov test

  One-sample Kolmogorov-Smirnov test

data: shrimp
D = 0.16837, p-value = 0.6873
alternative hypothesis: two-sided
```

Note that you nearly always get a message about ties!

14.2 Tests of differences

A major "class" of statistical tests look at differences between groups of data. There are tests for comparing:

- One sample to a reference point.
- Two samples.
- Multiple groups.

The distribution of your sample groups is a key factor in determining which test is most appropriate.

14.2.1 Student's t-test

The t-test is used when you have normally distributed samples. There are three main versions, all of which are run via the t.test() function:

- One-sample – where you compare your data to a known "reference point".
- Two-sample – where you compare two independent samples.
- Paired – where your samples are in matched pairs of observations.

```
t.test(x, y = NULL, alternative = "two.sided", mu = 0, paired = FALSE,
       var.equal = FALSE, ...)
```

The various parameters allow you to choose the type of test and give other options (Table 14.1).

Table 14.1 Some parameters of the t.test() function.

Parameter	Description
x	A numeric vector. Can be a formula of form response ~ predictor.
y	A numeric vector. If not specified a one-sample test is carried out, unless x is a formula.
alternative	The alternative hypothesis, the default is "two.sided", you can also specify "less" or "greater".
mu	The "true" value of the mean (for 1-sample test) or difference in means for 2-sample test (default = 0).
paired	If TRUE a paired test is performed.
var.equal	If TRUE the variance of the 2 samples is assumed equal. The default, FALSE carries out the Welch (Satterthwaite) correction.
...	Other parameters are possible.

One-sample t-test

In a one-sample test your aim is to compare the mean of your sample with a "known" value. In the t.test() command you specify your sample and the mean to which it should be compared.

Example:

One sample t-test

```
shrimp

[1] 32.2 33.0 30.8 33.8 32.2 33.3 31.7 35.7 32.4 31.2 26.6 30.7 32.5 30.7 31.2
[16]  30.3 32.3 31.7

# Is the % of shrimp > 30%?
t.test(shrimp, mu = 30, alternative = "greater")


   One Sample t-test

data: shrimp
t = 4.1299, df = 17, p-value = 0.00035
alternative hypothesis: true mean is greater than 30
95 percent confidence interval:
   31.03859   Inf
sample estimates:
mean of x
   31.79444
```

Two-sample t-test

The most common use for the t-test is to compare the means of two (independent) samples. Your data may be in one of two forms:

- Separate vectors (possibly in a list or data.frame).
- As a response variable and a grouping (predictor) variable.

Example:
Student's t-test with equal variance assumption

```
shoes

$A
[1]  13.2 8.2 10.9 14.3 10.7 6.6 9.5 10.8 8.8 13.3

$B
[1]  14.0 8.8 11.2 14.2 11.8 6.4 9.8 11.3 9.3 13.6
t.test(shoes$A, shoes$B, var.equal = TRUE)

  Two Sample t-test

data: shoes$A and shoes$B
t = -0.36891, df = 18, p-value = 0.7165
alternative hypothesis: true difference in means is not equal to 0
95 percent confidence interval:
-2.744924 1.924924
sample estimates:
mean of x mean of y
   10.63   11.04
```

In the preceding example the parameter var.equal was used to run a version of the test that assumes both samples have the same variance. The default is not to assume this, as in the following example.

Example:

Welch two sample t-test

```
head(cats, n = 3)

    Sex   Bwt   Hwt
1    F     2    7.0
2    F     2    7.4
3    F     2    9.5

t.test(Hwt/Bwt ~ Sex, cats)

  Welch Two Sample t-test

data: Hwt/Bwt by Sex
t = 0.22255, df = 94.618, p-value = 0.8244
alternative hypothesis: true difference in means between group F
and group M is not equal to 0
95 percent confidence interval:
-0.1629455 0.2040890
sample estimates:
```

```
mean in group F mean in group M
      3.915119     3.894547
```

In the preceding example the variance is not assumed to be equal. You can see that the data were specified as a `formula`, with the response being heart-weight/body-weight. Try each of the variables `Bwt` and `Hwt` separately and see what differences you find.

Paired t-test

In a paired test the observations are matched up, an item in one sample has a corresponding item in the second sample. The observations often have an "identifier" as a variable. You may also get data with two columns (e.g. before, after), which correspond to the paired measurements.

> ### Note: Matched pairs and repeated measures
>
> Paired (or matched pairs) tests are sometimes called *repeated measures* tests.

In the following example, there is a single response variable and an "identifier".

Example:

Paired t-test with an ID variable

```
str(sleep)

'data.frame':   20 obs. of 3 variables:
 $ extra: num 0.7 -1.6 -0.2 -1.2 -0.1 3.4 3.7 0.8 0 2 ...
 $ group: Factor w/ 2 levels "1","2": 1 1 1 1 1 1 1 1 1 1 ...
 $ ID   : Factor w/ 10 levels "1","2","3","4",..: 1 2 3 4 5 6 7 8 9 10 ...

t.test(extra ~ group, data = sleep, paired = TRUE)

    Paired t-test

data: extra by group
t = -4.0621, df = 9, p-value = 0.002833
alternative hypothesis: true difference in means is not equal to
0
95 percent confidence interval:
-2.4598858 -0.7001142
sample estimates:
mean of the differences
           -1.58
```

In the preceding example, `extra` is our main response variable (hours of extra sleep). The `group` variable represents two types of soporific drug. The `ID` variable represents the individuals.

In the next example, the data are in two columns; `Prewt` and `Postwt`. There is also a `Treat` column, which contains 3 different treatments. We'll use a `subset` to explore just one of these.

Example:

Paired t-test using two variables

```
str(anorexia)
```

```
'data.frame':   72 obs. of 3 variables:
$ Treat : Factor w/ 3 levels "CBT","Cont","FT": 2 2 2 2 2 2 2 2 2
2 ...
$ Prewt : num 80.7 89.4 91.8 74 78.1 88.3 87.3 75.1 80.6 78.4 ...
$ Postwt: num 80.2 80.1 86.4 86.3 76.1 78.1 75.1 86.7 73.5 84.6 ...

with(anorexia, t.test(Prewt, Postwt, paired = TRUE,
    subset = Treat == "Cont"))

  Paired t-test

data: Prewt and Postwt
t = -2.9376, df = 71, p-value = 0.004458
alternative hypothesis: true difference in means is not equal to
0
95 percent confidence interval:
-4.6399424 -0.8878354
sample estimates:
mean of the differences
     -            2.763889
```

Note: we should probably not have used a t-test for the preceding example, as there are 3 Treat levels, but it does illustrate how to use subset in the t.test function. The data should probably need dealing with using a linear mixed-effect model, which is a rather more advanced method!

Tip: Critical values

You can get critical values for the t distribution using the qt () function:

```
qt(p, df, lower.tail = TRUE, ...)
```

Where: p is the probability, df is the degrees of freedom, lower.tail is the "end" you want the value for. Bear in mind that you are looking at one end so for 5% you need to set p = 0.05/2.

Example:

critical values for t

```
qt(p = 0.05/2, df = Inf, lower.tail = FALSE)

[1] 1.959964

qt(0.01/2, df = Inf)

[1] -2.575829
```

14.2.2   U-test

The U-test has a similar role to the t-test, but is used for when your data are not normally distributed. The wilcox.test() function will carry out the three main kinds of U-test: one-sample, two-sample, and paired.

```
wilcox.test(x, y = NULL, alternative = "two.sided",
            mu = 0, paired = FALSE, ...)
```

The `wilcox.test()` function can accept a range of parameters (Table 14.2).

Table 14.2 Some parameters of the `wilcox.test()` function.

Parameter	Description
x	A numeric `vector`. Can be a `formula` of form `response ~ predictor`.
y	A numeric `vector`. If not specified a one-sample test is carried out, unless x is a `formula`.
alternative	The alternative hypothesis, the default is `"two.sided"`, you can also specify `"less"` or `"greater"`.
mu	The "true" value of the median (for 1-sample test) or difference in medians for 2-sample test (default = 0).
paired	If `TRUE` a paired test is performed.
...	Other parameters are possible.

> ## Note: U-test synonyms
>
> The U-test is known by several names. The two-sample test may be called the Mann-Whitney test or Wilcoxon rank sum test. The paired version is sometimes called Wilcoxon signed rank test. The prevalence of Wilcoxon is the reason the function is called `wilcox.test()` in R.

One-sample U-test

In the one-sample test you compare the median of your sample to a "fixed reference".

Example:

One sample U-test

```
wilcox.test(DDT, mu = 3.1)
Warning in wilcox.test.default(DDT, mu = 3.1): cannot compute
exact p-value with
ties


    Wilcoxon signed rank test with continuity correction

data: DDT
V = 95, p-value = 0.04997
alternative hypothesis: true location is not equal to 3.1
```

Two-sample U-test

The classic two-sample U-test compares two independent samples. Note that you can use a `subset` argument in the `wilcox.test()` command to "pick out" two samples.

Example:

Two-sample U-test

```
wilcox.test(count ~ spray, data = InsectSprays,
            subset = spray %in% c("C","D"))

Warning in wilcox.test.default(x = c(0, 1, 7, 2, 3, 1, 2, 1, 3, 0,
1, 4), :
cannot compute exact p-value with ties

   Wilcoxon rank sum test with continuity correction

data: count by spray
W = 20, p-value = 0.002651
alternative hypothesis: true location shift is not equal to 0
```

Note: U-test and tied ranks

You may see a warning message if your data contains tied values. In such cases it is common to apply a correction to your U-test. However, the routines are not in the base distribution of R, and they are generally quite small. You can try using `exact = FALSE` as a parameter. Alternatively, the package *coin* has functions that will allow exact p-values in the presence of ties.

Paired U-test

Matched pair tests (repeated measures) are handled in a similar manner to using `t.test()`, by adding the `paired = TRUE` parameter.

Example:

Paired U-test

```
# Anxiety scores before & after treatment
before <- c(1.83, 0.50, 1.62, 2.48, 1.68, 1.88, 1.55, 3.06, 1.30)
after <- c(0.878, 0.647, 0.598, 2.05, 1.06, 1.29, 1.06, 3.14, 1.29)

wilcox.test(before, after, paired = TRUE)

   Wilcoxon signed rank exact test

data: before and after
V = 40, p-value = 0.03906
alternative hypothesis: true location shift is not equal to 0
```

The preceding example shows depression scores for 9 patients before and after treatment (tranquilizer drug). In this example the `alternative` parameter was left at the default value ("two.sided").

> ## Note: Critical values for U
>
> You can get critical values for the U-test with `qwilcox()`. For example:
>
> ```
> qwilcox(p = 0.05/2, n = 9, m = 8, lower.tail = TRUE)
> [1] 16
> ```
>
> You supply p, the probability (remember that you are dealing with one end of the distribution), and the sample sizes n and m.

14.2.3 Analysis of variance

When you have multiple groups (more than 2) of data that are normally distributed you cannot use the t-test to look at differences between groups. The "big brother" of the t-test is analysis of variance (ANOVA), which you can run via the `aov()` command.

```
aov(formula, data, ...)
```

The driving force of the `aov()` command is the `formula`, which is used to specify how the *response* and *predictor* variable(s) are related (Table 14.3).

Table 14.3 Some parameters of the `aov()` function.

Parameter	Description
formula	A formula giving the terms for the ANOVA model. The general form is y ~ x where y is the *response* variable and x is the *predictor* variable.
data	The data.frame that holds the variables in formula.
...	Other parameters are possible.

There are various kinds of ANOVA you might undertake, you'll see two main types here; one-way and two-way.

One-way ANOVA

The simplest form of `formula` is: y ~ x. This sets out a one-way ANOVA, where y is the *response* and x is a single *predictor* variable (i.e. a grouping variable).

Example:

One-way ANOVA

```
str(chickwts)

'data.frame':   71 obs. of 2 variables:
$ weight: num 179 160 136 227 217 168 108 124 143 140 ...
$ feed : Factor w/ 6 levels "casein","horsebean",..: 2 2 2 2 2 2 2
2 2 2 ...

mod <- aov(weight ~ feed, data = chickwts)
summary(mod)
```

```
            Df   Sum Sq   Mean Sq   F value        Pr(>F)
feed         5   231129     46226     15.37     5.94e-10***
Residuals   65   195556      3009
---
Signif. codes:  0 '***' 0.001 '**' 0.01 '*' 0.05 '.' 0.1 ' ' 1
```

The result of the aov() command in an object that holds a special class. When you use summary() on the result you get the classic ANOVA summary table.

The summary table shows you that the main effect (feed) has a significant effect on the response (weight). However, it doesn't tell you anything about differences between the various feed types. You need to carry out a supplementary analysis to delve a bit deeper, this is called a *post hoc* analysis.

It is also helpful to visualize your data, in this case a box-whisker plot would be ideal (see Figure 11.7 for a boxplot of the example dataset).

Tip: Checking normal distribution

When you have multiple groups you should determine the normality of each and all of them. The shapiro.test() only works on a single sample vector. However, you can use aggregate() to split your data into chunks. You need a simple function to do this:

```
aggregate(weight ~ feed, data = chickwts,
    FUN = function(x) shapiro.test(x)$p.value)
```

The shapiro.test() produces a result with a p.value component, so you can extract the p-values alone (the $ at the end).

Post hoc analysis in 1-way ANOVA

Your main ANOVA result gives an overview of the main *predictor* but the *post hoc* delves a bit deeper and examines the pairwise comparisons. There are special analyses that carry out the required calculations.

To carry out a *post hoc* test you can use the TukeyHSD() function (Table 14.4). This conducts Tukey's Honest Significant Difference test on pairwise samples. This is the most common form of *post hoc* test.

```
TukeyHSD(x, which, ordered = FALSE, conf.level = 0.95, ...)
```

Table 14.4 Some parameters of the TukeyHSD() function.

Parameter	Description
x	A model result, usually the result of aov().
which	A character vector giving the names of the terms to use in the *post hoc* comparisons. The default is all terms.
ordered	If TRUE the pairwise comparisons are ordered such that differences in means are all positive.
conf.level	The confidence level, the default is 0.95 i.e. 95%.
...	Other parameters can be used.

Example:

Post hoc test for 1-way ANOVA

```
TukeyHSD(mod, ordered = TRUE)
  Tukey multiple comparisons of means
    95% family-wise confidence level
    factor levels have been ordered

Fit: aov(formula = weight ~ feed, data = chickwts)

$feed
```

	diff	lwr	upr	p adj
linseed-horsebean	58.550000	-10.413543	127.51354	0.1413329
soybean-horsebean	86.228571	19.541684	152.91546	0.0042167
meatmeal-horsebean	116.709091	46.335105	187.08308	0.0001062
casein-horsebean	163.383333	94.419790	232.34688	0.0000000
sunflower-horsebean	168.716667	99.753124	237.68021	0.0000000
soybean-linseed	27.678571	-35.683721	91.04086	0.7932853
meatmeal-linseed	58.159091	-9.072873	125.39106	0.1276965
casein-linseed	104.833333	39.079175	170.58749	0.0002100
sunflower-linseed	110.166667	44.412509	175.92082	0.0000884
meatmeal-soybean	30.480519	-34.414070	95.37511	0.7391356
casein-soybean	77.154762	13.792470	140.51705	0.0083653
sunflower-soybean	82.488095	19.125803	145.85039	0.0038845
casein-meatmeal	46.674242	-20.557722	113.90621	0.3324584
sunflower-meatmeal	52.007576	-15.224388	119.23954	0.2206962
sunflower-casein	5.333333	-60.420825	71.08749	0.9998902

The result has various columns, the first and last are the ones we are most interested in: diff shows the difference in group means (in this case they are all positive as ordered = TRUE was used), and p adj is the adjusted p-value for the pairwise comparisons.

Note: Post hoc plot

There is a plot method for the result of TukeyHSD() to allow a visualization of the *post hoc* comparisons.

Two-way ANOVA

In a 2-way ANOVA you have two predictor variables. The formula can specify the two predictors either *independently* or with *interaction*:

- y ~ x + z – independent, x and z act without interaction.
- y ~ x * z – interaction, x and z interact.
- y ~ x + z + x:z – alternative way of specifying the interaction.

In most circumstances you would begin with a model that specified interactions; if the summary showed the interaction to be not significant you then re-run the analysis with an independent model.

Example:

Two-way ANOVA with interactions

```
str(warpbreaks)

'data.frame':  54 obs. of 3 variables:
 $ breaks : num 26 30 54 25 70 52 51 26 67 18 ...
 $ wool   : Factor w/ 2 levels "A","B": 1 1 1 1 1 1 1 1 1 1 ...
 $ tension: Factor w/ 3 levels "L","M","H": 1 1 1 1 1 1 1 1 1 2 ...

mod <- aov(breaks ~ wool * tension, data = warpbreaks)
summary(mod)
              Df  Sum Sq  Mean Sq  F value   Pr(>F)
wool           1     451    450.7    3.765  0.058213 .
tension        2    2034   1017.1    8.498  0.000693 ***
wool:tension   2    1003    501.4    4.189  0.021044 *
Residuals     48    5745    119.7
---
Signif. codes: 0 '***' 0.001 '**' 0.01 '*' 0.05 '.' 0.1 ' ' 1
```

This time the `summary()` shows you multiple rows, corresponding to the different *predictor* variables and the *interaction*. Before you attempt a *post hoc* test you ought to visualize the data (look back at Figure 11-9).

Post hoc analysis in 2-way ANOVA

The `TukeyHSD()` function can deal with 2-way ANOVA, but the output from a *post hoc* test can be quite long. In general you are interested only in the results for the interaction term. You can limit the results using the `which` parameter.

Example:

Post hoc for 2-way ANOVA

```
TukeyHSD(mod, ordered = TRUE, which = "wool:tension")

  Tukey multiple comparisons of means
    95% family-wise confidence level
    factor levels have been ordered

Fit: aov(formula = breaks ~ wool * tension, data = warpbreaks)

$`wool:tension`
                 diff         lwr       upr      p adj
A:M-B:H     5.2222222  -10.084100  20.52854  0.9114780
A:H-B:H     5.7777778   -9.528544  21.08410  0.8705572
B:L-B:H     9.4444444   -5.861877  24.75077  0.4560950
B:M-B:H    10.0000000   -5.306322  25.30632  0.3918767
A:L-B:H    25.7777778   10.471456  41.08410  0.0001136
A:H-A:M     0.5555556  -14.750766  15.86188  0.9999978
B:L-A:M     4.2222222  -11.084100  19.52854  0.9626541
B:M-A:M     4.7777778  -10.528544  20.08410  0.9377205
A:L-A:M    20.5555556    5.249234  35.86188  0.0029580
```

B:L-A:H	3.6666667	-11.639655	18.97299	0.9797123
B:M-A:H	4.2222222	-11.084100	19.52854	0.9626541
A:L-A:H	20.0000000	4.693678	35.30632	0.0040955
B:M-B:L	0.5555556	-14.750766	15.86188	0.9999978
A:L-B:L	16.3333333	1.027012	31.63966	0.0302143
A:L-B:M	15.7777778	0.471456	31.08410	0.0398172

In 2-way ANOVA we are often interested in the *interaction* term. You can visualize the interactions using an interaction plot (for example Figure 13-7). Refer back to section 13.8 for a reminder of how to use the `interaction.plot()` command.

Tip: ANOVA contrast options

It is common to alter the contrasts options before undertaking ANOVA.

```
options("contrasts") # see current settings

$contrasts
[1] "contr.helmert" "contr.poly"

options(contrasts = c("contr.treatment", "contr.poly")) # default
options(contrasts = c("contr.sum", "contr.poly")) # sum
options(contrasts = c("contr.helmert", "contr.poly")) # orthogonal
```

Which option you choose is up for debate, either `sum` or `helmert` are usually deemed most suitable for ANOVA. The `treatment` contrast is usually best for linear modelling (see later).

14.2.4   Kruskal-Wallis test for multiple sample differences

If you have more than 2 samples and at least one of them is not normally distributed, you cannot use ANOVA. The "equivalent" of the one-way ANOVA is the Kruskal-Wallis test. You carry it out using the `kruskal.test()` command.

```
kruskal.test(formula, data, subset, ...)
kruskal.test(x, g, ...)
kruskal.test(x, ...)
```

The `kruskal.test()` allows you to specify your data in several ways (Table 14.5).

Table 14.5 Some parameters for the `kruskal.test()` command.

Parameter	Description
formula	A formula of form `response ~ predictor`.
data	Where to look for the data in the `formula` (usually a `data.frame`).
subset	A subset.
x	A `vector` of values, or a `list` of `vector` values.
g	A grouping variable, used if x is a single `vector`.
...	Other parameters may be used.

The different forms of kruskal.test() allow you to carry out the test when your data are in several layouts. Most commonly you will either have a data.frame or matrix with multiple numeric columns, or you will have a data.frame with a *response* variable and a grouping (*predictor*) variable.

Example:
Kruskal-Wallis test

```
str(InsectSprays)

'data.frame':  72 obs. of 2 variables:
$ count: num 10 7 20 14 14 12 10 23 17 20 ...
$ spray: Factor w/ 6 levels "A","B","C","D",..: 1 1 1 1 1 1 1 1 1 1 ...

kruskal.test(count ~ spray, data = InsectSprays)

  Kruskal-Wallis rank sum test

data: count by spray
Kruskal-Wallis chi-squared = 54.691, df = 5, p-value = 1.511e-10
```

Post hoc testing for Kruskal-Wallis

There is no dedicated method for conducting *post hoc* tests with Kruskal-Wallis. The easiest solution is to carry out multiple U-tests, and to adjust the p-values to take into consideration the multiple testing. You can do with with the pairwise.wilcox.test() function.

```
pairwise.wilcox.test(x, g, p.adjust.method, ...)
```

In this function, x and g are as they are for kruskal.test(). You can carry out various "adjustments" via the p.adjust.method argument. The options are: "holm", "hochberg", "hommel", "bonferroni", "BH", "BY", "fdr", "none". Type help("p.adjust") to see what R has to say about the options. Essentially "bonferroni" is most conservative and "fdr" (or "BH") is least conservative.

Example:
Post hoc for Kruskal-Wallis using pairwise U-tests

```
with(InsectSprays, pairwise.wilcox.test(count, g = spray, p.adj = "BH",
  exact = FALSE))

  Pairwise comparisons using Wilcoxon rank sum test with
continuity correction

data: count and spray
```

	A	B	C	D	E
B	0.62273	–	–	–	–
C	9.6e-05	9.6e-05	–	–	–
D	0.00013	0.00013	0.00398	–	–
E	9.6e-05	9.6e-05	0.07169	0.21806	–
F	0.50103	0.90775	9.6e-05	0.00013	9.6e-05

```
P value adjustment method: BH
```

If you have multiple *predictor* variables and your data are not normally distributed… you have some problems! The solutions are beyond the scope of this book but you might like to look at generalized linear modelling using `glm()`.

14.3   Tests for relationships

There are two main branches of analysis when it comes to exploring links and relationships between things.

- Correlation and regression – when variables are numeric.
- Association and Goodness of Fit – when variables are categorical.

Of course this is a gross over-simplification, but it is a good rule of thumb.

14.3.1   Correlation

In a correlation you are looking for the strength and direction of the relationship between two numeric variables. There are three main analyses, all of which can be handled by the `cor()` and `cor.test()` functions:

- Pearson's Product Moment – for normally distributed data.
- Spearman's Rho – for non-parametric data.
- Kendall's Tau – for non-parametric data.

```
cor(x, y, use = "everything", method = "pearson")
cor.test(x, y = NULL, method = "pearson", ...)
```

There are various potential parameters (Table 14.6).

Table 14.6 Some Parameters of the `cor()` and `cor.test()` functions.

Parameter	Description
x	A vector of numerical data. For cor.test can be a formula of form ~ x + z where x and z are the variables to correlate.
y	A vector of numerical data.
use	How to deal with missing values (for cor). The default is "everything", alternatives are: "all.obs", "complete.obs", "na or complete" or "pairwise.complete.obs".
method	The correlation method (default "pearson"), alternatives are "spearman" or "kendall".
...	Other parameters may be used.

The `cor()` function simply returns the correlation coefficient, whilst `cor.test()` goes a step further and assesses the statistical significance of the relationship.

For `cor()` you can only enter the data as separate x and y components.

Example:

Simple correlations

```
cor(cars$speed, cars$dist, method = "pearson")

[1] 0.8068949
```

```
with(swiss, cor(Fertility, Catholic, method = "spearman"))

[1] 0.4136456
```

If you have a data.frame or matrix with all-numeric columns you can obtain a correlation matrix, showing all the pairwise correlations.

Example:

Correlation matrix

```
round(cor(attitude, method = "spearman"), digits = 2)

            rating complaints privileges learning raises critical advance
rating        1.00       0.83       0.48     0.62   0.60     0.05    0.20
complaints    0.83       1.00       0.53     0.58   0.65     0.11    0.22
privileges    0.48       0.53       1.00     0.51   0.46     0.11    0.34
learning      0.62       0.58       0.51     1.00   0.62     0.13    0.54
raises        0.60       0.65       0.46     0.62   1.00     0.29    0.49
critical      0.05       0.11       0.11     0.13   0.29     1.00    0.26
advance       0.20       0.22       0.34     0.54   0.49     0.26    1.00
```

If you want a statistical significance test then cor.test() allows you to enter a formula, but note that the form is ~ x + z (i.e. without anything to the left of the ~).

Example:

Correlation significance tests

```
cor.test(~speed + dist, data = cars, method = "pearson")

	Pearson's product-moment correlation

data: speed and dist
t = 9.464, df = 48, p-value = 1.49e-12
alternative hypothesis: true correlation is not equal to 0
95 percent confidence interval:
 0.6816422 0.8862036
sample estimates:
      cor
0.8068949
```

```
with(attitude, cor.test(x = rating, y = learning, method = "kendall",
      exact = FALSE))

	Kendall's rank correlation tau

data: rating and learning
z = 3.4336, p-value = 0.0005956
alternative hypothesis: true tau is not equal to 0
sample estimates:
      tau
0.4491231
```

Note: Correlation and causation

A correlation (even if statistically significant) does not necessarily mean that there is a causal link between the two variables. You ought to draw the relationship to visualize it, using `plot()`. However you should not try to add a line of best-fit (because this implies cause and effect). It is probably acceptable to add a locally weighted scatter plot smoother. Look back at Chapter 12 (section 12.3) for examples.

14.3.2 Regression

Regression (or linear modelling) is an extension of correlation where you *do* assume a mathematical relationship between the variables. The `lm()` function allows you to carry out linear modelling when your data are normally distributed.

```
lm(formula, data, subset, ...)
```

To "drive" the function you need a `formula`, of form `y ~ x`, where `y` is your *response* variable and `x` is your *predictor* variable. Note that you can define a `subset`. There are other potential arguments but they are "more advanced".

You can specify your model `formula` in various ways, but here you'll see a couple of basic options:

- `y ~ x`
- `y ~ x1 + x2 + x3`

In the first instance there is a single *predictor* variable. In the second there are three (so you have multiple regression), which are separated by +. There are other formulae that can be used, and it is possible to carry out a wide range of analyses.

Note: Data distribution and `lm()`

For `lm()` your data need to be normally distributed. It *is* possible to carry out regression if your data conform to some other (known) distribution, in which case you can use generalized linear modelling with the `glm()` command.

Example:

Simple regression models

```
colnames(cars)

[1] "speed" "dist"

m0 <- lm(dist ~ speed, data = cars)

colnames(LifeCycleSavings)

[1] "sr"  "pop15" "pop75" "dpi"  "ddpi"

m3 <- lm(sr ~ pop15 + pop75 + ddpi, data = LifeCycleSavings)
```

Model results

The result of lm() is an object that has various components, which may be useful (including a summary() function).

```
summary(m0)

Call:
lm(formula = dist ~ speed, data = cars)

Residuals:
    Min      1Q  Median      3Q     Max
-29.069  -9.525  -2.272   9.215  43.201

Coefficients:
            Estimate  Std. Error  tvalue  Pr(>|t|)
(Intercept)  -17.5791     6.7584  -2.601    0.0123 *
speed          3.9324     0.4155   9.464  1.49e-12 ***
---
Signif. codes: 0 '***' 0.001 '**' 0.01 '*' 0.05 '.' 0.1 ' ' 1

Residual standard error: 15.38 on 48 degrees of freedom
Multiple R-squared: 0.6511,  Adjusted R-squared: 0.6438
F-statistic: 89.57 on 1 and 48 DF, p-value: 1.49e-12

summary(m3)

Call:
lm(formula = sr ~ pop15 + pop75 + ddpi, data = LifeCycleSavings)

Residuals:
    Min      1Q  Median      3Q     Max
-8.2539 -2.6159 -0.3913  2.3344  9.7070

Coefficients:
            Estimate  Std. Error  t value  Pr(>|t|)
(Intercept)  28.1247     7.1838    3.915  0.000297 ***
pop15        -0.4518     0.1409   -3.206  0.002452 **
pop75        -1.8354     0.9984   -1.838  0.072473 .
ddpi          0.4278     0.1879    2.277  0.027478 *
---
Signif. codes: 0 '***' 0.001 '**' 0.01 '*' 0.05 '.' 0.1 ' ' 1

Residual standard error: 3.767 on 46 degrees of freedom
Multiple R-squared: 0.3365,  Adjusted R-squared: 0.2933
F-statistic: 7.778 on 3 and 46 DF, p-value: 0.0002646
```

The part labelled Coefficients shows the statistic for the various model terms. For the m0 model there is only one (speed), whilst for the m3 model there are three. The columns show the actual coefficient (Estimate) as well as other values, including the statistical significance.

The bottom shows how "well" the model describes variability in your *predictor*. The values of particular interest are the Adjusted R-squared and the p-value. The former tells you what proportion of the variability is "explained" by your model. The latter tells you if the over-all model is statistically significant.

Other potentially helpful components in the `lm()` result are:

- Coefficients – use `coef(mod)` or `mod$coef`.
- Residuals – use `resid(mod)` or `mod$resid`.
- Fitted values – use `fitted(mod)` or `mod$fitted`.

The helper functions `coef()`, `resid()` and `fitted()` can access the components, which you can also extract using the $ syntax.

Example:

Model coefficients

```
coef(m3)

(Intercept)      pop15        pop75         ddpi
28.1246633   -0.4517775   -1.8354083    0.4278317

m0$coefficients

(Intercept)      speed
-17.579095    3.932409
```

You can also obtain the confidence intervals using `confint()`.

```
confint(object, parm, level = 0.95, ...)
```

The `parm` argument allows you to choose the variables you want to get the confidence intervals for (give a `character vector` of names), the default being all. You may also choose a different confidence level.

Example:

Confidence intervals for regression coefficients

```
confint(m3, parm = c("pop15", "pop75"), level = 0.99)

                 0.5 %          99.5 %
pop15     -0.8304629      -0.07309219
pop75     -4.5181214       0.84730492
```

The residuals represent "how far" each original data point is from the corresponding fitted model value.

Example:

Model residuals

```
# A summary of the residuals
summary(resid(m0))

   Min.  1st Qu.   Median    Mean  3rd Qu.     Max.
-29.069   -9.525   -2.272   0.000    9.215   43.201
```

The fitted values are calculated using the model coefficients, you get one value for each original observation.

Example:

Model fitted values

```
# The first 6 fitted values
fitted(m3)[1:6]
```

```
Australia  Austria   Belgium   Bolivia     Brazil    Canada
10.825248  11.176440  10.875817  6.228694   9.491693  9.602998
```

> ## Note: Regression model diagnostic plots
>
> The result of `lm()` has a `plot()` method. When you run `plot` on a model result you will get a series of diagnostic graphics. Type `help("plot.lm")` in R to see more details.

Altering models

Your dataset may contain variables that are not statistically significant. You may well have various options and need to try different combinations of variables to get the "best" model. You can make new models by editing the command line (use ↑ on your keyboard). You can also use the `update()` command to change a model.

```
update(model, formula, ...)
```

The `formula` allows you to add or remove model components. In the `formula` the `.` period character acts as a wildcard (meaning "all terms").

Example:

Altering a model using `update()`

```
# Add all possible terms to a new model
m4 <- lm(sr ~ ., data = LifeCycleSavings)
formula(m4)

sr ~ pop15 + pop75 + dpi + ddpi

# Subtract a single term (dpi) from the model
m3 <- update(m4, formula = ~. - dpi)
formula(m3)

sr ~ pop15 + pop75 + ddpi

# Remove another term
m2 <- update(m3, ~. - ddpi)
getCall(m2)
lm(formula = sr ~ pop15 + pop75, data = LifeCycleSavings)
```

The `formula()` command allows you to see the `formula`, whilst `getCall()` shows you the "result" of running `update()`, i.e. the new command as if you'd typed it in full yourself.

Note: Regression model building

There are tools that allow you to build the "best" regression models. The add1() function allows you to see the effect of adding a single variable to an existing model. You can then select the "best" option. The drop1() command allows you to see the effect that dropping a single variable would have on your existing model.

Comparing models

If you have different regression models you can compare them using the anova() command. Your models can only be compared if they are from the same dataset (with the same *response*). You give the names of the models, separated by commas.

Example:

Compare regression models

```
anova(m4, m3)
Analysis of Variance Table

Model 1: sr ~ pop15 + pop75 + dpi + ddpi
Model 2: sr ~ pop15 + pop75 + ddpi
  Res.Df  RSS Df Sum of Sq    F Pr(>F)
1    45 650.71
2    46 652.61 -1   -1.8932 0.1309 0.7192

anova(m3, m2, m1)

Analysis of Variance Table

Model 1: sr ~ pop15 + pop75 + ddpi
Model 2: sr ~ pop15 + pop75
Model 3: sr ~ pop15
  Res.Df   RSS Df Sum of Sq    F Pr(>F)
1    46 652.61
2    47 726.17 -1   -73.562 5.1851 0.02748 *
3    48 779.51 -1   -53.343 3.7599 0.05864 .
---
Signif. codes: 0 '***' 0.001 '**' 0.01 '*' 0.05 '.' 0.1 ' ' 1
```

In the first case the loss of the dpi term had no significant effect on the model. In the second case, 3 models were evaluated. The loss of ddpi has a significant impact (so m2 is worse than m3) but there is nothing much to choose between m2 and m1.

Tip: Regression model variables

It can be hard to "remember" what all the components of your data and models are. You can use colnames() (and rownames() if appropriate) to keep track of data. The "equivalents" for regression models are: variable.names() and case.names().

Prediction from models

The predict() function allows you to plug-in predictor values to a regression model and get predicted response values.

```
predict(object, newdata, se.fit, interval, ...)
```

There are various arguments to the function to give you some control over the output (Table 14.7).

Table 14.7 Some parameters of the predict() function.

Parameter	Description
object	The result of a lm model.
newdata	A data.frame containing variables that match those in the model. If omited the function returns fitted values.
se.fit	If TRUE the standard errors are also returned (default = FALSE).
interval	The type of interval calculation: "none" (the default), "confidence", or "prediction".
...	Other parameters are possible.

The important thing to note is that the newdata argument *must* be in the form of a data.frame, even if you have a single value.

Example:

Prediction from a regression model

```
mod <- lm(sr ~ pop15, data = LifeCycleSavings)
range(LifeCycleSavings$pop15)

[1] 21.44 47.64

unkn <- data.frame(pop15 = c(20, 30, 40, 50))
predict(mod, newdata = unkn)

        1          2          3          4
13.036246  10.806070   8.575895   6.345719

# Get confidence intervals
predict(mod, newdata = unkn, interval = "confidence")

        fit        lwr        upr
1  13.036246  10.810141  15.262351
2  10.806070   9.491753  12.120388
3   8.575895   7.272528   9.879261
4   6.345719   4.139014   8.552423
```

Note: Prediction for other analysis types

The predict() function is general and there are different forms for different analyses. When you run predict(), the class of your result is assessed and the appropriate variant of the function is executed, for lm this is predict.lm(). You can see what other variants are on your system using methods().

```
methods("predict")
```

14.3.3 Tests of association

When you have count data or frequencies you need particular kinds of analytical routines. Because you do not have *replicated* data you use probabilistic methods. The Chi-Squared test, developed by Pearson, is such a method. There are two main "versions":

- Chi-Squared test of association.
- Goodness of Fit test.

Both of these can be run using the `chisq.test()` function. You specify which type of test using the appropriate arguments (Table 14.8).

Table 14.8 Some Parameters of the `chisq.test()` function.

Parameter	Description
x	The data, usually a `matrix` or `vector` but can be a `factor`.
y	Data, ignored if x is a `matrix`.
correct	If TRUE (the default) a Yates' correction is applied for a 2x2 contingency table.
p	A vector of probabilities, used for Goodness of Fit test.
rescale.p	If TRUE the values in p are re-scaled to sum to unity.
simulate.p.value	If TRUE a Monte Carlo simulation is used to generate p-values.
B	The number of permutations to use if `simulate.p.value = TRUE`.

Chi-Squared test for association

When you have frequency data, based on observations of various categories you use `chisq.test()` to carry out a Chi-Squared test of association, and explore relationships between categories.

```
chisq.test(x, y = NULL, correct = TRUE, p, rescale.p = FALSE,
    simulate.p.value = FALSE, B = 2000)
```

The Chi-Squared test is usually carried out on a two-dimensional matrix-like table, known as a *contingency table*. You are looking to see if there are associations between the various categories.
The `chisq.test()` command will accept frequency data (usually as a `matrix`) but you can specify two `factor` variables, which will be tabulated as part of the computations.
The result contains various elements, including:

- `$observed` – the original data as a contingency table.
- `$expected` – the expected values (under the null hypotheses).
- `$residuals` – the Pearson residuals. These are approx. normally distributed with a critical value of ~ 1.96.

Example:

Chi-Squared test for association

```
# Visits of bumble bees to 2 different colours of flower
bees <- matrix(c(68, 14, 7, 8, 1, 11),
       ncol = 2,
       dimnames = list(
                    c("B.ter", "B.lus", "B.hyp"),
                    c("Violet", "Orange")))
       )
```

```
addmargins(bees)  # Add marginal totals
```

```
        Violet   Orange    Sum
B.ter      68        8      76
B.lus      14        1      15
B.hyp       7       11      18
Sum        89       20     109
```

```
(X <- chisq.test(bees))
```

```
Warning in chisq.test(bees): Chi-squared approximation may be
incorrect
```

```
    Pearson's Chi-squared test
```

```
data: bees
X-squared = 26.44, df = 2, p-value = 1.814e-06
```

```
round(X$expected)
```

```
        Violet   Orange
B.ter      62       14
B.lus      12        3
B.hyp      15        3
```

```
X$residuals
```

```
            Violet      Orange
B.ter    0.7546750   -1.591989
B.lus    0.5007022   -1.056232
B.hyp   -2.0077862    4.235430
```

In the preceding example you can see a contingency table (a matrix) giving counts for three bumblebee species and the visits to two different colours of flower (addmargins() was used to give marginal totals). The overall X^2 result is statistically significant. The $residuals show you that the only bee with a significant preference is *B.hyp*, which has a negative association with the Violet colour, and a positive one with the Orange coloured flowers.

Tip: Visualizing Chi-Squared results

There are various ways to visualize your results. The Pearson residuals are the best "result" to plot. A bar chart (see section 11.6 for the barplot() command) could work well, but a dot-chart (see section 11.11 for the dotchart() command) is highly efficient. Try this on the bees data.

```
dotchart(X$resid, pch = 23, bg = "black", pt.cex = 1.5)
title(xlab = "Pearson residuals", ylab = "Bee species and flower
colour")
abline(v = c(-2, 0, 2), lty = "dotted", col = "gray50")
```

Goodness of Fit tests

A *Goodness of Fit* test is similar to a regular association test, but you see if one set of frequencies "matches" another set. A goodness-of-fit test compares a set of observations with a "known" or theoretical set. In the chisq.test() command you specify p to carry out the test (Table 14.8). The result contains the same components as for a regular association test.

Example:

Goodness of Fit test

```
# Phenotype of pea plants
pea <- c(116, 40, 31, 13)
ratio <- c(9, 3, 3, 1) # expected ratio under Mendel theory
nam <- c("Gn:sm", "Yl:sm", "Gn:wr", "Yl:wr")
names(pea) <- nam
pea

Gn:sm  Yl:sm  Gn:wr  Yl:wr
  116     40     31     13

# Carry out test
(X <- chisq.test(pea, p = ratio, rescale.p = TRUE))

  Chi-squared test for given probabilities

data: pea
X-squared = 1.4222, df = 3, p-value = 0.7003

round(X$exp)

Gn:sm  Yl:sm  Gn:wr  Yl:wr
  112     38     38     12

X$res

    Gn:sm        Yl:sm        Gn:wr        Yl:wr
0.3299832    0.4082483   -1.0614456    0.1414214
```

In the preceding example you see counts of 4 phenotypes of pea plant. Under genetic theory you would expect the ratio to be 9:3:3:1. The result shows that the observed values are not significantly different from this. The Pearson residuals show that none of the categories showed a departure from the expected ratio.

14.4 Miscellaneous other tests

This is not a book about statistics, so it is not possible to include all the statistical analyses that R can conduct. Here is a brief list (Table 14.9) of some other functions that you might want to explore for yourself.

Of course the many command packages available for R add a huge number of analytical possibilities. Table 14.9 lists just a few of these that are "built-in" to the base distribution of R, which you can run without loading any additional libraries.

Table 14.9 Some of the statistical analysis functions possible in base R, not illustrated in this book.

Function	Description
glm	generalized linear modelling (like lm but can use non-Gaussian distribution).
pairwise.t.test()	multiple t-tests with p-value corrections.
friedman.test	for non-parametric data, where you have an un-replicated block design.
oneway.test	test differences in group means for normally distributed data.
quade.test	for non-parametric data, where you have an un-replicated block design.
fisher.test()	an "exact" test for association for 2D contingency tables.
mantelhaen.test()	association for 3D contingency tables
mcnemar.test()	this test looks at the symmetry of rows and columns in a two dimensional contingency table.
binom.test()	assess the probability of success when there are only two potential outcomes.
poisson.test()	a test of the rate parameter or the ratio between two rates.
prop.test()	test the null that the proportions (probabilities of success) in several groups are the same, or that they equal certain given values.
pairwise.prop.test()	carry out pairwise tests of differences in proportions.
prop.trend.test()	look for changes in proportions in a consistent pattern from one group to another.
ansari.test()	test differences in scale parameters between two samples.
bartlett.test	test homogeneity of variance between groups.
fligner.test	a test for homogeneity of variance between groups.
mood.test	differences in scale parameters between two samples.
mauchly.test	a test for sphericity. This is used in repeated measures analyses to assess pairwise differences in variance.
var.test	compare the variance of two (Gaussian) samples.
Box.test	independence in time series. These are sometimes known as 'portmanteau' tests.
PP.test	test for the null hypothesis that a time series has a unit root against a stationary alternative.
power.t.test()	explore power in the t-test.
power.anova.test()	explore power in the F-test (ANOVA). This only works for 1-way ANOVA.
power.prop.test()	perform power calculations for proportion tests (2-sample tests).
prcomp	principal components analysis.
princomp	principal components analysis.

EXERCISES:

Self-Assessment for Statistical analyses

1. Which of the following can be used to test for normal distribution?
   a. `qq.test()`
   b. `ks.test()`
   c. `shapiro.test()`
   d. `t.test()`
2. You can carry out a one-sample test on a non-parametric sample with the ____ function and the ____ argument.
3. When performing ANOVA your input must be a `formula`.. TRUE or FALSE?
4. You can compare `lm` models using `aov()`.. TRUE or FALSE?
5. Tests of association are performed with the ____ function. You can use Monte Carlo simulation for p-values with the ____ argument.

Answers to exercises are in the *Appendix*.

14.5   Chapter Summary: Statistical analyses

Topic	Key Points
Distribution	Use `shapiro.test()` for the Shapiro-Wilk test of normality. Use `ks.test()` for the Kolmogorov-Smirnov test to compare two samples (one of which can be a randomly generated distribution).
Distribution families	Different distribution families can be handled using `rxxx()` (random), `dxxx()` (density), `pxxx()` (probability), and `qxxx()` (quantile) functions. Type `help(Distributions)` to see the supported distribution families.
Differences	For tests of differences between samples you need: t-test, U-test, ANOVA or Kruskal-Wallis tests.
Student's t-test	Use `t.test()` for the t-test. You can carry out one-sample, two-sample or paired versions. Input can be in the form of a `formula` or separate variables. Use argument `mu` for a one-sample test. Use `paired = TRUE` for the paired version. The default `var.equal = FALSE` does not assume equal variance.
U-test and Wilcoxon	Use `wilcox.test()` to carry out 1/2/paired versions of the U-test. Use argument `mu` for a one-sample test. Use `paired = TRUE` for the paired version.
Multiple sample tests	Use Analysis of Variance (ANOVA) for normally distributed data. Use the Kruskal-Wallis test for non-parametric data (but only for a 1-way analysis).
Analysis of Variance	Use `aov()` to carry out ANOVA on multiple samples. Input *must* be via a `formula`. You can specify more complex tests with the `formula` e.g. `y ~ a * b` to indicate a two-way analysis with interactions. Use `TukeyHSD()` for *post hoc* testing.
Kruskal-Wallis	Use `kruskal.test()` for a non-parametric version of one-way ANOVA. Input can be in several forms, including a `formula`, multi-sample `data.frame`, or sample and grouping variables. There is no *post hoc* so use `pairwise.wilcox.test()`, which is quite conservative.
Relationships	For tests of relationships you need: Correlation, regression (linear modelling), or Association (and Goodness of Fit) tests.

(Continued)

(Continued)

Topic	Key Points
Correlation	Simple correlation between two numeric variables can use pearson (default), spearman, or kendall coefficients via the method argument. Use cor() for simple coefficients, or cor.test() for significance tests.
Regression	Linear modelling (regression) is carried out via the lm() function. Input via a formula of the form y ~ a + b + ... Get model results using summary(), along with other components such as: coef(), resid(), and fitted(). Compare models using anova(). Use predict() for predictions based on the model. Use confint() for confidence intervals.
Association	Use chisq.test() for Chi-Squared tests of association. Data are usually in the form of a matrix. Add a vector of probabilities, p, for Goodness of Fit tests. Results components include $expected, and $residuals (Pearson residuals).
Other analyses	There are many other statistical tools (see Table 14.9).

15. Programming tools

The concept of *programming* can seem rather daunting to many people. However, programming is simply giving a list of instructions to a device. If you've ever used a spreadsheet then you will have done some programming, such as entering a formula. A shopping list is a kind of programming, containing instructions about what to buy. Whoever does the shopping interprets the list and makes the purchases.

If you have followed some of the examples in this book then you'll also have done some programming already. In this chapter you'll see some of the ways you can use special programming tools to help you make the most of R. This is not an exhaustive thesis about programming, but you'll see some of the basic tools that will carry you a long way.

What's in this chapter

- » R Scripts
- » Functional Programming
  - » Input parameters
  - » Function results
  - » User intervention
  - » Conditional expressions
  - » Error trapping
  - » Loops
  - » Complex result objects
  - » Custom classes
- » Managing Functions
- » R Environments

One of the strengths of R is you can customize it for your own solutions. You can do this in two main ways:

1. Custom scripts.
   - Run using `source()` or from within a "helper" program.
   - Can use as a copy/paste resource.
   - Do the same thing over and over.
   - Limited user intervention.
2. Custom commands/functions.
   - Allow great flexibility.
   - Allow user intervention.
   - Custom functions saved as `.RData` files.
   - Loaded using `load()` command.

Note: Support material

See the ⬊ for links to material on the support website.

15.1 Scripts

A script is a document that contains R code. You can use this as a "cut-and-paste" resource, where you keep useful routines. Alternatively, you can use a script as a "record" of the steps you used and the R code you executed.

An R script is plain text and can be made in various ways:

- From the R console.
- A text editor (anything that can save plain text).
- The R script editor (Mac and Windows).
- An IDE script editor (e.g. RStudio).

Any text editor can be used to create R scripts. However, there are specialized programs that have features that make writing and producing scripts easier. The standard R GUI in *Windows* has a script editor but it is fairly basic (Figure 15.1).

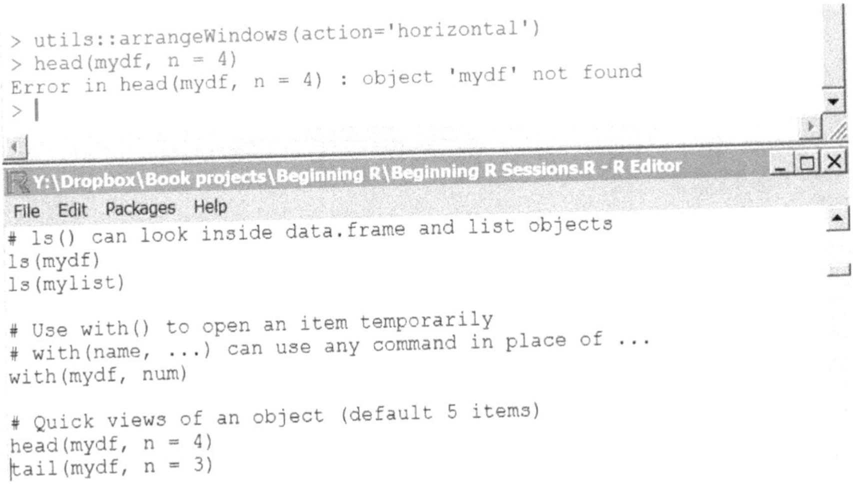

```
> utils::arrangeWindows(action='horizontal')
> head(mydf, n = 4)
Error in head(mydf, n = 4) : object 'mydf' not found
> |
```

```
Y:\Dropbox\Book projects\Beginning R\Beginning R Sessions.R - R Editor    _ □ ×

File  Edit  Packages  Help
# ls() can look inside data.frame and list objects
ls(mydf)
ls(mylist)

# Use with() to open an item temporarily
# with(name, ...) can use any command in place of ...
with(mydf, num)

# Quick views of an object (default 5 items)
head(mydf, n = 4)
tail(mydf, n = 3)
```

Figure 15.1 The Windows GUI script editor is easy to use but has few features and no syntax highlighting.

A more advanced script editor is part of the *RStudio* IDE. This makes a good starting point for script development (Figure 15.2).

You can use more or less any text editor, but you need to be careful with programs like Microsoft Word, as this has a habit of altering formatting in ways that "confuse" R. There are many text editors designed to work with other computer programs, these may have features that allow you to send R code lines directly to R, and to highlight R syntax.

Scripts are useful for many purposes e.g.:

- Keeping track of your work.
- Producing copy/paste solutions.
- Making a library of useful commands for future use.

15.1.1 Managing R scripts

R scripts are plain text files, so you can read/write them using any text editor or word processor. Usually you should give your script files a .R name extension, as this will be recognized by your Operating System.

You can also write a script from the Script Editor in Mac or Windows GUI or from RStudio. There are *save* options from the menu.

To load a script – and execute the commands within it – use the source() command from the console. You can also open a text file in the script editor window and run it from there (either all in one go, or one line/block at a time).

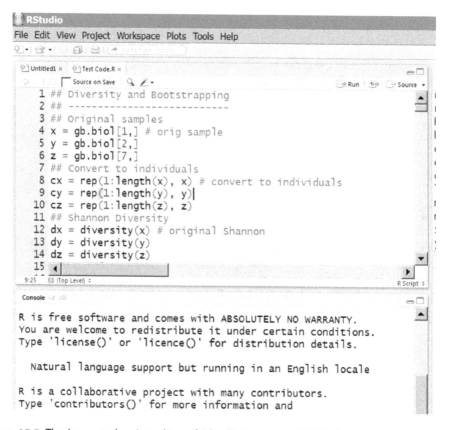

Figure 15.2 The integrated script editor of RStudio has syntax highlighting and other advanced features.

Tip: Script information

It seems obvious but... when you write an R script make sure that the first few lines are comment lines that describe what your script does. It is easy to forget!

15.2 Functional programming

One of the strengths of R is that you can create your own functions – R is essentially a programmable calculator.

A function that you write yourself is a potentially powerful entity. You get greater flexibility over a plain script. Make a custom function in several ways:

- Direct from the R console.
    - the function is visible as an R object when you use `ls()`.
    - run the function like any built-in command.
    - save to disk with `save()` as .RData (or `save.image`).
    - reload using `load()`.
- In a sctipt/text editor.
    - Use `source()` to import.

Custom functions are flexible as you can:

- Have set default values.
- User can set variable values.
- Use custom classes to allow `print`, `summary` and `plot` methods.

A custom function is set using the `function()` command and has three elements:

- The name.
  - use regular naming conventions.
  - try to ensure names do not duplicate "important" functions or data.
- The input parameters.
  - the main inputs.
  - you can have set defaults.
- The main body.
  - the R commands that produce the result.

You create custom functions directly in the console or via a script editor but the `function()` command is the key element:

```
name <- function(arglist) expr
```

The `arglist` part is where give the names of the arguments, and any default values, use `name = value` to set defaults.

The `expr` part is the main body of the command and can be very simple or very complicated and spread over many lines. When using multiple lines for input enclose the `expr` in { and }.

You can use more or less any regular R commands in your custom functions. Some R commands are especially useful in creating functions, as you will see next.

15.2.1 Input parameters/arguments

Any arguments (parameters) that you want to use need to be "defined" in the main `function`. Use `name = value` pairs, where `name` is the parameter and `value` is the default (if you want to set a default).

Example:

A `function` with multiple arguments and defaults

```
manning <- function(r, grad, coef = 0.1125) r^(2/3) * grad^0.5/coef

# Now run the function
manning(r = 5, grad = 0.05)

[1] 5.811824

manning(r = 5, grad = 0.05, coef = 0.2)

[1] 3.269151
```

In the preceding example (a formula to estimate the speed of fluids in pipes) there are three parameters, r, `grad` and `coef`. The latter has a default value, which will be used in the calculation if the user does not enter an explicit value.

Note: The . . . argument

The three dots . . . is a special kind of argument/parameter. It allows you to have one or more unspecified parameters. It can be useful for example if you want to plot something and do not want to include all the possible graphical parameters (e.g. cex, col or lty). Essentially you are inviting the user to include other parameters that might work.

15.2.2   Multiple code lines

In most cases your R code will require more than a single line, in which case you enclose everything between curly brackets {}. It is possible to have other pairs of {} in your function, for subroutines, as you will see shortly.

If you are using multiple lines you are likely to need intermediate objects to be calculated. These objects are transient, and only exist in the function environment. These transient objects can have the same names as other objects in your workspace (as they are kept separate), and won't be saved/stored.

Example:

A multi-line function.

```
func3 <- function(x = 2) {
  x2 <- x^2
  x3 <- x^3
  x4 <- x^4
   c(x2, x3, x4)
   }

func3(3)
[1] 9 27 81
```

In the preceding example there are three main lines of code, which raise the input value to different powers. The final line joins them to make a vector. When you run the function, the vector is returned (to screen).

Note: Argument names

Your function will contain at least one argument name. You do not need to type the name of any argument, as R will interpret the first input as the first argument, and so on. With longer names you can use abbreviations, as long as they are unique. R is case sensitive so you must match case (but see later). In practice you ought to type the parameter names, as it makes it easier to see exactly what you have done.

15.2.3   Function results

The "result" of your function can be dealt with in various ways (Table 15.1). What happens to the result depends on a combination of three things:

- If the result object is assigned a name within the function.
- What command you use to "end" your function.
- If you assigned an object to the function.

If your function ends with an un-named "result", this will be returned to screen unless you "store" the result by assigning a name to it.

Example:

Assign an object to a function

```
f3 <- func3(x = 6)
f3

[1]  36 216 1296
```

> ## Note: Assign and display
>
> You can force a result to be displayed, even when you assigned it to an object, by enclosing the entire command in () parentheses.
>
> ```
> (f3 <- func3(x = 3))
> [1] 9 27 81
> ```

If your result has a name within the function it will *not* be automatically returned to screen. You can deal with the result in various ways (Table 15.1).

Table 15.1 Programming functions useful in displaying results.

Function	Description
print	Sends the object to screen. The class of the object will affect how it is printed. You can define your own print function.
return	Returns the object to screen and ends the function.
invisible	Returns an object but invisibly. This allows you to formally return a result but not have it go to the screen.
cat	Concatenates objects, then sends to screen. You can use this to send simple "messages".

In general you would use return only in very simple cases where you wanted the result to go to screen. The two most sensible options are print and invisible. Use the former when you generally want the result to go to screen. Use the latter when you generally don't want the result to go to screen!

Example:

Dealing with results in a function

```
func3a <- function(x = 2) {
  x2 <- x^2
  x3 <- x^3
  x4 <- x^4
  result <- c(x2, x3, x4)
  }

# Result is not displayed by default
func3a(x = 2)
```

```
func4 <- function(x = 2) {
  x2 <- x^2
  x3 <- x^3
  x4 <- x^4
    result <- c(x2, x3, x4)
      print(result)
    }

# Result is now displayed
func4(x = 4)
[1] 16 64 256
func5 <- function(x = 2) {
  x2 <- x^2
  x3 <- x^3
  x4 <- x^4
    result <- c(x2, x3, x4)
      invisible(result)
    }


# Result is not displayed
func5(x = 3)

# Save result to named object for display later
f5 <- func5(x = 3)
f5

[1] 9 27 81
```

> **Tip: End of `function` results**
>
> It is always a good idea to have an explicit statement at the end of your function that deals with the result.

The cat function is used to send "messages" to screen (although you can send to disk files). It concatenates objects and then "prints" them.

```
cat(..., sep = " ")
```

Essentially you supply various objects (...) separated by commas, and a separator character (default is a space). Other parameters are available. It is most useful to use cat as part of a print function (see later for examples of custom class and printing), but there are occasions when you want a simple message to go to screen.

Example:

Simple screen message via cat.

```
func6 <- function(x = 2, pwr = c(2, 3, 4)) {
  x1 <- x^pwr[1]
  x2 <- x^pwr[2]
  x3 <- x^pwr[3]
    cat("Powers used:", pwr, "\n")
    result <- c(x1, x2, x3)
      print(result)
    }
```

```
func6()  # Using all defaults

Powers used: 2 3 4
[1] 4 8 16

func6(3, pwr = c(2, 4, 6))

Powers used: 2 4 6
[1]   9 81 729
```

In the preceding example "\n" was used to create a newline, otherwise the actual result gets printed to screen on the same line.

Note that your message will be sent to screen even if you use invisible!

Convert a named object to text

Text input will be interpreted as a named object in cat() so you need to "convert" to text. To do this you can use deparse(substitute(your_input))

Example:

Text representation of named object

```
func8 <- function(x, MARGIN = 2, FUN = mean, ...) {
  result <- apply(x, MARGIN = MARGIN, FUN = FUN, ...)
  fun <- deparse(substitute(FUN))
   cat("Function:", fun, "\n")
    print(result)
 }

func8(airquality)

Function: mean
    Ozone    Solar.R      Wind      Temp     Month        Day
      NA         NA  9.957516 77.882353  6.993464  15.803922

func8(airquality, FUN = median, na.rm = TRUE)

Function: median
   Ozone   Solar.R   Wind  Temp   Month    Day
    31.5     205.0    9.7  79.0     7.0   16.0
```

In the preceding example you would get an error if you tried to use cat with FUN. The deparse(substitute()) line ensures that the object is handled as text. Note also that the ... was used to allow additional parameters to be entered. In this case it allows the user to enter na .rm = TRUE even though the function hasn't got this argument explicitly.

15.2.4   User intervention

You can pause the execution of a function and allow the user to input something. The read-line() command is what you need:

```
readline(prompt = "a_message")
```

In the prompt use \ as an escape character e.g.

- \n – newline.
- \t – tab.
- \" – quote mark.

Example:

User intervention via `readline()` command

```
func10 <- function(x, MARGIN = 2, FUN = mean) {
result <- apply(x, MARGIN = MARGIN, FUN)
 readline(prompt = "Press any key to continue \n")
  print(result)
 }
func10(BOD)

Press any key to continue

   Time      demand
3.666667   14.833333
```

In the preceding example no specific user entry was needed, function execution is simply halted until some key is pressed.

You can use `readline` to request specific entry, which would require you to include some conditional expressions.

15.2.5 Conditional expressions

You can use `if()` to create conditional expressions for various circumstances.

- `if(condition_expr) {subroutine}` – for subroutines.
  - the {} form subroutine blocks in your code.
- `if() expr_1 else expr_2` – for short one-or-another routines.

Use the "usual" conditionals e.g.:

- `&` – AND
- `|` – OR
- `==` – Equals
- `!` – NOT

You use `if()` to set some sort of condition that can return either FALSE or TRUE. If the condition is TRUE the subroutine is executed. If the condition evaluates as FALSE then the command steps past the subroutine. You can create several `if()` statements, so providing multiple choices.

The `if() else` combination permits you to make a simple "one or the other" choice.

Example:

Use of `if() else`

```
func11 <- function(x, MARGIN = 2, FUN = mean, ...) {
YorN <- readline(prompt =
        "Press Y to use mean or N to use median: ")
  if(YorN == "Y" | YorN == "y") FUN <- mean else FUN <- median
  result <- apply(x, MARGIN = MARGIN, FUN = FUN)
    print(result)
 }
```

```
func11(BOD, FUN = median)

Press Y to use mean or N to use median: y
    Time      demand
3.666667    14.833333
```

Tip: Line indentation in scripts

It is useful to indent lines in your R scripts. Using different numbers of spaces can help you see "sections" within your script, and helps with readability. Remember that R does not bother about spaces (except within quotes), so use spaces for your benefit.

Subroutines

If you "chain" several if() statements you'll probably need to enclose the business-end in curly brackets {} to form subroutines. The code within the {} can spill over multiple lines.

Example:

Using {} to define subroutine blocks

```
# If all options are FALSE the default will be run..
# ..unless an alternative was entered by user
func12 <- function(x, MARGIN = 2, FUN = mean, ...) {
  YorN <- readline(prompt =
        "Press Y to use mean or N to use median: ")
  if(YorN == "y" | YorN == "Y") { # If Y given
    FUN <- mean
    }
  if(YorN == "n" | YorN == "N") { # If N given
    FUN <- median
    }
  result <- apply(x, MARGIN = MARGIN, FUN = FUN, ...)
  print(result)
  }

func12(BOD)

Press Y to use mean or N to use median: n
Time    demand
 3.5      15.8
```

Note that the mean is the default value returned if the user enters anything other than "Y" or "N" (because it is specified in the argument list FUN = mean).

Short subroutines

If your subroutines "fit" on one code-line you can omit {} completely.

Example:

Subroutines without {}

```
func12a <- function(x, MARGIN = 2, FUN = mean, ...) {
  YorN <- readline(prompt =
                   "Press Y to use mean or N to use median: ")
  if(YorN == "y" | YorN == "Y") FUN <- mean
  if(YorN == "n" | YorN == "N") FUN <- median
  if(YorN == "S" | YorN == "s") FUN <- sum
  result <- apply(x, MARGIN = MARGIN, FUN = FUN, ...)
  print(result)
}

func12a(BOD)

Press Y to use mean or N to use median: s
Time    demand
  22       89
```

In the preceding example there is an option "S" that is not mentioned in the function! It is important to make sure you give your users the correct information.

Convert input case

In the preceding examples you can see that the if() conditions were somewhat cumbersome as | was used to allow both upper or lower case entry. It is much easier to convert all input to either upper or lower.

You can convert input case:

- tolower() – to lower case
- toupper() – to upper case

Example:

Convert user input to lower case

```
func12b <- function(x, MARGIN = 2, FUN = mean, ...) {
  YorN <- readline(prompt =
          "Press Y to use mean or N to use median: ")
  YorN <- tolower(YorN)
  if(YorN == "y") FUN <- mean
  if(YorN == "n") FUN <- median
  result <- apply(x, MARGIN = MARGIN, FUN = FUN, ...)
  print(result)
}

func12b(BOD)

Press Y to use mean or N to use median: x
  Time       demand
3.666667   14.833333
```

Case conversion helps simplify things when users have to input.

15.2.6 Error trapping

You can attempt to anticipate user "errors" and exit "gracefully".

- `missing()` – check for missing inputs
- `stop()` – stop execution and display a message

Note: in the `missing()` function you don't need `==`.

Example:

Error trapping with `missing` and `stop`

```
func13 <- function(x, FUN, ...) {
 if(missing(FUN)) stop("Specify a function")
  result <- apply(x, 2, FUN = FUN, ...)
   print(result)
  }

func13(BOD, mean)  # No problem, FUN specified

   Time      demand
3.666667   14.833333

func13(BOD)          # Error: FUN not specified

Error in func13(BOD): Specify a function
```

Suppress R error messages

If you are using the `stop()` command you can also modify how the R error message is displayed. Use the parameter `call. = FALSE` to prevent the R error message being displayed.

Example:

Suppress R error message in an error trap

```
func14 <- function(x, FUN, ...) {
 if(missing(FUN)) {
  stop("Specify a function", call. = FALSE)
  }
  result <- apply(x, 2, FUN = FUN, ...)
   print(result)
  }

func14(BOD, mean)  # No problem, FUN specified

   Time      demand
3.666667   14.833333

func14(BOD)          # Error: FUN not specified

Error: Specify a function
```

15.2.7 Argument matching

Sometimes you have a limited choice of arguments to present. You can restrict the user to one of the choices via the `match.arg()` function.

```
match.arg(arg, choices)
```

Note: it is helpful to convert user input to lower (or upper) case, which simplifies the matching.

Example:

Match arguments for user input

```
func16 <- function(x, FUN = "mean", ...) {
 funcs <- c("mean", "median", "sum") # The choices for FUN
  FUN <- tolower(FUN)                 # Make lower case
  FUN <- match.arg(FUN, funcs)        # Match input to funcs options
   result <- apply(x, MARGIN = 2, FUN = FUN)
    print(result)
 }

func16(BOD)                                  # Defaults to "mean"

    Time        demand
3.666667    14.833333

func16(BOD, FUN = "median")             # Use "median"

Time    demand
 3.5      15.8

func16(BOD, FUN = "IQR")                # Error message
Error in match.arg(FUN, funcs) :
 'arg' should be one of "mean", "median", "sum"

func16(BOD, FUN = "Sum")                # OK

Time    demand
 22       89
```

If using `match.arg()` input must be in quotes:

```
func16(BOD, FUN = sum)

Error in as.character(x) :
 cannot coerce type 'builtin' to vector of type 'character'
```

The original commands might accept either quoted or unquoted:

```
apply(BOD, MARGIN = 2, FUN = "sum")

Time    demand
 22       89
apply(BOD, MARGIN = 2, FUN = sum)

Time    demand
 22       89
```

15.2.8 Loops

Loops are created using the `for()` command. These "subroutines" can be enclosed in {} if required. The `for()` command sets up an "index", which is used in the loop.

Example:

Using a loop – to make a cumulative median

```
func17 <- function(x) {
  tmp <- seq _ along(x)        # A temporary object
    for(i in 1:length(tmp)) {  # Start the loop
     tmp[i] <- median(x[1:i])  # Build the cumulative median
    }                          # End the loop
   print(tmp)
  }
```

```
shrimp
```

```
 [1] 32.2 33.0 30.8 33.8 32.2 33.3 31.7 35.7 32.4 31.2 26.6 30.7 32.5 30.7 31.2
[16]  30.3 32.3 31.7
```

```
func17(shrimp)
```

```
 [1] 32.20 32.60 32.20 32.60 32.20 32.60 32.20 32.60 32.40 32.30 32.20 32.20
[13] 32.20 32.20 32.20 31.95 32.20 31.95
```

Loops are frowned upon by some programmers. If you *can* find a way to achieve your result without a loop, then that may be more elegant, or time/RAM efficient. However, a loop can often be the simplest way to do what you need.

15.2.9   Complicated result objects

Sometimes your calculations will produce multiple results, which you may not wish to have presented all at once. There are various things you can do to help limit the screen display, whilst retaining the maximum information in the result.

Quite often the best solution is to create a `list` object to hold the components of your result. A `list` is very flexible, and allows you to hold disparate objects together.

Making results into `list` objects

The `list` is a useful object type as it can deal with different sorts of object and is simply a bundle of "stuff".

Example:

Make the result of a function into a `list` object

```
func18 <- function(x) {
 mn <- mean(x)
 md <- median(x)
 qt <- quantile(x)
 hi <- max(x)
 lo <- min(x)
  result <- list(mean = mn, median = md, quantile = qt,
          max = hi, min = lo)
  return(result)
 }
```

```
func18(shrimp)
$mean
[1] 31.79444
```

```
$median
[1] 31.95

$quantile
    0%      25%      50%      75%     100%
26.600   30.900   31.950   32.475   35.700

$max
[1] 35.7

$min
[1] 26.6
```

Display some of a result but retain everything

If you have multiple "results" but only wish to display some part, then a list is useful. What you do is:

1. Make the result into a list
2. Use print() to present the part(s) you want to the display
3. Use invisible() to "keep" the entire list result

Example:

Make a result with multiple parts but display only some to screen

```
func19 <- function(x) {
  mn <- mean(x)
  md <- median(x)
  qt <- quantile(x)
  hi <- max(x)
  lo <- min(x)
   result <- list(mean = mn, median = md, quantile = qt,
          max = hi, min = lo)
     print(result$mean)
       invisible(result)
   }

func19(shrimp)          # Shows mean only

[1] 31.79444

func19(shrimp)$max      # Display mean and max only

[1] 31.79444
[1] 35.7

f19 <- func19(shrimp)   # Shows mean but saves the rest

[1] 31.79444

f19                     # Complete result

$mean
[1] 31.79444

$median
[1] 31.95
```

```
$quantile
     0%       25%      50%      75%     100%
26.600   30.900   31.950   32.475   35.700


$max
[1] 35.7


$min
[1] 26.6


names(f19)                    # View result elements

[1] "mean"    "median"  "quantile" "max"    "min"

class(f19)                    # Confirm result is list

[1] "list"

f19$quantile                  # view the quantile part only

     0%       25%      50%      75%     100%
26.600   30.900   31.950   32.475    35.700
```

Example:

Add a message/label to a presented result

```
func19a <- function(x) {
 mn <- mean(x)
 md <- median(x)
 qt <- quantile(x)
 hi <- max(x)
 lo <- min(x)
  result <- list(mean = mn, median = md, quantile = qt,
        max = hi, min = lo)
   cat("The mean is:", result$mean, "\n")
    invisible(result)
 }

func19a(abbey)          # Shows mean & message

The mean is: 16.00645

f19a <- func19a(abbey)  # Shows mean & message and stores the rest

The mean is: 16.00645

f19a
$mean
[1] 16.00645

$median
[1] 11

$quantile
  0%   25%   50%   75%    100%
 5.2   8.0  11.0  15.0   125.0
```

```
$max
[1] 125

$min
[1] 5.2

f19a$quantile

  0%    25%    50%    75%    100%
 5.2    8.0   11.0   15.0   125.0
```

Example:

Make display for print and save list invisibly

```
func19b <- function(x) {
mn <- mean(x)
md <- median(x)
qt <- quantile(x)
hi <- max(x)
lo <- min(x)
  result <- list(mean = mn, median = md, quantile = qt,
        max = hi, min = lo)
   disp <- c(result$min, result$quantile[2], result$median,
        result$mean, result$quantile[4], result$max)
   names(disp) <- c("Min", "LQ", "Median", "Mean", "UQ", "Max")
   print(disp)            # Result must be printed, return() no good
     invisible(result)
  }

func19b(chem)           # Main result printed now
```

Min	LQ	Median	Mean	UQ	Max
2.200000	2.775000	3.385000	4.280417	3.700000	28.950000

```
f19b <- func19b(chem)  # Result printed and stored
```

Min	LQ	Median	Mean	UQ	Max
2.200000	2.775000	3.385000	4.280417	3.700000	28.950000

```
f19b

$mean
[1] 4.280417

$median
[1] 3.385

$quantile
  0%    25%    50%    75%    100%
2.200   2.775  3.385  3.700  28.950

$max
[1] 28.95

$min
[1] 2.2
```

15.2.10 Custom class

Use a custom class attribute to permit print, summary and plot methods. This can give you great flexibility, as you can produce a complicated result that can be plotted or summarized using separate functions, that you write.

1. In your function make a result of some kind.
2. Assign the result to a class (check your class name is unique).
3. display messages as required.
4. Store result invisibly or print to screen if you prefer.
5. Make custom print, summary or plot functions to handle the result as you need.

When you create a custom class you should append the name to your plot, print or summary functions (with a period as a separator). For example: plot.myclass(), summary.myclass().

Example:

Make a function with a custom class attribute

```
func20 <- function(x) {
mn <- mean(x)
md <- median(x)
qt <- quantile(x)
hi <- max(x)
lo <- min(x)
  result <- list(mean = mn, median = md, quantile = qt,
        max = hi, min = lo)
   cat("Function complete.\n")
    class(result) <- "myclass"
      invisible(result)
  }
```

```
func20(chem)         # Only message gets displayed
Function complete.
(func20(chem))       # Force display, note class attribute
Function complete.
   Min    LQ Median    Mean    UQ    Max
 2.200000 2.775000 3.385000 4.280417 3.700000 28.950000
f20 <- func20(chem)  # Save result to named object
Function complete.
class(f20)            # Result has custom class
[1] "myclass"
f20

      Min         LQ   Median       Mean       UQ        Max
 2.200000    2.775000   3.385000   4.280417  3.700000   28.950000
```

Example:

Create custom print() method for your new class

```
print.myclass <- function(x) {
 disp <- c(x$min, x$quantile[2], x$median, x$mean,
     x$quantile[4], x$max)
   names(disp) <- c("Min", "LQ", "Median", "Mean", "UQ", "Max")
    print(disp)
  }
```

```
func20(abbey)              # As before, message shown, result stored

Function complete.

f20 <- func20(abbey)       # Store result

Function complete.

f20                                # Calling the result runs the print() method
      Min        LQ      Median       Mean        UQ         Max
  5.20000    8.00000    11.00000   16.00645   15.00000  125.00000

print(f20)                         # Uses print.myclass()

      Min        LQ      Median       Mean        UQ         Max
  5.20000    8.00000    11.00000   16.00645   15.00000  125.00000

print.default(f20)         # Force the default print display

$mean
[1] 16.00645

$median
[1] 11

$quantile
  0%   25%   50%    75%    100%
  5.2   8.0  11.0   15.0   125.0

$max
[1] 125

$min
[1] 5.2

attr(,"class")

[1] "myclass"

print.myclass(f20)         # Use the class name explicitly if you want

      Min        LQ      Median       Mean        UQ         Max
  5.20000    8.00000    11.00000   16.00645   15.00000  125.00000
```

Example:

Add options to your custom print class

```
print.myclass <- function(x, digits = NULL) {
  disp <- c(x$min, x$quantile[2], x$median, x$mean,
      x$quantile[4], x$max)
    names(disp) <- c("Min", "LQ", "Median", "Mean", "UQ", "Max")
    print(disp, digits = digits)
  }


print(f20)                         # Uses default sig. figs.

      Min        LQ      Median       Mean        UQ         Max
  5.20000    8.00000    11.00000   16.00645   15.00000  125.00000
```

```
print(f20, digits = 2) # Use 2 sig. figs.

Min    LQ  Median    Mean     UQ      Max
5.2   8.0    11.0    16.0   15.0    125.0

getOption("digits")    # The current default sig. figs.

[1] 7
```

15.2.11 Finding custom methods

View all the methods available for print, summary or plot with the methods() command:

```
methods(generic.function, class = "name")
```

Example:

View methods for a specific class

```
methods(class = "myclass")

[1] print
see '?methods' for accessing help and source code
```

If you use generic.function instead of class you'll see all the methods for that function (e.g. print, summary or plot).

Tip: Hidden methods

Some methods are hidden (the methods() function will show you which ones with an asterisk *). This means you cannot view the code. Use getAnywhere(method.name) to view the underlying code.

15.3 Managing functions

Custom function objects generally appear when you type ls(). When on disk a custom function may be in binary form as an .RData file, or as text (usually as .R). There are various commands that can help manage function objects (Table 15.2).

Table 15.2 Commands to help manage custom functions.

Function	Description/Result
save	Saves to disk as .RData binary file.
load	Loads a .RData binary file.
dump	Saves a text representation of a function. Use .R file extension.
source	Loads a text file (.R) and runs the contents as if typed from the console.
dput	Saves a text representation of an object (such as a function).
dget	Loads a text file – the opposite of dput.

> **Note: .RData and .RDS files.**
>
> The save() command will save objects as .RData on disk. An alternative is to use saveRDS(), which will save a *single* object. Restore the object using readRDS(). An advantage of .RDS format is that you can assign a different name to the object when you read it.
>
> ```
> saveRDS(object, file, ...)
> readRDS(file, ...)
> ```

15.4   R environments

Usually your custom functions are visible in the workspace when you type ls(). Functions in packages are not visible directly.

You can bundle custom functions into a new R environment. This largely tidies them away so they are not generally visible. To make the functions available you attach() the environment.

There are several ways to make a new environment and manage it (Table 15.3 shows some of the simpler commands).

Table 15.3 Commands to help manage R environments.

Function	Description/Result
new.env	Make a new (empty) environment.
env$x <- x	Add x to the environment env.
rm(x, envir = env)	Remove x from the environment env.
ls(env)	List the contents of the environment env.
attach(env)	Adds the environment env to the search path.
save(env, file = name)	Save the environment env to a disk file (use .RData file extension).
load(file = name)	Load a file that is an R environment.

An R environment can be helpful, to keep objects out of your regular workspace for example. You might have some custom functions that you want to bundle together as a kind of toolbox. Keeping them in a separate environment helps to de-clutter your main workspace.

Your environment acts like a separate object, which you can save to disk (and load anytime). It can be helpful to attach() the loaded environment to the search path, which means that the contents are easily accessible.

Example:

An R environment as a toolbox

```
# Make some functions
F1 <- function(x) x^2
F2 <- function(x) x^3
F3 <- function(x) sqrt(x)

# New environment
NE <- new.env()
NE
```

```
<environment: 0x7fc33ce282e8>

# Add items to NE
NE$F1 <- F1
NE$F2 <- F2
NE$F3 <- F3

# Remove funs from original workspace
rm(F1, F2, F3)

# Attach NE to search path
attach(NE)

# View contents of environment
ls(NE)
[1] "F1" "F2" "F3"
# un-link environment from workspace
detach(NE)
```

EXERCISES:

Self-Assessment for Programming Tools

1. You can use a word processor to create R scripts.. TRUE or FALSE?
2. To set a default for an argument you use ____.
3. When using if() and setting a conditional expression, which of the following would be valid expressions?
   a. x => 99
   b. x <= 99
   c. x !99
   d. x = 99
4. To "save" function results you need ____, ____, or ____ functions.
5. As part of an error trapping routine you need the stop() function.. TRUE or FALSE?

Answers to exercises are in the *Appendix*.

15.5   Chapter Summary: Programming tools

Topic	Key Points
Scripts	An R script is a plain text document (use .r extension). Use source() to run an entire script. Use GUI script editor in Windows or Mac to run selected lines or entire script. The RStudio IDE has a good script editor.
Functions	Use function() for custom functions. There are 3 elements: name, arguments, and body. Save a function using save(), load using load(). Functions are visible in the workspace with ls().
Function arguments	Arguments are separated by commas. Use name = value to set default values. Use ... as an unspecified argument, which can be matched in the body of the function.
Multiple lines	Use {} to enclose the body of the function, allowing multiple lines. Additional {} can define sub-routines/blocks.

(Continued)

(Continued)

Topic	Key Points
Results	Last evaluated expression is displayed as result. Assign the `function` to a named object to "store" it. Use `print()`, `return()` and `invisible()` to save results more conveniently.
Messages	Use `cat()` to send an object (which could be a message or an object/result) to screen. Use `deparse(substitute(x))` to "convert" an object x to text.
User intervention	Use `readline()` to pause and send a `prompt` to screen.
Escape characters	Use \ as an escape character: \n = newline, \t = tab, \" quote marks.
Conditional expressions	Use `if()` to make conditional statements. Use `if()` `else` for simple one-condition subroutines. Common conditionals are: & (AND), | (OR), == (equals), and ! (NOT).
Case change	Use `tolower()` and `toupper()` to change case.
Error trapping	Use `missing()` and `stop()` to help in error trapping. Use argument `call. = FALSE` in `stop()` to suppress R error message (but still display your own).
Argument matching	Use `match.arg(arg, choices)` to match input `arg` to set `choices`.
Loops	Use `for(var in seq)` to create loops that run until `var` is no longer in seq.
Result objects	Make a `list` of the "results" from your `function`, then use `print()` or `invisible()` to manage what results are sent where.
Custom class	Define a custom `class` to hold a `function` result. Then you can make a custom `print()`, `summary()` or `plot()` function to deal with it. Append `.myclass` to the `print`, `summary` or `plot` name (where `myclass` is your custom `class` name). Use `methods()` to see `classes` already defined.
Manage functions	Use `save()`, `load()`, `dump()`, `source()`, `dput()`, and `dget()` to help manage functions. Use `saveRDS()` and `readRDS()` to save/load single object (which may be a `function`). Unlike `save()` and `load()` you can assign a different name to the object when reading.
Environments	Use an R environment to "bundle" R objects together. Use `new.env()` to make an environment. Use `env$x <- x` to add x to env. Use `attach()` to add the environment to the `search` path.

Appendix

Here you can find the answers to the end-of-chapter exercises.

Chapter 1
1. TRUE. R is Open Source software, backed by a large team.
2. FALSE. R is available for all operating systems; Widows, Macintosh, and many kinds of Linux.
3. To open the help system type: `help.start()` from the console.
4. To add a command package use the `install.packages()` function.
5. b use the ↑ key to scroll back through previous commands.

Chapter 2
1. The calculation order is: () / * + – (often recalled by the acronym BODMAS).
2. A convenience function for log to base 10 is `log10()`.
3. FALSE. Whilst trigonometry is in radians you can use pi to help you convert degrees to radians and vice versa. Multiply radians by `pi/180` to get degrees, and use `180/pi` to return to radians.
4. The result of `floor(47.555)` is: 47 as all the decimal part is removed.
5. The default number of decimal places for the `round()` function is 0. Use the `digits` parameter to set a different value.

Chapter 3
1. TRUE. R names *may* include numbers *but* a name should not begin with a number. You can also use . or _ but no other special characters.
2. You can tell what kind an object is by using the `class()` function.
3. c A `matrix` object can hold `numeric` or `character` (or `logical`) data *but* all the contents must be the same `class`.
4. A `factor` object is a kind of `grouping` or `categorical` variable.
5. FALSE. The `logical` kind of object *must* be TRUE or FALSE. R may "recognize" 1 or 0 in lieu (similarly T or F) in commands, *but* the actual contents must be TRUE or FALSE.

Chapter 4
1. The `c()` function is the simplest way to combine items.
2. You can use the `length.out` argument in `seq()` to make a sequence with a certain number of elements.
3. All of the options allow you to read disk files:
   a. `read.table()` spreadsheet-like files
   b. `scan()` a text file
   c. `load()` an R-encoded datafile
   d. `source()` a text file of R commands
4. To import a tab separated file you specify the separator with "\t".
5. FALSE. Whilst the working directory is the default place R looks to get/save items, you can specify any path (only forward slashes / are allowed in path names).

Chapter 5

1. You can view the contents of your workspace using `ls()` or `objects()` functions.
2. FALSE the `class()` function shows you the kind of an object.
3. FALSE the `rm()` function will remove anything visible in your workspace but you cannot remove core components (such as example data or functions).
4. b the `save()` function usually writes data in a binary-encoded format. It *is* possible to get the function to write ASCII but it is not generally helpful.
5. To export a `data.frame` you need the `write.table()` or `write.csv()` functions.

Chapter 6

1. To view the type of an object use `class()`, but to test for a particular type use the `inherits()` function.
2. FALSE the `dim()` function shows rows and columns (in that order).
3. To view or alter the column names for a `matrix` you use the `colnames()` function.
4. d to add a "citation label":
   a. would add a comment
   b. would add the citation but remove any other attributes
   c. would add a `citation` element to the main data, exactly what depends on the kind of object
   d. this adds a `citation` attribute. You could also have used: `attributes(my_data)$citation <- "Gardener 2022"`
5. FALSE you can set the number of rows using n parameter (the default n = 6).

Chapter 7

1. FALSE you *can* use `attach()` but there are other methods including: $, square brackets [], and the `with()` function.
2. You can get the proportion of missing items using `sum(is.na(x)) / length(x)`.
3. TRUE the `replace` parameter "returns" each random pick back to the pool, so it could be used again. In other words, the items are replaced after being picked.
4. b To sort a `data.frame` you need to get an index via `order()`, using the column you want to sort on (and any tie-breakers). Then use the index to rearrange the data.
5. You can conver to upper case with `toupper()`, or to lower case with `tolower()`.

Chapter 8

1. To get 25 random values from the uniform distribution, between 0 and 100, type `runif(n = 25, min = 0, max = 100)`.
2. FALSE you need the `byrow` parameter to build a `matrix` row-by-row.
3. None all of the options could add a column to a `data.frame`!
4. FALSE you need the `strptime()` function. The `format()` function converts `character` to POSIX.
5. To switch between "wide" and "long" layouts you might use `stack()`, `unstack()`, or `reshape()` functions.

Chapter 9

1. FALSE commands in R are case sensitive; the function is `cumsum()`.
2. To get column means for a `numeric matrix` you cold use `colMeans()`, or `apply()` functions.
3. c You use `tapply()` for grouping variables.
   a. `apply()` works for simple column means
   b. `sapply()` works like a and also for `list` objects
   c. `tapply()` allows you to specify a grouping variable
   d. `lapply()` is for `list` objects

4. To get a marginal statistic for a table-like object, you can use `addmargins()`.
5. TRUE you can use `sweep()` as an alternative to `scale()` in standardization.

Chapter 10

1. To make a `table` more readable you can change 0 to something else via the `zero.pri nt` argument. You can also use `print()` with the `zero.print` argument for `ftable` and `xtabs` objects.
2. TRUE you can use `ftable()` to reshape an exiting `table` object.
3. TRUE the `xtabs()` function will only accept input as a `formula`.
4. c the `attr()` function is the only way to get names attributes from a flat table (`ftable`) object.
5. If you "un-pivot" a `table` object using `as.data.frame()` you can rename the frequency column using the `responseName` argument.

Chapter 11

1. The classic method for visualizing data distribution is a histogram, which you can plot using the `hist()` function.
2. FALSE you can plot a `vector` *but* only as a single series. If you require multiple data series you will need a `matrix`.
3. a and b (`dotchart` and `barplot`):
   a. The dot chart is the most "useful" and allows you to add a group statistic
   b. you could use a bar chart with `beside = FALSE` to make a stacked chart, and if you used `proportions()` your `barplot()` would be scaled to unity
   c. The box-whisker plot is best suited for visualizing differences
   d. the strip chart is best as a general overview
4. FALSE the `range` parameter is what you need. The default (1.5) extends the whiskers to 1.5 x the inter-quartile range. Points beyond that are shown as outliers.
5. To alter the rotation of the axis annotations you need the `las` parameter.

Chapter 12

1. TRUE you can use `points()` to add lines if you use the `type = "l"` argument.
2. FALSE the `abline()` function *can* add straight lines of best-fit but you can also use `low-ess()` to add locally weighted best-fit lines.
3. You can use the `mtext()` function to add text in the plot margin areas. Justify text using the `adj` argument.
4. Suppress axes using the `axes = FALSE` argument from most graphical functions. Alternatively you can suppress a single axis with `xaxt = "n"` or `yaxt = "n"` arguments.
5. a, b, and d but a and b need d:
   a. `italic()` makes text *italic* but needs to be inside an `expression()` function.
   b. `sqrt()` can be used to make a $\sqrt[y]{x}$ math symbol (root with optional base) but needs to be inside an `expression()` function.
   c. `mean()` is not used, but an over-bar can be drawn with `bar()` in an `expression()` function.
   d. `expression()` is the basic function that "wraps around" other symbol functions to produce "fancy text".

Chapter 13

1. FALSE you can refer to a colour by its position on the `palette()`.
2. You can split a plot window with `par()`, `split.screen()`, or `layout()` functions.
3. b closes a device, and potentially writes the graphic on disk:
   a. `dev.cur()` shows the current device
   b. `dev.off()` closes the current device; if this is being used on-disk, the file is closed and "written"

    c. `x11()` opens a graphical window using the X11 system

    d. `wmf()` does not exist (although there is a `win.metafile()` function in Windows that does create .wmf files)

4. You can plot a multiple time series using separate panels using the `plot()` (or `plot.ts()`) function with `plot.type = "multiple"` argument.

5. TRUEusing `graphics.off()` will restore the graphical defaults; it also closes all open graphical windows and devices.

Chapter 14

1. c and b:

    a. There is no function `qq.test()` (`qqnorm()` is a graphical function)

    b. The `ks.test()` can be used to run a Kolmogorov-Smirnov test against a normal distribution

    c. The `shapiro.test()` is the basic test for normality

    d. The t-test is for differences

2. You can carry out a one-sample test on a non-parametric sample with the `wilcox.test()` function and the `mu` argument.

3. TRUE the `aov()` function only accepts input as a `formula`.

4. FALSE you compare `lm` models with the `anova()` function.

5. Tests of association are performed with the `chisq.test()` function. You can use Monte Carlo simulation for p-values with the `simulate.p.value` argument.

Chapter 15

1. TRUE you *can* use a word processor to create R scripts, **but** you need to ensure that the saved file is plain text.

2. To set a default for an argument you use `name = default`.

3. b and c

    a. You need `>=`

    b. `<=` is correct

    c. `!` is correct

    d. You need `==` (double `=`)

4. To "save" `function` results you need `print()`, `return()`, or `invisible()` functions.

5. FALSE the `stop()` function will stop the execution and optionally send a message, so you probably would use it. However, it is possible to contrive other ways to deal with errors.

Index

CPSIA information can be obtained
at www.ICGtesting.com
Printed in the USA
JSHW060822270623
43809JS00001B/1